## PRAISE FOR *GET BETTER FASTER*

"In *Get Better Faster*, Bambrick-Santoyo powerfully guides leadership teams to provide novice teachers with expert coaching. He reveals beyond the shadow of a doubt that leaders not only *can* diagnose and overcome the challenges their new teachers are facing, but *must* do so for schools to realize their promise to students."

—William Robinson, executive director, Darden/Curry Partnership

"Our journey with Paul Bambrick-Santoyo began five years ago when our school district had six out of the ten worst-performing schools in the state. Paul's first book, *Driven by Data*, became our district bible for school turnaround, followed soon after by the implementation of the seven levers shared in *Leverage Leadership*. Now, with *Get Better Faster*, Paul shows more clearly than ever how educators can drive learning through true instructional leadership. I highly recommend this book to anyone who strives to lead a school, not as an evaluator, but as a coach."

—Sandy Coroles, superintendent, Ogden School District

"*Get Better Faster* is a powerful tool for anyone who supports new teachers. Every part of this book is designed to be eminently usable for leaders who strive to spend their time on what matters most for learning. It's rich with practical, detailed advice that empowers coaches to give teachers highly individualized support."

—Dawn R. Robinson, Ed.D, chief school performance officer, Charlotte-Mecklenburg Schools

"Gallup McKinley County Schools has spent the past two years rededicating itself to transformational school improvement, and *Driven by Data* and *Leverage Leadership* by Paul Bambrick-Santoyo are the tools at the forefront of our positive results. *Get Better Faster* has made our destiny even brighter. Shifting our leaders from evaluation mode to coaching mode is already fueling a cycle of change in our classrooms. It's creating better leaders, who are then building better teachers, who are using better techniques to make every student a stronger learner."

—Frank Chiapetti, superintendent, Gallup McKinley County Schools

"Only Paul Bambrick-Santoyo could have written this book. *Get Better Faster* is practical guidance from a leader with a history of success for educators determined to change students' lives. It's easy-to-use and relentlessly focused on practices proven to move progress—and yes, it will drive achievement *faster* than ever!"

—Billy Snow, district transformation and innovation officer,
Caddo Parish Public Schools

"We've all seen *that* teacher—the one who kindles student learning and does the most important daily work in our schools. But too often, we fail to acknowledge *that* school leader—the needle-moving, difference-making, transformative force of nature that helps *every* teacher become *that* teacher. If you believe this is the *what*, then the book you hold is the *how*. Read it. Do it. Harness the power to become *that* leader."

—Brian Conley, chief school improvement officer,
Salt Lake City School District

"Paul Bambrick-Santoyo is making a profound difference in the lives of leaders and teachers. His approach to this work is framed by a vision that all children will succeed if we improve learning every day, in every classroom, in every lesson, for every child. Thank you, Paul, for sharing your work, so that we can all get better—and smarter—for our children."

—Eric J. Becoats, assistant superintendent, Turnaround Network

"New teachers and the principals who hire them can leave their fears at the door! Paul Bambrick-Santoyo's new book is a must-read for all educators who develop, impact, and influence teachers in the art of teaching and learning. New teachers need a roadmap to success: this is it."

—Mauriciere de Govia, district #23 superintendent,
New York City Department of Education

# Get Better Faster

## A 90-Day Plan for Coaching New Teachers

Paul Bambrick-Santoyo

Foreword by Jon Saphier

**JB JOSSEY-BASS™**
A Wiley Brand

**Uncommon Schools** | Change History.

Published by Jossey-Bass
A Wiley Brand
One Montgomery Street, Suite 1000, San Francisco, CA 94104-4594—www.josseybass.com

Jossey-Bass books and products are available through most bookstores. To contact Jossey-Bass directly
call our Customer Care Department within the U.S. at 800-956-7739, outside the U.S. at 317-572-3986,
or fax 317-572-4002.

Wiley publishes in a variety of print and electronic formats and by print-on-demand. Some material included
with standard print versions of this book may not be included in e-books or in print-on-demand. If this book
refers to media such as a CD or DVD that is not included in the version you purchased, you may download this
material at my.paulbambrick.com. For more information about Wiley products, visit www.wiley.com.

**Library of Congress Cataloging-in-Publication Data**

Names: Bambrick-Santoyo, Paul, 1972- author.
Title: Get better faster : a 90-day plan for developing new teachers / Paul
    Bambrick-Santoyo.
Description: San Francisco, CA : John Wiley & Sons, Inc., [2016] | Includes
    bibliographical references and index.
Identifiers: LCCN 2016008688| ISBN 9781119278719 (pbk.) | ISBN 9781119279013
    (epub)
Subjects: LCSH: First year teachers—Handbooks, manuals, etc.
Classification: LCC LB2844.1.N4 B29 2016 | DDC 370.71/1—dc23 LC record available at
    https://lccn.loc.gov/2016008688

Cover design: Wiley
Cover photograph by ©Jacob Krupnick

Printed in the United States of America
FIRST EDITION
*PB Printing*          10 9 8 7 6 5 4

# Contents

# DVD Video Contents

The video clips are also accessible online at my.paulbambrick.com.
Here is an overview of the video clips for your quick reference.

**Introduction**

| Clip | Teacher Action Step | Key Leadership Move | Description |
|------|---------------------|---------------------|-------------|
| 1 | Teacher Radar—Scan | Plan/Practice | **"I look for eyes, hands, and feet."**<br>Nikki Bridges coaches Jackson Tobin in identifying the key student actions to look for when he scans the room. |

**Principles of Coaching 2: Plan, Practice, Follow Up, Repeat**

| Clip | Teacher Action Step | Key Leadership Move | Description |
|------|---------------------|---------------------|-------------|
| 1 | Teacher Radar—Scan | Plan/Practice | **"I look for eyes, hands, and feet."**<br>Nikki Bridges coaches Jackson Tobin in identifying the key student actions to look for when he scans the room. |
| 2 | Exemplar and Aggressive Monitoring | Leading PD | **"The quality of your prework dictates the quality of your students' classwork."**<br>Kelly Dowling leads PD using an exemplar annotated handout to identify what makes aggressive monitoring effective. |

| Clip | Teacher Action Step | Key Leadership Move | Description |
|------|---------------------|---------------------|-------------|
| 3 | Habits of Discussion | Plan/Practice | **"Roll out a hands-down discussion."** Syrena Burnam and Norvella Dunwoody script language for rolling out the habits of discussion. |
| 4 | Mark Up Student Work and Cue Students | Leading PD, Practice | **"The three Fs: feedback, fix it, and follow up."** Ramy Abdel-Nabi and Jackie Rosner work with Jasmine Romero to improve her feedback to students during independent practice. |
| 5 | Develop Effective Lesson Plans 101 | Follow-Up | **"Film your lesson in upcoming weeks."** Julie Jackson and Rachel Kashner plan how they'll review Rachel's lessons for the upcoming week, starting with the independent practice. |

**Principles of Coaching 3: Make Feedback More Frequent**

| Clip | Teacher Action Step | Key Leadership Move | Description |
|------|---------------------|---------------------|-------------|
| 6 | Go Conceptual | Real-Time Feedback | **"Can I ask a question? Does that show progress over time?"** Art Worrell asks Michael Cheely's students an important critical thinking question at the end of a class discussion. Then the two debrief how that question increased rigor. |
| 7 | Teacher Radar—Pause and Scan | Real-Time Feedback | **[Written on whiteboard] "Track (Scan)."** Ashley Anderson coaches Ijeoma Duru without pausing the lesson by holding up a whiteboard in the back of the room that cues Ijeoma when to scan. |

| Clip | Teacher Action Step | Key Leadership Move | Description |
|---|---|---|---|
| 8 | What to Do and Teacher Radar—Scan | Real-Time Feedback | **"When I put my hand over [the student's head], stop, make eye contact, and give a What to Do direction."** Nikki Bridges gives whispered and nonverbal feedback to Jackson Tobin while students work independently. |

**Phase 1 (Pre-Teaching)**

| Clip | Teacher Action Step | Key Leadership Move | Description |
|---|---|---|---|
| 9 | Routines and Procedures—Plan and Practice | Leading PD, Practice | **"Try one more time, and use fewer words."** Serena Savarirayan models opening classroom procedures for a cohort of new teachers, and then coaches new teacher Noel Borges as he tries to replicate those procedures. |
| 2 | Exemplar and Aggressive Monitoring | Leading PD | **"The quality of your prework dictates the quality of your students' classwork."** Kelly Dowling leads PD using an exemplar annotated handout to identify what makes aggressive monitoring effective. |
| 10 | Strategic Prompting | Leading PD, Practice | **"Teacher 1, please stand and begin practice."** Kelly Dowling leads teachers to role-play teaching reading in PD. |

| Clip | Teacher Action Step | Key Leadership Move | Description |
|---|---|---|---|
| 11 and 12 | Routines and Procedures—Rollout | Leading PD, Practice | **"Tracking me with those laser eyes."** Julie Jackson and Andrea Somerville model rolling out routines, and then Alison Komorowski repeatedly practices getting students to transition from the cafeteria to their classroom. |
| 13 | Square Up, Stand Still | Leading PD, Practice | **"I need to work on my posture."** Nikki Bridges gives Jackson Tobin immediate feedback to square up and stand still as he practices monitoring breakfast. |
| 5 | Develop Effective Lesson Plans 101 | Follow-Up | **"Film your lesson in upcoming weeks."** Julie Jackson and Rachel Kashner plan how they'll review Rachel's lessons for the upcoming week, starting with the independent practice. |

**Phase 2**

| Clip | Teacher Action Step | Key Leadership Move | Description |
|---|---|---|---|
| 8 | What to Do and Teacher Radar—Scan | Real-Time Feedback | **"When I put my hand over [the student's head], stop, make eye contact, and give a What to Do direction."** Nikki Bridges gives whispered and nonverbal feedback to Jackson Tobin while students work independently. |

| Clip | Teacher Action Step | Key Leadership Move | Description |
|------|---------------------|---------------------|-------------|
| 14 | Do It Again | Real-Time Feedback, Follow-Up | **"What's the value of doing it again?"** Ashley Anderson prompts Ijeoma Duru to initiate a Do It Again at key points in the lesson. Then they debrief what made those moments the right time for a Do It Again. |
| 7 | Teacher Radar—Pause and Scan | Real-Time Feedback | **[Written on whiteboard] "Track (Scan)."** Ashley Anderson coaches Ijeoma Duru without pausing the lesson by holding up a card in the back of the room that cues Ijeoma when to scan. |
| 1 | Teacher Radar—Scan | Plan/Practice | **"I look for eyes, hands and feet."** Nikki Bridges coaches Jackson Tobin in identifying the key student actions to look for when he scans the room. |
| 15 | Teacher Radar—Break the Plane | Plan/Practice | **"What is the drawback of that position?"** Erica Lim and Laquan Magruder rehearse the way Laquan will circulate as students are working independently. |
| 16 | Write the Exemplar | Leading PD, Practice | **"Who can share a piece of feedback they just got from their partner?"** Jesse Corburn leads a group of teachers in writing exemplar responses to prework questions. |

| Clip | Teacher Action Step | Key Leadership Move | Description |
|------|---------------------|--------------------|-------------|
| 17 | Monitor Aggressively: Mark Up Student Work and Cue Students | N/A (Math teaching clip) | **"How did you know to use addition?"** Sari Fromson aggressively monitors as her students complete their independent practice in math, giving meaningful feedback to each student multiple times in one lesson. |
| 18 | Monitor Aggres-sively—Mark Up Student Work and Cue Students | N/A (Reading teaching clip) | **"I'm coming around now."** Julia Goldenheim aggressively monitors her reading class to greatly enhance the quantity and quality of feedback her students receive. |
| 19 | Monitoring Pathway and Collect Data | Plan/Practice | **"Why do we go to the higher students first?"** Syrena Burnam and Norvella Dunwoody make a concrete strategic plan for Norvella to collect data while monitoring aggressively. |
| 4 | Mark Up Student Work and Cue Students | Leading PD, Practice | **"The three Fs: feedback, fix it, and follow up."** Ramy Abdel-Nabi and Jackie Rosner work with Jasmine Romero to improve her feedback to students during independent practice. |

**Phase 3**

| Clip | Teacher Action Step | Key Leadership Move | Description |
|------|---------------------|--------------------|-------------|
| 20 | Weekly Data Meetings—Unpack the Exemplar | Looking at Student Work | **"Break down what you see the student doing."** Nikki Bridges has her teachers review student work that reflects mastery to identify what an ideal student response looks like. |

| Clip | Teacher Action Step | Key Leadership Move | Description |
|------|---------------------|--------------------|-------------|
| 21 | Weekly Data Meetings—Identify the Gaps | Looking at Student Work | **"They're adding rather than expanding."** During their weekly data meeting, Nikki Bridges guides her teachers in identifying the gaps in student understanding. |
| 22 | Weekly Data Meetings—Plan the Reteach | Looking at Student Work | **"What is the ideal that you would see in their work?"** Nikki Bridges and her teachers identify the components of the ideal student response they will seek out when they reteach the content they are reviewing. |
| 23 | Turn and Talk, Middle School | Plan/Practice | **"How do you turn that into a Turn and Talk that's meaty?"** Jesse Rector and Allison Kelly review her plan to include a Turn and Talk in an upcoming lesson. |
| 24 | Turn and Talk, Elementary School | Real-Time Feedback | **"This would be a good Turn and Talk moment."** Juliana Worrell quickly whispers to Najee Carter to alert him to a powerful opportunity to use Turn and Talk, and then lets him know what to look for in a response as students are conferring. |
| 25 | Narrate the Positive | Plan | **"Where should you have been looking?"** Juliana Worrell and Clare Perry watch footage of Clare's lesson to identify where her eyes should have gone as she narrated the positive. |

| Clip | Teacher Action Step | Key Leadership Move | Description |
|------|--------------------|--------------------|-------------|
| 26 | Check for Understanding | Real-Time Feedback | **"How many chose A?"** Serena Savarirayan polls the room during Allyson Reynolds's lesson, and then debriefs what made this strategy effective. |
| 27 | Target the Error and Close the Loop | N/A (Teaching clip) | **"Would that help or hurt the poor?"** Ryan Miller asks a series of probing questions to correct his students' misunderstanding of the impact of a law created in the aftermath of the revolution. |
| 28 | Think-Aloud—Set Listening Task | N/A (Teaching clip) | **"I want you to write down what I'm doing."** Art Worrell prepares his students to take notes during the think-aloud. |
| 29 | Think-Aloud—Model the Thinking | N/A (Teaching clip) | **"When I think about the Era of Good Feelings, right away I'm thinking about nationalism."** Art Worrell walks his students through the thought process he uses to read a history text effectively, modeling annotation skills and providing the rationale for them step-by-step. |
| 30 | Think-Aloud—Model the Thinking | Plan | **"Uh-oh. Now I'm starting to understand why these bones are so important."** Juliana Worrell models a think-aloud for Sarah Sexton, who is teaching her elementary students about the skeletal system. |

**Phase 4**

| Clip | Teacher Action Step | Key Leadership Move | Description |
|------|---------------------|---------------------|-------------|
| 31 | Strategic Prompting— Call on Students Based on Their Learning Needs | Real-Time Feedback | **"I'm going to show the class how to do it more efficiently."** Nikki Bridges and Sarah Engle identify the errors students are making during independent math practice, and roll out a strategy for correcting student misunderstanding during the next part of the lesson. |
| 32 | Guided Discourse— Show Call (Math) | N/A (Teaching clip) | **"One-third black, one-third white, one-third gray."** Andrew Schaefer shows students three different examples of how their classmates have solved a math problem, pushing them to determine through discourse which one is correct. |
| 33 | Guided Discourse— Show Call (Literacy) | N/A (Teaching clip) | **"Which is the best evidence?"** Nicole Willey guides her students to identify the best evidence in the story they have been reading. |
| 34 | Prompting: Universal (Roll Back) and Strategic (Provide a Resource) | Plan | **"Let's go back to this moment with Jessica."** Nikki Bridges and Nicole Willey watch footage of Nicole teaching her students the definition of the word *vindicate*, and plan what Nicole could do differently to correct misunderstanding more thoroughly for a greater number of students. |

| Clip | Teacher Action Step | Key Leadership Move | Description |
|---|---|---|---|
| 27 | Target the Error and Close the Loop | N/A (History teaching clip) | **"Would that help or hurt the poor?"** Ryan Miller asks a series of probing questions to correct his students' misunderstanding of the impact of a law created in the aftermath of the revolution. |
| 26 | Check for Understanding | Real-Time Feedback | **"How many chose A?"** Serena Savarirayan polls the room during Allison Reynolds's lesson, and then debriefs what made this strategy effective. |
| 35 | Close the Loop | Plan | **"I didn't go back and tell them why those aren't real reasons."** Serena Savarirayan and Allyson Reynolds plan how Allyson can close the loop to make sure her students comprehend the true difference between histograms and bar graphs. |
| 3 | Habits of Discussion | Plan/Practice | **"Roll out a hands-down discussion."** Syrena Burnam and Norvella Dunwoody script language for rolling out the habits of discussion. |

**Stretch It**

| Clip | Teacher Action Step | Key Leadership Move | Description |
|---|---|---|---|
| 34 | Prompting: Universal (Roll Back) and Strategic (Provide a Resource) | Plan | **"Let's go back to this moment with Jessica."** Nikki Bridges and Nicole Willey watch footage of Nicole teaching her students the definition of the word *vindicate*, and plan what Nicole could do differently to correct misunderstanding more thoroughly for a greater number of students. |
| 31 | Strategic Prompting— Call on Students Based on Their Learning Needs | Real-Time Feedback | **"I'm going to show the class how to do it more efficiently."** Nikki Bridges and Sarah Engle identify the errors students are making during independent math practice, and roll out a strategy for correcting student misunderstanding during the next part of the lesson. |
| 6 | Go Conceptual | Real-Time Feedback | **"Can I ask a question? Does that show progress over time?"** Art Worrell asks Michael Cheely's students an important critical thinking question at the end of a class discussion. Then the two debrief how that question increased rigor. |

# DVD Additional Materials

The video clips are also accessible online at my.paulbambrick.com.
Here is quick overview of additional materials available on the DVD.

| Resource | Description |
|---|---|
| Get Better Faster Scope and Sequence | A print-friendly version of the sequence of all the action steps in the book in one document. Ideal for carrying around with you when observing classes and trying to identify the highest-leverage action step. |
| Get Better Faster Coach's Guide | The all-in-one summary document of the entire book: each action step with the best probing questions, scenarios for practice, and cues for real-time feedback. The best guide to have by your side when planning your feedback meetings with your teachers. |
| Real-Time Feedback PD | All the materials needed to lead a professional development session for instructional leaders on real-time feedback:<br>• Session plan agenda<br>• PowerPoint presentation<br>• Handouts (including one-pager on real-time feedback) |
| Leader resources to accompany coaching principles/tips | Latest version of guides to accompany the coaching principles/tips throughout the book:<br>• Six Steps for Effective Feedback (updated version of original guide that appeared in *Leverage Leadership*)<br>• Time/task management tools to use with teachers |
| Teaching resources to accompany coaching of specific skills | Useful materials to accompany the coaching of specific skills in the Get Better Faster Scope and Sequence:<br>• Routines and procedures planning template (Phase 1)<br>• High School Habits of Academic Discourse (Stretch It) |

# Foreword

If you are an educator, you probably remember that at the end of your first year of teaching, you had many new resolutions and strategies lined up for the start of the next year. Year two would be different. Class expectations would be clear; routines would be established quickly; transitions would be seamless. You knew how to structure lessons so that pace and interest would diminish management problems from the get-go.

You had endured that midyear funk when you thought all was lost—perhaps this was not the profession for you after all—and you had finally risen from the fatigue of nonstop work that had left you drained and craving respite. Now you were ready.

But what if you had mastered all these aspects of classroom management in your first ninety days? What if not only management but classroom dialogue with robust student thinking and high participation were hallmarks of your instruction—all because you had received expert coaching? Your first year would have been profoundly different. But more important, your students would have experienced productive learning for far more of their year, because downtime, distraction, delays, and inattention would have all but disappeared. This is the promise and the possibility of Paul Bambrick-Santoyo's *Get Better Faster*.

Not all beginning teachers experience the debilitating scenario I described, but a large and significant portion of newly minted teachers do. The cost to students and to the retention of promising adults in the profession is huge. And it does not have to be. As Paul says in the introduction, "For a teacher, succeeding early is more than a predictor of the trajectory his or her career will take. It's a matter of immense urgency."

This is a book for coaches as well as beginning teachers. It would have been easy to write another book about routines, getting attention, and structuring lessons. *Get Better Faster* is vastly more than that: it is a coach's guide to step-by-step instruction, support, and development of teachers' thinking and planning skills, scaffolded in bite-sized pieces.

Because there is a predictable sequence to what a rookie teacher will need to master for sound management, there is a sequential blueprint for what the coach will undertake. Those who are supporting beginning teachers can use it as a diagnostic tool to decide where to begin with rookies who aren't starting from absolute scratch.

The approach to coaching is an artful blend of directive and nondirective techniques that one sees in coaches of performers and premier athletes. The focus is on small, specific, and focused moves and responses ("Go Granular") that make a marginally big difference. These are followed by direct rehearsal and practice of the moves with the coach ("Plan, Practice, Follow Up, Repeat"). This actual practice and feedback, sometimes in role-playing mode without students present, is a distinguishing feature of this "playbook" for successful teaching. Yet the learning for the beginning teacher is not rote or formulaic; it is like coaching a football quarterback in how to anticipate and adjust. The objective is mindful behavior with proficiency and rigor.

Review of lessons is framed by probing questions that are congruent with more nondirective approaches. Samples of questions and dialogues are provided for the many concrete situations beginning teachers face.

Real-time feedback (side-by-side co-teaching) is illustrated with more concrete examples and presents a model in which the students cannot tell who is the coach and who is the teacher. This approach makes feedback more frequent and more actionable.

Paul never loses sight of the importance of rigor with the content and constant teacher learning about how to teach it. Embedded within the experience of the beginning teacher is the presumption that academic proficiency for *all* students is a must. Thus coachees learn how to define for students what good performance and good work look like. Similarly, they learn to spread out student work and analyze for patterns of errors as a standard prep event for the next day's lesson. This is essential value-based learning for teachers new to the profession, for this analysis is then followed by planning with the coach for small-group reteaching for students who didn't get it the first time. If that were expected of every teacher in America, we would be in a very different position with closing the achievement gap.

Carrying out the complete coaching regimen of this book will seem time-intensive and incredibly rigorous to some readers. That it is. But don't let that hold you back. With whatever time one has, cultivating thinking-rich classrooms is the agenda with beginning teachers, and it is achievable. Coaches and mentors are teachers of teachers. The capacity to fill that role with effectiveness, integrity, and commitment is significantly increased by the expertly crafted contributions of Paul Bambrick-Santoyo.

Jon Saphier

*Jon Saphier is the founder and president of Research for Better Teaching, Inc., and the author of many books on education, including* The Skillful Teacher

# Acknowledgments

It is hard to believe how much has happened since the publication of *Driven by Data* in 2010. I have enjoyed the gift of interacting with thousands of educators across the globe, and they are the heroes of this book. I firmly believe that if we get better at sharing our best practices across one another's schools, we can transform education. Thank you to each and every one of you who took the time to share with me your struggles and successes: your words of wisdom pervade this book that couldn't have been written without you.

Without realizing it, I ended up sharing more personal stories in this book than in previous ones. That probably reveals how my world feels so dependent on my family. I wrote this book while my wife was completing residency (a dream fifteen years in the making) and my three children were at three different grade spans—elementary, middle, and high. This context gave me a unique window into the life of an adult learner (my wife) as well as extra at-bats at trying to be a good father. Many a night, my children and I would sit side by side at the dinner table, they completing homework while I was writing. The interruptions—working through challenging problems on parabolas, conducting a line-level analysis of *A Tale of Two Cities,* engaging the complexities of adding fractions, or getting emotional over the scenes in *Wonder*—kept me rooted: they reminded me of the daily struggle and subsequent joy of learning. I was also constantly aware of the importance of great teachers. I've said repeatedly: Gaby and the kids make me a better person. Without them, the world wouldn't shine as it does.

On the writing side, I couldn't have had a better partner than Alyssa White. This was the first book project where she took the lead of our team from the beginning, and the fruit of her work is present throughout the text. She regularly came up with new angles and hooks that helped bring the text alive. We've now worked alongside each other for five years, and I hope for many more to come. Your imprint is everywhere!

Back in 2012, we launched a new teacher working group at Uncommon Schools focused on what highly effective leaders do to develop new teachers quickly. Those original leaders have gone on to do extraordinary things. Nikki Bridges, Juliana Worrell (co-author with me on *Great Habits, Great Readers*), Julie Jackson, Jesse Rector, Serena Savarirayan—each showed us a higher level of excellence than we had seen before. The foundational work that we did required countless hours of filming, critiquing, and redoing. We didn't realize at the time that we were embodying what would become Principle 2 of this book: Plan, Practice, Follow Up, Repeat. This virtuous cycle of continuous improvement is the foundation on which the book was built. Thank you to every leader who contributed to this book (too many to count!) over the past years: from my first leadership family (keep bleeding blue! Mike Mann, Kelly Dowling, Jody-Anne Jones, Eric Diamon, Vernon Riley, Tonya Ballard, Yasmin Vargas, Lauren Moyle, Desiree Robin, Tameka Royal, Andrew Schaefer, Autumn Figueroa, Tildi Sharp, and Keith Burnam) to my second leadership family (Julie Jackson, Kathleen Sullivan, J. T. Leaird, Maya Roth, Paul Powell, Dana Lehman, and all forty-four principals), your example lives on in the videos and words you contributed here.

Finally, a shout-out to the large team of support around me that allowed me to thrive in my work and complete this project: Brett Peiser, Angelica Pastoriza, Michael Ambriz, Jacque Rauschuber, David Deatherage, Jared McCauley, Steve Chiger, Sarah Engstrom, Britt Milano, Kate Gagnon, and every other principal and leader who worked with us: thank you. You all kept me focused and made this possible. Thank you one and all!

# About the Author

**Paul Bambrick-Santoyo** is the chief schools officer for high schools and K–12 content development at Uncommon Schools. Prior to assuming that role, Bambrick-Santoyo spent thirteen years leading Uncommon's North Star Academies in Newark, New Jersey. During his tenure at North Star, the schools grew from serving fewer than three hundred students to more than three thousand, while at the same time making dramatic gains in student achievement. North Star's results make them among the highest-achieving urban schools in the nation and winners of multiple recognitions, including the U.S. Department of Education's National Blue Ribbon Award. Author of *Driven by Data, Leverage Leadership,* and *Great Habits, Great Readers,* Bambrick-Santoyo has trained more than fifteen thousand school leaders worldwide in instructional leadership, including multiple schools that have gone on to become the highest-gaining or highest-achieving schools in their districts, states, and/or countries. On the basis of that success, Bambrick-Santoyo cofounded the Relay National Principals Academy Fellowship and is founder and dean of the Leverage Leadership Institute, creating proofpoints of excellence in urban schools nationwide. Prior to joining North Star, Bambrick-Santoyo worked for six years in a bilingual school in Mexico City, where he founded the International Baccalaureate Program at the middle school level. He earned his BA in social justice from Duke University and his MEd in school administration via New Leaders from the City University of New York—Baruch College.

# About Uncommon Schools

At Uncommon Schools, our mission is to start and manage outstanding urban public schools that close the achievement gap and prepare low-income scholars to enter, succeed in, and graduate from college. For the past twenty years, we have learned countless lessons about what works in classrooms. Not surprisingly, we have found that success in the classroom is closely linked to our ability to hire, develop, and retain great teachers and leaders. That has prompted us to invest heavily in training educators and building systems that help leaders to lead, teachers to teach, and students to learn. We are passionate about finding new ways for our scholars to learn more today than they did yesterday, and we work hard to ensure that every minute matters.

We know that many educators, schools, and school systems are interested in the same things we are interested in: practical solutions for classrooms and schools that work, can be performed at scale, and are accessible to anyone. We are fortunate to have had the opportunity to observe and learn from outstanding educators—both within our schools and from around the world—who help all students achieve at high levels. Watching these educators at work has allowed us to derive, codify, and film a series of concrete and practical findings about what enables great instruction. We have been excited to share these findings in such books as *Teach Like a Champion 2.0* (and the companion *Field Guide*); *Reading Reconsidered*; *Practice Perfect*; *Driven by Data*; *Leverage Leadership*; *Great Habits, Great Readers*; and now *Get Better Faster*.

Paul Bambrick-Santoyo has committed his career to identifying the key levers that can support and develop great teachers. In *Get Better Faster,* he provides an instructional manual, designed specifically for school leaders, that provides a comprehensive ninety-day plan for training first-year teachers to proficiency. Based on ideas developed together with teachers and leaders from across Uncommon

Schools, the book includes powerful techniques that make teacher coaching more effective, as well as concrete skills necessary for all new teachers to be successful.

We are very thankful to Paul, the Uncommon Schools New Teacher Working Group, and the entire Uncommon Schools team for all the hard work that led to such an influential and inspiring book. We are confident that the material covered will help teachers and leaders become even better, faster!

Brett Peiser
Chief Executive Officer
Uncommon Schools

Uncommon Schools is a nonprofit network of forty-nine high-performing urban public charter schools that prepare nearly sixteen thousand low-income K–12 students in New York, New Jersey, and Massachusetts to graduate from college. A 2013 CREDO study found that for low-income students who attend Uncommon Schools, Uncommon "completely cancel[s] out the negative effect associated with being a student in poverty." Uncommon Schools was named the winner of the national 2013 Broad Prize for Public Charter Schools for demonstrating "the most outstanding overall student performance and improvement in the nation in recent years while reducing achievement gaps for low-income students and students of color." To learn more about Uncommon Schools, please visit our website at http://uncommonschools.org. You can also follow us on Facebook at www.facebook.com/uncommonschools, and on Twitter and Instagram at @uncommonschools.

# Get Better Faster Scope and Sequence

## Top Action Steps Used by Instructional Leaders to Launch a Teacher's Development

| Management Trajectory | | Rigor Trajectory |
|---|---|---|
| | **Phase 1: Pre-Teaching (Summer PD)** | |
| **Develop Essential Routines & Procedures** | | **Write Lesson Plans** |

**Develop Essential Routines & Procedures**

**1. Routines & Procedures 101:** Design and roll out

- Plan and practice critical routines and procedures moment by moment:
  - Explain what each routine means and what it will look like.
  - Write out what teacher and students do at each step, and what will happen with students who don't follow the routine.
- Plan & practice the rollout: how to introduce the routine for the first time:
  - Plan the "I Do": how you will model the routine.
  - Plan what you will do when students don't get it right.

**2. Strong Voice:** Stand and speak with purpose

- Square Up, Stand Still: when giving instructions, stop moving and strike a formal pose.
- Formal register: when giving instructions, use formal register, including tone and word choice.

*Note: Many other topics can be introduced during August training. What are listed above are the topics that should be addressed to reach proficiency. Other topics to introduce—even if teachers will not yet master them—could be:*

*Least Invasive Intervention*

*Narrate the Positive*

*Build the Momentum*

*Teacher Radar: know when students are off task*

*Do It Again: practice routines to perfection—have students do it again if it is not done correctly (and know when to stop Do It Again)*

**Write Lesson Plans**

**1. Develop Effective Lesson Plans 101:** Build the foundation of an effective lesson rooted in what students need to learn

- Write precise learning objectives that are
  - Data driven (rooted in what students need to learn based on analysis of assessment results)
  - Curriculum plan driven
  - Able to be accomplished in one lesson
- Script a basic "I Do" as a core part of the lesson.
- Design an Exit Ticket (brief final mini-assessment) aligned to the objective.

**2. Internalize Existing Lesson Plans:** Make existing lesson plans your own

- Internalize & rehearse key parts of the lesson, including the "I Do" and all key instructions.
- Build time stamps into the lesson plan and follow them.

**Roll Out and Monitor Routines**

**3. What to Do:** Give clear, precise directions

- Economy of language: give crisp instructions with as few words as possible (e.g., 3-word directions). Check for understanding on complex instructions.

**4. Routines & Procedures 201:** Revise and perfect them

- Revise any routine that needs more attention to detail or is inefficient, with particular emphasis on what students and teachers are doing at each moment.
- Do It Again: have students do the routine again if not done correctly the first time.
- Cut It Short: know when to stop the Do It Again.

**5. Teacher Radar:** Know when students are off task

- Deliberately scan the room for off-task behavior:
  - Choose 3–4 "hot spots" (places where you have students who often get off task) to scan constantly
  - Be Seen Looking: crane your neck to appear to be seeing all corners of the room.
- Circulate the room with purpose (break the plane):
  - Move among the desks and around the perimeter.
  - Stand at the corners: identify 3 spots on the perimeter of the room to which you can circulate to stand and monitor student work.
  - Move away from the student who is speaking to monitor the whole room.

**6. Whole-Class Reset**

- Implement a planned whole-class reset to reestablish student behavioral expectations when a class routine has slowly weakened over previous classes.
- Implement an "in-the-moment reset" when a class veers off task during the class period.
  - Example: Stop teaching. Square up. Give a clear What to Do: "Pencils down. Eyes on me. Hands folded in 3-2-1. Thank you: that's what Harvard looks like." Pick up tone & energy again.

**Independent Practice**

**3. Write the Exemplar:** Set the bar for excellence

- Script out the ideal written responses you want students to produce during independent practice.
- Align independent practice to the rigor of the upcoming interim assessment.

**4. Independent Practice:** Set up daily routines that build opportunities for students to practice independently

- Write first, talk second: give students writing tasks to complete prior to class discussion, so that every student answers independently before hearing his/her peers' contributions.
- Implement a daily entry prompt (Do Now) to either introduce the day's objective or review material from the previous day.
- Implement and review a longer independent practice and/or a daily Exit Ticket (brief final mini-assessment aligned to your objective) to see how many students mastered the concept.

**5. Monitor Aggressively:** Check students' independent work to determine whether they're learning what you're teaching

- Create & implement a monitoring pathway:
  - Create a seating chart to monitor students most effectively.
  - Monitor the fastest writers first, then the students who need more support.
- Monitor the quality of student work:
  - Check answers against your exemplar.
  - Track correct and incorrect answers to class questions.
- Pen in Hand: mark up student work as you circulate.
  - Use a coding system to affirm correct answers.
  - Cue students to revise answers, using minimal verbal intervention. (Name the error, ask them to fix it, tell them you'll follow up.)

Engage Every Student

## 7. Build the Momentum

- Give the students a simple challenge to complete a task:
  - Example: "Now, I know you're only 4th graders, but I have a 5th-grade problem that I bet you could master!"
- Speak faster, walk faster, vary your voice, & smile (sparkle)!

## 8. Pacing: Create the illusion of speed so that students feel constantly engaged

- Use a handheld timer to stick to the times stamps in the lesson & give students an audio cue that it's time to move on.
- Increase rate of questioning: no more than 2 seconds between when a student responds and teacher picks back up instruction.
- Use countdowns to work the clock ("Do that in 5, 4, 3, 2, 1").
- Use call and response for key words.

## 9. Engage All Students: Make sure all students participate

- Make sure to call on all students.
- Cold-call students.
- Implement brief (15–30 second) Turn & Talks.
- Intentionally alternate among multiple methods in class discussion: cold calling, choral response, all hands, and Turn & Talks.

## 10. Narrate the Positive

- Narrate what students do well, not what they do wrong.
  - "I like how Javon has gotten straight to work on his writing assignment."
  - "The second row is ready to go: their pencils are in the well, and their eyes are on me."
- While narrating the positive and/or while scanning during a redirect, look at the student(s) who are off task.
- Use language that reinforces students' getting smarter:
  - Praise answers that are above and beyond, or strong effort.

Respond to Student Learning Needs

## 6. Habits of Evidence

- Teach students to annotate with purpose: summarize, analyze, find the best evidence, etc.
- Teach and prompt students to cite key evidence in their responses.

## 7. Check for Whole-Group Understanding: Gather evidence on whole-group learning:

- Poll the room to determine how students are answering a certain question.
  - "How many chose letter A? B? C? D?"
  - Students answer the question on whiteboards: "Hold up your whiteboards on the count of three . . ."
- Target the error: focus class discussion on the questions where students most struggle to answer correctly.

## 8. Reteaching 101—Model: Model for the students how to think/solve/write

- Give students a clear listening/note-taking task that fosters active listening to the model, and then debrief the model:
  - "What did I do in my model?"
  - "What are the key things to remember when you are doing the same in your own work?"
- Model the thinking, not just a procedure:
  - Narrow the focus to the thinking students are struggling with.
  - Model replicable thinking steps that students can follow.
  - Model how to activate one's own content knowledge and skills that have been learned in previous lessons.
  - Vary the think-aloud in tone and cadence from the normal "teacher" voice to highlight the thinking skills.
- We Do and You Do: give students opportunities to practice with your guidance.

**11. Individual Student Corrections**

- Anticipate student off-task behavior and rehearse the next two things you will do when that behavior occurs. Redirect students using the least invasive intervention necessary:
  - Proximity
  - Eye contact
  - Use a nonverbal
  - Say student's name quickly
  - Small consequence

**Phase 4 (Days 61–90)**

**Set Routines for Discourse**

**12. Engaged Small-Group Work:** Maximize the learning for every student during small-group work

- Deliver explicit step-by-step instructions for group work:
  - Make the group tasks visible/easily observable (e.g., a handout to fill in, notes to take, product to build, etc.).
  - Create a role for every person (with each group no larger than the number of roles needed to accomplish the tasks at hand).
  - Give timed instructions, with benchmarks for where the group should be after each time window.
- Monitor the visual evidence of group progress:
  - Check in on each group every 5–10 minutes to monitor progress.
- Verbally enforce individual & group accountability:
  - "You are five minutes behind; get on track."
  - "Brandon: focus."

**Lead Student Discourse 101**

**9. Reteaching 201—Guided Discourse:** Let students unpack their own errors & build a solution

- Show-Call: post student work (either an exemplar or incorrect response) & ask students to identify why that answer is correct/incorrect.
- Stamp the understanding:
  - "What are the keys to remember when solving problems like these?" or "Can someone give me a rule?" (Students use their own words.)
- Give them at-bats: give students opportunities to practice with your guidance.

**10. Universal Prompts:** Push the thinking back on the students through universal prompts that could be used at any point

- Provide wait time after posing challenging questions.
- Precall: let a student who needs more time know you're calling on him/her next.
- Roll back the answer: repeat the wrong answer back to the student. (Give the student time to think and you time to build a plan!)

- Ask universal prompts to push the student to elaborate:
  - "Tell me more."
  - "What makes you think that?"
  - "How do you know?"
  - "Why is that important?"
- Close the loop: after correcting their error, go back to students with wrong answers to have them revise their answers.

11. **Habits of Discussion:** Teach and model for students the habits that strengthen class conversation
- Keep neutral/manage your tell: don't reveal the right/wrong answer through your reaction to the student response.
- Agree and build off: "I agree with _____, and I'd like to add . . ."
- Disagree respectfully: "While I agree with [this part of your argument], I disagree with _____. I would argue . . ."

| Stretch It (Next Steps) |
| --- |

**Lead Student Discourse 201**

12. **Strategic Prompts:** Ask strategic questions to targeted students in response to student error
- Prompt students to access previously learned knowledge:
  - Point students to resources (notes, posted concepts and content, handouts).
  - "What do we know about _____ [content learned in previous classes]?"
  - Use a prompting guide (e.g., *Great Habits, Great Readers* Guided Reading Prompting Guide) to design questions.
- Call on students based on their learning needs (data driven).
  - Call on lower- and middle-achieving students to unpack the question.

None!
Once you get this far, you can focus entirely on rigor and deepening your content knowledge.

- If they struggle, try a higher-achieving student.
- If they are easily unpacking, try a lower-achieving student.
- Create a sequence of students to call on based on the rigor of each prompt (e.g., first ask middle student, then low, then high, etc.).

- Students prompting students: push students to use habits of discussion to critique or push one another's answers.
  - Probe deeper: "[Peer], have you considered this point . . .?"

13. **Go Conceptual:** Get students to do the conceptual thinking

- Ask students to verbalize a conceptual understanding of content, not just the answer to a specific question:
  - "That's the procedure. Now tell me why that works."
  - "Can you generalize that idea to apply to all problems like this one?"
  - "Use the following terms [terms learned in previous classes] in restating your answer."

- Upgrade vocabulary: ask students to use technical/academic language when answering questions:
  - "That's the right idea generally. Now state it again using proper mathematical/historical/scientific language."
  - "Correct. Now state it again using your Academic Word Wall as a resource."

- Stretch it: ask particular students to answer a more difficult extension to a given question:
  - "What would the answer be if I changed it to [change the problem to something more complex]?"
  - "Is there an alternative way to solve this problem/do this task?"
  - "What do you think is the strongest counterargument to yours, and how would you refute it?"

# Introduction

"Which one do you want to practice?" asks elementary principal Nikki Bridges. She's talking about the list she and new teacher Jackson Tobin have just made together: a list of the instructions Jackson most often delivers during reading lessons, and the actions he expects his students to take in response. They're the kind of small actions that can make or break his reading lesson—actions as simple as looking up at the teacher when listening to instructions or saving your place in a book you're not finished reading.

And Nikki's not one to let reading instruction—or any other kind of instruction—wait. Her school, Leadership Preparatory Ocean Hill (LPOH), serves students in Brooklyn who don't normally have educational success. Ninety-two percent of the students qualify for a free or reduced lunch, and few are reading when they enter kindergarten. Yet Nikki has a phenomenal track record for overcoming these obstacles: by the end of fourth grade, LPOH students were number one in the entire state of New York on the state math exam and in the top 1 percent for reading. But for all her prowess, Nikki could never traverse this path alone: to get results like these, she needs every teacher to fly.

That's where Jackson comes in. Right now, he's furrowing his brow at the list Nikki referred to a moment ago. "God," he says, laughing ruefully, "I want to practice all of them." Jackson's in his first month of teaching second grade, and although he's focused and eager to learn, he's somewhat anxious, too. Like any teacher, Jackson longs for a classroom where all the simple instructions on the list before him are followed swiftly and smoothly, with every student ready and willing to learn. And like any new teacher, he's intimidated as well as driven by the enormity of that task.

But when Jackson chooses the first direction on the list—Finger Freeze, which requires students to mark their place in the book they're reading with a finger, then look up from the page to watch for their teacher's directions—something changes. Nikki settles at a desk to role-play the part of one of Jackson's students. Jackson rises, taking on the role of teacher.

Watch clip 1 to see what happens next.

---

 Watch clip 1: Teacher Radar—Scan
(Key Leadership Move: Plan/Practice)

---

Jackson ends up practicing the Finger Freeze maneuver three times. The first time, Nikki suggests that he add a quick positive narration as he checks that all students are performing Finger Freeze correctly ("Nikki's got it!"). The second time, a bit flustered, he goes through the motion of praising Nikki's responsiveness without realizing that, in fact, she's staring at her book and not at him. But the third time, when Nikki gazes into the distance rather than following Jackson's directions, he makes eye contact with her, then leans in and points to the spot on the page where she should be placing her finger. He has her full attention.

"How'd that feel?" Nikki asks, slipping back out of character. Jackson grins. "Better," he admits.

It's true: Jackson has just become a better teacher. Without his realizing it, his voice, and even his posture, have grown stronger. He's internalized a new teaching skill that he will be able to access immediately when he returns to his classroom tomorrow morning. What's more, he's learned this skill after teaching for a remarkably short time. Nikki didn't wait until a midyear review of Jackson's teaching to coach him on this skill; instead, she practiced it with him in depth just a handful of weeks into his career. The result? Jackson got better faster than he could have without her guidance.

It would be easy to underplay the impact of Jackson's learning such a small skill. Teaching is a vast, complex art—there's still so much more for Jackson to master on that list of reading lesson procedures alone. Considering this long path ahead, Jackson and Nikki could throw up their hands in discouragement, forgoing coaching and leaving Jackson to learn almost exclusively by trial and error. Or, just as dangerously, Nikki could give Jackson a long list of broadly worded feedback, leaving him with fifteen things to work on at once on the grounds that each is too important to implement later. Despite the good intentions of both leader and teacher, Jackson would be hard put to respond to all this feedback at once; the likely result would be all fifteen pieces of teaching wisdom falling through the cracks.

But what Nikki and Jackson's work goes to show is that there is another way: that skill by skill and week by week, teachers can get better far faster through coaching than they ever could without it. Over the course of Jackson's first year, improvements like these, ones that looked infinitesimal on their own, had an enormous impact. By June, when the second graders Jackson worked with were preparing to make their way to third grade, all his students were reading at or above grade level. The following year, Jackson had even more success. Jackson's results matched those of a seasoned virtuoso, even though it would take many more years for him to reach that level of artistry himself. He's like a violinist who wouldn't yet book a solo concert, but who can certainly contribute great music to an orchestra of other musicians who are among the most skilled in the nation.

This book tells the story of how school leaders guide new teachers to success. It reveals the practices of master teaching that every new teacher can learn and replicate within a few months of beginning to teach, and it breaks down the tools great leaders use to pass those practices on. More important, it will show you how you can use these tools, too.

## CHANGING THE GAME

"What made you better?" Nikki asks Jackson next. "What enabled you to be so effective just now?" At first, Jackson focuses on the specifics of how he redirected Nikki when she was off task. He gave clear, precise instructions, he remembers; and he made direct eye contact with Nikki when she didn't comply, letting her know that his instructions applied to her.

But while all these actions are important, the one that interests Nikki most is something much more basic. All Jackson's newfound success was possible because of two key root actions: identifying what he would have to do to implement Finger Freeze effectively, and practicing doing exactly that.

Imagine if Nikki had instructed Jackson simply to "make sure your students are following your instructions." That sounds like a straightforward direction, but in fact, it's fairly abstract. What does a teacher actually have to *do* to "make sure they're following"? Exactly what actions—or inactions—on the part of the students constitute nonresponsiveness? Even the leader delivering this direction may not know, and the first-year teacher almost certainly doesn't. But checking that all students have their fingers on their books, their feet on the floor, and their faces forward—that's something Jackson could, and did, master with great precision. And more important still, it's something he could, and did, master in an empty classroom, in the isolated space between one school day and the next. By practicing the concrete actions that would improve his ability to lead his class, Jackson gave his students the gift of not having to wait for him to grow as a teacher. He returned to them the next day already measurably better.

It's this focus on the actionable—the "practice-able"—that drives the success of Nikki's coaching.

> ### Core Idea
> Focusing on the actionable—the "practice-able"—
> drives effective coaching.

When Nikki works with her teachers, her focus is not merely on motivating and inspiring them (though she's more than capable of that, too): it's on teaching them concrete skills they can practice, perfect, and put into action. That's how she ensures that the time she dedicates to leading professional development sessions, supporting lesson planning, and observing classes is time well spent—time that has a direct impact on what teachers do and how well students learn. It's how she boils down the wisdom of her own experience as an educator into concrete skills that any new teacher can practice—and perfect—one by one.

Nikki's approach is a great departure from what teacher training usually looks like. As Robert Marzano and colleagues noted in *Effective Supervision,* the vast majority of teachers are observed one or two times per year at most—and even among those who are observed, scarcely any are given feedback as to how they could improve.[1] The bottom line is clear: teachers aren't receiving much coaching. As a consequence, educators are very rarely asked to practice the micro-skills that will make them better at teaching—especially not under the supervision of an expert who can help them get better on the spot. Unlike soccer players, actors, or doctors, teachers tend to have to learn on their own. And when they do get some attention, it comes in the form of a single annual observation and a multipage list of written feedback: an evaluation rather than a coaching session.

Nikki revolutionizes this paradigm by making her goal not to evaluate teachers but to develop them. She gets in the game with her teachers, focusing relentlessly on the specific, crucial actions she knows will win them the championship.

---

### Core Idea

The purpose of instructional leadership is not to evaluate teachers but to develop them.

---

The challenge of such microcosmic coaching is that in addition to boiling down the wisdom of her experience into specific, practice-worthy actions, Nikki must engineer her feedback to land like a perfectly placed set of dominoes. Going into immense depth on one skill at a time, each building on the last, is precisely what makes Nikki's approach to coaching effective. Pile on too many skills at once, and the chain of dominoes will tumble and scatter: the teacher will run out of both the time and the energy to internalize them all as we saw Jackson do with Finger Freeze. But teach the right skill at the right time, and the result is a steady chain reaction of success.

The short-term result is what looks like agonizingly slow growth. But what would have happened if Nikki had instead asked Jackson to practice everything on the list they had made—if she'd attempted to provide a fully outfitted teaching toolkit instead of a single helpful strategy? The same thing that usually happens when you give someone a large box of unfamiliar tools. At worst, the box will go unopened. At best, the person will eventually figure out how to use the most essential tools—but not as many of them, as quickly, or with as rich a level of understanding as if you'd introduced him or her to each tool one by one.

This book is far from the first in recent years to attest to the power of isolating and practicing individual skills in depth. Among the most significant has been Daniel Coyle's groundbreaking *The Talent Code,* which sets out to identify the secrets of the most successful professionals in fields from athletics to astronautics and regions from Japan to Brazil. What, Coyle asks, do top-twenty tennis players, pop stars from Dallas, and the Brontë sisters—three canonized writers all from the same "poor, scantily educated British family"—have in common?[2]

The answer: not in-born talent, but practice. At Moscow's Spartak Tennis Club, trainees practice holding their racquets in just the right position for untold hours before they even try swinging completely or hitting a ball. At the Septien Vocal Studio, singers spend years perfecting their vocal technique piece by piece—a preteenage Jessica Simpson worked for two years specifically to eliminate the vibrato from her voice. And in the small British town of Haworth, the seeds of *Jane Eyre* were planted as young Charlotte Brontë and her siblings entertained themselves by scribbling fantastical tales in the series of notebooks scholars call "the tiny books," giving each other an unconscious but highly intensive training in the art of building a story. Olympic athletes, chart-topping pop stars, and literary giants alike became great not through innate gift but through hard, smart work: by practicing minute aspects of their craft over and over and over again.

What Nikki accomplishes in the field of education is no less remarkable than what the athletes and artists Coyle observed have done—and her methods are no different. In the moment we just witnessed, Jackson rehearsed like those Olympic tennis players with their frozen racquets: he practiced one essential component of teaching a great lesson until it was cemented into his muscle memory so deeply that tomorrow, when he returns to his students, he'll put it into action almost automatically. And over the course of his first year, Jackson will repeat this process with dozens of other skills. His newly improved ability to scan for responsiveness will make it far easier for him to, for example, scan students' independent writing assignments as they work on them, so that he can give them the in-the-moment support they need. The one skill he learned today will make an immediate impact on his teaching, will pave the way for him to grow even more as a teacher, and—above all—will stick. That's what makes that skill powerful.

> ## Core Idea
>
> Great instructional leadership isn't about discovering master teachers ready-formed.
> It's about coaching new teachers until the masters emerge.

This book is based on the success not just of Nikki and Jackson but of a rapidly growing community of educators like them. From the coast to coast (and beyond the sea), thousands of educators are finding extraordinary achievement as a result of building—not just finding—great teachers. Some of these are individuals you'll get to know over the course of this book: they hail from the following cities (listed from west coast to east):

| | |
|---|---|
| San Jose, CA | Rochester, NY |
| Ogden, UT | Alexandria, VA |
| Denver, CO | Philadelphia, PA |
| Dallas, TX | Wilmington, DE |
| Tulsa, OK | Newark, NJ |
| Shreveport, LA | Brooklyn and Queens, NY |
| New Orleans, LA | New Haven, CT |
| Chicago, IL | Boston, MA |
| Santiago, Chile | |

These teachers and leaders come from nearly every type of public school: small, large, district, charter, turnaround, start-up—and many other designations unique to their cities. They have pioneered the practices in this book and have either provided their testimonials or graciously (courageously) volunteered to have some of their best work filmed to show what truly exemplary coaching looks like.

Over the course of the book, we will break down the most critical actions leaders and teachers must enact to achieve exemplary results. We'll show what skills new teachers must learn to ensure that their students' learning never has to wait, separating what's important generally for them to know from what's urgent for them to know now. We'll reveal the coaching techniques that school leaders can use to teach them those skills. And perhaps most important of all, we'll provide every tool you need to make all these strategies work for you so that you can guide your own cohort of teachers to the same levels of success.

# WHY FOCUS ON NEW TEACHERS?

Teacher coaching is a vast topic—and, at the time of writing, a hot one. In the past few years, thinkers in education have published on everything from who should be responsible for conducting training[3] to the role of technology in training[4] to whether teaching is a trainable skill at all.[5] Why, in the midst of all this conversation, would this book be focused so heavily on *first-year* teacher development? Why does the first year, in particular, matter?

## Success for All Students

First and foremost, the first year matters because a first-year teacher is a professional in action, doing the urgent daily work of teaching. He or she is entrusted with students who will be in first-grade language arts or tenth-grade chemistry only once. It may be their teacher's first year of delivering instruction, but it's the students' *only* year to learn the content.

The risk that great teaching won't happen that year, then, is one those students can't afford for us to take. It's all too likely that the result will be a year of learning lost to them forever. And while this would be an intolerable outcome in any circumstances, it would be nothing short of disastrous at this moment in the United States, because more classrooms than ever are being led by new teachers.

As Richard M. Ingersoll has put it, our nation is currently experiencing an overall "greening" of its teaching workforce; that is, more teachers have fewer years of experience than was the case in previous decades. The most common teacher in 1988 had fifteen years of teaching experience; but by 2008, the most common teacher was a first-year teacher, and a quarter of all teachers had been teaching for five years or fewer.[6]

So if we leave the development of new teachers to chance, we're putting a greater-than-ever proportion of our students at an unacceptable disadvantage. This book is about our best and only other option: embracing the task of getting new teachers better faster with determination and focus, so that they and their students will both thrive. It's about passing down whatever we can of our experience as educators, because if we leave our new teachers to learn exclusively from their own experience, we're leaving students in a position where they might or might not get great instruction this year. Instead, we must insist that they *will*. As the leaders cited throughout the book will testify, the work with new teachers is fundamental for guaranteeing consistent student achievement from year to year.

## Success for New Teachers

Giving quality guidance to new teachers is critical to the development not only of the students but also of the new teachers themselves. In fact, coaching may be one of the most important factors that determines both how successful a teacher's career is and whether the teacher chooses to continue along that career path at all.

Recently, prominent sources such as *Education Week* and the National Commission on Teaching and America's Future (NCTAF) have chronicled a worrying trend: more U.S. teachers than ever before—40 to 50 percent—are leaving the profession within their first four or five years of teaching.[7] Worse still, these sky-high attrition rates tend to peak at the schools that can least afford to spend time handpicking a new crop of teachers every year. "The consequences of high teacher turnover are particularly dire for our nation's low-performing, high-poverty schools," the NCTAF reports. "Many of these schools struggle to close the student achievement gap because they never close the teaching quality gap—they are constantly rebuilding their staff."

What's spurring this mass exodus? The experts agree: our newest teachers aren't getting enough on-the-ground support.[8] When new teachers take on their first teaching jobs, they too often land in much less collaborative communities than the ones they thrived in while earning their college degrees. In college, they are open to a constant stream of insights from both leaders and peers. When they reach the school classroom, however, they are asked to do the real work behind closed doors; they have nowhere to turn when challenges arise. When they need guidance the most, it's hard to find it.

Even at schools that promise guidance and teamwork, the pervasiveness of this closed-door teaching culture can inhibit attempts to deliver on those promises.[9] "Many states offer some form of mentoring for brand new teachers," concedes the National Education Association's Cynthia Kopkowsi—indeed, she adds, twice as many new teachers are mentored now as were ten years ago. "But there's a broad range from an involved, routine presence to a sporadic visitor." With ineffective coaching, as with no coaching at all, new teachers tend to jump ship.

But with *good* coaching on their side, new teachers stick around. As extensive studies by Ingersoll show, when schools do provide new teachers with meaningful leadership and partnership, the new teachers are significantly more likely to remain in the profession.[10] In fact, Ingersoll discovered, the more support we provide, the more new teachers we tend to hang on to. Teachers who receive just one or two basic forms of support—such as "regular supportive communication" with a school leader—are only slightly more likely to continue teaching than their peers who aren't given any support at all; but those who receive a comprehensive induction package that also includes professional development and lesson planning support are dramatically less likely to do so.

Why would coaching make teachers want to stay—more, even, than financial incentives do? Because by and large, teachers are motivated by their desire to do well by their students. When they're left floundering, they see little hope of accomplishing what they set out to do. But when, with the help of a leader, their start-of-year anxieties are swiftly transformed into triumphs, their desire to teach is fueled rather than diminished. They're working hard in either case, but this way, they're working smart, making progress that's just as visible to them as it is to their coaches. They see their success reflected in that of their students, and they remain eager to do more.

What all this means is that if we want to keep new teachers teaching—if we want to build a generation of educators who will do their work well and passionately for many years—we must reach them when they come to us, not a few years down the road. We must spend the first year guiding every teacher to build outstanding teaching habits by trying the right strategies and watching them work. If we don't, they're likely to leave us; but when we do, they can become the all-stars our children need.

## Success for All Teachers—and Yourself

Not only new teachers can benefit from the guidance in this book. Given that most teachers were not supported effectively in the early stages of their career, many of the skills and practices in this book apply to them as well. In fact, when we piloted this sequence of skills in our schools, we noticed that most teachers had areas where they could improve their instruction, and these skills helped close that gap. In the end, great coaching works for all teachers, and getting better at coaching new teachers makes you better at coaching any of your teachers.

Over the course of the past ten years, we have coached more than fifteen thousand school leaders. When discussing the challenges of leadership, we have seen an overwhelmingly common pattern emerge: the classrooms of a small handful of teachers create 80 percent of the problems for a leader. They contribute to more discipline problems, more office referrals, more disgruntled parents, and disproportionately more work. Just as teachers leave the profession when they struggle, so do leaders: according to a 2014 study by the School Leaders Network, scarcely more than 50 percent of principals remain in the profession for more than three years, and many flee specifically because they hunger to spend more meaningful time on instructional leadership tasks than is typical in the culture of our nation's schools today. Learning to target your coaching on these teaching "hot spots" can dramatically improve not only your success rate but also your satisfaction as an instructional leader.[11] Successful coaching has a positive ripple effect on every aspect of school leadership.

## MYTHS AND REALITIES OF COACHING NEW TEACHERS

Every action recommended in this book emanates from an unshakeable core belief: effective coaching makes people better at what they do. This may sound like something it would be easy for any educator—anyone who believes in the power of teaching—to agree with, but the rarity with which coaching is used effectively to train teachers reveals that that's not necessarily the case. What follows are a few common myths that frequently prevent school leaders from using coaching to drive teacher development—and the realities that debunk them.

### Myth 1: Practice Doesn't Make Perfect—Experience Does

How long does it take to become proficient at teaching? Many in the profession would say that the answer is ten years. In this view, it's only experience that can teach you how to teach.

Yet that commonplace answer isn't sustained when looking at the teaching profession. Ten-year teachers are not all alike: some are vastly more developed and successful than others by any measure.[12] Teachers develop at extremely different rates for many reasons. The one thing we do know, however, is that effective coaching can greatly accelerate that growth. Great teaching isn't limited to those who have a certain amount of experience or some innate, indefinable spark of talent. It's accessible to those who can learn what makes great teaching, and practice it until it becomes their teaching.

### Myth 2: Just Any Practice Will Make Perfect

Recently, what had been a widely accepted truism about practice came under debate. Known as the 10,000-hour rule and popularized by Malcolm Gladwell, this common wisdom held that it takes 10,000 hours of practice to master any given skill. Get thousands of hours of practice in, and virtuoso-level success is all but guaranteed.

Now, a team of scientific researchers believes that they have proven this to be false. The findings have been displayed in many publications with titles like "Practice Doesn't Always Make Perfect."[13] The number of hours logged practicing, this study finds, is erratic at best as a predictor of future success. The popular conclusion many professionals have drawn from this information is that innate talent must be a better indicator of success than practice.

In fact, both versions oversimplify the reality: practice does make perfect, but it has to be *quality* practice. The quality of the time you spend practicing a skill, rather than the sheer quantity of time, is what affects your results. We'll describe in more detail what quality practice looks like in the second section of the Principles of Coaching chapter of this book, "Plan, Practice, Follow Up, Repeat." For now, however, suffice it to say that perfect practice does make perfect, and a knowledgeable coach can make sure perfect practice happens all the time.[14]

---

### Core Idea

Practice doesn't make perfect, but perfect practice does.

---

## Myth 3: Teachers Need to Master Management Completely Before They Can Focus on Learning

Too many educators assume that an early focus on school culture and classroom management must trump student learning altogether—you must wait for months to think about learning. But in reality, fostering student learning is like planting a seed. It's true that certain environmental factors need to be in place for what you're trying to grow to become strong and thrive: students need an ordered classroom to learn, just as seeds need water, air, and light to bloom. But the seed doesn't magically shoot up into a fully grown plant all at once when the seed has been nourished by a set amount of water, air, or light. Instead, you water it for a few days, and its roots emerge. You continue a bit longer, and the plant begins poking up out of the soil. Keep watering and place the new sprout in the right spot on the windowsill, and leaves appear. The creation of the right environment and the growth of the plant are ongoing processes that happen side-by-side.

In just the same way, student learning can't wait to take root until after the perfect classroom environment has been established. That's why we've set up the management and rigor skills that we believe teachers must learn within the first few months of the school year to be mastered in tandem. They're two separate threads of teacher development, to be sure, and are presented in this book accordingly; but our students cannot afford for us to wait even a few weeks to begin attending to their learning, regardless of whether flawless classroom management is in place. Management needs to be a greater focus in the earliest days of the year than it will need to be after the first ninety days, but rigor is a focus at all times, and the results of the teachers in this book show that making room for learning from the beginning pays off.

## WHAT IS "BETTER," AND HOW FAST IS "FASTER"?

### Better: A Scope and Sequence of Skills

We set out to determine what a teacher needs *first* in order to be better at his or her job as quickly as possible. What do we mean by "better"? More able to meet students' most immediate needs. If we do our work with new teachers well, their students should be able to learn as effectively in their classrooms as in those of more experienced teachers, never having the chance to fall behind.

There are many others who have documented the skills of better teaching—in particular, Doug Lemov in *Teach Like a Champion* and Jon Saphier in *The Skillful Teacher*. These are both invaluable books for any educator interested in *Get Better Faster*; many of the skills that appear in this book are ones that could never have been identified without them.

But neither book will tell an overwhelmed new teacher what's most important to master first. Prioritizing all these incredibly important teaching skills is the goal of this book. *Get Better Faster* orders essential teaching skills in terms of what is most important for new teachers to learn first. These skill areas are then broken down into even more specific actions a teacher needs to take to perform each skill effectively. As you'll see, those specific actions are what a leader practices with a teacher, as Nikki did with Jackson. This level of specificity is what made Jackson's practicing effective, and having determined those types of actions for all these most highly prioritized skills is what this book does for you so that you can get to the work of coaching teachers around those actions.

## Faster: Ninety Days

*Get Better Faster* also proposes a ninety-day timeline for mastering the skills. This book is far from the first to zoom in on this period of time. In his professional handbook *The First 90 Days*, Michael Watkins claims that close to 75 percent of leaders he interviewed agreed with the statement, "Success or failure during the first few months is a strong predictor of overall success or failure in the job."[15]

*Get Better Faster,* however, focuses on the first ninety days with a slightly different philosophy. For a teacher, succeeding early is more than a predictor of the trajectory his or her career will take. It's a matter of immense urgency, because the more quickly a teacher masters the most important skills of teaching, the more quickly students get to develop the skills of being students. Getting to that level of competence within the first three months of teaching is an extraordinarily ambitious feat—but it's possible for a teacher who follows the methods in these pages, and for the sake of our students, it's well worth striving for.

While most applicable to the first ninety days of school, this sequence of skills and trainings can be started at any time. If a teacher starts later or develops less rapidly, this ninety-day plan can be used to close the gap. More experienced teachers could pick a later starting point on the trajectory (if they've mastered everything listed in the first thirty days, they could start with the next thirty days). The coaching techniques presented here will help teachers develop at an accelerated rate wherever they begin, and can help throughout the year.

## HOW THIS BOOK IS STRUCTURED

Here is a quick overview of how this book is structured.

### Principles of Coaching

| Technique | Description |
|---|---|
| Go Granular | Lasting growth doesn't come from trying to learn everything at once: it comes from working on just one or two skills at a time and polishing those skills down to the smallest detail. |
| Plan, Practice, Follow Up, Repeat | The plan-practice-repeat cycle—planning how the teacher will implement a piece of feedback, guiding him or her in practicing, and repeating this with the next piece of feedback—is the essence of getting better faster. |

| Technique | Description |
|---|---|
| Make Feedback More Frequent | Some feedback is best delivered in the moment. The section on principle 3 describes how to give real-time feedback—a practice already embraced in disciplines from medicine to music—to teachers. |

### The First Ninety Days in Five Phases

| Phase: Date | Coaching Blueprint | Management Trajectory | Rigor Trajectory |
|---|---|---|---|
| **Phase 1:** Dress Rehearsal | Professional development, including the final PD before school: the "dress rehearsal" | Develop Essential Routines and Procedures | Write Lesson Plans |
| **Phase 2:** Days 1–30 | Feedback schedule and first feedback meeting | Roll Out and Monitor Routines | Independent Practice |
| **Phase 3:** Days 31–60 | Weekly data meeting | Engage Every Student | Respond to Student Learning Needs |
| **Phase 4:** Days 61–90 | Real-time feedback for rigor | Set Routines for Discourse | Lead Student Discourse 101 |
| **Stretch It** | (All the above!) | None (focus on rigor!) | Lead Student Discourse 201 |

This book is divided into two basic parts: an introductory guide to the leadership principles that make coaching powerful, and a breakdown of the skill-by-skill coaching that is most urgent for a new teacher to receive during each of four phases. Let's take a more detailed look at what each part of the book will include.

## Principles of Coaching

The following are the core principles of coaching described in the first major section of the book:

- **Go Granular.** Coaching new teachers on just one or two skills at a time and polishing those skills down to the smallest detail may feel tedious, but it's the key to dramatic, lasting growth. This section will show why precise feedback is so powerful—and how to tell if your granular feedback is granular enough.

- **Plan, Practice, Follow Up, Repeat.** In a nutshell, the cycle of planning, practicing, and repeating is the essence of getting better faster. Once you have the right piece of granular feedback in hand, the key is perfect practice: planning the execution, implementing the plan, and repeating until mastered. This part of the book will explain how.

- **Make Feedback More Frequent.** The more immediate the feedback, the quicker the turnaround. This section shows the value of a practice already embraced in disciplines from medicine to music: giving real-time feedback. The section provides a guide for bringing real-time feedback to the classroom while still respecting the teacher's role as the class leader.

## Phase 1 (Pre-Teaching)—A Dress Rehearsal

Phase 1 takes place in summer before students even enter the classroom. Summer professional development incorporates as many opportunities for new teachers to practice new skills as possible, culminating in an all-staff dress rehearsal of the first day of school from start to finish.

- **Coaching Blueprint.** Phase 1 focuses on leading summer professional development, and particularly the final PD before school starts: the dress rehearsal.

- **Management Skills: Develop Essential Routines and Procedures.** New teachers will design, to the smallest possible detail, the routines and procedures that will keep their classrooms running smoothly, so that they can roll them out when students arrive.

- **Rigor Skills: Write Lesson Plans.** New teachers need routines for one reason: to be able to teach the content. In Phase 1, teachers set the foundation for rigor by learning the basics of writing and revising lesson plans: starting from the end goal (assessment and objective) and building the most essential pieces.

## Phase 2—Instant Immersion

School has started! While a few new skill areas will be introduced to new teachers during Phase 2, the major focus will be on getting new teachers to perfect what they began learning during Phase 1, now in the context of having their students on board as well.

- **Coaching Blueprint:** Phase 2 focuses on building an observation and feedback schedule and planning the first feedback meeting.

- **Management Skills: Roll Out and Monitor Routines.** Having designed their classroom routines and procedures during Phase 1, new teachers must now roll them out with the students and polish them so that they work just as well in practice with the students as they did when planned during the summer. New teachers revise or tweak any routines that aren't translating well into the classroom and develop the basic classroom management skills needed not only to get students to follow basic procedures but also to keep them on task for the work that matters most.

- **Rigor Skills: Independent Practice.** Effective independent practice is the end game of student learning: if students aren't practicing, they won't learn. This stage is about providing adequate time for independent practice and monitoring whether students are completing it proficiently. Learning how to monitor independent practice is the foundation for targeting instruction to students' most urgent learning needs.

## Phase 3—Getting into Gear

By the second month of the year, new teachers have enough foundations in their class to start pushing for 100 percent: 100 percent of students on task, 100 percent intellectually engaged, and 100 percent learning.

- **Coaching Blueprint:** Phase 3 focuses on using student work to drive teaching, and on a powerful way for leaders and teachers to support each other in doing so: the weekly data meeting.

- **Management Skills: Engage Every Student.** At this phase, management is in a place such that most students are on task and the classroom generally looks well managed, and the new teacher's focus is on bringing the remaining off-task students up to match the pace of the rest. This will allow the learning to take off.

- **Rigor Skills: Respond to Student Learning Needs.** With more students fully engaged, a teacher can start to target instruction to identify and close the gaps in student learning. It all starts by collecting the evidence: getting students to reveal their thinking both individually and as a group, and verbally as well as in writing. This information gives the teacher the ability to reteach on the spot when students need something modeled again.

## Phase 4—The Power of Discourse

With lessons now highly attuned to the needs of every student, a teacher can start to turn the heaviest intellectual work over to the students. The key to accomplishing this is to foster rigorous student-driven discourse.

- **Coaching Blueprint:** Phase 4 focuses on giving real-time feedback for rigor, a natural but often overlooked resource for the leader.

- **Management Skills: Set Routines for Discourse.** The importance of management is always that it creates a foundation on which rigor can be built stably. The link between the two becomes ever clearer over the course of the Scope and Sequence, and is never more evident than during Phase 4, when the management techniques a teacher will need the most all directly function to set the stage for rich student discussions. These include perfecting pacing to create ample time for student talk, and facilitating engaged small-group work to pave the way for better whole-class discourse.

- **Rigor Skills: Lead Student Discourse 101.** Leading class discussions effectively is one of the greatest art forms of instruction—and one of the most difficult. The challenge arises when students give incorrect responses. Here teachers will learn how to accelerate and target learning through the fine art of asking the right student the right question at the right time.

## Stretch It—Ready to Paint

Congratulations! You and your teachers have built a foundation for effective teaching for years to come. Where to go next? Stretch It is just that: an opportunity to stretch oneself further on the journey to lifelong learning as a teacher and leader. What's included in the Stretch It section of this book is by no means an exhaustive list of everything else teachers can learn after the first ninety days (that would entail multiple books!). Instead, it describes our recommendations for the *next*-most-urgent skills to begin tackling. Here's what those skills are, and why they're so important.

- **Coaching Blueprint:** The primary coaching focuses of Stretch It are ensuring that all the progress that the teacher has already made remains in place, and continuing to shift the bulk of the intellectual work being done during class to the students.

- **Rigor Skills: Lead Student Discourse 201.** Phase 4 Rigor focused on getting the teacher to prompt students to voice great insights during discussion. Stretch It Rigor takes this a step further, focusing on getting students to do the prompting themselves, too. The teacher will train the students in the habits of discussion that allow intellectuals of every age to collaborate—not compete—to arrive at meaningful conclusions.

## HOW TO USE THIS BOOK

This book is designed to be a toolbox you reach for again and again in your work as a leader and coach—to give you all the materials you need to build a cohort of successful new teachers in ninety days. It strives to pass on the expertise of educators who are scaling the greatest heights in teacher coaching and student achievement on a national level. In theory, a written instruction manual for school leaders should be sufficient. But our experience in coaching tells us there will always be more to perfecting a skill than reading about it. Leaders learn much more when they can "see" it, and they become masters by doing.

To that end, *Get Better Faster* is designed to help you see it, name it, *and* do it. Each chapter described in the previous section of this introduction includes not only text (naming each skill) but also a selection of videos of leaders in action (letting you see it). The final step—doing it—falls to you. With the right guidance included, you will know you are not alone in achieving this level of success!

Here are a few guidelines for using all this material to your advantage.

## Have a Pencil Handy

The goal of *Get Better Faster* isn't just to read about all this—it's to be able to put it into action. So the text is broken up by tools that will help you see, plan, and implement each technique that is being described. These include:

- Videos. These show how the skills presented in this book look in action. Just as a student (or a new teacher) needs modeling, most of us need to see what a skill really looks like in order to be able to DO it. The clips capture the techniques we're describing better than words ever could. They take you directly into the classrooms of the top teachers and leaders in the nation who are getting the results which show that these techniques work.

- Stop and Jots. These are moments to process, think critically, and develop conclusions on your own before reading on. We remember more when we write while we read; this is a way to "learn by doing" even as you're reading this book.

These are meant not as bonuses but as core aspects of the book—the thinking and planning you get to do yourself as you go. The book is written, but you're writing the story of your school—so keep a pencil in hand and use it!

## Don't Skip the Coaching Principles and Blueprints

The coaching principles that launch this book—and the coaching blueprints found in each phase—aren't the cherry on top to the specific coaching actions recommended in each phase. Rather, they're essential techniques without which delivering the coaching actions will be much less likely to bring about lasting change. If you skip ahead to one of the phases, you will be missing the coaching foundation that will allow you to dive effectively into the specific coaching techniques listed for each teaching skill.

We recommend this even for readers who already know about the coaching techniques from a workshop or from the observation and feedback chapter of *Leverage Leadership*. Here, each principle has been honed to focus on specific, critical aspects of teacher development in more detail. Going granular, practicing relentlessly, and giving more frequent feedback are practices we always knew were powerful, but we have learned more recently exactly how much they determine the impact of observation and feedback, and why.

In addition to those blueprints, there are over fifty "Findings from the Field" embedded throughout the text from educators just like yourself: coaches, principals, and even teachers sharing their own tips based on using this material. Enjoy each unique nugget of wisdom!

## Use It—Your "Blueprints"

Once you've read the book, it will be easy to pick off the shelf and turn to the most important sections for your use. To make those sections even more accessible, we have consolidated the key points of the book into a few documents (some embedded in the book and others in the appendix and on the DVD) that can be printed and carried around as you walk the school.

Here's an overview of the most critical ones:

- **Get Better Faster Scope and Sequence.** This document is the most frequently referenced throughout *Get Better Faster,* and the summary Scope and Sequence breaks down every action new teachers must be performing in order for them to master each of the teaching skill areas this book presents. This is the perfect resource to have at hand when conducting classroom observations.

- **Get Better Faster Coach's Guide.** The Get Better Faster Coach's Guide takes the Get Better Faster Scope and Sequence and adds key probing questions, scenarios for practice, and cues for real-time feedback. This is the go-to guide for planning your feedback meetings with your teachers.

- **Six Steps for Effective Feedback.** First introduced in *Leverage Leadership,* the Six Steps for Effective Feedback one-pager has been revised and improved to reflect the best practices of the highest-achieving leaders. It is a one-page guide for giving feedback effectively.

- **Real-Time Feedback PD.** On the DVD you'll find full PD materials to coach instructional leaders around the keys to effective feedback and real-time feedback. These materials, including session plans, PowerPoints, and handouts, will allow you to run your own PD on feedback for the leadership team in your school.

Please note that both the Scope and Sequence and the Coach's Guide are designed to be as printing-friendly as possible, which means that the information they provide will be slightly more concise than the corresponding sections in the book.

> ### Q Findings from the Field: Print Them Out and Create a "Rainbow Guide"
>
> I've found for myself and fellow school leaders that the greatest barrier to using the tools is the start. To eliminate that barrier, I created a "Rainbow Guide": a bound version of the [listed resources], each one on a different colored paper as we were given in Leverage Leadership Institute, and then I added a simple tab to each resource. The impact has been palpable. Now, during our monthly principals' training, we have our Rainbow Guides in hand and jump right to the Get Better Faster Scope and Sequence. It has made my leaders' ability to access their tools both fun and more expedient. Now famous, the Rainbow Guide is like the Sorcerer's Stone: it made my leaders better faster.
>
> —Erin McMahon, principal manager, Denver, Colorado

## DIVE IN—MEET YOUR TEACHERS WHERE THEY ARE

Once you internalize the coaching principles and move on to the part of this book that breaks down the Get Better Faster Scope and Sequence piece by piece, it's less crucial to read straight through each chapter of the book from beginning to end. If you have time to do this, then by all means do so! If, however, you're in the midst of coaching a teacher and need to just dive right in, the book is set up to accommodate that. Simply begin by reading over the Scope and Sequence itself, then jump to the part of the book that specifically addresses in greater detail what your teachers need the most.

Here's the best way to navigate the book.

**If you are using the Scope and Sequence before the school year begins . . .**

- **Read the Coaching Principles and then the Phase 1 Coaching Blueprint.** The Phase 1 coaching tips will help you prepare summer PD sessions that train teachers in the skills they'll need most from the first day of school onward.

- **Start from the top—the first Phase 1 action step.** A strong foundation is critical to beginning the year. Therefore, start with the first action steps in Management (Routines and Procedures 101 and Strong Voice) and Rigor

(Develop Effective Lesson Plans 101 and Internalize Existing Lesson Plans). Do not move forward until a teacher is proficient in these areas!

**If you are using the Scope and Sequence at any other point in the year . . .**

- **Read the Coaching Principles.**

- **Identify your teacher's action step.** Go to the Get Better Faster Scope and Sequence (first pages of the book; a printable version is on the DVD) and determine the highest-leverage action step for your teacher. Remember to think waterfall: start from the top and stop as soon as you hit a problem area for the teacher.

- **Go to the appropriate phase and read the Coaching Blueprint.** For example, if your teacher is struggling with getting students to cite evidence, jump to Phase 3 and start with the Phase 3 Coaching Blueprint.

- **In that same phase, jump to the Rigor or Management section (depending on your action step) and go to the page that matches your teacher's struggle.** Use the Quick Reference Guide that appears at the beginning of each Management and Rigor section to identify the challenges that the teacher is most struggling with, and skip to the corresponding section that presents the skills that will help him or her overcome those specific challenges.

## READY TO DIVE IN!

Every school year will bring new challenges and opportunities that are unique to each school. But one thing is constant: worldwide, a legion of new teachers will enter schools, fresh from college or other jobs, ready to make a difference but not sure how. That's where you step in.

Let's begin the journey of serving each of our teachers to maximal impact! Time to turn the page.

# Principles of Coaching

What do professional soccer players, heart surgeons, and stand-up comics all have in common? They make their living in performance professions: jobs that require them to perform a task with perfect accuracy in the moment. The soccer player has to score that winning goal amid the chaos of opposition on all sides, with fans screaming in the stands. The actor has to deliver that stirring monologue on command night after night, with just as much passion and sincerity each time. The surgeon has just one chance to repair a patient's body—often in emergency conditions.

Teaching is a performance profession, too. Just like the soccer player going for the goal, the actor delivering the monologue, and the surgeon performing an emergency operation, teachers have to deliver excellent instruction *live*: not only delivering on a great lesson plan but also modifying it swiftly and surely in response to whatever challenges or triumphs the students bring to the classroom that day. Every moment in the classroom is one irreplaceable chance to teach students what they need to learn, just as every second of a soccer match is a chance to push the team closer to victory.

Because of this, it's vital that teachers be trained in the same way as their fellow performance professionals: with an eye to preparing them for the live game.

Athletes, performance artists, and doctors all receive coaching that gives them as many opportunities as possible to practice the tasks they'll need to complete under the gun, so that when the critical moments come, they're ready. There's a great deal of focus in the field of education on how leaders should *evaluate* their teachers. But particularly when we recognize teaching as a performance profession, we see that what's more important than assessing how teachers did yesterday is making sure they will succeed today, tomorrow, and throughout their careers. Like any great soccer coach or play director, we must shift our focus from *evaluating* to *coaching*—making sure our teachers will do dazzling work in the moments that matter most, when their classrooms are packed with students and the clock is ticking.

---

### Core Idea

Follow the lead of the maestros in every field:
evaluate less and coach more.

---

This Principles of Coaching section will cover the essential techniques of great teacher coaching, revealing what every leader needs to know in order to train teachers as performance professionals. It includes three principles:

- **Principle 1: Go Granular.** Break teaching down into discrete skills to be practiced successively and cumulatively.

- **Principle 2: Plan, Practice, Follow Up, Repeat.** Coach a teacher through effective practice.

- **Principle 3: Make Feedback More Frequent.** Make the most of every observation by increasing the frequency of feedback.

These three topics don't comprise everything there is to know about coaching, but they cover all the most basic foundational skills: everything you need to know to make the shift to a system in which teachers receive the training and guidance they deserve and thrive as performance professionals. In our discussions of the subsequent phases, we'll dive even deeper into these principles with concrete Coaching Blueprints relevant to that stage in a teacher's development. But first let's dive into the principles that can transform not only your approach to developing teachers but also your whole role as a school leader. Following these three principles ensures that your work with teachers has a direct and consistent impact on student achievement.

## PRINCIPLE 1: GO GRANULAR

One of the high schools I manage was born in exceptionally cramped quarters: a small handful of classrooms on the top floor of an existing school in Newark. We knew we would soon need more space, and we had the perfect spot picked out: the empty lot right behind the school.

So for the next eighteen months, all of us watched our high school's new home take shape literally from the ground up. The construction crew began by digging a foundation, then laying an intricate framework of beams that looked more like a skeleton than a building. But after that, as they added walls, floors, and a roof, it was remarkable how quickly the school became a school.

I still think often about one conversation I had with the manager of the construction crew, back when the beams of the high school were still being laid. "We have to be really careful at this phase," he told me. "If the beams are off by a quarter of an inch, it'll compromise the whole structure of the building."

At the time, I was astounded. A quarter of an inch could make or break the stability of a building over a hundred feet long? But the more I think about this, the more sense it makes. After all, architecture is far from the only field in which perfecting bite-sized tasks is the key to completing a much bigger, more ambitious project. It's the same way with the calculations that make a space shuttle structurally space-worthy, or with the precise curvature of a concert pianist's fingers that enables him or her to perform an entire concerto. If we don't get the right foundation in place, we can't get far; but once we do, we fly.

The process for building a school is the same as the process for building up someone's teaching skills. Imagine the teacher you want your new teachers to be, and you probably don't see the equivalent of foundation beams: you see the finished building in all its glory. The teacher you envision is the ideal combination of warmth and strictness, flawlessly organized yet also able to adjust on the fly to unanticipated events. He or she conveys joy at every moment and gets students beyond the memorization of facts to critical thinking and academic creativity. Most important of all, no student ever slips through this teacher's classroom without getting the instruction he or she needs.

When we approach the task of developing teachers, we often struggle to get this shining image of the perfect teacher out of our minds. This is reflected by the prevalence of teacher evaluation rubrics that require the observer to track a teacher's success in forty, fifty, or even seventy areas at once. Such rubrics portray our comprehensive vision of what great teaching looks like. It may well be true, as their advocates argue, that they "honor the complexity of teaching."[1]

But what these rubrics fail to honor is the complexity of *learning* to teach. In focusing on painting a picture of the final building in complete accuracy, they haven't spent much time on how to get the beams placed with precise accuracy. If our goal is to develop and coach those teachers, we need to start with the beams.

> ## Core Idea
>
> Want to build something with lasting strength?
> Start with the foundation and sweat the small stuff.

The foundational skills of teaching need to be perfected to the last quarter-inch before we begin the task of building walls around them. In short, we need to go granular: give bite-sized feedback on the specific skills a teacher most needs to work on, rather than sweeping feedback that covers a broad range of topics.

The most successful leaders I've worked with give feedback in this way: they observe teachers frequently and assign them just one or two action steps per week. It feels excruciatingly slow at first—just as the building of the high school did—but little by little, the steps build momentum, quickly adding up to a great, strong structure with a meticulously rendered foundation that will keep it standing tall for years to come.

## Action Steps: The Quarter-Inch View

The art of delivering the right bite-sized action step to a teacher at the right time is the heart of going granular—and it's often incredibly challenging. How can you know the right step? Let's practice. We'll look at a case study of a leader who tried to identify a solid action step. Then we'll name criteria for strong action steps, and we'll conclude by giving you a chance to practice putting them into action—both with classroom management and with rigor.

Imagine a first-year teacher—let's call him John—who is working to develop his classroom management skills. His principal—let's call her Christina—is coaching him. Here's what Christina saw yesterday when she observed John at work.

---

## Case Study 1: The Observation

It's 10:30 on Wednesday morning, and as Christina slips into the back of John's classroom, everything seems to be going smoothly. John's ninth-grade students are quietly finishing up an exercise on systems of equations. "Time is up! Put your pencils down," John says a few moments after Christina has entered. "I need all eyes on me."

Most students look up. Daniel, however, is still working on one of the problems, and Isabel twirls her pencil between her fingers, gazing dreamily toward the door. In another corner of the room, Tracy is fiddling with a piece of paper under her desk. As John moves on, asking who knows the answer to the first question on the worksheet, a number of other students drift out of focus too, one by one.

John calls on Darius, who has identified the need to add the two equations to eliminate the x variable but has made some errors in adding negative integers. John asks Darius how he got his answer. As Darius begins his explanation, however, more students lose focus. Tracy has shown the paper she was playing with to the classmates around her, and now they are murmuring among themselves. Their voices soon begin to compete with Darius's.

"Wait, Darius," John interjects, looking around the room to see which students are causing the disruption. He prompts Darius to continue when the noise reduces slightly, but background noise lingers as Darius continues answering John's question.

At this point, Christina steps out of the classroom and contemplates what should be John's next step for improvement.

---

Imagine you are Christina. How would you assess John's performance? It is likely that John has come a long way in classroom management since he first began teaching. He had all of his students working quietly and independently at first, and he started with most students engaged during whole-class discussion before they started drifting off. What could Christina ask John to do that would be sure to increase learning for everyone in his classroom?

Perhaps Christina's first instinct is to say:

---

**Christina's Action Step, Version 1**

"Improve your classroom management using a variety of techniques."

---

You can probably immediately see the flaw in Christina's advice. All of John's management is not off, and where John is struggling, he is unlikely to improve if he doesn't know how. This action step doesn't give John any guidance on what to do—and if Christina observed his class again a week later, it would probably look exactly the same.

What if Christina gave John this feedback instead?

---

**Christina's Action Step, Version 2**

"Be sure to _immediately_ redirect any students who are off task during your class. That will help you keep other students on task, so you don't end up with an even bigger management problem."

---

Christina's second attempt is definitely stronger. She has narrowed her focus to the moment where the problems start to emerge: when John does not address the first students who go off task. She has selected a more specific aspect of great classroom management: redirecting individual off-task students. Because John started off with almost all of his students on task, she's correct in thinking that mastering these first moments of off-task behavior is an important next step for John.

However, Christina still hasn't guaranteed improvement in John's classroom next week. Many questions remain. What did she mean when she referred to "off-task" behavior? How, exactly, should John "redirect" a student who displays it? John needs to know the answers to these questions to improve his teaching craft—and Christina will need to recognize them when she observes his class again, so that she can tell for sure if the change she identified has taken place.

How could Christina further improve her feedback? Let's see what her action steps for John look like when she rewrites them to be even narrower:

> ### Christina's Action Step, Version 3
>
> "Deliberately scan the room for on-task behavior:
>
> - Choose three or four 'hot spots' (places where you have students who often get off task) to constantly scan.
> - 'Be Seen Looking': crane your neck to appear to be seeing all corners of the room."

> ### Stop and Jot: Christina Goes Granular
>
> What makes Christina's third attempt at an action step more effective?
>
> _____
> _____
> _____
> _____
> _____
> _____

### Criteria for Effective Action Steps

These final action steps would be much more likely to improve John's classroom management than the others Christina considered. Why? Three big characteristics made the difference.

- **Observable and practice-able.** The action steps listed are unmistakably clear. What makes them clear is that you could observe them in action. If Christina returned to John's classroom at any moment, she'd know almost immediately whether he'd implemented either of them. She could see if he is looking at specific "hot spots" or craning his neck. She'd be able to tell right away whether he needed more coaching around those actions or whether he's ready to learn another habit of great teaching. Being observable also makes the action step practice-able: John could easily practice either of these actions prior to teaching again.

- **Highest leverage.** Christina could have named any number of other action steps that would have improved classroom management and increased student learning, but the ones she ultimately identified address the most urgent challenges in John's classroom: John needs to "see" the problem—and be seen looking by the students—before he can fix it. Improving what we could call his "radar" is a foundational skill to help a teacher identify the problem. Imagine if Christina had given John an action step about what to tell a student who is off task, but John isn't able to see that behavior in the first place (a very real likelihood for a new teacher!). Then the action would be for naught. Improving a teacher's radar is a prerequisite for fixing the problem. As such, it is higher leverage and will lay the groundwork for more improvements in the future.

- **Bite-sized.** Neither of these action steps is a broad, murky suggestion like "Get more kids on task." They're specific things John could go back to his classroom and do right away. Instead of struggling to do something big and nebulous, he can immediately make a habit of something small and concrete. To determine whether a granular action step is granular enough, ask yourself, "Could this action step be accomplished in one week?" If not, the action step isn't small enough. (I'll explain more about the value of the weekly action step in a moment.)

---

### Criteria for the Right Action Step

1. Is it observable and practice-able?
2. Is it the highest-leverage action you could ask the teacher to perform?
3. Is it bite-sized enough that the teacher could accomplish it in one week?

---

#### The Get Better Faster Scope and Sequence of (Granular) Action Steps

If this was your first time generating a specific action step, you might have found it difficult to create an action step that met the three criteria. If you did, you are not alone! Most leaders we have worked with are uncertain, at first, about identifying the right granular action step during each observation. It can feel overwhelming to imagine choosing the single task that will drive the most learning in a teacher's classroom in the course of a single week, particularly when you have to do it for dozens of teachers at a time.

But you don't have to dive into the process of observation and feedback blindly. As the construction manager with whom I had the conversation would agree, a building project of the magnitude of a high school building would never come together without a blueprint to guide your way. And while there's no perfect blueprint for developing a teacher—no single document could ever account for the vast variety of paths different human professionals follow when they set out to master a craft—there's still an extent to which you can foresee what will help a new teacher the most.

We have spent the past few years with our colleagues culling through the videos and notes from thousands of observations of new teachers by hundreds of different instructional leaders. In that process, we looked most closely at principals who had the strongest track record of developing new teachers—leaders like Nikki Bridges. When we walked around the schools of principals like Nikki, we were stunned at the development of their teachers: none of the new teachers looked like new teachers!

As we studied these leaders' observation notes and their action steps, we noticed patterns that distinguished their feedback from other, less effective school leaders. Their action steps not only were more precise, high leverage, and bite-sized (meeting the aforementioned three criteria ) but also followed a similar order. Although not every teacher's feedback was the same, these leaders maintained an eerie level of consistency in the order in which they worked on actions with teachers. They consistently followed sequences—for example, developing a teacher's radar before teaching him or her how to redirect a student, and working on independent practice before managing a class discussion.

The fruit of this investigation was the development of a scope and sequence of action steps for new teachers that has since been used by thousands of leaders. Continuously refined each year to reflect the latest trends, this resource gives you a blueprint—and order—to help you in choosing and developing the right action steps. Here is an overview of the sequence (a complete version appears just before the Introduction of this book):

Get Better Faster Scope and Sequence of Action Steps to Launch a Teacher's Development

| Phase | Management Trajectory | Rigor Trajectory |
|---|---|---|
| **Phase 1 (Pre-Teaching)** | **Develop Essential Routines and Procedures** | **Write Lesson Plans** |
| Dress Rehearsal (Summer PD) | 1. **Routines and Procedures 101**: Design and roll out<br>2. **Strong Voice**: Stand and speak with purpose | 1. **Develop Effective Lesson Plans 101**: Build the foundation of an effective lesson rooted in what students need to learn<br>2. **Internalize Existing Lesson Plans**: Internalize and rehearse key parts of the lesson |
| **Phase 2** | **Roll Out and Monitor Routines** | **Independent Practice** |
| Instant Immersion (Days 1–30) | 3. **What to Do**: Give clear, precise directions<br>4. **Routines and Procedures 201**: Revise and perfect them<br>5. **Teacher Radar**: Know when students are off task<br>6. **Whole-Class Reset**: Get a whole class back on task | 3. **Write the Exemplar**: Set the bar for excellence<br>4. **Independent Practice**: Set up daily routines that build opportunities for students to practice independently<br>5. **Monitor Aggressively**: Check students' independent work to determine whether they're learning what you're teaching |
| **Phase 3** | **Engage Every Student** | **Respond to Student Learning Needs** |
| Getting into Gear (Days 31–60) | 7. **Build the Momentum**: Motivate students to complete a task<br>8. **Pacing**: Create the illusion of speed so that students feel constantly engaged | 6. **Habits of Evidence**: Teach students to identify and cite evidence<br>7. **Check for Whole-Group Understanding**: Gather evidence on whole-group learning |

| Phase | Management Trajectory | Rigor Trajectory |
|---|---|---|
| | 9. **Engage All Students:** Make sure all students participate<br><br>10. **Narrate the Positive:** Describe what students do well, not what they do wrong<br><br>11. **Individual Student Corrections** | 8. **Reteaching 101—Model:** Model for the students how to think/ solve/write |
| **Phase 4** | **Set Routines for Discourse** | **Lead Student Discourse 101** |
| The Power of Discussion (Days 61–90) | 12. **Engaged Small-Group Work:** Maximize the learning time for every student in group work | 9. **Reteaching 201—Guided Discourse:** Let students unpack the error and build a solution<br><br>10. **Universal Prompts:** Push the thinking back on the students through universal prompts that could be used at any point<br><br>11. **Habits of Discussion:** Teach and model for students the habits that strengthen class conversation |
| **Stretch It** | | **Lead Student Discourse 201** |
| Ready to Paint (Days 91+) | None!<br><br>Once you get this far, you can focus entirely on rigor and deepening content knowledge. | 12. **Strategic Prompts:** Ask strategic questions to targeted students in response to student error<br><br>13. **Go Conceptual:** Get students to do the conceptual thinking |

*Note:* This is the abbreviated version; the full Get Better Faster Scope and Sequence is located at the front of the book and on the DVD. The video clips are also accessible online at my.paulbambrick.com.

The Get Better Faster Scope and Sequence is divided into four phases of teacher development to mirror the first months of a teacher's career (thus the four sections that drive this book). Each phase has a core focus—the major areas in which a teacher needs to develop—and granular action steps listed with each action area. For example, the focus of Phase 1 Rigor is writing lesson plans. Number 1 of the Phase 1 Rigor action steps is Develop Effective Lesson Plans 101. The following are the bite-sized action steps listed for this area:

- Write precise learning objectives that are data driven (rooted in what students need to learn based on analysis of assessment results).
- Deliver an effective I Do as a core part of the lesson.
- Design an exit ticket (brief final mini-assessment) aligned to the objective.

Every step of the way, you have an action step to use with teachers to help them get better faster.

To be sure, the action steps in the Scope and Sequence do not constitute an exhaustive list of everything a new teacher needs to master at every point in the year; rather, they focus on the highest-leverage steps identified through on-the-ground observation of exceptional leaders. Moreover, you might discover effective action steps yourself that aren't in this guide. If so, please pass them on! This guide has evolved and improved because of input from thousands of instructional leaders. You can help make it stronger as well.

We should also note that not every teacher will develop at the pace the Scope and Sequence proposes. But if they follow the sequence, the ultimate measure of your success will be the improvement you see in their classroom.

What the Scope and Sequence offers, then, is not an end-point evaluation tool, but a coaching blueprint—it shows the granular increments by which to measure success, and the ideal order in which to put each piece in place.

---

### Core Idea

The Get Better Faster Scope and Sequence is not an evaluation tool but rather a blueprint for building better teachers.

---

Although these steps don't address the "how" of coaching (that's the next section!), they are critical for your success. Usually, when a feedback session goes poorly, the trouble is rooted in a weak action step. When you don't know where you're headed in a feedback meeting, neither will the teacher.

To give you the opportunity to practice generating granular action steps, what follows are two real-world case studies based on actual observations of new teachers. Pull out your Scope and Sequence and get ready to practice identifying the right action step!

### Putting It into Practice—Case Study on Management

Let's take a look at how you can use the Scope and Sequence with a case study of a teacher struggling with classroom management.

---

### Case Study 2: Management

Darnell has worked hard with you to set up his opening routines. He created a routine of greeting students at the door and set the expectation for students to enter quietly. He had a Do Now (a five-minute written task) already placed on students' desks so that they could start work immediately, and set a timer for five minutes to create urgency about completing it. Whereas the routine worked successfully at the beginning of the year, as you observe him today you notice that the routine has deteriorated.

As each student enters the room, Darnell greets them, but as they move toward their desks, some students dawdle or wander to other parts of the classroom before pulling out their chairs. Others talk among themselves or even lightly scuffle with each other—one or two binders fall to the floor amid giggles. Hardly anyone has begun work on the Do Now.

Darnell moves to the front of the class, stands still, and calls out: "Class, remember that everyone should be heading to his or her own seat, not someone else's." There is little change. "We should be working silently on our Do Nows," he tries again a moment later—to no avail. Two minutes later, when nearly everyone is seated but only half the class is completing their Do Now, Darnell tells the class that they have collectively lost half a point already in the system of classroom consequences they use. Some of the shuffling dies down then, but some murmurs remain.

---

With this observation in mind, pull out your Scope and Sequence. What would be the observable and practice-able, highest-leverage, bite-sized action step you could give him? As you contemplate your action step, remember the following:

- The Get Better Faster Scope and Sequence was written in priority order. Consider it like a waterfall: start from the beginning and stop when you hit the area where the teacher is starting to struggle.

- The action steps in the Scope and Sequence are written generally for any teacher. You should adapt them to even more specifically target the teacher in question.

- What makes an action bite-sized is not the number of words but whether or not you can accomplish it in one week. Sometimes adding words can add clarity and precision.

With these tips, write down your action step:

### Stop and Jot: Case Study 2

Write down the bite-sized action step you would give to Darnell to improve his teaching next week:

_____

_____

_____

_____

 **Stop here.** Keep reading only after you've drafted your action step!

Let's break down the case study. From the information presented, Darnell has already designed and rolled out an effective routine; the problem is that students have stopped following it. He seems to have decent implementation of Strong Voice (granted that in a written case study, it is much more difficult to ascertain his posture and register than in a real classroom observation!). Since Phase 1 action steps don't seem to be the core issue, we move to Phase 2. Here we start to see some real possibilities. Does the root of the problem lie in

- A lack of clear instructions in what students need to do in the procedure? (management action step 3)
- An imperfect procedure? (step 4)
- Darnell's ability to see the problem? (step 5)
- Darnell's ability to reset the class once the routine has failed? (either step 4, Do It Again, or step 6, Whole Class Reset)

In many ways, each of these would be a legitimate area of focus; your choice would depend a lot on what you already know about Darnell's areas of weakness, and the insights you would gain by being in the actual classroom. If your proposed action step fell in the Phase 2 section, you are on the right track.

The following is the top action step we would recommend based on the real case of Darnell:

---

### Case Study 2 Action Steps

**Phase 2 Management—Whole-Class Reset:**

- Implement a planned "reset" of the entry routine:
  - Issue clear What to Do directions: "Stop. Everyone back outside. All eyes on me. [Wait for everyone to head back outside the class.] That is not what this class can look like. As you enter, you need to do three things: (1) Enter silently. (2) Immediately take your seat. (3) Begin your Do Now and don't stop until the timer sounds. We'll do it until we get it right. Ready? Go."
  - Narrate two students who do it well ("Thank you, Maria. That's what seventh graders look like.").
  - Circulate the room, moving toward students who are not on task.

---

What do you notice about this action step?

- It takes the language of the action steps in the Scope and Sequence and tailors it to Darnell's specific needs.

- It is cumulative: it remains centered on the whole-class reset (action step 6) but includes elements from previous action steps Darnell has already worked on and been proficient in, in other settings (in this case, What to Do directions and circulating with purpose). Just as a piano player will keep practicing her posture, hand location, and chords with each new piece she learns, so too the teacher will continue to practice earlier action steps as he learns new ones.

- It remains bite-sized: Darnell could clearly practice and implement this immediately, mastering it in the upcoming week. This is the heart of building an effective action step.

> ### Findings from the Field: Spend Less Time on the "What" and More Time on the "How"
>
> When I started using the Get Better Faster Sequence for action steps, my whole approach to teacher development changed. Before, I felt like my feedback was a little like "whack-a-mole": tackle a random problem over here, only to have another one pop up over there. I felt pretty directionless. Now I have a clear starting point—has my teacher mastered Phase 1? Phase 2?—and a clear trajectory. This allows me to spend less time on "what" my feedback should be and more time on "how" to deliver that feedback and how to practice. In the process, I have seen my new teachers move so much faster than before.
>
> —Patrick Pastore, principal, Rochester, New York

### Putting It into Practice—Case Study on Rigor

Now that you've taken a crack at management, let's try rigor. For some, this will be easier; for others, harder. Let's give it a try!

---

### Case Study 3: Rigor

Ashley is a high school English teacher, and when you walk into the classroom, you see her giving instructions for an independent writing task. "OK. Now that we have established the basic meaning of Sonnet 65, I want you to answer the following question: How does Shakespeare's use of figurative language contribute to establishing the theme of the sonnet? Please annotate your poem with the best evidence and organize your ideas before writing. You will have fifteen minutes. You may begin."

As you look at Ashley's lesson plan, you can see that the task is nicely aligned to her objective and to the rigor of upcoming writing assignments. She is clearly pushing her students.

As she sets the timer for fifteen minutes, students get to work immediately. You see them annotating their poem, drafting an outline of their response, and beginning to write. Ashley stands at the front of the room, scanning to make sure students appear to be writing, and looking down at her lesson plan. About five minutes in, she notices that one of her most struggling students hasn't begun writing, so she goes over to him and stays talking to him for five minutes. Then she reminds the class that they have five more minutes and waits for students to finish.

The timer goes off, and Ashley calls the class to attention. "So, now that you've finished writing, what you do think: How does Shakespeare's use of figurative language contribute to establishing the theme of the sonnet?" Three students raise their hands, and Ashley calls on them one at a time. Michael begins, and although he identifies a core example of figurative language in the poem, he's not able to identify a central theme to the poem. Anna contributes and agrees with Michael, which causes Ashley to pause the discussion. "Both of you have chosen good figurative language, but you haven't connected to the theme. James, can you help out?" James proceeds to make the same error as his peers, and Ashley gets a little frustrated. She goes on to explain how Shakespeare used figurative language, and the class nods approvingly. A number of students comment that they had that answer themselves.

At the end of the class, when Ashley collects the writing assignments, she notices that three students in the class were able to identify a proper theme and support it with figurative language, three more had answers that were getting close, and most of the rest were confused: they had not finished writing and had poor evidence selected.

---

Referring to your Scope and Sequence and remembering the tips from the previous case study, write down your action step. Again, start from the top and stop where the first major error occurs.

**Stop here.** Read on only after you've drafted your action step!

As we look at this case study, we see that many things are going well for Ashley. Her routines and procedures are on point and students are engaged, which immediately allows us to focus on the action steps for rigor. If we look at Phase 1, she seems to have proficiency: she has a quality objective aligned to her upcoming assessments and a quality task that is also aligned (step 1). Moving forward to Phase 2, the class conversation indicates that Ashley seems to know what she is looking for in their responses (step 2). Independent practice is well set up, with an appropriate amount of time and on-task behavior (step 4).

A clear area of struggle is in managing class discussion, which could pull you to look at action steps in Phase 3 (step 6, not getting students to cite good evidence) or Phase 4 (step 9, not guiding students to unpack their errors themselves; or step 11, not using good habits of discussion). In fact, in our work with many instructional leaders, this is precisely where most will go.

Yet if you look closely at the root cause of the lack of quality discussion, it centers around Ashley's lack of knowledge of where her students were prior to the beginning of the discussion. Because she looked only at the most struggling student's work during independent practice, she had no idea that only three students had decent analysis and only three more had selected quality figurative language to make their point. If she had walked around the room and paid attention to student work, she could have seen their errors and coached them in the moment, *prior* to the class discussion. She also could have diagnosed the class's struggles and targeted the discussion to address it.

By looking at the root cause of the problem—where it began—we landed on the following top action step.

---

### Case Study 3 Action Step

**Phase 2 Rigor—Monitor Aggressively:** Check students' independent work to determine whether they're learning what you're teaching

- Create and implement a monitoring pathway:
  - Create a seating chart to monitor students most effectively.
  - Monitor the fastest writers first, then the students who need more support.
- Monitor the quality of student work:
  - Check answers against your exemplar.
  - Track right and wrong answers to class questions.
- Pen in Hand: mark up student work as you circulate.
  - Use a coding system to affirm a correct answer.
  - Cue students to revise answers, using minimal verbal intervention.

---

Did you come up with a similar action step? If so, congratulations! If not, here are some final takeaways that could help:

- If we go in order from top to bottom (the waterfall approach), aggressive monitoring (step 5) is the first area of error. Although there are many other areas of growth, getting this right will contribute to improving student learning and laying a foundation for the rest. Use the order of the sequence to your advantage.

- Every one of us has "go-to" areas of instruction about which we are naturally drawn to giving feedback. Because of this, we have also become quite adept at giving feedback in these areas. Yet these areas are not always the highest leverage for that teacher. Utilizing the Get Better Faster Scope and Sequence can open our horizons to giving feedback about other areas of instruction that normally haven't been our forte, and in turn, that develops our expertise to serve even more teachers.

## Conclusion

Going granular with our action steps can be a significant change if we are used to whole evaluation observations. And there's no doubt that at first this change will feel as though you are moving at a glacial pace. That was certainly the case with the high school building—watching the foundation be put into place inch by inch made it seem as if the building would never be completed. But somehow, what began by looking like a slow start transforms within months into something extraordinary: a monument to making learning happen.

Once you've identified the right action step, you've won half the battle. The second half is guiding a teacher to mastery of it. That's covered by the next principle.

### Final Reflection: Go Granular

What are your biggest takeaways for identifying the right action step for a teacher?

_____

_____

_____

_____

What action steps from the Scope and Sequence would most enhance your repertoire and make you better at giving feedback?

_____

_____

_____

_____

Think of a new teacher you've worked with recently and an area in which that teacher struggled. What would be an effective series of action steps for that teacher?

_____

_____

_____

_____

## PRINCIPLE 2: PLAN, PRACTICE, FOLLOW UP, REPEAT

A couple of years ago, my older daughter began competing in Forensics (public speaking competitions). She's confident and outgoing by nature, but still, when it came time for her to present a speech before a panel of judges, she was nervous. What if she made a mistake, right there during her presentation? It was intimidating to be judged on something she'd have only one chance to get right.

What ultimately reassured my daughter was the amount of practicing she did before she competed. Together, my daughter and I (and subsequently her high school coach) practiced until she'd built every skill of delivering a great speech right into her muscle memory—adding a dramatic pause at just the right moment, dropping in volume for effect while still remaining audible, and appearing to make eye contact with every member of the audience. When the time came for my daughter to present her speech, it had become something she knew exactly how to do, because she'd done it flawlessly so many times before. Practicing each skill in isolation, and then gradually putting them together, made all the difference.

Just like delivering a speech—or playing a sport or performing surgery or acting in a play—teaching happens live. So how can teachers overcome that same worry my daughter struggled with—that feeling of having only one chance to perform correctly? The same way she did: by practicing specific skills over and over until practice has made perfect. In every field, the more effectively we practice, the better we perform.

The Scope and Sequence provides the skills of getting better at teaching; practicing is the way to learn them faster.

How does that look in the field of coaching teachers? Let's refer back to the opening clip you saw in the introduction of Nikki Bridges working with her teacher Jackson.

 Rewatch clip 1: Teacher Radar—Scan
(Key Leadership Move: Plan/Practice)

When Jackson walked into Nikki's office, he had no idea how to scan for student behaviors and keep his students on point to follow instructions. When he walked out, he had practiced multiple times and was more prepared than ever to implement that skill in the classroom. He built up his expertise outside the classroom, and that meant he had it ready to use when it counted most.

What Nikki and Jackson just proved—that teachers can grow dramatically by practicing outside the classroom—gets at the heart of transforming the dangerous myth that teachers cannot become great in any less than ten years.[2] At the root of this myth is the assumption that teachers learn primarily—or even exclusively—from experience. And while experience is indeed a great teacher, we cannot afford to accept the premise that the process of becoming a master is impossible to accelerate. The new teachers of the most effective leaders didn't have to wait ten years, because their leaders lived by a simple mantra that has been repeated since the early 1900s: practice until you cannot get it wrong.[3]

> ### Core Idea
>
> Contenders practice until they get it right.
> Champions practice until they cannot get it wrong.

So what separates the practice of contenders from those of champions? There are a few basic principles Nikki used that made her practice effective. You can emulate them:

- **Define "perfect"**—determine what ideal practice will look like.
- **Plan before you practice**—build an effective script before you take it live.

- **Practice**—take it live.
- **Follow up and repeat**—observe implementation to make sure the action is performed as flawlessly for the students as it is behind the scenes.

## Define "Perfect": Know How the Skill Must Look

Imagine a swimming instructor who tells her students that today, they're going to learn how to do a basic flutter kick (the classic kick that accompanies front crawl strokes). She hands everyone a kickboard and stands at the edge of the pool. "OK, kids," she says, with no further introduction. "Let's go! Show me your best kick!"

What follows would not truly be practice. It would get students into the water with their kickboards, but they wouldn't know what to do when they got there, and the instructor wouldn't have any way of assessing their success. There would be a lot of splashing in the pool, but probably not much learning.

Now imagine that instead, the instructor has every child lie on his or her side outside the pool. "Keep your legs straight," she might say, "like dry spaghetti, not cooked spaghetti; and point your toes like a ballerina. Now separate your legs like scissors: one leg forward and the other leg back. Switch legs—the first one back and the other forward. Now move them back and forward in quick strokes: keep cutting paper with your scissor legs. Kick hard when you kick down, and soft when you kick up!" She could walk around and correct the movements of students who are struggling. By the time the students actually get in the water, they've already improved their strokes and greatly increased their likelihood of success. The difference is night and day, for many important reasons. One of the first reasons is that the coach knew exactly what she was looking for. Without a vision of the basic flutter kick, she could not have gotten her students to practice what mattered.

> ### Core Idea
>
> You can't make practice perfect
> until you define what "perfect" looks like.

Think back to some of the action steps you read or designed in the previous section. When your action steps are observable and practice-able, high leverage, and bite-sized, they specify exactly what needs to be perfected—but the task of defining each component of "perfect" remains. For example, think about Nikki's work with Jackson. The action step was scanning the room for responsiveness. Breaking that down, Nikki has to get Jackson to do the following. First they selected the moment in class where he wanted to practice (when he says, "Finger Freeze: track me"). Then they detailed each component:

- What the teacher is doing:
  - Walk around before the direction to monitor students.
  - Say "Finger Freeze: track me."
  - Scan for responsiveness.
  - Narrate the positive of students who got it right.
  - Point to the book of someone who doesn't have his finger in place or where his hands should be.

- What the student is doing when direction is given:
  - Feet on floor
  - Eyes on teacher
  - Finger in the book pointing to a spot or holding sides of the book

This definition of "perfect" breaks down the action step to make it relevant to the teacher's classroom, and you now have a clear vision of what teacher and student actions will spell success for that action step. This also allows you to know what to look for when you observe the teacher.

The same holds true for rigor. In the Phase 1 Coaching Blueprint (focused on leading PD), we will show a video (clip 2) of Kelly Dowling leading a PD workshop around aggressive monitoring while doing close reading. You'll learn more about effective techniques for leading PD in Phase 1, but look at how she makes certain to define "perfect."

---

 Watch clip 2: Exemplar and Aggressive Monitoring
(Key Leadership Move: Leading PD)

---

## Plan Before You Practice

Once you have a clear vision of what perfect looks like, the next step is to make sure your teacher has that same vision *before* starting to practice. It's easy to overlook this step, yet doing so is the number one factor that leads to ineffective practice.

Imagine that your sixth-grade teacher is working on the Phase 3 Rigor action step of habits of evidence: teaching students to annotate the best evidence in a text as they read and having them cite that evidence during class discussion. You state this action step and then you say to your teacher, "Let's practice." Your teacher stands up and delivers the instructions to annotate for the best evidence, and then practices calling on students to cite evidence. Sounds effective, right?

Yet here is the problem: what makes this action step difficult is not telling students to do the task of annotating and citing evidence but building the habit of finding the *best* evidence. The practice described here was nothing more than the teacher saying the instructions. What will likely happen in class, then, is that the teacher will give instructions, not everyone will be successful in following them, and the teacher will have to figure out how to respond on her own. How would that be different with a plan?

Imagine that same teacher, this time building a plan. You pull out her lesson plan for an upcoming class and see that she will be working with the following excerpts from *Warriors Don't Cry*, a memoir from Melba Beals about her experience as one of the students to integrate Little Rock's Central High during the civil rights movement. Working with chapter 7, the teacher is focusing on the students' ability to identify the author's emotional state in four key passages on the first day of school. Please refer to the excerpts.

---

## Warriors Don't Cry

*Key Excerpts from Chapter 7*

*Melba Patillo Beals*

Mrs. Bates told us to remain seated until everyone else left the room. I sat very still for a long moment as everybody around me began moving. So, God, you really do want me to go back to that school. For a time it seemed as if I were all alone in a silent tunnel, and everyone else was way at the other end. I would always remember that judge and his huge, piercing dark eyes. There must be something wonderful in his heart, I thought. (68)

I was racing to keep pace with a woman who shouted orders over her shoulder to us. Nobody had yet told us she was someone we could trust, someone we should be following. I tried to move among the angry voices, blinking, struggling to accustom my eyes to the very dim light. The unfamiliar surroundings reminded me of the inside of a museum—marble floors and stone walls and long winding hallways that seemed to go on forever. It was a huge, cavernous building, the largest I'd even been in. I made my legs carry me quickly past angry white faces, dodging fists that struck at me. (72)

We quickly compared notes. Each of us was assigned to a different homeroom. "Why can't any of us be in the same homeroom or take classes together?" I asked. From behind the long desk, a man spoke in an unkind booming voice. "You wanted integration . . . you got integration." (73)

As I entered the classroom, a hush fell over the students. The guide pointed me to an empty seat, and I walked toward it. Students sitting nearby quickly gathered their books and moved away. I sat down, surrounded by empty seats feeling unbearably self-conscious. Still, I was relieved to be off my feet. I was disoriented, as though my world were blurred and leaning to the left, like a photograph snapped from a twisted angle and out of focus. A middle-aged woman, whom I assumed to be the teacher, ignored me. (75)

---

Instead of stopping with the selection of key excerpts, you ask her to identify what is the best evidence she wants to see the students gather. She takes her handout and annotates it herself, circling the key evidence she will monitor. She also includes her exemplar response to the writing prompt and highlights the key parts of that response as well. After she has done so, you script out her instructions and a plan for her to walk around the classroom to see whether students selected that evidence. Then you plan what she will say to students who are not finding good evidence.

Figure 1 shows what the teacher's copy of the handout looked like after the class. In light ink are her original annotations; in thicker ink are her notes that she took while monitoring the students' annotations.

What just happened? You dramatically accelerated the teacher's ability to get her students to cite the best evidence by building a full plan *before* she entered the classroom. If the teacher had tried to practice looking for good evidence without an annotated handout, the practice would have been much more superficial.

By creating a plan, you create a vision for the teacher of what the class could look like before she even experiences it in practice. In doing so, you increase the odds of the teacher practicing—and teaching—successfully.

Figure 1

Figure 1

---

Name: _____     Date: _____
Section: NU               Team: _____

WARRIORS DON'T CRY CHAPTER 7 CLOSE READ

**DISCUSSION PREPARATION**

**Close Read Focus: Diction**

**Key Question:**

Directions: While you read the passage below, pay close attention to Beals' diction. What words/phrases does Beal use in the four excerpts below that:
a) Convey how she feels?
b) Convey an essential theme in the novel?

*[handwritten: Odie, identified - call on him for this + "unbearably self-conscious"]*

| Page 68 | Page 72 | Page 73 | Page 75 |
|---|---|---|---|
| Mrs. Bates told us to remain seated until everyone else left the room. I sat very still for a long moment as everybody around me began moving. So, God, you really won't do want me to go back to that school. For a time it seemed as if I were all alone in a silent tunnel and everyone else was way at the other end. I would always remember that judge and his huge, piercing dark eyes. There must be something wonderful in his heart, I thought. | I was racing to keep pace with a woman who shouted orders over her shoulders to us. Nobody had yet told us she was someone we could trust, someone we should be following. I tried to move among the angry voices, blinking, struggling to accustom my eyes to the very dim light. The unfamiliar surroundings reminded me of the inside of a museum – marble floors and stone walks and long winding hallways that seemed to go on forever. It was a huge, cavernous building, the largest I'd ever been in. Breathless, I made my legs carry me quickly past angry white faces, dodging fists that struck at me." | Three thirty-nine, that was the number of the homeroom card; I was assigned to the third floor. We quickly compared notes. Each of us was assigned to a different homeroom. "Why can't any of us be in the same homeroom or take classes together?" I asked. From behind the long desk, a man spoke in an unkind booming voice. "You wanted integration...you got integration." | As I entered the classroom, a hush fell over the students. The guided pointed me to an empty seat, and I walked toward it. Students sitting nearby quickly gathered their books and moved away. I sat down, surrounded by empty seats feeling unbearably self-conscious. Still, I was relieved to be off my feet. I was disoriented, as though my world were blurred and leaning to the left, like a photograph snapped from a twisted angle and out of focus. A middle-aged woman, whom I assumed to be the teacher, ignored me. |

*[handwritten left: Call on Jabriel for this]*
*[handwritten middle: Bese has several pieces of diction]*

**Pre-Discussion Question** *[handwritten: Call on Janyi if we struggle — review this box — random words]*

How is Beals' emotional state similar in all 4 of these excerpts?

*[handwritten response:]* In each of these excerpts, Beal is experiencing alienation. She describes feeling "all alone" in "unfamiliar surroundings" to depict her isolation. Her descriptions of the physical setting include "winding hallways," "cavernous," and "museum," highlighting the cold distance she felt in the school.

---

**Core Idea**

Plan before you practice to prevent practicing imperfectly.

---

This process is no different than planning great lessons. Grant Wiggins and Jay McTighe are among the many pioneers who highlight the importance of "back-wards planning": starting with your objective for what students will be able to do at the end of the lesson, and working backwards to plan a lesson that will get you there.[4] Planning how to coach a teacher on a skill is similar. Defining perfect is identifying your destination, and this next piece of the puzzle—planning how the teacher will practice it—is mapping the route there.

Syrena Burnam does this when working with Norvella, her biology teacher. Syrena is working with Norvella to increase the quality of student discourse. To build the students' habits of discussion when discussing the results of a laboratory experiment, they are working together to plan the implementation of a "hands-down discussion": one where Norvella asks the students to build off of one another's answers without her intervention. Norvella is not used to stepping back and letting the students do the thinking. Watch clip 3 to see the process that Syrena uses to make sure that Norvella's rollout of this new procedure is effective.

 Watch clip 3: Habits of Discussion
(Key Leadership Move: Plan/Practice)

Here are the most important elements that make Syrena's—and anyone's—planning effective:

- **Come prepared to plan.** Syrena already knew what routine they were going to practice, and she'd planned accordingly. She planned what an effective roll-out could be so that she would be ready to recommend precise language when her teacher struggled. You can also see in the video that she'd made sure the teacher had brought her lesson plans. The two of them made the revisions right into the lesson plan, which dramatically increased the likelihood that the teacher would remember to implement the action in her class.

- **Write a detailed script.** Syrena planned the specific words and actions Norvella would use to reach her goal, rather than relying on vague directives. She made sure to nail down the language and steps her teacher would take, and they wrote it down to hold on to it. This way, Norvella knew exactly what to do a few moments later when she took it live.

- **Get out in front of error.** Syrena knew that the difficulty for her teacher was motivating the students around the excitement of a hands-down discussion, so she focused on that part of the script. In other cases, it could be a teacher's pacing, or the behavioral challenges that could arise. As much as possible, the plan you develop should lock in success in the roughest as well as the smoothest of circumstances.

By implementing these three elements before live practice, your teacher is much more likely to succeed.

---

### Findings from the Field: Plan Side by Side and Then Compare

When I was a new teacher, one of the most important things my principal did for me was plan alongside me and then compare and contrast. For example, he would say, "Let's plan out your questioning sequence for your next class. You and I will both write sequences separately and then let's share and compare." This was so powerful because it allowed me to try to build a plan myself first and then to learn how he was thinking about the same problem. I found that my plans became so much stronger as a result.

—Lauren Catlett, principal, Troy, New York

---

### Stop and Jot: Plan before You Practice

Plan how you'd practice the skill for which you defined practice earlier, including challenges.

_____

_____

_____

_____

_____

_____

---

### Practice: "Let's Take It Live"

Once you have your plan for success in place, it's time to take it live! Let's watch the video of Ramy Abdel-Nabi and Jackie Rosner leading teachers in practicing aggressive monitoring: the art of giving students precise feedback during independent practice. Watch the highlights of their PD session (clip 4) and how they get the teachers to practice authentically.

 Watch clip 4: Mark Up Student Work and Cue Students
(Key Leadership Moves: Leading PD, Practice)

A few key characteristics were especially critical to making Ramy and Jackie's practice with the teachers so effective:

- **Just do it.** The point bears repeating: for practice to be powerful, the teacher has to practice what she will have to do during class. If the teacher being coached had played the part of the students, or if she and the coach had both just discussed what she would have to do instead of physically doing it, she would not have learned what she needed to learn. She might have been mentally prepared to implement the action step, but the precise goal of practice is for the teacher to build muscle memory: experiencing what it feels like to implement successfully.

- **Cut off imperfect practice.** The instant the teacher's monitoring was slightly off, the leader cut her practice off. This meant that the teacher never had a chance to internalize any habits that would impede the success of her opening procedures. The practicing was dedicated to coaching her on performing the skill correctly, not incorrectly.

> ### Findings from the Field: The Third Time Is the Charm
>
> The most important moments with my teachers are where I can help them perfect their practice—this is where they make the biggest jumps in their development. A simple formula helped over and over again: model the technique, interrupt the practice at the first moment of error, and practice a third time to incorporate any final adjustment. In that way, a teacher goes from novice to proficient quite quickly.
> —Jimena Saavedra Fernandez, coach, Santiago, Chile

- **Add complexity.** In the first round, they just focused on looking at many students' work. In the second round, they focused on improving her feedback to individual students. By the end of the exercise, the teacher had steadily built up better, tighter skills.

- **Repeat until successful.** The opening of this chapter described how my daughter practiced her speech many times successfully so that she would be completely assured of delivering it successfully when she was being graded on it. It probably comes as little surprise that the same is true of practicing teaching skills. By the time the teacher returns to her classroom, a great procedure for monitoring student work won't just be something she thinks she might be able to do correctly sometimes: it will be something she simply *does* correctly. It's this deep internalization that ultimately makes practice the game-changing tool it is.

---

### Findings from the Field: Practice Often and with Humility

Sometimes the most impactful idea is the one that's most obvious. If you want to be sure they can do it repeatedly well, they must practice. Teachers need to not just learn new skills but practice those skills until they can do them to perfection and as a habit. Planning ahead and practicing that plan to perfection has had the biggest impact on my growth and the development of my teachers and leaders.

My advice to instructional leaders is to create an environment of constant growth and self-reflection by modeling this with humility. Leaders need to be seen as the lead learner in their buildings and publicly own their mistakes and their growth areas, and demonstrate their improvement in those areas over time.

—Dr. Lamont Browne, principal manager, Wilmington, Delaware

---

### Core Idea

To make teaching effective, plan before you practice, and practice before you teach.

---

## Follow Up and Repeat: Lock in Success

To ensure that the teacher effectively implements the plan you've made together, follow-up is essential. Simply look specifically for successful implementation of this skill the next time you observe the teacher, and let the teacher know what you've seen the next time you meet with him or her. Areas in which the teacher is successfully implementing the skill can become sources of precise praise; any spots that are still a challenge for the teacher can be practiced over again.

Look at how Julie Jackson does that with her teacher Rachel (clip 5). In this meeting, they have been working on Develop Effective Lesson Plans 101—namely, improving the alignment of Rachel's objectives with her exit ticket and the "I Do" of the lesson. After spending time practicing writing objectives, exit tickets, and the I Do for upcoming lessons, Julie locks in this learning by establishing the follow-up they will take:

Watch clip 5: Develop Effective Lesson Plans 101
(Key Leadership Move: Follow-Up)

So many things are remarkable about this clip. For starters, this follow-up work took Julie no more than two minutes, but these two minutes guaranteed much more likely success for Rachel. Here are a few elements that distinguish quality follow-up:

- **Set a time to observe it in action.** Julie's simple question of asking when she could observe Rachel's implementation sends a powerful message: she cares about Rachel's success, and she expects these actions to be implemented. Such a message didn't take a heavy hand at all: it was just a question.

### Findings from the Field: Film It to Lock in Follow-Up

My principal was really struggling with getting her teacher to implement the action step. The teacher would never fully act on the action plan they established in the feedback meeting. That's when we decided to film the teacher's classroom. At the next meeting, they looked at the film, and they were immediately able to identify exactly how the teacher got off track. By seeing it, the teacher was much more eager to start implementing it. A week later, the principal observed and the plan was working. The teacher actually continues to implement this strategy.

—Sondra Jolovich-Motes, principal manager, Ogden, Utah

- **Lock in the tasks.** One of the hardest things for a newer teacher—or any educator, for that matter!—is to remember all the tasks that have to be accomplished. Rather than leave this to chance, Julie and Rachel both write down the tasks and timeline. (We will discuss this in more detail in the Phase 2 Coaching Blueprint section, "Set the Tone: The First Feedback Meeting.")
- **Use your resources.** Julie makes sure to use any resources available to her to support her teacher, whether it be a copy of a teaching guide or a video camera to self-critique the lesson.

Follow-up is the natural segue into your next cycle of practice. Grab what the teacher did well and build on that in practicing and mastering the next action step. The result is an ongoing cycle of growth, with each piece of the foundation you're building firmly in place before the next is cemented on top of it.

> ### Findings from the Field: Follow Up, and Teachers See That You Care
>
> I have always been a strong believer in observing and in giving feedback. But the Get Better Faster approach brought something new: following up. When you start following up consistently, your teachers get to a point where if you don't get back into their classroom with the follow-up action, they're calling you out on it! It becomes really important to them, and they really appreciate it. They know when you're going to be in to look at it again, and they look forward to the additional feedback. It's bite-sized—not too much information—and it creates a culture of teachers and leaders working together.
>
> —Ginger Conroy, principal, Denver, Colorado

## Conclusion

When a challenge arises, the person you want on the scene to help is the person who's already been prepared to manage it. This is why the power of practice in PD cannot be overstated. Practicing relentlessly before you need to use your skills is the key to guaranteeing they'll be ready for you when you do need them. If you want to *hope* to overcome a massive challenge, trusting an unfamiliar miracle to see you through certainly works sometimes. But if you want to *guarantee* triumph, practicing to perfection leaves little to chance.

We've now covered two of the core coaching tools that leaders must harness to get teachers better faster: granular action steps that give a teacher clear knowledge of what to do, and opportunities to practice those actions outside the classroom so that he or she can put them to work inside it. Now we move on to the third and last coaching technique we'll present in detail: making feedback more frequent.

---

### Stop and Jot: Plan, Practice, Follow Up, Repeat

Look back at your earlier Stop and Jots and select one of the action steps you designed.

Step 1 (Plan): What planning could you do with the teacher to set up the practice to be effective? Write out the script, task, and exemplar:

_____

_____

_____

Step 2 (Practice): What is the most important part of the practice with which the teacher will likely struggle?

_____

_____

_____

Step 3 (Follow Up): What are the key follow-up tasks that you and the teacher should do to lock in the learning?

_____

_____

_____

---

## PRINCIPLE 3: MAKE FEEDBACK MORE FREQUENT

When hospital residents begin to perform their first surgeries, they never do so alone. Instead, they work alongside a more experienced doctor who will speak up—and, if necessary, intervene—the moment anything looks like it could possibly go wrong.[5] Most of us take this level of care for granted. When it comes to the field of medicine, we fully comprehend that the presence of the more experienced professional is a lifesaver—for a doctor *not* to do anything to correct an error in the moment would be unconscionable. The underlying premise is that a patient's life is of the utmost importance in medical care, and a teaching doctor can keep that sacred—while also training residents—by simply stepping in when needed. But there is another premise at work as well: by stepping in and coaching in the moment, the experienced doctors deliver more feedback to the residents, and as a result, the residents get better faster. They fix their mistakes and become experts more quickly. Anyone who has accompanied a doctor through residency can attest to the dramatic speed in their development as physicians. This is not a luxury but a necessity: without it, we would not have enough trained doctors to met the need. As past, current, and future patients, we are all benefactors of this accelerated development.

New teachers are not very different from hospital residents: they are green, yet they immediately have to work with actual people. What would happen if we decided to honor the same two premises of residency?

Hanushek and Rivkin, among many others, have demonstrated that consecutive years of good or bad teaching can have dramatic impacts on learning.[6] While those impacts are not as significant as the life-and-death circumstances of a doctor, the stakes are still high for our children, and more effective coaching can make the difference. To attest to this, Ross, Bennett, and others have shown that academic achievement increased for students whose teachers were coached more frequently.[7]

What would happen if we gave teachers feedback far more frequently, stepping in when needed with a new teacher, just as we expect doctors to do for residents? We would not only improve learning in the moment but also accelerate a teacher's growth.[8]

---

### Core Idea

A resident doctor develops at an accelerated rate and serves patients better because of the hands-on coaching of an attending physician. To accelerate a new teacher's development and to help learning thrive, follow the doctor's lead.

---

In today's education landscape, however, the frequent and real-time feedback that we assume is essential for surgeons is often missing or even taboo. Just prioritizing more frequent feedback is challenging (we address that further and in more detail in the Phase 2 Coaching Blueprint). More notably, there is an unspoken rule that when instruction is under way, a school leader's role should be that of a silent observer at most—that there's something untouchable, even sacred, about that moment when a teacher steps to the front of the classroom. The rule is rooted in a genuine risk: real-time feedback done poorly can undermine the teacher's authority or reduce his or her sense of leadership in the classroom.

Real-time feedback done well, however, can take the best of medical practice and help teachers get better. This is essential precisely because there *is* something sacred about class time: the intellectual lives of the students. If we see something going wrong during a lesson that is hurting student learning, we do both those students and their teacher a disservice by not correcting it before the students lose valuable learning time. When we leave real-time feedback out of the picture, important learning moments are lost for students and teachers alike. Just as we would fear what might happen with a surgeon, a teacher who is never given real-time feedback runs a risk of not performing his or her job properly at a critical time—and repeating that mistake multiple times in the future. The people whose lives have been entrusted to the teacher may suffer as a result. What begins as well-intentioned respect for teachers' ownership of their own classrooms ends by deprioritizing the primary goal of education: students' learning.

The leaders who excel at quickly developing teachers prioritize student learning in the moment by improving teaching *as it happens*—and do so without undermining the teacher. The teacher can then incorporate those improvements into his or her practice for many hours to come, continuing to reach more students more effectively long after the leader who first delivered the feedback has left the room.

### Findings from the Field: Shift from What You Could Have Done to What You're Doing

Real-time feedback changes the conversation from "what you should have done" to "what we are doing." It can create a relationship where the teacher and coach are in the moment together, instead of thinking about what could have been done, or what might be. It takes a level of comfort and trust, but it can lead to huge gains.

—Jennifer Jackson, principal, Denver, Colorado

For a baseline idea of how great real-time feedback can drive instruction to the next level, let's see how Art Worrell coached his global history teacher Michael to go deeper with his content. They are working on the Stretch It skill of Go Conceptual: getting students to articulate a larger conceptual understanding beyond basic comprehension. In this particular class, the students are comparing Hammurabi's Code with the Torah (written four hundred years later) to analyze what degree of continuity or change has occurred between these eras. Michael is getting stuck in having the students make simple comparisons between the two documents. Watch how Art jumps in and how he uses that moment in the debrief afterwards (clip 6).

---

 Watch clip 6: Go Conceptual
(Key Leadership Move: Real-Time Feedback)

---

> ### Stop and Jot: Real-Time Feedback
>
> What did Art do to model for the teacher as seamlessly as possible? Jot down the actions you saw him take.
>
> _____
>
> _____
>
> _____
>
> _____

Art's decision to step into the class at this moment creates an immediate improvement in student learning—and it was also a breakthrough moment for Michael to see the impact of questioning for conceptual understanding. They could have talked about this in a check-in, but seeing it live with his own students creates a quicker, more lasting impression. This is the power of real-time feedback at its best: it facilitates the growth of students and teachers simultaneously. It puts the improvement process on fast-forward, making changes immediately that would otherwise take days or weeks for a teacher to implement.

To be sure, reaping the rich rewards of real-time feedback—especially when so many teachers are unused to it—requires a careful touch. This section will cover every essential step of making real-time feedback not only effective but also respectful to all within a school community. These are the steps:

- **Prepare the surgical room—create a culture of real-time feedback.** In order for real-time feedback to work, leaders must be transparent about it—and teachers must anticipate it. Fortunately, with the help of a well-prepared PD session, this can be accomplished at the beginning of the school year.

- **Pick the right moment.** Select the right time to deliver real-time feedback that will most leverage student and teacher development.

- **Use the least invasive approach.** Deliver real-time feedback quickly, clearly, and as noninvasively as possible (just like surgery!).

- **Conduct a follow-up visit.** Debrief the moment of real-time feedback to identify what made the new teaching practice effective.

## Create a Culture

Teachers who have never before encountered real-time feedback may find it disarming at first—especially if they're not expecting it. The surest way to keep this from happening is to create a culture of feedback. This involves making it clear from the very beginning of the year that you regularly give real-time feedback while you observe lessons and that real-time feedback is a typical piece of the coaching process that does not reflect badly on the teacher receiving it. Transparency about what real-time feedback means—and how every teacher can make the most of it—will go a long way toward making it a piece of your school's culture that teachers can expect and appreciate.

A crucial element in ensuring that real-time feedback becomes part of your school's culture is to make it a habit. If you give regular real-time feedback, your consistency will make it a norm. To grease the skids, it is highly beneficial to launch the year with a short PD session on the power of real-time feedback (which can be combined with the power of practice if that is also not a norm for teachers). See "Launch Real-Time Feedback—Opening PD" for a simple form of PD you could deliver.

## Launch Real-Time Feedback—Opening PD

- **Show a video of real-time feedback being delivered in another profession.** Show how this feedback comes as an aid rather than as an accusation, and enables both the coach and the new teacher to make sure their job is done as well as it possibly can be. (You can look for videos of sports coaching, resident doctors, lawyers conferencing during a trial, pilots-in-training, and the like.)
- **Show a video of a leader giving real-time feedback to a teacher— and the teacher immediately implementing it.** Ideally, you would be the leader in this video, but if you're rolling out real-time feedback for the first time, you can use one of the videos in this book. Have teachers reflect on how the real-time feedback helps the teacher improve instruction.
- **Make the connection between the real-time feedback you'll be providing and the feedback your teachers give their students every day.** "Imagine that you're teaching solving quadratic equations through factoring," you might say, "and a student makes an error. It would be a lot more powerful to coach her to fix it in the moment, rather than waiting to mark it wrong on that student's homework later. I give real-time feedback for the same reason. It gives you as the teacher a chance to learn something right away, and it ensures that your students get the most out of that lesson."
- **Model real-time feedback.** During the PD, have a teacher join you at the front of the room. Role-play a lesson observation in which this teacher plays the teacher, you play yourself, and some of the other teachers participating in the PD play the students. At some point, give the teacher real-time feedback and have him or her implement it in the moment. Then, as summer PD goes on, continue to occasionally give real-time feedback while teachers are rehearsing. Ideally, every new teacher would get to experience real-time feedback at least once in rehearsal before the first day of school.

*Note:* In the DVD, you'll find materials for real-time feedback PD that can help you implement this PD. Although these are written for instructional leaders, you could pull materials to reorient toward your teachers. Online access at my.paulbambrick.com.

Phase 1—the pre-teaching phase—will describe in more detail the value of holding PD sessions before students arrive that prepare teachers for all they'll need to do in the earliest days of school. These sessions are the ideal time to brief teachers on real-time feedback.

Once you've prepared teachers for real-time feedback, all that remains is to actually do it—and to do it consistently. As with anything else, it's this repeated follow-up that makes a good practice into a habit. Before long, you will have established the cultural expectation that real-time feedback will happen in your school, with every member of the community anticipating it and benefiting from it.

## Pick the Moment

The most important determinant for picking the right moment for real-time feedback is whether it will help student learning and make the lesson go more smoothly. Imagine, for example, that a teacher you're observing begins teaching a lesson with a poor objective. Coaching the teacher to write stronger objectives would be an extremely valuable exercise, but real time isn't the time to do it. To do so would pull the rug out from under the lesson the teacher has planned, likely leaving him or her very uncertain as to how to proceed with the rest of the lesson. The students would lose more learning to a derailed lesson than to a lesson with an imperfect objective. In contrast, if one student is off task and you can get the teacher to change the student's behavior, you have increased student learning in that moment and in the future without a negative consequence.

The second determinant of whether it's the right moment for real-time feedback is whether the feedback is small enough to be implemented right away without practice. The first coaching principle, Go Granular, focused on the power of making action steps as small and practice-able as possible, so that teachers can immediately implement them. When it comes to giving feedback in real time, going even more granular—that is, delivering only feedback that's bite-sized enough for the teacher to implement it right then and there, with no practice whatsoever—becomes a necessity. If a teacher won't get it right in the moment, you will benefit from waiting until you can work on it more extensively in your feedback meeting.

> ### Keys to Picking the Right Moment for Real-Time Feedback
> 1. Keeps lesson on track and improves student learning
> 2. Can be implemented immediately without practice

When you've picked the right moment, your next task is to communicate the feedback to the teacher.

## Deliver the Feedback

Just like the surgeons we described at the opening of this chapter, leaders giving real-time feedback to teachers have to do so in the least invasive way possible—that is, the way in which the teacher remains in control of as many of the actions as possible. Here are a series of techniques for delivering your real-time feedback, ranked in order of their invasiveness. The quickest, least invasive ones are always the best to use; in more challenging situations, the more invasive ones may be necessary.

### Quickest and Least Invasive: Nonverbals

Ashley Anderson's teacher Ijeoma Duru is working in Phase 2 of her teacher development, particularly the ability to scan the room and identify student non-responsiveness. As we see in clip 7, Ashley is in the back of the room supporting Ijeoma in the first days of teaching.

 Watch clip 7: Teacher Radar—Pause and Scan
(Key Leadership Move: Real-Time Feedback)

Ashley demonstrated by far the least invasive way to communicate with a teacher during class: silent signals. By keeping a whiteboard handy, she was able to alert Ijeoma when her students weren't paying attention by simply holding up a sign with the word "track." Then she added "scan" to remind the teacher of the action to take. Not a single student noticed what was happening, and the flow of the lesson did not falter.

Because they are so noninvasive, silent signals are an incredibly powerful tool of real-time feedback. They can take many forms in addition to the whiteboard that Ashley used, such as

- A hand gesture—for example, touching forefingers to each other to indicate an opportunity to Turn and Talk

- A visual cue—for example, holding up a red card to flag a particular error you've already set up with the teacher, such as when the teacher is doing more of the talking than should be the case

- Another physical nonverbal cue—for example, exaggerating your own erect posture to indicate to a teacher to Square Up, Stand Still

Using a silent signal to deliver real-time feedback does require a bit of preparation, as you need to let the teacher know what your signal will be and what it will mean. When you know in advance what you plan to coach teachers to do in real time, you can touch base with them before class about the signal you plan to use. Once you and the teacher have set these expectations, nonverbal real-time feedback moves at lightning speed. A quick gesture from the leader translates all but seamlessly into the teacher's performing an action that will have lasting positive impact in his or her classroom.

### Still Not Very Invasive: Whisper Prompt

Nikki Bridges takes the nonverbal form of real-time feedback and combines it with a second technique: a whisper prompt. Here we see Nikki working with Jackson in Phase 2. He has mastered What to Do directions, but he doesn't know when to use them because he doesn't see the moments when students are off task, so Teacher Radar is his focus. Watch as Nikki works with Jackson on noting student off-task behavior (clip 8).

---

 Watch clip 8: What to Do and Teacher Radar—Scan
(Key Leadership Move: Real-Time Feedback)

---

> ### Stop and Jot: Whisper Prompts
>
> What did Nikki do to help Jackson develop even faster? Jot down the actions you saw her take.
>
> _____
> _____
> _____
> _____

Right before she used a silent signal, Nikki used a second technique to let Jackson know what she was planning during class: she whispered feedback to him. When carried out effectively, a whisper prompt can be just as subtle as a nonverbal signal, even though it involves speaking out loud. You can communicate a message to the teacher without interrupting his or her teaching. Two keys will make whispering work:

- Pick a moment when students are working.
- Be quick: state the action and your rationale.

The best moments for whispering feedback are clear: during independent practice, small group work, or Turn and Talks. This way, the students won't be distracted by the teacher-leader interaction; and with the students occupied, the teacher will be able to focus much more fully on what the leader is saying. In a workshop I led recently, one astute leader pointed out that when Nikki gives Jackson feedback, she even positions herself so that she is facing the students, and Jackson is looking away from them. "At first I didn't understand why Nikki would do that," said the leader, describing how counterintuitive it seemed that a leader would ask a teacher to turn away from his class, "but then I realized that if Jackson were still looking at the class, he would have been trying to monitor student work at the same time as he was listening to Nikki's feedback. He couldn't do both at once, so she had him look away just long enough to get her message across."

All of this is valuable only if you are very concise in your feedback—saying probably no more than three sentences. A teacher can't devote his or her full attention to a leader for very long while class is going on. So keep it simple: state the action step and the evidence/rationale. A surgeon will always choose the most efficient surgery; your words should be no different.

### Findings from the Field: A Simple Fix with Just a Few Words

One of my teachers was struggling to work on fluency during guided reading. She was having students doing round-robin reading rather than giving each student a chance to focus in on the text and practice reading themselves. With a short, simple whisper prompt

("Have them all whisper-read"), the teacher had all students whisper-reading and truly engaging with the text rather just waiting their turn. What my teachers love about real-time feedback is that they see and feel success immediately—and the students reap all the benefits. The small change the teacher makes sticks faster than it does when we practice in our coaching conversations, meaning the teacher can move on to their next action step more quickly.

—Tera Hering, principal, Tulsa, Oklahoma

### More Invasive: Model

Sometimes words are not enough, and a teacher really needs to see it to understand. This is where modeling comes in. Modeling can be just as quick as the other two types of feedback, and it can be done without challenging the teacher's leadership. In the opening clip of this chapter (clip 6), we saw how Art Worrell did just that.

 Rewatch clip 6: Go Conceptual
(Key Leadership Move: Real-Time Feedback)

In effect, Art took on the role of teacher nonintrusively by first taking on the role of student. He followed all the same protocols his teacher's students have to follow when they wish to participate in class: he raised his hand and then asked permission. When the teacher affirmed that Art could ask the class a question in that moment, Art explicitly addressed the students as a fellow participant, rather than giving the teacher directives in front of them. This meant that for the entire time Art was modeling, the teacher retained control of her classroom.

Modeling has the added benefit of allowing a teacher to see in the moment exactly what he or she could have done. Many of the new teachers we have interviewed have called this the best part of all of their PD. Once they see a master teacher model for them with their own students, they start to believe more in what is possible for them to do. It may feel awkward at first, but the payoff of respectful modeling—both in the moment you do it and in the teacher's career for years to come—is immense.

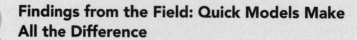

## Findings from the Field: Quick Models Make All the Difference

As a new teacher, I struggled with having a formal tone. (Strong Voice): I had to learn that my voice needed to match expectations. My coach helped me master this by giving me real-time feedback and jumping in when my tone was off—she did an awesome job of modeling quickly what I needed to do. When she modeled something small and quick, I was able to jump right in and pick it back up. Without real-time modeling, I wouldn't have seen the problem with my tone.

—Rachel Kashner, teacher and leader, Newark, New Jersey

Most Invasive: Extensive Model

Sometimes you need to model for longer than in the previously described situation described in order to get the class on track. Simply continue leading the class for an extended period of time, probably getting students through a particular critical moment in the lesson that is proving challenging, before inviting the teacher back in. Be sure to debrief with the teacher later to ensure that the teacher was able to identify why you did that and what was effective.

## Testimonial from a Teacher: Modeling Makes It Click

My first year of teaching was a tremendous challenge. No matter how many hours I spent poring over my lesson plans and processing the emailed feedback I had been given, I could not make the necessary progress I needed to become the effective teacher that my students deserved. Each day I prepared as much as possible and internalized the feedback given, and yet it seemed that I made little to no progress. I simply was not getting it, and just when I began to question my decision to teach, my instructional leader gave me feedback in a way that finally clicked for me.

I had just finished giving students a countdown to put their pencils down and direct their attention to me; however, a majority of the students were not meeting my expectations. My instructional leader jumped in and said to the class, "Let's try that again." She then mod-eled having a strong stance, counted down with a firm tone, and clearly made direct eye contact with the students to gain compliance. To my surprise, she then handed back the reins and whispered to me, "Now you try! Feet planted. Use a firm tone and have them pass papers in." Even though she walked to the far side of the classroom to communi-cate to the students that I was back in control, I was comforted to know that she was still there. I tried again, and all of a sudden, it clicked! Seeing her in action, seconds before with my very own students, made it crystal clear to me exactly what I needed to adjust. Her body lan-guage and her tone when speaking—it all made sense. As I mimicked exactly what she did, I could not believe how responsive students were.

I immediately implemented these same actions when I was on my own with my students. It was like magic! It worked! From that day forward, I welcomed my instructional leader and principal jumping into my lessons. After each instance, it seemed that my effectiveness grew instantaneously. I wasn't at home alone trying to figure out what the written feedback meant, or if my instructional leader and principal perhaps had only seen the worst part of my lesson. Instead, I was seeing masters in action with a small chunk of my lesson, seeing how it should be done and then immediately jumping back in to try again. The cycle of seeing master teachers model, then immediately implementing their best practices with my own students, in real time, is what has made me the effective teacher I am today.

—Sara Shanahan, teacher, Newark, New Jersey

## Close the Loop

Real-time feedback is so effective because the teacher ends up putting it into practice right there in the moment. The outcome is better student learning and faster teacher growth. You can supercharge this learning even further by debriefing with the teacher after giving real-time feedback. You saw that in the first clip with Art. Even if you see the teacher implement the feedback during class without faltering, you also need to be sure that the teacher knows *why* the feedback led to improvement, or it won't stick. The debrief may take place either during that same class period or, more easily, at the teacher's next feedback meeting. You might begin by saying something like, "When you were checking for understanding, I had you call on Prishanti first, and then on Darius. How did that affect the way you taught the rest of the lesson?"

This allows the teacher to name the action and understand its impact, increasing the likelihood that he or she will continue that action in the future.

## Conclusion

Real-time feedback is a practice that puts professional development on fast-forward. It shortens the feedback loop with teachers, which means students learn more. And, as Sara Shanahan described in her testimonial, it is also often the breakthrough moment for a teacher's own reflection on his or her development.

When delivered effectively, real-time feedback adds a powerful tool to the repertoire of an instructional leader. Just as a resident starts to fly with real-time feedback from his or her attending physician, so too can teachers fly with your support.

The Get Better Faster Coach's Guide in the appendix (and on the DVD) has recommended real-time feedback strategies aligned to each action step in the Get Better Faster Scope and Sequence. In addition to that, here is a summary guide for when and how to use real-time feedback.

### Delivering Real-Time Feedback—Making It Stick

| Least Invasive to Most Invasive | Examples |
|---|---|
| **Nonverbals**<br>• Preestablished signal or nonverbal cue<br>  – Hand gesture<br>  – Visual cue (whiteboard, red card)<br>  – Physical nonverbal cue (posture) | • Hand gesture:<br>  – Point at student from the back of the room: student off task<br>  – Hands folded = check for posture; fingers pointing to eyes = scan the room for responsiveness<br>  – Write in the air = give the students an "everybody writes" task<br>• Visual cue:<br>  – Red card = too much teacher talk<br>  – Cards/whiteboards with words: "Cold call," "Why" (ask why), "Scan"<br>• Physical nonverbal cue:<br>  – Exaggerate posture to indicate Square Up, Stand Still |

| Least Invasive to Most Invasive | Examples |
|---|---|
| **Whisper Prompt**<br><br>• Right moment: when students are working or the teacher is not in front—during Turn and Talks or independent work<br>• What to do: state what to do, the evidence, and the rationale in less than thirty seconds | • Students are not tracking:<br>  – "You have a handful of students who aren't tracking you when you give directions. Stop, say 'track me,' and scan for responsiveness. Don't move on until those students comply."<br>• Ratio (teacher is doing too much of the work):<br>  – "When they come out of Turn and Talk, have four students share every time before you respond."<br>  – "Tiana has a medium answer and Ramon has a strong one. Call on Tiana, then Ramon to share their answers to the class." |
| **Model**<br><br>• Right moment: learning or management will weaken without intervening<br>• Ask the teacher: raise hand to ask to jump in<br>• Model, exaggeratedly: use language of effective teaching, narrate what you do<br>• Debrief in meeting afterwards:<br>  – "Why did I jump in, and what did I do?"<br>  – "What was the impact on instruction?" | • Ask a question to the class:<br>  – "So when you start writing, what are the important things Ms. X will be looking for?"<br>  – "What should I do if I finish my work early?"<br>• Right it right: prompt students for better answers:<br>  – Writing task: "Scholars, nice job citing evidence from the text in your answers. My challenge to you is to revise your answer to explicitly connect your evidence to your argument."<br>  – "Scholars, track me. I want to challenge you to use the language from the question as you are responding. I'm going to listen for the next few to see if you can do it."<br>• Model the skill:<br>  – "Eyes on me." Model Be Seen Looking and whisper to the teacher: "Watch how I use Be Seen Looking to monitor the students."<br>  – "I want to ask a few break-it-down questions because I'm not sure everyone understands."<br>  – During independent work, conduct three conferences with students, modeling breaking it down.<br>  – "I want to narrate the positive things I'm seeing in this room because I see [student] [praise]." |

| Least Invasive to Most Invasive | Examples |
|---|---|
| **Extensive Model**<br><br>• Right moment: circumstances require you to lead the class for an extended period of time<br>• Planned: select time beforehand to do model teaching for part or all of the lesson | • Jump in:<br>  – "Ms. B, you're making a key point. Would you mind if I added on to it?"<br>  – "I want to ask the next two questions. I want to make sure each answer is 'all the way right.'"<br>  – "Mr. X, that doesn't seem quite right. The definition is missing one key nuance." |

---

### Stop and Jot: Delivering Real-Time Feedback

Think of a time when real-time feedback would have helped you coach a teacher you were working with. Of the four strategies described in the "Delivering Real-Time Feedback—Making It Stick" table, which would have been the most effective for delivering your feedback in that moment? Circle one:

Nonverbal
Whisper prompt
Model
Extensive model

Plan your next observation with real-time feedback. What will you say or do with this teacher?

_____

_____

_____

 **STOP**    Congratulations! Stop here to evaluate where to go from here.

Reaching the end of this chapter means you've learned the foundations for *how* to coach a teacher effectively. Now we'll examine more closely *what* skills that coaching must cover in each phase of a teacher's development. Recall from the introduction that from this point forward, it's less crucial to read straight through each chapter of the book from beginning to end. If you have time to do this, then by all means do so; but if you're in the midst of coaching a teacher and need to just dive right in, simply begin by reading over the Scope and Sequence itself and then jump to the part of the book that specifically addresses in greater detail what your teachers need the most.

Here's the best way to navigate this part of the book.

**If you are using the Scope and Sequence before the school year begins . . .**

- **Read the Phase 1 Coaching Blueprint:** The Phase 1 Coaching Blueprint will help you prepare summer PD sessions that train teachers in the skills they'll need most immediately from the first day of school onward.

- **Start from the top—the first Phase 1 action step:** A strong foundation is critical to beginning the year. Thus, start with the first action steps in Management (Routines and Procedures 101 and Strong Voice) and Rigor (Develop Effective Lesson Plans 101 and Internalize Existing Lesson Plans). Do not move forward until a teacher is proficient in these areas!

**If you are using the Scope and Sequence at any other point in the year . . .**

- **Identify your teacher's action step.** Go to the Get Better Faster Scope and Sequence (in the first pages of the book; a printable version is on the DVD) and determine the highest-leverage action step for your teacher. Remember, think waterfalls: start from the top and stop as soon as you hit a problem area for the teacher.

- **Go to the appropriate phase and read the coaching blueprint.** For example, if your teacher is struggling with getting students to cite evidence, jump to Phase 3 and start with the Phase 3 Coaching Blueprint.

- **In that same phase, jump to the rigor or management section (depending on your action step) and go to the page that matches your teacher's struggle.** Use the Quick Reference Guide that appears right before the Phase 1 Management and Rigor sections to identify the challenges that the teacher is most struggling with, and skip to the corresponding section that presents the skills that will help him or her overcome those specific challenges.

# START HERE QUICK REFERENCE GUIDE

Here's a cheat sheet that shows where to go from here.

**The Scope and Sequence Cheat Sheet: Where to Go to Meet Your Teachers' Needs**

| Challenge | Skill Area |
|---|---|
| **If your teacher is struggling to . . .** | **Jump to . . .** |
| Develop essential routines and procedures | Phase 1 Management |
| Write effective lesson plans | Phase 1 Rigor |
| ***If and once* the teacher has mastered all of Phase 1, and he or she is struggling to . . .** | **Jump to . . .** |
| Roll out and monitor routines | Phase 2 Management |
| Establish effective independent practice | Phase 2 Rigor |
| ***If and once* the teacher has mastered all of Phase 2, and he or she is struggling to . . .** | **Jump to . . .** |
| Engage 100 percent of students | Phase 3 Management |
| Tailor lessons to respond to in-the-moment student learning needs | Phase 3 Rigor |
| ***If and once* the teacher has mastered all of Phase 3, and he or she is struggling to . . .** | **Jump to . . .** |
| Make time for students to discuss material as a group | Phase 4 Management |
| Lead student discussions | Phase 4 Rigor |
| ***If and once* the teacher has mastered all of Phase 4, and he or she is struggling to . . .** | **Jump to . . .** |
| Shift leadership of discussions from the teacher to the students | Stretch It Rigor |

*Note:* A more detailed guide with more specific challenges will appear at the beginning of each section.

# (Pre-Teaching): Dress Rehearsal

A few weeks before school started in his first year, Noel Borges was as unprepared for his first day of teaching as many new teachers. He'd graduated from a good university, observed great teachers in action, and studied the most up-to-date literature on great education strategies. Yet despite all of this preparation, an upcoming Monday in September would be the very first time Noel had stood in front of a classroom full of middle school students and taught completely on his own.

As leaders, how can we see someone like Noel through this dramatic transition from learning to teach to actually teaching? How can we make sure Noel will earn his students' respect? Command their attention? Use that focus to teach them their first sixth-grade history lesson?

Noel's principal, Serena Savarirayan, takes these questions to heart. Her solution? Give the first day of school the Broadway treatment. In the weeks before school begins, Serena will get Noel and his fellow teachers ready by rehearsing the school day as if it were a hotly anticipated new play: piece by piece, over and over, in the same amount of time and space as each teacher will have to do it when the show opens.

Teaching and the performing arts share a critical similarity: both depend on *responsive performance.* They require professionals to do their most important work live, while simultaneously and appropriately modifying it based on the reactions of those watching. To deliver an excellent responsive performance—the kind that deserves a standing ovation—you need to master two sets of actions: the variations you'll make depending on audience response, and the planned constants you'll do no matter what. Variations are challenging to prepare for, and because you can never anticipate all of them in advance, knowing they could appear at any time can make even highly experienced performers freeze up before the curtain rises (or the school doors open). But if you've rehearsed the constants so many times that you can get through them as automatically as you brew your morning coffee, you'll have what you need to gather your forces, emerge from backstage, and give your audience what they came for no matter what. Your muscle memory will see you through your stage fright, and the show will go on.

On the first day of school, that's exactly what we need from every teacher. Yet unlike an actor, singer, or dancer, a new teacher is all too likely to arrive at the head of a classroom without ever having physically rehearsed for the first day of school. Like Noel, these teachers have likely been exposed to the general demands of leading a classroom, but have not been prepared for the specific demands of leading their own. As Deborah Loewenberg Ball and Francesca M. Forzani put it in "Building a Common Core for Learning to Teach," it's common practice in the United States to focus more on hiring "better" teachers up front than on training teachers as they dive into their work. This practice, Ball and Forzani explain, is a "gamble," betting each teacher's actual success in the classroom on qualifications that don't necessarily make him or her a "better" teacher.[1]

Serena refuses to gamble. Her summer rehearsal sessions lock in her teachers' success precisely because they require all teachers to perfect the precise teaching actions they'll need in the classroom, and to do so *before,* not after, they need them. That's why Phase 1 of the Get Better Faster Scope and Sequence takes place in the days before students arrive for the first day of school. Teachers need to master these skills before they even meet their students, because the skills are the starter kit for a successful school year.

> ## Core Idea
>
> A new teacher in the first days of school will freeze up.
> Relentless rehearsing will break the ice.

So what does a dress rehearsal for teaching look like? Let's see how Serena does it. In clip 9, Serena has asked Noel to practice his first greeting to his students when they gather outside his classroom.

 Watch clip 9: Routines and Procedures—Plan and Practice
(Key Leadership Moves: Leading PD, Practice)

> ## Stop and Jot
>
> What actions does Serena take to lead an effective dress rehearsal with Noel?
>
> _____
> _____
> _____
> _____

Serena leaves nothing to chance: she models an effective entry routine and then gives Noel the opportunity to practice himself—not once but multiple times. He is visibly more confident the second time he practices his greeting, with steadier posture and no hesitation in his voice. More important, he's earned that confidence. He knows a little bit more now about how to deliver the performance he really needs to give when he meets his students, and that concrete piece of knowledge has already made him a better teacher.

Let's take a look at the Phase 1 Coaching Blueprint to see what techniques will help you train your teachers in these skills.

# PHASE 1 COACHING BLUEPRINT: LEADING PD

Recall the three essential coaching skills this book has already covered:

- Go Granular
- Plan, Practice, Follow Up, Repeat
- Make Feedback More Frequent

How do those look before the school year begins? They are embedded in the professional development (PD) training you lead during that time. Because teachers don't yet have students in front of them, all the training occurs in workshop or simulated form. This training can culminate in a dress rehearsal of the first days of school that will let teachers put all those skills into action at once.

## Leading Professional Development

The best way to learn something is to live it. Adults learn new skills not by passively hearing or reading content but by putting the skills into action. This idea turns traditional PD on its head. The key to effective PD is not the delivery of the content but the quality of the practice.

> ### Core Idea
> Your PD is only as good as what your participants practice.

In the simplest terms, effective PD gives participants a chance to see it, name it, and do it. Here, we provide a brief overview of the essential components of a PD that accomplishes this. For more information about leading PD, turn to *Leverage Leadership,* which includes a full-length chapter on this subject.[2]

1. **See it.** Seeing is believing, and that is nowhere more apparent than in effective PD. Teachers need to see a model of what a skill looks like when it's done well, whether they see it by watching video of a master teacher in action or by reading an exemplar lesson plan. That model will be the basis for them to understand how to implement the skill.

2. **Name it.** Seeing it is to believe it; naming it is to remember it. When participants are given the opportunity to share what they saw in the model and then

given a common language to describe it, they internalize the model even more effectively. You also create a shared language that a school community can use to support each other in implementing a skill.

The "see it, name it" combination is incredibly impactful in delivering PD. In clip 2, Kelly Dowling is leading PD on how to lead an effective close reading lesson. She is focusing on how to prepare for aggressive monitoring (a Phase 2 Rigor skill). Look at how she uses the "see it, name it" pedagogy to help participants understand the core preparation needed to monitor effectively.

Rewatch clip 2: Exemplar and Aggressive Monitoring
(Key Leadership Move: Leading PD)

Rather than just telling teachers to prepare for monitoring, she shows an exemplar teacher handout that is annotated with all the key notes she will be looking for when monitoring student work. Teachers look at this model and name the important action steps. Throughout this process, Kelly makes it her goal to get the teachers to come up with as many of the actions as possible independently, rather than telling them. Once they've generated the key points, she "stamps" their understanding with a core idea that they can hold on to when practicing.

3. **Do it (practice).** Once teachers have seen a model and named the important steps, they can get out of their chairs and practice. This is one of the most straightforward yet underutilized components of great PD. It can't be said too many times: if teachers don't practice the skill during the PD, they will not learn it.

Watch in clip 10 how Kelly continues her PD once they have learned additional skills as well.

Watch clip 10: Strategic Prompting
(Key Leadership Moves: Leading PD, Practice)

The teachers in this PD have not just learned passively about effective teaching practices; they've had a chance to practice, give and receive feedback, and try again. In a single PD session, Kelly has dramatically changed outcomes for the teachers. Just as in the first clip of Serena with Noel (clip 9), they followed a cycle of "see it, name it, do it" to profound impact.

> ### 🔍 Findings from the Field: Use a Cheat Sheet to Perfect the Feedback on Practice
>
> Getting teachers to practice during PD is critical to helping them develop. One challenge can be after the role play when you ask teachers to give each other feedback: often their feedback is vague and not very helpful. To prevent that from happening, we give participants a "feedback cheat sheet" which gives them typical errors teachers make while practicing and suggested action steps. If you think through the concrete feedback you would give the teacher, you can create a simple cheat sheet and make the peer feedback on practice so much more effective!
>
> —Kelly Dowling, principal, Newark, New Jersey

Leading PD sessions like these prior to teaching trains new teachers on every isolated skill in the Phase 1 (Pre-Teaching) Scope and Sequence. This form of PD also functions well because it introduces those skills incrementally, so that teachers can begin (for example) by scripting a routine, continue by scripting how they'll teach that routine, and ultimately role-playing teaching *and* executing the routine.

If you are overwhelmed by the thought of planning and developing PD sessions with this framework in mind, have no fear. There are outstanding resources available that have those PD sessions planned for you. *Teach Like a Champion 2.0*, *Teach Like a Champion Field Guide*, and *The Ten-Minute In-Service* all have developed teacher-facing PD sessions with session plans and handouts.[3] You can use these to jump-start your PDs and make it much easier to get up and running!

> ### 🔍 Findings from the Field: All You Need Is Forty-Five Minutes
>
> Even when you have a clear action step, a teacher doesn't fully understand it until they can see it and practice it. It is in the practice when teachers realize what they have to do. As such, you don't need a long PD to accomplish this. With a very simple structure—opening Do Now, watch a few short videos, role play (practice, practice, practice!), and Exit Ticket—you can make significant strides in teachers' development.
>
> —Claudia Ricciulli, coach, Santiago, Chile

## The Final PD Before School Starts: The Dress Rehearsal

After all this, though, there's still something missing. New teachers still lack the experience of putting together all the skills they're learning as they'll need to do on the first day of school: leading routines, teaching lessons, and commanding student attention in real time, sustaining their best work over a period of six to eight hours. To fill that gap, Julie Jackson and other leaders like her take the Broadway mind-set a step further: they lead a dress rehearsal. Clips 11 and 12 show how it looks as the teachers rehearse the morning routines. Particularly in kindergarten, teaching students how to move from the cafeteria to their classrooms can save a tremendous amount of time. Watch as a lead teacher models and coaches her newer teacher in these opening routines.

Watch clips 11 and 12: Routines and Procedures—Rollout
(Key Leadership Moves: Leading PD, Practice)

The dress rehearsal gathers all staff two or three days before school begins to practice Day One from start to finish. Just as would happen if the teachers were actors, this dress rehearsal begins with everything in place—all materials set up, all staff in position—and plays out minute by minute exactly as it would if the students were there, too. Where possible, the presence of students can even be mimicked by teachers who play the role of students when they don't have other dress-rehearsal duties to perform; otherwise, every staff member can simply imagine that the students are in the building and proceed exactly as if this were the case.

The dress rehearsal is the bow on top of summer PD. It ties together all the other preparation new teachers have done, and gives everyone a final chance to make sure that every aspect of the school day—and of every lesson, every hallway transition, and every arrival and dismissal within it—will fit in its place. Then, if any part of the plan is still rough around the edges—if any routines still need additional work, for example—teachers still have time to perfect them before opening night.

### Findings from the Field: When Turning Around School Culture, Cut the Fluff and Start with Arrival

At first, there were a lot of holes in implementation of schoolwide routines throughout the school. We started by redoing how we do the arrival routines. This was ideal because it started off the day and everyone was involved. We practiced the routines with the whole staff. Some of them were definitely confused at first. But we practiced and practiced, and we used Narrate the Positive, and we said, "OK, we want our students to have a positive experience when they come to school. We're going to do this so that by the time they get to their classrooms every morning, they'll have 'Five before 1st': five adults welcome them in a positive way before 1st period."

With only a limited number of PD days before school started, we made time for this by cutting everything that was the "stuff we always do." I decided what I could put in an email/document rather than present so that we would have the time to focus on what mattered most.

—Danielle Petters, principal, Dallas, Texas

We've now thoroughly covered *how* leaders like Julie train new teachers in key skill areas during Pre-Teaching. Now let's dive more deeply into *what* new teachers will learn in summer PD, starting with management skills and then moving on to rigor.

## Teaching Skills Overview

The core skills in Phase 1 correspond to the key areas to rehearse prior to beginning teaching. We narrow that focus to just three core skill areas to tackle during Phase 1: setting routines and procedures, establishing a strong presence in the classroom, and writing lesson plans.[4] Following is the excerpt of the Get Better Faster Scope and Sequence that shows in more detail what each of these skill areas includes.

**Phase 1 Action Step Sequence**

| Management Trajectory | Rigor Trajectory |
|---|---|
| **Develop Essential Routines & Procedures**<br><br>1. **Routines & Procedures 101:** Design and roll out<br>  • Plan and practice critical routines and procedures moment by moment:<br>    – Explain what each routine means and what it will look like.<br>    – Write out what teacher and students do at each step, and what will happen with students who don't follow the routine.<br>  • Plan & practice the rollout: how to introduce the routine for the first time:<br>    – Plan the "I Do": how you will model the routine.<br>    – Plan what you will do when students don't get it right.<br>2. **Strong Voice:** Stand and speak with purpose<br>  • Square Up, Stand Still: when giving instructions, stop moving and strike a formal pose.<br>  • Formal register: when giving instructions, use formal register, including tone and word choice. | **Write Lesson Plans**<br><br>1. **Develop Effective Lesson Plans 101:** Build the foundation of an effective lesson rooted in what students need to learn<br>  • Write precise learning objectives that are<br>    – Data driven (rooted in what students need to learn based on analysis of assessment results)<br>    – Curriculum plan driven<br>    – Able to be accomplished in one lesson<br>  • Script a basic "I Do" as a core part of the lesson.<br>  • Design an Exit Ticket (brief final mini-assessment) aligned to the objective.<br>2. **Internalize Existing Lesson Plans:** Make existing lesson plans your own<br>  • Internalize & rehearse key parts of the lesson, including the "I Do" and all key instructions.<br>  • Build time stamps into the lesson plan and follow them. |

*Note:* Many other topics can be introduced during August training. What are listed above are the topics that should be addressed to reach proficiency. Other topics to introduce—even if teachers will not yet master them—could be:

• Least Invasive Intervention

• Narrate the Positive

• Build the Momentum

• Teacher Radar: know when students are off task

• Do It Again: practice routines to perfection—have students do it again if it is not done correctly (and know when to stop Do It Again)

# PHASE 1 MANAGEMENT—DEVELOP ESSENTIAL ROUTINES AND PROCEDURES

**Quick Reference Guide**

| If your teacher is struggling to . . . | Jump to . . . |
|---|---|
| **Routines and Procedures 101** | |
| Establish clear routines for the classroom | Plan and practice critical routines and procedures moment by moment |
| Teach a routine that is new for the students | Plan and practice the rollout |
| **Strong Voice** | |
| Establish body language that communicates leadership (e.g., teacher is slouching, shifting, facing away from class) | Square Up, Stand Still |
| Speak with calm authority | Formal register |

**Phase 1 Scope and Sequence**

| Management Trajectory | Rigor Trajectory |
|---|---|
| **Develop Essential Routines & Procedures** | Write Lesson Plans |
| 1. **Routines & Procedures 101:** Design and roll out | 1. **Develop Effective Lesson Plans 101:** Build the foundation of an effective lesson rooted in what students need to learn |
| • Plan and practice critical routines and procedures moment by moment: | • Write precise learning objectives that are |
| – Explain what each routine means and what it will look like. | – Data driven (rooted in what students need to learn based on analysis of assessment results) |
| – Write out what teacher and students do at each step, and what will happen with students who don't follow the routine. | – Curriculum plan driven |

| Management Trajectory | Rigor Trajectory |
|---|---|
| • Plan & practice the rollout: how to introduce the routine for the first time:<br>  – Plan the "I Do": how you will model the routine.<br>  – Plan what you will do when students don't get it right.<br>**2. Strong Voice:** Stand and speak with purpose<br>  • Square Up, Stand Still: when giving instructions, stop moving and strike a formal pose.<br>  • Formal register: when giving instructions, use formal register, including tone and word choice. |   – Able to be accomplished in one lesson<br>  • Script a basic "I Do" as a core part of the lesson.<br>  • Design an Exit Ticket (brief final mini-assessment) aligned to the objective.<br>**2. Internalize Existing Lesson Plans:** Make existing lesson plans your own<br>  • Internalize & rehearse key parts of the lesson, including the "I Do" and all key instructions.<br>  • Build time stamps into the lesson plan and follow them. |

*Note:* Many other topics can be introduced during August training. What are listed above are the topics that should be addressed to reach proficiency. Other topics to introduce—even if teachers will not yet master them—could be:

- Least Invasive Intervention
- Narrate the Positive
- Build the Momentum
- Teacher Radar: know when students are off task
- Do It Again: practice routines to perfection—have students do it again if it is not done correctly (and know when to stop Do It Again)

## Introduction to Phase 1 Management Skills: Develop Essential Routines and Procedures

In his writing, Nobel prize–winning author Orhan Pamuk is a wild card. His sweeping novels might include anything from a chapter narrated by a piece of chalk (in *My Name Is Red*) to ten pages over the course of which every single sentence begins with the word "sometimes" (in *The Museum of Innocence*). But in his writing *process,* Pamuk is a stickler for regularity. In a 2005 interview, he described how much his work depends on his having a discrete space in which to write—and remembered, with lingering distress, one long-ago year when he wasn't able to rent an office. "My wife and I were living in an apartment for married students and didn't have any space, so I had to sleep and write in the same place," he said. "This upset me."[5]

So Pamuk devised an eccentric solution to his problem. Every morning, he would dress and bid his wife good-bye as if he were leaving for work. Then, he said, "I'd leave the house, walk around a few blocks, and come back like a person arriving at the office." The act of returning to his home as if it were his office gave Pamuk the ability to sit down and write with energy, focus, and skill—despite the fact that in reality, he'd simply walked out and then back in through the same door.

At first glance, the daily routine that enabled Pamuk to imagine one space as two seems bizarre, even delusional. But from another angle, it makes sense. Pamuk had to create a routine that allowed him to see the space in a new way, explicitly telling himself, "This is my time for writing; my other tasks will wait until later in the day." And most of us aren't so different: the right routines make our daily work more thorough, efficient, and innovative. Far from stifling cognition and creativity, the right routines and procedures nurture our greatest ideas, giving them the freedom to develop and flourish.

The same is true for our students. A classroom is only a room—nothing more. But with the right routines in place, they become spaces designed to let our students' minds soar.

---

### Core Idea

A classroom is only a room—but roll out the right routines,
and it becomes a place where students' minds can soar.

---

What follows are the key skills a new teacher must master in Phase 1 to establish the right routines in the first weeks of the school year. These are the routines and procedures that make the classroom a space that nurtures learning, and the strong voice that enables you to teach your students those routines. We'll break them down in a way that shows specifically how to prepare your teachers to make this vision a reality.

**Routines and Procedures 101**

---

### Teacher Professional Development Goal

**Routines and Procedures 101:** Design and roll out every essential classroom routine so that you can bring students on board from Day One.

---

The number one glitch that leads to broken-down routines is insufficient planning. When a teacher doesn't know with absolute clarity, inside and out, what a routine should look like when the students are doing it properly, there's no way to get the real students to match the vision. That's why writing up and rehearsing the routine is the starting point for getting management right.

### Findings from the Field: Practicing Procedures Sets Common Expectations

Never underestimate the power of practice before the first day of school. During our opening PD, we engaged our teachers around planning and practicing critical schoolwide routines and procedures. We outlined each routine into a three-step process and gave each teacher a guide that described these steps in detail. In addition, we spent an entire day practicing each routine over and over until we were 100 percent clear on what the routine should look like.

There were many benefits to doing this, but the biggest testimony to the impact that this had on our school was when our first-year teachers said, "We really didn't know what to expect going into the first day of school, but now we feel comfortable." By frontloading the routines practicing precisely, we are having the best year that we have had in my four years at East Central Junior High. The practice laid the foundation, and soon we had strong managers in our classrooms.

—Joshua Regnier, principal, Tulsa, Oklahoma

The following are the top challenges these routines and procedures will help new teachers overcome:

- The teacher does not have clear routines established for the classroom.
- The routine is new for students—either because it's the beginning of the year or because the teacher is changing the routine.

# ROUTINES AND PROCEDURES 101: PLAN AND PRACTICE CRITICAL ROUTINES AND PROCEDURES MOMENT BY MOMENT

 *Coaching Tips*

## Teacher Context

### Challenge

The teacher does not have clear routines established for the classroom.

### Action Step

Plan and practice critical routines and procedures moment by moment:

- Explain what each routine means and what it will look like.
- Write out what teacher and students do at each step, and what will happen with students who don't follow the routine.

### Action Step Overview

The best-planned classroom routines are those that get thoroughly out in front of these three questions:

- What will the teacher be doing at every moment of the routine?
- What will the students be doing?
- What will the teacher do when a student does not respond?

For every critical routine, the new teacher will have to write out exactly what this procedure will accomplish and what it will look like, scripting precisely what both the teacher and the students will do every step of the way.

The value of focusing on routines and procedures during summer PD is that it gives teachers a chance to script, script, and script their routines some more, leaving no foreseeable stone unturned. New teachers will complete the planning process because you've already given them the time to do it. By the time they're finished, they may have a ten- or fifteen-page document that captures each of their essential classroom routines in detail. If that sounds excessive, just imagine what you'd have given for a guide like that during your first year of teaching!

*Quick Tip from a Coach—Don't Skip the Basics*

*When I first was an instructional assistant principal at a turnaround school, we had over twenty new teachers, all of whom needed support in management when the year began. After the first few weeks, I realized that my teachers were meeting the weekly goals I gave them around the Phase 2 and 3 action steps (What to Do, scanning, whole-class reset, and narrating the positive), but the percentage of students who were on task was not increasing. Eventually, I went back into the Get Better Faster Scope and Sequence. After turning to Phase 1 of the guide, it hit me! Many of my teachers did not have a clear idea of what each routine looked like in the classroom and what students should be doing at each step. Although my teachers were mastering other skills, I had not gotten them to master the first. Once I went back and set up critical routines and procedures, my teachers were able to build on previously mastered skills, and the students in my school learned more.*

—Tom Weishaupt, principal, Philadelphia, Pennsylvania

| | KEY LEADERSHIP MOVES |
|---|---|
| **Probing Questions** | • [Show a model video or do a live model of an effective routine] "What is each step the teacher takes in this routine? Write down what the teacher is doing and what the students are doing." |
| | • "Describe what you want [certain routine] to look like. Ideally, what would students do during that transition/routine? What would you be doing?" |
| **Planning and Practice** | • Complete a template for the key routines in the teacher's classroom (most important: student entry and exit, transitions, materials distribution, and listening). At each moment, what will the teacher be doing? What will the students be doing? What will the teacher do when students don't comply? |

- Rehearse in the classroom setting:
  - Round 1: basic mastery: focus on the specific words and actions the teacher will use, such as where he or she will look and stand, and key ways he or she could break the routine down into smaller steps for the students.
  - Round 2: add minor student misbehaviors or errors in following instructions (not too much: you want to build muscle memory!).

 Rewatch clip 9: Routines and Procedures—Plan and Practice (Key Leadership Moves: Leading PD, Practice)

# ROUTINES AND PROCEDURES 101: PLAN AND PRACTICE THE ROLLOUT

 *Coaching Tips*

## Teacher Context

### Challenge

The routine is new for students—either because it's the beginning of the year or because the teacher is changing the routine.

### Action Step

Plan and practice the rollout: how to introduce routine for the first time:

- Plan the "I Do": how you will model the routine.
- Plan what you will do when students don't get it right.

### Action Step Overview

Scripting every routine will ensure that the teacher knows what students must do in the classroom. Planning how to roll out each routine ensures that the students will know what to do, too. The number one error new teachers can make with students is assuming that they know what to do. What's most important for the new teacher to plan is how he or she will model the routine, and what to do when students stumble.

The most essential components of an effective rollout[6] include the following:

- **I Do.** It can be uncomfortable for many teachers (not just new ones) to fully model a routine as if they were a student. Doing so, however, can make all the difference in clarity. The I Do should break the routine down into small actions the students can follow easily, with a pause between each action. A tight and precise I Do makes the practice much more effective.
- **We Do/You Do.** The I Do is followed by opportunities for students practice the routine in parts and then independently. Although planning the I Do is most critical, the bulk of rollout time should be spent on the We Do and the You Do, with students practicing the routine or procedure repeatedly until they are performing it correctly.
- **Positive framing.** Celebrate what students do well as they learn the routine, rather than narrating what goes wrong.

- **A challenge factor.** Even the most seemingly dull routine can be transformed into a more exciting challenge. Having students engage in friendly competition as they practice each piece of the routine won't just make learning more fun for them—it'll ensure that they remember what to do and do it with joy all year long.

What does it look like to plan such a detailed rollout with a teacher? The main key here is to script the instructions the teacher will give and how he or she will model. Skip this step, and you're likely to end up practicing something irrelevant to the challenges this particular teacher is facing. Then, when you get to the practicing phase, anticipate practicing multiple times (probably three or four) until the teacher leads the rollout flawlessly. Don't lower the bar! Just as this rollout will determine how students conduct themselves in the classroom for the rest of this year, the tone of your practice in these moments will set that of all your future meetings with the teacher. Later in the year, you will see this teacher progress to the point where you need to practice only one or two times—but it's much easier to make the shift to less practice than to more of it.

*Quick Tip from a Coach—Get Veteran Teachers to Model Roll-Outs*
*During our new-teacher PD, our team leaders will model what it looks like to introduce procedures to your class. Then we do "layup drills" that give our new teachers a chance to practice rolling out the procedure themselves. We initially focus on having them practice rolling out existing routines because our new teachers say that's one of the hardest parts. You don't realize until you get there how hard it is going to be to talk to your students for the first time.*

—Whitney Hurwitz, principal, Dallas, Texas

| | **KEY LEADERSHIP MOVES** |
|---|---|
| **Probing Questions** | • [Show a model video or do a live model of an effective rollout] "What did you notice about that rollout that made it effective?"<br>• "What will be the most difficult parts of the routine for you to deliver and for students to master?"<br>• "What are the key micro-actions for you to model to perfect this part of the routine?" |

| Planning and Practice | • Focus on scripting the I Do of the rollout and the What to Do instructions. Best practices for the model I Do: break it down, pregnant pause, repeat piece by piece |
| | • Plan the positive language the teacher will use to narrate the roll-out |
| | • Plan the challenge factors the teacher will use to engage the students in the rollout |
| | • Memorize the rollout speech, then stand up and practice (too much to do both at once!). |
| | • If teachers are working on this action step in peer groups, have teachers take turns playing the students to make it more authentic. |
| Real-Time Feedback | If the modeling is ineffective, prompt: "Mr. Smith, am I following your model effectively?" [then model the correct actions and narrate what you're doing]. |

Rewatch clips 11 and 12: Routines and Procedures—Rollout
(Key Leadership Moves: Leading PD, Practice)

## Routines and Procedures 101

| Action Step | When to Use It | Probing Questions | Scenarios to Practice | Cues for Real-Time Feedback |
|---|---|---|---|---|
| Plan and practice critical routines and procedures moment by moment | Teacher does not have clear routines established for the classroom. | • [Show a model video or do a live model] "What is each step the teacher takes in this routine?" "What is the teacher doing, and what are the students doing?"<br><br>• "Describe what you want [certain routine] to look like. Ideally, what would students do during that transition/routine? What would you be doing?" | Complete a template for the key routines in the teacher's classroom (most important: student entry and exit, transitions, materials distribution, and listening). Rehearse in the classroom setting.<br><br>• Rd 1: basic mastery: focus on the specific words and actions the teacher will use, such as where to look and stand, and key ways to break the routine down into smaller steps for the students.<br><br>• Rd 2: add minor student misbehaviors or errors in following instructions (not too much: you want to build muscle memory!). | N/A |
| Plan and practice the rollout | The routine is new for the students (beginning of the year or when changing a routine). | • [Show a model video or do a live model of an effective rollout] "What did you notice about that rollout that made it effective?"<br><br>• "What will be the most difficult parts of the routine for you to deliver and for students to master?"<br><br>• "What are the key micro-actions for you to model to perfect this part of the routine?" | • Focus on scripting the I Do: break it down, pregnant pause, repeat piece by piece.<br><br>• Keep the language positive and enthusiastic, including a challenge.<br><br>• Memorize the rollout speech, then stand up and practice.<br><br>• Leader or peers should play roles of students to make practice more authentic. | Model: If the teacher modeling is ineffective, prompt: "Mr. Smith, am I following your model effectively?" [then model the correct actions and narrate what you're doing]. |

## Strong Voice

> ### Teacher Professional Development Goal
>
> **Strong Voice:** Stand and speak with purpose and power to establish control of the classroom.

Imagine the president of the United States striding up to a podium to deliver a speech. The president you picture can be present, past, or fictional—any person you envision will have the straight back, the steady shoulders, and the sure, even paces that declare, "I'm in command here." You can probably even imagine what the speech will sound like when the president begins to deliver it: you know that his words will be spare yet powerful, and delivered in strong, even tone. Every pair of eyes within view of the podium is locked on the president, and it's not just because of the position this person holds—it's also because presidents carry themselves presidentially. Stand like a leader, and people will pay attention.

In *Teach Like a Champion,* Doug Lemov refers to this presidential quality as "it"—a quality that usually seems intangible and elusive, possessed by some teachers and not by others. Teachers who have "it," Lemov says, "enter a room and are instantly in command. Students who moments before seemed beyond the appeal of reason suddenly take their seats to await instructions."[7]

However, Lemov goes on to say, "it" is in fact a concrete set of actions, ones that any teacher can put to use. You don't need a specific personality or level of experience to command your students' attention just as surely as the president commands the citizens' attention. Instead, the teachers who lead their classrooms with confident strength do so through specific, concrete actions that Lemov lists in *Teach Like a Champion,* from avoiding raising your voice to refusing to engage nonresponsive students.

Like Lemov, we've grouped those actions together in the skill area of Strong Voice. Naturally, during pre-teaching, new teachers must learn some of the most fundamental skills of Strong Voice, but there isn't enough time during this phase for them to master all of those skills at once. The 101-level techniques of Strong Voice we'll address here—striking a confident posture and speaking at a formal register—will give a new a powerful jump-start in the art of "it." These two deceptively small actions carry all the impact of a strong first handshake with a new colleague: they inspire immediate respect that paves the way to a fruitful partnership with the individuals in question. The descriptions that follow show how.

> ### Findings from the Field: Use Your Height to Your Advantage
>
> As a new teacher, I always had energy and enthusiasm, but I didn't have the ability to command a room. I didn't know how to use my height to my advantage. So my coach would take the lead in my classroom and change one variable, which was her posture. She squared up, she used her height, she put her hands behind her back, and her voice was more powerful. When she talked, the students would actually listen. Then she would throw it back to me, and I would try to replicate what she just did. It changed my teaching completely.
>
> —Lauren Moyle, principal, Newark, New Jersey

The core challenge Strong Voice sets out to overcome is teacher body language that comes across as lax, intimidated, or anxious. Specifically, Strong Voice will address weaknesses in the teacher's:

- Posture: the teacher undermines his or her leadership presence by slouching, shifting from foot to foot, or facing at an angle away from the students.

- Tone: the teacher's vocal register is too casual or informal.

# STRONG VOICE: SQUARE UP, STAND STILL

 *Coaching Tips*

## Teacher Context

### Challenge

Posture: the teacher undermines his or her leadership presence by slouching, shifting from foot to foot, or facing at an angle away from the students.

### Action Step

Square Up, Stand Still: when giving instructions, stop moving and strike a formal pose.

### Action Step Overview

Early in their careers, teachers may not recognize the ways in which deceptively subtle body language—such as slouching, shifting from foot to foot, or clasping an arm behind their back—undermines their ability to take charge of a classroom. What's more, they're likely not to be accustomed to receiving feedback on their posture or vocal register, because the fields in which we typically give people feedback on their physical behavior are few and far between. Leaders usually need to be extremely specific and direct in order to get teachers to properly incorporate the two smallest, most powerful things they can do to get their students to listen to them: stop moving and stand up straight.

*Tip from a Teacher—Show Me How It Feels*

*I remember standing with my coach in her office side by side, and her moving my shoulders into the exact position her shoulders were in, and lifting my chin so I would understand exactly how to square up and stand still. It definitely is very awkward at the beginning, having someone put you in that position—if someone is helping you do it, it's obviously something you don't do naturally. One thing my coach and the other leaders in our school do is they say: 'This is probably going to feel awkward.' That prepares you before it actually happens. It's really helpful to recognize that's what's coming and it's probably going to feel awkward and that's OK. And then the practice felt so powerful to me because after that I could see what she meant. People kept telling me square up, stand still, square up, stand still, but feeling what it felt like to square up and stand still wasn't something I could do until someone else showed me.*

—Jackie Rosner, teacher and instructional leader, New York, New York

Watch clip 13: Square Up, Stand Still
(Key Leadership Moves: Leading PD, Practice)

    Nikki's actions in this clip reveal that getting a teacher to square up and stand still means fundamentally changing the body movements of that teacher. Notice the power of her actions: she walks right up to Jackson and adjusts his shoulders, showing him exactly how it will feel to take on the posture that defines him as the leader of his classroom. Without feedback this direct, it's incredibly difficult to develop a true awareness of how we hold ourselves in the first place, let alone how we need to adjust our posture to make it more solid.

---

### KEY LEADERSHIP MOVES

**Probing Questions**

- [Watch model video] "How does the teacher use her body language to communicate leadership in her classroom?"
  - Elementary clip: Rachel King, clip 53, *Teach Like a Champion 2.0*
  - Middle school clip: Patrick Pastore, clip 54, *Teach Like a Champion 2.0*
  - High school clip: Mike Taubman, clip 69, *Teach Like a Champion 2.0*
- [Model giving directions with a relaxed posture, then while squaring up and standing still] "What is the difference in the way I communicated the first way versus the second way?"
- "What is the value in communicating leadership with our body language?"

| Planning and Practice | • Have new teachers practice delivering the opening routines for their earliest lessons while squaring up and standing still. |
| | • Film the practice—or use a mirror—so that the new teacher can see what he or she looks like while delivering instructions. |
| Real-Time Feedback | • Nonverbal: model exaggerated posture and stance—shift your body upward and arch shoulders to remind the teacher to square up and stand still. |

# STRONG VOICE: FORMAL REGISTER

 *Coaching Tips*

## Teacher Context

### Challenge
Tone: the teacher's vocal register is too low or lax, or the directions the teacher delivers are wordy or overly casual.

### Action Step
When giving instructions, use formal register, including tone and word choice.

### Action Step Overview
The tone in which we speak, just like the way in which we carry ourselves, is something very difficult to self-identify. Yet it can be one of the first underminers of a teacher's authority. If the teacher speaks too casually, too softly, or too shrilly, he or she can lose the students in the first few minutes. Using many of the same techniques that work well for formal register, however, a leader can coach a teacher to the same levels of success in this aspect of his or her physical presentation as well.

## KEY LEADERSHIP MOVES

**Probing Questions**

- "Imagine you had to say 'It's time to leave' to three different audiences—your friend after dinner, a symphony concert audience at the end of a performance, or when a building is on fire. Speak out loud how you would deliver those words differently to each audience." [After the teacher does so] "What is the value and purpose of the middle one: your formal register?"

- "When is it important to use formal register? What message does it send to the students?"

- For a teacher who already knows formal register: "What are the keys to formal register?"

- [Watch video of the teacher's classroom] "What conditions lead you to drop your formal register?"

**Planning and Practice**

- Videotape the teacher during practice, and review the footage so the teacher can hear when he or she is maintaining a formal register, and when his or her register begins to become casual/informal.

- Practice maintaining a formal tone while delivering a lesson on routines and procedures. Note when the teacher is maintaining a formal register, and when the teacher's register becomes too informal or casual.

**Real-Time Feedback**

Nonverbal: combine Square Up, Stand Still gesture with pointing to your mouth to remind the teacher to speak in a formal register.

## Strategies for Coaching

### Strong Voice

| Action Step | When to Use It | Probing Questions | Scenarios to Practice | Cues for Real-Time Feedback |
|---|---|---|---|---|
| Square Up, Stand Still | Posture: teacher undermines his/her leadership presence by slouching, shifting from foot to foot, or facing at an angle away from the students. | • [Watch video] "How does the teacher use her body language to communicate leadership in her classroom?"<br><br>• [Model giving directions with a relaxed posture, then while squaring up and standing still] "What is the difference in the way I communicated the first way versus the second way?"<br><br>• "What is the value of communicating leadership with our body language?" | • Practice maintaining a formal posture while delivering a lesson on routines and procedures. Note when the teacher is squaring up and standing still, and when the teacher's body begins to become informal/weak.<br><br>• Film the practice—or use a mirror—so that the new teacher can see what he or she looks like while delivering instructions. | Nonverbal: model exaggerated posture and stance—shift your body upward and arch shoulders to remind the teacher to square up and stand still. |
| Formal register | Tone: teacher's vocal register is too casual or informal. | • "Imagine you had to say 'It's time to leave' to three different audiences: your friend after dinner, a symphony concert audience at the end of a performance, or when a building is on fire. Speak out loud how you would deliver those words differently to each audience." [After teacher does so] "What is the value and purpose of the middle one: your formal register?"<br><br>• "When is it important to use formal register? What message does it send to the students?"<br><br>• For a teacher who knows formal register: "What are the keys to formal register?"<br><br>• [Watch video of the teacher's classroom] "What conditions lead you to drop your formal register?" | • Videotape the teacher during practice, and review the footage during the check-in so that the teacher can hear when he/she is maintaining a formal register, and when his/her register begins to become casual/informal.<br><br>• Practice maintaining a formal tone while delivering a lesson on routines and procedures. Note when the teacher is maintaining a formal register and when the teacher's register becomes too informal or casual. | Nonverbal: combine Square Up, Stand Still gesture with pointing to your mouth to remind the teacher to speak in a formal register. |

**Stop and Jot**

What are the three top coaching ideas you plan to use to train your teachers in these Phase 1 Management skills? Jot them down here.

_____

_____

_____

_____

_____

_____

# PHASE 1 RIGOR—WRITE LESSON PLANS

## Quick Reference Guide

| If your teacher is struggling to . . . | Jump to . . . |
|---|---|
| **Develop Lesson Plans 101** | |
| Write lesson objectives that are data driven, manageable, and measurable | Write precise learning objectives |
| Deliver basic information to the students | Script out what to say during the "I Do" part of the lesson |
| **Internalize Existing Lesson Plans** | |
| Remember what to do next in the lesson | Internalize key parts of the lesson |
| Protect time for independent practice at the end of the lesson | Build time stamps into the lesson plan |

## Phase 1 Scope and Sequence

| Management Trajectory | Rigor Trajectory |
|---|---|
| **Develop Essential Routines & Procedures**<br><br>1. **Routines & Procedures 101:** Design and roll out<br>  • Plan and practice critical routines and procedures moment by moment:<br>    – Explain what each routine means and what it will look like.<br>    – Write out what teacher and students do at each step, and what will happen with students who don't follow the routine.<br>  • Plan & practice the rollout: how to introduce the routine for the first time:<br>    – Plan the "I Do": how you will model the routine.<br>    – Plan what you will do when students don't get it right. | **Write Lesson Plans**<br><br>1. **Develop Effective Lesson Plans 101:** Build the foundation of an effective lesson rooted in what students need to learn<br>  • Write precise learning objectives that are<br>    – Data driven (rooted in what students need to learn based on analysis of assessment results)<br>    – Curriculum plan driven<br>    – Able to be accomplished in one lesson<br>  • Script a basic "I Do" as a core part of the lesson.<br>  • Design an Exit Ticket (brief final mini-assessment) aligned to the objective. |

| Management Trajectory | Rigor Trajectory |
|---|---|
| 2. **Strong Voice:** Stand and speak with purpose<br><br>• Square Up, Stand Still: when giving instructions, stop moving and strike a formal pose.<br><br>• Formal register: when giving instructions, use formal register, including tone and word choice. | 2. **Internalize Existing Lesson Plans:** Make existing lesson plans your own<br><br>• Internalize & rehearse key parts of the lesson, including the "I Do" and all key instructions.<br><br>• Build time stamps into the lesson plan and follow them. |

## Introduction to Phase 1 Rigor Skills: Write Lesson Plans

When education scholars Bradley A. Ermeling and Genevieve Graff-Ermeling conducted research on the Japanese practice of lesson plan study, they discovered a simple, logical shift in focus that made an enormous difference.[8] Lesson plan study is a practice that entails developing lessons for specific content over a long period of time. The instructors involved in a particular study work to closely observe how students respond to an initial lesson, revising both that lesson and those that follow it to meet student needs better.

What intrigued the authors most was the evidence Japanese instructors used to inform their lesson plan revisions. "While our background and training in the USA included some emphasis on assessment and references to evidence-based decision making, we had no prior experience focusing on evidence with this level of depth and rigor," they marveled. "When asked to reflect and make revisions, our first instinct was to comment on whether the lesson went as planned and whether students were generally engaged." Shifting their method to more closely match that of their Japanese colleagues—using *data* to drive lesson planning, data collected not only through tests and quizzes but also by listening to what answers students generated in class—enabled them to write more effective lesson plans than they had ever developed before.

In truth, it should come as no surprise that keying into student results in this way would lead to game-changing lesson planning. If anything, it should surprise us that it comes as such a revelation. The planning process recommended in *Driven by Data* is based on this same philosophy, and several other American educators—such as Jon Saphier in *The Skillful Teacher*—have also written extensively about data-based planning and the impact it could have on American classrooms. Knowing where students are and adjusting instruction to match their needs are at the heart of great teaching.

But what's significant about Ermeling and Graff-Ermeling's study in the context of new teacher training is that it acknowledges how long it can take to collect the data that makes a lesson plan powerful. New teachers can't dive into the very first day of school with the same depth of insight into student needs that they'll have gathered after a month or two in the classroom. What they can do, however, is begin by building on the work their colleagues have done before their arrival: making time for independent student work; designing lesson topics that match the objectives on a strong curriculum plan; and, when possible, adapting lesson plans already used by more experienced teachers for their own use.

---

### Core Idea

Brand-new teachers won't immediately have insight into whether students have learned after a lesson.
What they can do right away is plan lessons that illuminate those insights as their eyes get sharper.

---

That's what the lesson planning skills new teachers will learn during Phase 1 will ensure they're able to accomplish. By the time new teachers get to the point where they can plan around individual student data, they'll have a background in lesson planning that will ensure that the shift to data-based lesson planning will be far less dramatic for them than it was for Ermeling and Graff-Ermeling. They'll have been working from the right mind-set from the beginning—an ideal way to start on the road to classroom rigor.

The Phase 1 Rigor skills capture the actions that will develop this mind-set. First, we'll determine the key skills new teachers need to learn in order to plan a great lesson from scratch. Then we'll discuss a few additional skills that are important if the new teacher is adapting an already existing lesson plan for use in his or her own classroom.

## Develop Effective Lesson Plans 101

> ### Teacher Professional Development Goal
>
> **Develop Effective Lesson Plans 101:** Build the foundation of an effective lesson rooted in what students need to learn.

In learning how to write new lesson plans from scratch, new teachers will learn how to build three basic elements of a great lesson plan:

- A data-driven objective

- An "I Do" that gets students moving in the right direction

- An Exit Ticket that lets the teacher know if they made it all the way

These three parts of the lesson plan are ideal to begin with because they are the easiest for a teacher to manage and control at the beginning of his or her career.

### Findings from the Field: Act It Out

When it came to lesson planning, we saw a lot of teachers feeling very overwhelmed. We started by creating some guiding questions they could ask themselves: "If I'm looking for an inference, what exactly am I going to do? Get in the mind of the student: What do you do as a reader?" Ultimately, this "how"—what the students needed to do— was the biggest roadblock. So we acted it out as students. We'd find a piece of text, and I would act like the student: "I don't know what to do with it." The teacher would then say, "Well, think about everything you already know about cars." I'd say, "Great, what did just you have me do?" And we'd write it down: have students activate prior knowledge. Over time, with the help of lesson plan feedback protocols like these, teachers got better.

—Kate Lynn Wilke, principal, Dallas, Texas

These basic skills of great lesson planning will get a new teacher past the following three challenges:

- The lesson objectives are not data driven, are not manageable and measurable, or have not been identified.
- The teacher stumbles or doesn't know what to say during the I Do part of the lesson.
- The teacher's Exit Ticket doesn't align to the objective.

# DEVELOP EFFECTIVE LESSON PLANS 101: WRITE PRECISE LEARNING OBJECTIVES

 *Coaching Tips*

## Teacher Context

### Challenge

The teacher does not know how to create a solid lesson objective. The lesson objectives are not data driven, are not manageable and measurable, or have not been identified.

### Action Step

Write precise learning objectives that are

- Data driven (rooted in what students need to learn based on analysis of assessment results)
- Curriculum plan driven
- Able to be accomplished in one lesson

### Action Step Overview

Let's unpack these criteria of an effective objective:

- **The objective is data driven.** It addresses what students most urgently need to learn, as demonstrated by assessment and analysis of data. The importance of this is thoroughly discussed in Driven by Data.
- **The objective is manageable and measurable.** It calls out one piece from a bigger topic or skill set students need to master—a piece small enough that the students will be able to master it in one lesson, and then move on to another small piece the following day. By the end of the lesson, there will be a clear way for the teacher to measure whether the students have learned the objective sufficiently.

The first key to writing a great objective is to start with your end goal of what you want students to learn—the final assessment defines your objective. Beyond this, the next most powerful way to help new teachers perfect the art of writing objectives is to have them complete an exercise in which they have to revise a too-broad objective to make it manageable in one lesson. After writing objectives that are not aligned to an end goal, writing objectives that are too broad is the most common error in planning objectives. Your probing questions will be key in getting teachers to narrow their objectives. Hold out for 100 percent quality objectives, because that will be the only way teachers can replicate them when you are not accompanying them.

*Quick Tip from a Coach—Have the Standards in Hand*
*Writing assessment-aligned objectives was the action step that made the biggest difference with teacher development and student learning. It allows teachers to develop their own conceptual understanding and more precisely target student learning. The biggest impact with teacher growth came by observing instruction with the standards in hand. This helped us to script precise action steps and practice writing learning objectives. We can not only see what is most important for students to learn with the standards in hand but also reflect on the alignment of instructional moves toward that needed student learning.*

—*Nicole Veltzé, principal, Denver, Colorado*

---

### KEY LEADERSHIP MOVES

| Probing Questions | • "Let's look at the upcoming assessment and the questions related to this objective. What do students have to know and do to be able to answer one of these questions correctly?"<br><br>• "If you asked them how they know their answer is correct, what key conceptual understanding do you want them to be able to articulate?"<br><br>• [After breaking down all the skills/knowledge required to answer the assessment tasks] "Of all the skills/knowledge, what are the most important parts for you to address in this lesson? Which do the students already have some mastery of, and which are the key next skills to push them further?" |
|---|---|

| Planning and Practice | • Pull out upcoming assessments to identify the right end goal, and break down too-broad objectives to make them manageable for individual lessons. |
| | • Planning and Practice are identical: plan a full week of upcoming objectives together so that the teacher has a solid beginning to his or her lesson planning. |
| | • Make sure you have all materials at hand during the meeting: upcoming lesson plans, curriculum scope and sequence, interim assessment, final exam/state test released items, and so on. |

 Rewatch clip 5: Objectives and Exit Tickets
(Key Leadership Move: Follow-Up)

# DEVELOP EFFECTIVE LESSON PLANS 101: SCRIPT A BASIC "I DO"

 Coaching Tips

## Teacher Context

### Challenge
The teacher stumbles or doesn't know what to say during the "I Do" part of the lesson.

### Action Step
Script a basic "I Do" as a core part of the lesson.

### Action Step Overview
The I Do is the point during any lesson where the least variance occurs—only the teacher is speaking. This makes it the part of the lesson that a new teacher can most easily prepare for. A well-scripted I Do can enable a teacher not only to teach effectively but also to establish his or her content knowledge and expertise with the students. The key is building a concise, precise script: teachers usually add too many extra words. Leave the exact wording of the I Do to chance, and the teacher is much more likely to stumble, be unclear, or otherwise undermine the students' ability to follow along. Particularly for a new teacher, scripting the I Do changes the game: it makes modeling an area in which he or she has locked in success, rather than risking derailment. (Note: We will revisit the I Do in Phase 3, where we will add more sophistication and respond to student learning needs. Right now we are just getting the teacher to master the basics of delivery of information.)

## KEY LEADERSHIP MOVES

**Probing Questions**

- "Let's look at your objective and the key understandings that students need to have in order to master it. How will you explain those key understandings?"
- "What will be the key points of confusion for many of the students? Given that answer, where should you emphasize your points most clearly to address that confusion?"
- "What are the key points you want to communicate during the I Do?"
- "How can you write out your I Do to make it easy to remember and deliver in the moment?"

**Planning and Practice**

- Plan (often accomplished by writing a quality objective): write out key understandings students must reach by the end of the lesson.
- Script the I Do into the lesson plan word for word. After the teacher has finished the script, ask him or her to see if there are any extraneous words that don't add value. Push the teacher to make the script tighter and shorter until every word has value. Don't begin practice until you have finished this part.
- Practice delivering the I Do. As you listen to the delivery, look for the teacher adding extraneous words or sentences that you could cut to reduce the model to what is essential.

**Real-Time Feedback**

- Nonverbal: hold out your palm and point to it with the other hand to indicate to the teacher to go back to his or her script and follow it.

# DEVELOP EFFECTIVE LESSON PLANS 101: DESIGN AN EXIT TICKET

 *Coaching Tips*

## Teacher Context

### Challenge
The teacher's Exit Ticket doesn't align to the objective.

### Action Step
Design an Exit Ticket (brief final mini-assessment) aligned to the objective.

### Action Step Overview
A critical fact for new teachers to learn as early as possible is that an Exit Ticket—a written end-of-class assignment that requires students to put to use what they've learned in class—is the ultimate way to measure whether your daily teaching was successful. If you don't assess what matters, you don't really know what happened when your lesson was translated from plan to practice. Exit Tickets solve this problem. They are directly aligned to the objective so that a teacher can look at them and truly be able to answer the question: Did the students meet the objective? The following are keys to a good Exit Ticket:

- Keep them short to make them easy to check.
- Make sure they align to the upcoming interim assessment and the most important parts of the objective that you are trying to measure.

Here is an example from a high school physics class. Note how the Exit Ticket meets the criteria: it's easy to check, but it also makes sure that students understand the concept:

*EXIT TICKET: Newton's Second Law*
1. State Newton's Second Law:
2. A 5 kg object has the free body diagram shown in Figure 2. Determine the net acceleration of the object. Show all work.

Figure 2

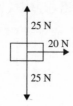

3. The graphs in Figure 3 are of net force versus acceleration for different objects. All graphs have the same scale for each respective axis. Rank the mass of the objects from greatest to least.

Figure 3

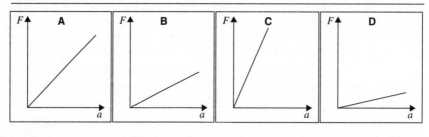

Greatest _____ _____     _____     _____ Least

---

### KEY LEADERSHIP MOVES

| | |
|---|---|
| **Probing Questions** | • "When you finish the class, what will students be able to do to show you that they have mastered the objective?" |
| | • "What key question/task could you give them at the end of the lesson to assess that mastery?" |
| | • "Look at the upcoming interim assessment/year-end test: How can we align your question to that level of difficulty and rigor?" |
| **Planning and Practice** | • Plan/revise a week's worth of Exit Tickets. Have the upcoming interim/year-end assessment questions in hand to help set the rigor of the Exit Ticket. |
| | • Look at previous Exit Tickets to see where students are struggling and what skills need to continue to be assessed. |

## Develop Effective Lesson Plans 101

| Action Step | When to Use It | Probing Questions | Scenarios to Practice | Cues for Real-Time Feedback |
|---|---|---|---|---|
| **Write precise learning objectives** | Lesson objectives are not data driven, are not manageable and measurable, or have not been identified. | • "Let's look at the upcoming assessment and the questions related to this objective. What do students have to know and do to be able to answer one of these questions correctly?"<br><br>• "If you asked them how they know their answer is correct, what key conceptual understanding do you want them to be able to articulate?"<br><br>• [After breaking down all the skills/knowledge required to answer the assessment tasks] "Of all the skills/knowledge, what are the most important parts for you to address in this lesson? Which do they already have some mastery of, and which are the key next skills to push them further?" | • Pull out upcoming assessments to identify the right end goal: break down too-broad objectives to make them manageable for individual lessons.<br><br>• Planning and practice are identical: plan a full week of upcoming objectives together.<br><br>• Make sure you have all materials at hand during the meeting: upcoming lesson plans, curriculum scope and sequence, interim assessment, final exam/state test released items, etc. | N/A |
| **Script a basic "I Do"** | Teacher stumbles or doesn't know what to say during the I Do part of the lesson. | • "Let's look at your objective and the key understandings that students need to have in order to master it. How will you explain those key understandings?"<br><br>• "What will be the key points of confusion for many of the students? Given that answer, where should you emphasize your points most clearly to address that confusion?"<br><br>• "What are the key points you want to communicate during the I Do?"<br><br>• "How can you write out your I Do to make it easy to remember and deliver in the moment?" | • Plan: write out key understandings students must reach by the end of the lesson.<br><br>• Script the I Do into the lesson plan word for word. Remove extraneous words. Don't begin practice until you have fully tightened the script.<br><br>• Practice delivering: look for the teacher adding extraneous words or sentences that you could cut to reduce the model to what is essential. | Nonverbal: hold out your palm and point to it with the other hand to indicate to the teacher to go back to his/her script and follow it. |

| Action Step | When to Use It | Probing Questions | Scenarios to Practice | Cues for Real-Time Feedback |
|---|---|---|---|---|
| **Design an Exit Ticket aligned to the objective** | Teacher's Exit Ticket doesn't align to the objective. | • "When you finish the class, what will students be able to do to show you that they have mastered the objective?" <br> • "What key question/task could you give them at the end of the lesson to assess that mastery?" <br> • "Look at the upcoming interim assessment/year-end test: How can we align your question to that level of difficulty and rigor?" | • Plan/revise a week's worth of Exit Tickets. Have the upcoming interim/year-end assessment questions in hand to help set the rigor of the Exit Ticket. <br> • Look at previous Exit Tickets to see where students are struggling and what skills need to continue to be assessed. | N/A |

## Internalize Existing Lesson Plans

> ### Teacher Professional Development Goal
>
> **Internalize Existing Lesson Plans:** Make already existing lesson plans your own.

My colleagues and I are huge advocates of sharing already existing great lesson plans with new teachers. Teaching is so difficult and such a complex art that it's impossible to underestimate the power of filling in even one piece of the teaching puzzle for a new teacher just getting on his or her feet. When that piece is planning the lesson, the teacher is freed to get better at everything from perfecting tone to developing routines—the pieces you *can't* do for them—in hours that would otherwise have been spent developing a brand-new lesson plan. In addition, if taken from a quality teacher, the already existing lesson plan will almost always be of better quality than what the new teacher would have developed on his or her own while also trying to prepare on all these other levels.

If you have access to quality lesson plans that you can share with a new teacher, the key is that the teacher must do more than just read through it. The action steps that follow will ensure that new teachers can take full advantage of an existing lesson plan.

Here are a few challenges associated with adapting an existing lesson plan for use in one's own classroom:

- The teacher hasn't internalized the lesson, and may stumble when delivering it.
- The teacher runs out of time, completing only part of the lesson plan and leaving large chunks untaught.

# INTERNALIZE EXISTING LESSON PLANS: INTERNALIZE KEY PARTS OF THE LESSON

 *Coaching Tips*

## Teacher Context

### Challenge

The teacher hasn't internalized the lesson, and may stumble when delivering it.

### Action Step

Internalize and rehearse key parts of the lesson, including the "I Do" and all key instructions.

### Action Step Overview

Just as we mention in developing new lesson plans, the first most important area of focus for a new teacher is the delivery of the parts of the lesson where he or she does most of the talking: the I Do and all key instructions. Often new teachers will assume that these are the easy parts, and they won't practice them sufficiently. Memorizing these key parts can be a game-changer, because once that's done, the teacher is freed to focus on other parts of the lesson—the ones that can't be memorized in advance.

Memorizing key parts of the lesson can be harder than it sounds: that's where your leadership is crucial.

*Quick Tip from a Coach—Make the Plan Come Alive by Annotating and Practicing*
*The risk of a teacher working with an existing plan is that they can think they can go on "auto-pilot": just read the plan at the moment of class. But that doesn't prepare you to teach effectively. We took the following steps to make sure they "owned" the lesson plan:*
- *Annotate the lesson plan: underline, write, or scribble on key parts that need to be highlighted when teaching (easy to observe!).*
- *Write the exemplar: identify the 100 percent correct responses the teacher wants from students, and stand by them! Identify where the students are and build the road to get to 100%.*

- *Define the times: a lesson plan on paper can include everything—real time isn't so kind. Teachers need to know where they'll cut if going over time or what to add if they run short.*
- *Rehearse the lesson: rehearsing will let the teacher see what is going to work and what needs to be improved!*

  In short, you have to make sure that what your teacher has planned on paper will endure in reality.

  *—Cristóbal Edwards, coach, Santiago, Chile*

---

### KEY LEADERSHIP MOVES

| | |
|---|---|
| **Probing Questions** | • "What parts of the lesson plan are most important for you to know cold? What is the value of memorizing these parts of the lesson?" |
| | • "How do you normally prepare and internalize a lesson plan?" |
| | • "What are the challenges to remembering these plans during delivery?" |
| **Planning and Practice** | • Give the teacher a set time to learn a specific chunk of the lesson cold, and then have him or her try delivering it to a partner without looking down at the lesson. |
| | • Practice one chunk of the lesson at a time. Once a teacher has it cold, put those chunks together until he or she has it completely memorized. |
| | • Build a lesson internalization routine and complete it together with the teacher: determine when he or she will spend time each day memorizing key parts of the lesson, how he or she will practice, and who will be his or her practice partner (even if the "partner" is as basic as a mirror). |
| **Real-Time Feedback** | • Model: when the teacher is struggling with the lesson plan, intervene and cue students to turn and talk. Give the teacher thirty to sixty seconds to skim the plan before jumping back into the lesson. |

---

# INTERNALIZE EXISTING LESSON PLANS: BUILD TIME STAMPS INTO THE LESSON

 **Coaching Tips**

## Teacher Context

### Challenge

The teacher runs out of time, completing only part of the lesson plan and leaving large chunks untaught.

### Action Step

Build time stamps into the lesson plan and follow them.

### Action Step Overview

Every teacher constantly negotiates with time: "How can I fit as much learning as possible into the time I have for this lesson?" The challenge for new teachers is that it normally takes them far longer to teach the same material. Everything is slower: their instructions, their delivery, their class discussion, and so on. One very simple strategy to help them is to put a time limit on every part of the lesson. If they know they should be done with homework review at 10:17 a.m., they will feel a sense of urgency about moving forward. Time stamps are a teacher's best friend: they let the teacher know immediately whether he or she is ahead of time or behind. It will be a while yet before teachers are necessarily able to meet all these time stamps—that's addressed further on in the Scope and Sequence. For now, what's important is that they make it a habit to set realistic time management goals that will, when met, ensure that what's most important happens in each lesson.

*Quick Tip from a Coach—Don't Let the Filet Mignon Go Cold*
*Time stamping lesson plans has been super high impact for my work with new teachers. The simple act of supporting teachers to name how long each part of the lesson should take—and then setting some firm boundaries (the Do Now must be over in less than five minutes)— dramatically accelerated the growth of many teachers. Without time stamps, too often new teachers would "serve the appetizers" of a lesson (the Do Now, a mini-lesson, other teacher talk) while letting the "filet*

*mignon" (the meatiest, most rigorous part of the lesson) go cold—or worse, uneaten. Time stamping helps new teachers serve a nice, juicy, warm filet of rigor every day.*

*—Doug McCurry, principal manager, New Haven, Connecticut, and Brooklyn, New York*

---

### KEY LEADERSHIP MOVES

| | |
|---|---|
| **Probing Questions** | • "What is the ideal amount of time you want for independent practice at the end? What are the challenges to making sure that students have that amount of time?"<br><br>• "What are the key tasks students need to do to be able to work independently effectively? What are the parts of the lesson we could cut short if you are running out of time?" |
| **Planning and Practice** | • Have the teacher write down exactly when he or she will reach each part of the lesson, adding the specific time stamps that apply to the teacher's own lesson to the lesson template he or she is working with. Also note which parts of the lesson could be trimmed or cut if the teacher is running over.<br><br>• Have the teacher rehearse the lesson with timer in hand, so that he or she can get a sense of what it will take to stick to those times. Cut unnecessary language that is slowing the teacher down. |
| **Real-Time Feedback** | • Nonverbal: hold up fingers for how many more minutes to spend in that section of the lesson. |

---

## Internalize Existing Lesson Plans

| Action Step | When to Use It | Probing Questions | Scenarios to Practice | Cues for Real-Time Feedback |
|---|---|---|---|---|
| **Internalize and rehearse key parts of the lesson** | Teacher hasn't internalized the lesson, and may stumble when delivering it. | • "What parts of the lesson plan are most important for you to know cold? What is the value of memorizing these parts of the lesson?"<br><br>• "How do you normally prepare and internalize a lesson plan?"<br><br>• "What are the challenges to remembering these plans during delivery?" | • Give the teacher a set time to learn a specific chunk of the lesson cold, and then have him/her try delivering it to a partner without looking down at the lesson.<br><br>• Practice one chunk of the lesson at a time. Once a teacher has it cold, put those chunks together until he/she has it completely memorized.<br><br>• Build a lesson internalization routine: determine when the teacher will spend time each day memorizing key parts of the lesson, how he/she will practice, and who will be his/her practice partner (even if the "partner" is as basic as a mirror). | Model: when the teacher is struggling with the lesson plan, intervene and cue students to turn & talk. Give the teacher 30–60 seconds to skim the plan before jumping back into the lesson. |
| **Build time stamps into the lesson** | Teacher runs out of time, completing only part of the lesson plan and leaving large chunks untaught. | • "What is the ideal amount of time you want for independent practice at the end? What are the challenges to making sure that students have that amount of time?"<br><br>• "What are the key tasks students need to do to be able to work independently effectively? What are the parts of the lesson we could cut short if you are running out of time?" | • Write down specific time stamps in the teacher's lesson plan. Note which parts of the lesson could be trimmed or cut if teacher is running over.<br><br>• Rehearse the lesson with timer in hand. Cut unnecessary language that is slowing the teacher down. | Nonverbal: hold up fingers for how many more minutes to spend in that section of the lesson. |

PHASE 1

RIGOR

**Stop and Jot**

What are the three top coaching ideas you plan to use to train your teachers in these Phase 1 Rigor skills? Jot them down here.

_____

_____

_____

_____

_____

_____

## CONCLUSION

The power of a grand entrance is impossible to underestimate. For the cast of a musical, that may mean a stunning dance number. For Orhan Pamuk, it means reentering an old room with a new mind-set. And for a new teacher, it means welcoming students into the classroom on the first day of school with purpose, urgency, and joy. Any of these entrances is a giant first step up the ladder to success: it won't get you all the way there, but it will prevent you from having to scramble to keep your footing.

Phase 1 will help new teachers nail their footing on the opening number: a first day of school with carefully planned routines and focused lesson plans. With the opening number complete, they can move on to Phase 2: Instant Immersion.

# Instant Immersion

My wife, Gabriela (Gaby for short), was born in Mexico and came to the United States to go to college on a scholarship. When we first got married, we moved back to Mexico City so that she could complete medical school. Whereas Gaby is completely bilingual, I was not even close when we first arrived. I still remember how at ease Gaby was in conversation with family, friends, and co-workers and how much I had to think before I could utter a coherent sentence. Gaby was right in her element in Mexico, but I was in a state of instant immersion.

I started working as an English teacher at a nearby school and stayed teaching there for six years. During that time, nearly all of my colleagues were Mexican and spoke only Spanish with me. The one exception was the faculty of the English Department, which was largely made up of recently arrived English speakers like myself who were all struggling to communicate effectively in Spanish.

Over the course of the next several months, our small English team began to divide. Some of us grew more proficient at a surprisingly rapid pace, while others never felt comfortable saying much more in Spanish than basic interactions and how they preferred their coffee. Even up to five years later, they struggled to communicate with their students' parents or to follow local politics.

What made the difference? It wasn't a matter of who among us were more outgoing, or even who had studied Spanish the longest before making the journey to Mexico. Instead, the teachers who were able to ride the waves of instant immersion—both functioning and learning as we went—had two key characteristics in common: they had learned a solid foundation of grammar and vocabulary to be able to string sentences together, and they took every opportunity to apply them each day.

I recall my own first days interacting with colleagues at my school. I listened intently to see what phrases they were using to describe certain things, and then I practiced. I didn't try to do it all at first (engaging in a dinner conversation was too difficult because of trying to keep up with the pace and all the different voices), but instead focused on one-on-one conversations where I had more time to think and formulate my words. Because of my own language limitations, I was most successful at first with using as few words as possible. When I got a blank stare or look of confusion, I went back and revised my words or conjugation until I was understood. I would often formulate whole phrases in my head first before speaking to have a better chance at success. I observed, took mental notes, and practiced. Each time I fell flat on my face, I would get up and try again.

The process didn't feel quick—it felt agonizingly slow!—but those around me could see the difference much more than I could.

Learning to teach is the same as learning a foreign language: you need a solid foundation, but then you need to dive in with the basics. Phase 1 was all about the foundation. Phase 2 is about diving in: using the experience of instant immersion into teaching not as a drowning experience but as an opportunity to tread water as you learn to swim.

---

### Core Idea

Learning to teach is like learning a language.
Phase 1 is about learning the rules.
Phase 2 is about using them to communicate.

---

Of course, instant immersion is a challenge even with this level of support. (Treading water can be terrifying when one is first learning to swim.) Jackson Tobin felt this acutely two years ago, when he'd just begun teaching. A few weeks into September, a colleague of mine asked him how things were going, and it was clear that he felt overwhelmed. "All the rehearsals, all the summer PD, it's all been really helpful," he explained, "but—well, there's just no substitute for when the kids are actually there." What Jackson was facing—what any new teacher, however well prepared, faces in September—was the challenge of learning how to speak a new language just as fluently in practice as in theory.

Phase 2 doesn't eliminate the stress and anxiety of a first-year teacher's experience (although it can definitely reduce it). When implemented well, Phase 2 allows a teacher to move toward swimming and away from drowning—and that makes all the difference.

# PHASE 2 COACHING BLUEPRINT: MAKE TIME FOR FEEDBACK

The number one thing you'll need to kick-start your year of delivering feedback is a schedule which ensures that you have time to do it. Here, we'll show how to schedule time to engage the coaching principles of Go Granular and Plan, Practice, Follow Up, Repeat. We'll also provide materials to make your very first feedback meeting with each of your new teachers a success.

## Make Time for Feedback

At a training I led recently, I had just shown a video of a coach giving a teacher feedback and had asked participants to share their responses to the video. Many participants commented on the positive tone of the feedback or on how specific it was; but one school leader was distracted by one specific word the coach in the video had used: "today."

"The first thing she said was, 'When I observed you *today*,'" he remarked. "Not 'way back before Halloween,' but 'today.' That teacher is going to remember exactly the moment she's talking about, and be able to do something about it tomorrow. What kind of scheduling makes it possible for a leader to have such fast turnaround on observation feedback?"

The answer takes up an entire chapter in *Leverage Leadership*—one that explains how to arrange your whole schedule around providing weekly observation and feedback to every teacher in your school. This section, however, will be more succinct, summing up just the most important steps to establishing a reliable observation and feedback schedule for all your new teachers. If you've already built a solid schedule that locks in observations of all your teachers, skip forward to the next section. If not, read through the following four steps. For best results, pull out your calendar and build your schedule as you read.

# DELEGATE, BLOCK, LOCK, AND BACKWARDS-PLAN

 *Four Steps to Scheduling Observation and Feedback*

1. **Delegate—distribute your teachers among the members of your leadership team.** The first step is to make sure you have a reasonable load of teachers to observe. Our experiences with leaders across the country have shown that getting to a ratio of thirty teachers to one instructional leader meets the needs of 90 percent of school leaders. The 30-to-1 ratio allows for biweekly observations; a 15-to-1 ratio allows for weekly observations. For new (and most!) teachers, that is far more ideal!

2. **Block out time when you're likely to be interrupted.** The next step to making feedback meetings stick in your schedule is a simple one: don't plan them for the times of day when you're likely to get interrupted. Meetings planned around breakfast, lunch, or after school usually become missed meetings, because that's when principals most often need to speak with students or parents about specific, immediate challenges. Block out moments like this, as well as any other hours of the week you can't devote to teachers. The time that remains is what you have to work with in planning the feedback meetings.

3. **Lock in feedback meetings first.** Locking in your feedback meetings *before* you plan when you'll observe each teacher is an excellent accountability tool: if you've already arranged to meet the teacher and you know he or she will be waiting in your office to receive your feedback, you have an added incentive to follow through. You also save yourself a ton of time: you remove long strings of email exchanges to try to find a time to meet. By pinning down regular check-ins with each teacher, you save time and create a solid structure around which teachers can plan.

4. **Plan your observation schedule.** The final step is obvious: plan when to observe. Observing your teacher in action as near as possible to your weekly feedback meeting with him or her will help you know firsthand what coaching the teacher most urgently needs that week—and the teacher will be able to implement it immediately. Plan a twenty- or thirty-minute slot—one that comes earlier in the week than the time you've planned to hold a feedback meeting with the new

teacher—during which to observe him or her. (Like the feedback meetings, observations may be planned back-to-back to increase efficiency.)

Once you've done this, here's what your schedule might look like if you manage fifteen teachers.

| | Monday | Tuesday | Wednesday | Thursday | Friday |
|---|---|---|---|---|---|
| 6 a.m. | | | | | |
| :30 | | | | | |
| 7 a.m. | | | | | |
| :30 | | | | | |
| 8 a.m. | | Meet Fallon | Meet Mears | | |
| :30 | | Meet West | Meet Dennis | | |
| 9 a.m. | Observe Fallon, West, Watson | Meet Watson | Meet Hamayan | | |
| :30 | | | | | |
| 10 a.m. | | | Observe McClain, Hagan, Daria | | Observe Kerstein, Lennox, Chan |
| :30 | | | | | |
| 11 a.m. | | | | | |
| :30 | | | | | |
| 12 p.m. | Observe Mears, Elliott, Morales | | | | Meet Kim |
| :30 | | | | | Meet Chan |
| 1 p.m. | | Meet Morales | | | Meet Lennox |
| :30 | | Meet Elliott | Meet Hagan | | Meet Kerstein |
| 2 p.m. | | Observe Kim, Dennis, Hamayan | Meet Daria | | |
| :30 | | | Meet McClain | | |

If you manage more than fifteen teachers—up to thirty teachers—the schedule still looks the same: you just set up a rotation, making sure you see each teacher every other week instead of every week. It doesn't take up any more time. The ratio of thirty teachers to one leader meets the needs of 90 percent of leaders my colleagues and I have met at schools across the country. If you're one of the remaining leaders with a greater number of teachers per leader than that, turn to *Leverage Leadership* for a set of tips for how to make observation and feedback happen in that context.

What have you accomplished when you set this schedule? You've committed to regularly completing the one step that will most fuel teacher growth: providing the specific coaching each teacher needs most urgently at all times. Building this coaching into your calendar is half the battle of making sure every teacher receives it.

> ## Core Idea
>
> When it comes to giving teachers feedback,
> setting up the schedule is half the battle.

Once you have a schedule and observe regularly, how do you keep from spending too much time in preparing to give your leaders feedback? If it takes hours to prepare each meeting, you will quickly find it unsustainable. In the next "Findings from the Field," Serena Savarirayan provides some helpful tips to save time and become more efficient in planning meetings.

## Findings from the Field: Need for Speed?
## Plan Your Feedback while Observing

If you start to block out your time to observe and give feedback regularly, the challenge is learning to prepare for each of those feedback meetings efficiently. If you don't, you'll never have enough time to do it all! After much trial and error, here are the steps I follow to make sure I'm prepared—efficiently—for each feedback meeting:

- **Have your tools in hand when observing.** Whenever I observe, I make sure I have my iPhone (so I can film the teacher if it is useful), my Get Better Faster Scope and Sequence (so I can select an action step efficiently), and a blank template for planning my feedback meeting. This way, while I'm observing, I can select the action step and start scripting the feedback that I will give. I make a point not to leave the observation until at a minimum I've selected the action step. That does two things: first, that it lets me develop my action steps while the observation is freshest in my mind; and second, it helps me build a habit of thinking: What would I do if I were teaching this lesson? Or: What would the best math teacher I know do if he or she were teaching this lesson?
- **Record the time stamps in the feedback script.** If I filmed the lesson, I record the time stamps into my meeting script of the best part to use in the feedback meeting. That way I don't have to watch the whole video but can zero in immediately on the part that captured the area of growth for the teacher.
- **Complete the meeting script in ten minutes.** Because of how I used the observation time, I am able to complete the script for my feedback meeting in just ten more minutes after the observation. I pull out my Get Better Faster Coach's Guide [in the appendix and on the DVD] to select appropriate prompts, practice scenarios, and real-time feedback cues. I have the lesson plan in hand in case we need it to make changes. I watch the critical moments in the video a second time to give me optimal clarity about what to address with the teacher.

At first it took me way more than ten minutes. But if you challenge yourself to be that efficient, you will get there in time. And it makes the habit of instructional leadership so much more doable!

—Serena Savarirayan, principal manager, Newark, New Jersey

(If you're interested in additional tools to help you monitor and maintain observation and feedback, *Leverage Leadership* includes a great deal more guidance and resources.)

## Set the Tone: The First Feedback Meeting

It's one thing to schedule your feedback meetings, and another to know what to do when a teacher who's never received this kind of feedback before is sitting right in front of you. We addressed the core areas of feedback in the opening chapter (coaching principle 2): Plan, Practice, Follow Up, Repeat. However, those will not come easily unless you've created a safe, productive meeting environment where teachers can thrive. Your first feedback meeting is critical for setting the tone for the year.

---

### Core Idea

You never get a second chance to make a first impression.
The quality of your first meeting sets the tone for the rest of the year.

---

What does it take to start on the right foot? The key is to focus on rolling out the specific routines that you want in place in every feedback meeting, all year round. If this strikes you as similar to the emphasis on teachers setting up student routines, which you worked on during Phase 1, you're dead on—adults need these types of routines just as much as students do. Let's take a look at the most important ones that will drive the first feedback meeting.

What's the greatest challenge new teachers face in the earliest part of the year? Managing the sheer amount of work it takes to teach. Personal organization may not sound momentous, but it can be the single hardest part of setting up a successful classroom—as many of us recall all too well. "I was spending too much time on materials, and staying too late," one new teacher remembered of her first month in the classroom. "My morale was taking a hit, and it was hard to get little tasks done when all I could do was think about how much I had to do."

The solution? Provide the teacher with tools for personal organization, and use them with him or her to track the teacher's priorities throughout the year. See the next "Findings from the Field" to consider the tools that Nikki Bridges used with Jackson and her other new teachers.

## Findings from the Field: Provide Tools for Personal Organization

My first move at my first meeting with a new teacher is to give him or her a binder full of all the materials he or she will need to stay organized throughout the year. That includes:

- **Task management tracker.** The task management tracker establishes what each teacher's tasks are, and the space to plan how he or she will complete them. Consolidating this information in one place is immensely helpful for a new teacher trying to remember so many different tasks at once.
- **Calendar.** Previewing a school calendar with a new teacher may seem like a mundane agenda item to include during a feedback meeting, but it's a critical one. Making sure the teacher has a calendar that shows important deadlines and upcoming school events—and has reviewed that calendar!—will go a long way toward ensuring that the teacher plans his or her time effectively.
- **Weekly meeting notes.** To be sure the teacher is able to make use of what you cover during your feedback meeting, provide him or her with a space to take notes while you're working together. Just like an observation tracker for you, the weekly meeting note space will remind the teacher of what's most important to work on right now, even in the midst of everything else going on during a busy school day.
- **Data-driven instructional plan.** With so many daily tasks for a new teacher to accomplish, it's easy to lose track of the big picture: the learning goals for every student for the year. A copy of the current instructional plan serves as a reminder that all these smaller daily and weekly actions align with student learning needs—something that can help both to motivate the teacher and to build his or her understanding of the "why" behind each week's action step.

When a new teacher has all of these located in one binder, I remove a major obstacle that could keep him or her from being successful.

—Nikki Bridges, principal, Brooklyn, New York

It needn't take more than five minutes to present these tools in your first meeting with a teacher—and once you've done it with one teacher, you can do it with everyone else, too.

Figures 4 and 5, as well as the sample Data-Driven Instructional Plan, are some examples you could use or adapt.

Figure 4  **Task Management Tracker**

## Monday

| | |
|---|---|
| 7:00-7:30 | |
| 7:30-8:10 | |
| 8:10-8:40 | |
| 8:40-9:25 | |
| 9:25-10:10 | |
| 10:10-10:40 | |
| 10:40-11:25 | |
| 11:25-12:10 | |
| 12:10-12:40 | |
| 12:40-1:30 | |
| 1:30-2:15 | |
| 2:15-2:30 | |
| 2:30-3:25 | |
| 3:25-4:05 | |
| After School | |

| Before I leave | Prep 1 |
|---|---|
| | |

| At home | Prep 2 |
|---|---|
| | |

## Figure 5  Meeting Notes Template

**Uncommon Schools**  **NORTH ★ STAR**

**Weekly Meeting Notes Page**

| Date: | | Meeting Type:<br>(feedback, data, co-teacher) | |
|---|---|---|---|
| **My Strengths** | | | |
| ☐ | | | |
| ☐ | | | |

| My Action Steps | Timeline |
|---|---|
| ☐ | |
| ☐ | |

| Notes for Planning & Practice |
|---|
| |

| Follow-up Steps |
|---|
| |

**Sample Data-Driven Instructional Plan**

| Part II. Five-Week Reteach Plan—Next 3 Weeks—Dates: 11/14 through 1/22 |
|---|
| Week 3 (11/25–11/30): SD, 2-2, Review of 10-1 Grammar IA, *The Piano Lesson* Act I, Quote Integration<br><br>Vocab: 2-1 and 2-2 Review<br><br>Literature: *The Piano Lesson* Act I (Symbol and Conflict)<br><br>Writing: Focus on Thesis Statements<br><br>Quiz: 2-1 and 2-2, Grammar Review |
| Week 4 (12/3–12/7): SD, 2-3, Pronoun Antecedent Agreement, *The Piano Lesson* Act I and Act II<br><br>Vocab: 2-3<br><br>Grammar: Pronoun Antecedent Agreement Guided Practice<br><br>Literature: *The Piano Lesson* Acts I and II (More Symbol and Conflict)<br><br>Writing: Integrating Citations more Fluidly<br><br>Quiz: 2-3, SD, Pronoun Antecedent Agreement |
| Week 5 (12/10–12/14): ER, 2-4, Pronoun Reflective/Reciprocal, *The Piano Lesson* Act II<br><br>Vocab: 2-4; Grammar: Pronoun Reflexive/Reciprocal Guided Practice<br><br>Literature: *The Piano Lesson* Act II (Theme)<br><br>Writing: Clinching Statements: So What?<br><br>Quiz: 2-4, ER, Pronoun Reflexive/Reciprocal |

## Core Idea

Give new teachers the tools to build time management systems, and you save them hours in a matter of minutes.

## Stop and Jot: Tools for Personal Organization

Which of the tools Nikki gave her new teachers do you plan to use with yours? Which do you have already, and which will you need to create from scratch?

_____

_____

_____

_____

Once you've set up the organization of your feedback meeting, it's time to set the tone with a preview of the format your meeting will follow. This is also the time to plant the roots of the relationship you intend to build with this teacher, one based on both professionalism and trust. Principal Desiree Robin follows an intentional sequence for her first meetings to set the right tone and make it easier for teachers to grow:

- **Preview the format.** Walking through what you will do in the meeting reduces anxiety and allows a teacher to focus on the current moment.

- **Create an emotional safe space.** Asking a teacher how he or she is doing—and genuinely listening to his or her response—is a vitally important foundation for feedback.

- **Provide tools for task management.** (This is the same as what Nikki described earlier.)

- **Preview the calendar.** (This is the same as what Nikki described earlier.)

- **Set PD goals.** Save the setting of professional goals until the end of the first meeting: a perfect segue into giving feedback.

- **Give feedback!**

These simple steps don't take much time, but they change outcomes. By acknowledging where teachers are emotionally and organizing their time, you free up mental space for them to focus on their teaching—this can make all the difference.

We're now ready to give Phase 2 feedback. Read on!

## Teaching Skills Overview

Phase 2 focuses on succeeding in the instant immersion of the first days of class: implementing the basic skills that allow teachers to tread water while they learn the rest. Teachers learned the foundation during Phase 1. Now they will dive in and use those skills. For Phase 2 Management, this means getting all routines solidly in place by making sure every student is on board. For Phase 2 Rigor, it means establishing effective independent practice as a daily component of each lesson. Although other aspects of teaching are more exciting on the surface (for example, delivering engaging content and facilitating quality student discussions), getting independent practice right first makes sure that whenever you send students off to work on something, you are getting maximal learning. You can be the greatest facilitator in the world, but if students don't practice what they've learned independently, they won't master it! (Remember the example from learning a language: I had to be able to talk one-on-one before I could master the dinner conversation.) And don't worry: Phases 3 and 4 will get you quickly into those other areas that make up great teaching.

**Phase 2 Action Step Sequence**

| Management Trajectory | Rigor Trajectory |
|---|---|
| **Roll Out and Monitor Routines** | **Independent Practice** |
| 3. **What to Do:** Give clear, precise directions <br><br>• Economy of language: give crisp instructions with as few words as possible (e.g., 3-word directions). Check for understanding on complex instructions. <br><br>4. **Routines & Procedures 201:** Revise and perfect them <br><br>• Revise any routine that needs more attention to detail or is inefficient, with particular emphasis on what students and teachers are doing at each moment. <br><br>• Do It Again: have students do the routine again if not done correctly the first time. <br><br>• Cut It Short: know when to stop the Do It Again. <br><br>5. **Teacher Radar:** Know when students are off task <br><br>• Deliberately scan the room for off-task behavior: <br><br>– Choose 3–4 "hot spots" (places where you have students who often get off task) to scan constantly <br><br>– Be Seen Looking: crane your neck to appear to be seeing all corners of the room. | 3. **Write the Exemplar:** Set the bar for excellence <br><br>• Script out the ideal written responses you want students to produce during independent practice. <br><br>• Align independent practice to the rigor of the upcoming interim assessment. <br><br>4. **Independent Practice:** Set up daily routines that build opportunities for students to practice independently <br><br>• Write first, talk second: give students writing tasks to complete prior to class discussion, so that every student answers independently before hearing his/her peers' contributions. <br><br>• Implement a daily entry prompt (Do Now) to either introduce the day's objective or review material from the previous day. <br><br>• Implement and review a longer independent practice and/or a daily Exit Ticket (brief final mini-assessment aligned to your objective) to see how many students mastered the concept. |

| Management Trajectory | Rigor Trajectory |
|---|---|
| • Circulate the room with purpose (break the plane): <br><br>   – Move among the desks and around the perimeter. <br><br>   – Stand at the corners: identify 3 spots on the perimeter of the room to which you can circulate to stand and monitor student work. <br><br> • Move away from the student who is speaking to monitor the whole room. <br><br> **6. Whole-Class Reset** <br><br> • Implement a planned whole-class reset to reestablish student behavioral expectations when a class routine has slowly weakened over previous classes. <br><br> • Implement an "in-the-moment reset" when a class veers off task during the class period. <br><br>   – Example: Stop teaching. Square up. Give a clear What to Do: "Pencils down. Eyes on me. Hands folded in 3-2-1. Thank you: that's what Harvard looks like." Pick up tone & energy again. | **5. Monitor Aggressively:** Check students' independent work to determine whether they're learning what you're teaching <br><br> • Create & implement a monitoring pathway: <br><br>   – Create a seating chart to monitor students most effectively. <br><br>   – Monitor the fastest writers first, then the students who need more support. <br><br> • Monitor the quality of student work: <br><br>   – Check answers against your exemplar. <br><br>   – Track correct and incorrect answers to class questions. <br><br> • Pen in Hand: mark up student work as you circulate. <br><br>   – Use a coding system to affirm correct answers. <br><br>   – Cue students to revise answers, using minimal verbal intervention. (Name the error, ask them to fix it, tell them you'll follow up.) |

# PHASE 2 MANAGEMENT—ROLL OUT AND MONITOR ROUTINES

Quick Reference Guide

| If your teacher is struggling to . . . | Jump to . . . |
|---|---|
| **What to Do** | |
| Deliver clear, concise directions | What to Do (economy of language) |
| **Routines and Procedures 201** | |
| Develop efficient routines | Revise routines |
| Get students to follow routines | Do It Again |
| Know when it is time to move on after a Do It Again | Cut It Short |
| **Teacher Radar** | |
| Notice the earliest actions of student nonresponsiveness | Scan hot spots |
| Demonstrate to the students that he or she is watching them | Be Seen Looking |
| Leave the front of the room and circulate | Circulate with purpose |
| Manage other students while one student is speaking | Move away from the student who is speaking |
| **Whole-Class Reset** | |
| Know what to do when the class becomes less engaged | Planned reset or in-the-moment reset |

**Phase 2 Action Step Sequence**

| Management Trajectory | Rigor Trajectory |
|---|---|
| **Roll Out and Monitor Routines** | Independent Practice |
| 3. **What to Do:** Give clear, precise directions | 3. **Write the Exemplar:** Set the bar for excellence |
| • Economy of language: give crisp instructions with as few words as possible (e.g., 3-word directions). Check for understanding on complex instructions. | • Script out the ideal written responses you want students to produce during independent practice. |
| 4. **Routines & Procedures 201:** Revise and perfect them | • Align independent practice to the rigor of the upcoming interim assessment. |
| • Revise any routine that needs more attention to detail or is inefficient, with particular emphasis on what students and teachers are doing at each moment. | 4. **Independent Practice:** Set up daily routines that build opportunities for students to practice independently |
| • Do It Again: have students do the routine again if not done correctly the first time. | • Write first, talk second: give students writing tasks to complete prior to class discussion, so that every student answers independently before hearing his/her peers' contributions. |
| • Cut It Short: know when to stop the Do It Again. | |
| 5. **Teacher Radar:** Know when students are off task | • Implement a daily entry prompt (Do Now) to either introduce the day's objective or review material from the previous day. |
| • Deliberately scan the room for off-task behavior: | |
| – Choose 3–4 "hot spots" (places where you have students who often get off task) to scan constantly | • Implement and review a longer independent practice and/or a daily Exit Ticket (brief final mini-assessment aligned to your objective) to see how many students mastered the concept. |
| – Be Seen Looking: crane your neck to appear to be seeing all corners of the room. | |
| • Circulate the room with purpose (break the plane): | 5. **Monitor Aggressively:** Check students' independent work to determine whether they're learning what you're teaching |
| – Move among the desks and around the perimeter. | |
| – Stand at the corners: identify 3 spots on the perimeter of the room to which you can circulate to stand and monitor student work. | |

| Management Trajectory | Rigor Trajectory |
|---|---|
| • Move away from the student who is speaking to monitor the whole room.<br><br>**6. Whole-Class Reset**<br>• Implement a planned whole-class reset to reestablish student behavioral expectations when a class routine has slowly weakened over previous classes.<br>• Implement an "in-the-moment reset" when a class veers off task during the class period.<br>  – Example: Stop teaching. Square up. Give a clear What to Do: "Pencils down. Eyes on me. Hands folded in 3-2-1. Thank you: that's what Harvard looks like." Pick up tone & energy again. | • Create & implement a monitoring pathway:<br>  – Create a seating chart to monitor students most effectively.<br>  – Monitor the fastest writers first, then the students who need more support.<br>• Monitor the quality of student work:<br>  – Check answers against your exemplar.<br>  – Track correct and incorrect answers to class questions.<br>• Pen in Hand: mark up student work as you circulate.<br>  – Use a coding system to affirm correct answers.<br>  – Cue students to revise answers, using minimal verbal intervention. (Name the error, ask them to fix it, tell them you'll follow up.) |

## Introduction to Phase 2 Management Skills: Roll Out and Monitor Routines

Bill Walsh was a legendary figure and one of the most successful football coaches of all time. He was aptly nicknamed "The Genius" for all of the innovations he led that transformed the sport. While most football fans know him as the creator of the West Coast Offense, his impact on the coaching world went much further. One of his biggest contributions was his method for game planning.

When Walsh was an assistant coach for the Cincinnati Bengals working under Paul Brown in the 1970s, he began scripting a set of two or three plays to open the game. It worked so well that when he moved on to head coaching, he expanded his script. He had ten to twelve scripted plays to start the game while coaching the Chargers, then twenty plays at Stanford, and twenty-five plays while coaching the Forty-Niners—that is nearly half the game! At the time, coaches viewed this approach as ludicrous. How can you possibly plan all your plays in advance when you should be adjusting to the flow of the game? Walsh's response is telling:

> Your ability to think concisely, your ability to make good judgments is much easier on Thursday night than during the heat of the game. So we prefer to make our decisions related to the game almost clinically, before the game is ever played . . . As the game is being played, to be honest with you, you are in a state of stress. Sometimes you are in a state of desperation and you are asked to make very calculated decisions. Your decisions made during the week are the ones that make more sense.[1]

If this approach works for one of the most insightful minds in sports, it certainly works for new teachers. When classes start, they are in the heat of the game and under great stress. Rather than try to make the best decisions in the moment, teachers thrive on having a set number of plays that will carry them through most of their lesson—just like Walsh.

PHASE 2

MANAGEMENT

---

### Core Idea

In Phase 2,
don't train teachers to make decisions in the heat of the moment.
Anticipate errors and make a plan you can follow.

---

Phase 2 Management is all about following Walsh's playbook. In the case of teaching, these "plays" are the moves teachers make at each part of the lesson: the words they say with each instruction, how they monitor and move around the classroom, and a generic "reset" for when the class is off track. Building and executing on these scripted plays can dramatically transform the classroom of a new teacher. Later, teachers will need to know how to modify that plan based on unforeseeable factors. For now, their energy is best allocated to learning the moves they can know in advance by heart. If we lead this phase effectively, their classrooms will be humming as well as Walsh's West Coast Offense.

## What to Do

> ### Teacher Professional Development Goal
>
> **What to Do:** Deliver even the most complex directions both succinctly and clearly.

One of the biggest impediments to great classroom management is a lack of precision in the quality of communication. Use too many words or too many unclear directions, and students will immediately start to check out.

The first step in building a classroom where all students are doing what they should be doing is having all students *know* what they should be doing. For this, you need a teacher who gives crystal-clear instructions, conveying even the most complex information in a way that leaves all students knowing what comes next.

> ### Q Findings from the Field: Tell Them What You Want to See
>
> What was hard for me as a teacher was becoming comfortable with the idea that as a teacher, your job is to tell children what to do. You're the adult in the room; you have to tell them what you want to see them doing in order for them to do it. I was right out of college when I started teaching, so that wasn't a natural thing for me to do. I would use way too many words, and they would get confused. But when I thought about what I wanted to see and how to say it clearly, I made it easier for my students to succeed—which they really want to do! But the only way they can is if you're really explicit about what they have to do.
> —Anne Albrecht, instructional coach, Brooklyn, New York

The following is the most common Phase 2 challenge that can typically be addressed by What to Do:

- The teacher's directions are unclear or use too many words.

# WHAT TO DO—ECONOMY OF LANGUAGE

 Coaching Tips

## Teacher Context

### Challenge

The teacher's directions, particularly when he or she leads routines and procedures, are unclear or use too many words. This can happen even with the best-planned routines: the teacher may have thought very carefully about the structure of the routine, but just not nailed down the right words to roll it out.

### Action Step

Economy of language: give crisp instructions with as few words as possible (for example, three-word directions). Check for understanding on complex instructions.

### Action Step Overview

Teachers can stumble over directions or use too many words for a variety of reasons:

- Their original plan did not have the words completely scripted.
- They get nervous and stumble over their script in the moment.
- They add more words without even realizing it.

Scripting and practicing directions before the lessons enable a teacher to deliver clear directions on the spot without having to pause and consider what to say. Sufficiently detailed directions might look something like this: "Eyes on me. Books closed. Now turn to page 47." Pause until all students are on the same page. "Please finish problems one through three. You have ten minutes. Begin."

For directions that are even more complex (for example, a difficult assignment), the teacher should also plan ways to check the students' understanding before sending them off to work.

*Quick Tip from a Coach—Use as Many Nonverbal Cues as Possible*
*Economy of language is so important—figuring out not only how to make your directions more concise but how to deliver them without even speaking. Some key nonverbal instructions are a thumbs-up and a smile for "start working," or opening up your palms for "start reading independently." Lessening teacher talk sends the message: "When I speak to you, it's focused on learning." It's a silent, "Let's get to work immediately." The key*

*to learning this technique is practicing it and seeing it modeled. During my classroom walk-throughs, I would model the motion and make eye contact with the teacher and observe them implementing it. For example, if a student was wearing his or her book bag, I would motion taking off the book bag, and the teacher would find the student who needed to do that and deliver the nonverbal motion. Teachers had to script every direction given during instruction, and students were taught the nonverbal gestures in whole-group settings with an emphasis on why this technique is essential.*

—Jody-Anne Jones, principal, Newark, New Jersey

---

## KEY LEADERSHIP MOVES

| | |
|---|---|
| **Probing Questions** | • "What happened yesterday when you asked your students to ___? What caused the confusion?" |
| | • "What is the value in using fewer words to describe what students should do?" |
| | • [Play video of teacher's instructions] "What is another way you could have restated these directions to make them clearer for students?" [or] "Write down all the directions you gave. Where did you use more words than needed?" |
| | • [If teacher struggles, model for him or her] "Let me deliver those same instructions. [Model] What do you notice about the difference between my delivery and your own?" |
| **Planning and Practice** | • Script clear, concise instructions together. Plan them out word by word: don't take shortcuts! Remove all extraneous words. |
| | • Provide feedback on clarity *before* practice: most errors can be fixed before your practice. |
| | • Rehearse key directions in the lesson. If necessary, model what the teacher could say to be most effective. |
| | • Focus on the pregnant pause between each component of the instruction: students often become confused when given too many directions at once. |

| Real-Time Feedback | • Nonverbal: hold up a red card for too many words. |
| | • Nonverbal: hold up a sign that says "What to Do." |
| | • Whisper prompt: "When you bring everyone back from this assignment, just say: 'Pencils down. Eyes on me!' No extra words." |
| | • Model: model giving concise directions using three to five words |
| | • Model: ask a student to repeat the teacher's instructions. |

 Rewatch clip 8: What to Do and Teacher Radar—Scan (Key Leadership Move: Real-Time Feedback)

## Strategies for Coaching

### What to Do

| Action Step | When to Use It | Probing Questions | Scenarios to Practice | Cues for Real-Time Feedback |
|---|---|---|---|---|
| **Economy of language** | Teacher's directions are unclear or use too many words. | • "What happened yesterday when you asked your students to ___? What caused the confusion?"<br><br>• "What is the value in using fewer words to describe what students should do?"<br><br>• [Play video of teacher's instructions] "What is another way you could have restated these directions to make them clearer for students?" [or] "Write down all the directions you gave. Where did you use more words than necessary?"<br><br>• [If teacher struggles, model for him or her] "Let me deliver those same instructions. [Model] What do you notice about the difference between my delivery and your own?" | • Script clear, concise instructions together. Plan them out word by word: don't take shortcuts!<br><br>• Provide feedback on clarity *before* practice: most errors can be fixed before your practice.<br><br>• Rehearse key directions: if necessary, model what the teacher could say to be most effective.<br><br>• Focus on the pregnant pause between each component of the instruction: students often become confused when given too many directions at once. | Nonverbal: hold up a red card for too many words.<br><br>Nonverbal: hold up a sign that says "What to Do."<br><br>Whisper prompt: "When you bring everyone back from this assignment, just say: 'Pencils down. Eyes on me!' No extra words."<br><br>Model: model giving concise directions using 3–5 words.<br><br>Model: ask a student to repeat the teacher's instructions. |

# Routines and Procedures 201

---

**Teacher Professional Development Goal**

**Routines and Procedures 201:** Revise routines to match student needs that emerge when the teacher rolls out the routine in the classroom.

---

Routines and Procedures 201 takes up where we left off in Phase 1. Although you and the teacher planned the opening routines as carefully as possible, you couldn't fully anticipate where the teacher or students would struggle in the implementation. The following are three challenges that new teachers most often encounter during the first week of school:

- Students are following the routine correctly, but it is inefficient or ineffective.

- The routine is effective, but students aren't following it.

- The teacher asks students to redo routines they have already performed sufficiently well.

Here are the three action steps that will most effectively help new teachers meet those challenges.

# ROUTINES AND PROCEDURES 201: REVISE ROUTINES

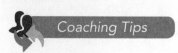
Coaching Tips

## Teacher Context

### Challenge
Students are following the routine correctly, but it is inefficient or ineffective.

### Action Step
Revise any routine that needs more attention to detail or is inefficient, with particular emphasis on what students and teachers are doing at each moment.

### Action Step Overview
When a routine fundamentally isn't working, the teacher will need to rewrite it altogether, identifying where it breaks down and generally adding much more detail. Opening routines and class transitions are particularly important for the teacher to revise during Phase 2, as they're the routines that will most set the tone of the classroom and increase time for learning.

## KEY LEADERSHIP MOVES

| | |
|---|---|
| **Probing Questions** | • "What has been the challenge in implementing this routine?"<br><br>• "Where does the breakdown begin: When is the first moment of students not following the routine?"<br><br>• [Watch video of a better routine] "What can you draw from this routine to make your own more effective?" |
| **Planning and Practice** | • Focus practice at the point where the routine has been going wrong. You'll notice when you observe and practice with the teacher that some parts of the routine have become natural and flow easily—don't keep practicing those! Instead, focus on the isolated part that's hard for the teacher. Conduct the role play with you playing the student and the teacher rolling out this routine. Model any student errors you anticipate.<br><br>• Pay attention to teacher positioning: stand in the ideal position to see as many students as clearly as possible.<br><br>• Make sure the teacher is incorporating all the actions he or she has already worked on with you: Strong Voice (posture, register), What to Do.<br><br>• Rehearse the first words to say to nonresponsive students. |
| **Real-Time Feedback** | • Model: "This is my favorite routine. Can I show our students the new way to do it?" |

# ROUTINES AND PROCEDURES 201: DO IT AGAIN[2]

## Teacher Context

**Challenge**

The routine is effective, but students aren't following it.

**Action Step**

Do It Again: have students do the routine again if not done correctly the first time.

**Action Step Overview**

Every time we allow a classroom routine to be performed incorrectly, we solidify imperfection. For this reason, the best response if students don't do the routine correctly is almost always to have them do it again until they get it exactly right. The following key sequence of instructions is what usually works most effectively for getting students to do it again and do it better.

1. Stop the routine at the moment of error.
2. Name the error (for example, "Students, we're not moving quickly enough to our seats.").
3. Go back to the beginning of the routine.
4. Give the students a challenge (for example, "I know you can do better. Let's try it again and see if we can beat our best time!").
5. Give the signal to restart the routine.

In *Teach Like a Champion*, Doug Lemov describes in more detail what makes Do It Again such an effective teaching technique; in brief, besides getting students to practice excellence, it does so in an immediate way that ends on the positive note of success.

## KEY LEADERSHIP MOVES

| | |
|---|---|
| **Probing Questions** | • "What are the keys to running a Do It Again effectively?"<br><br>• "Why is it important to have students repeat this routine when they haven't done it correctly?"<br><br>• [Watch video] "Where are the moments when students are incorrectly executing the routine? What would you like to see them do differently?" |
| **Planning and Practice** | • Plan each step of the Do It Again sequence:<br>　– Use Strong Voice (Square Up, Stand Still; use formal register).<br>　– Deliver the What to Do (name the error, name the correct action).<br>　– Challenge the students to do better.<br>　– Give the signal to restart the routine.<br><br>• Role-play the revised routine: make the same student errors from class and have the teacher practice implementing the Do It Again sequence until the routine looks flawless. |
| **Real-Time Feedback** | • Nonverbal: make a circle with your finger to cue the teacher to have students redo that part of the routine.<br><br>• Verbal: "Ms. Smith, I know the students can do that better. What would you like to see us do differently this time?"<br><br>• Model: "Can I show our students what we'd like them to do?" Whisper to the teacher what you are modeling. |

 Watch clip 14: Do It Again
(Key Leadership Moves: Real-Time Feedback, Follow-Up)

# ROUTINES AND PROCEDURES 201: CUT IT SHORT

 **Coaching Tips**

## Teacher Context

### Challenge
The teacher asks students to redo routines they have already performed sufficiently well.

### Action Step
Cut It Short: know when to stop the Do It Again.

### Action Step Overview
There's an art not only in knowing when to have students do it again, but also in knowing when to move on. By stopping students at the appropriate moment, teachers optimize the time spent on perfecting the routine.

---

### KEY LEADERSHIP MOVES

| | |
|---|---|
| **Probing Questions** | • "Remember when you had students do it again for the third time? Did they perform it even better after that?"<br><br>• "What is the purpose of having your students do it again? When is it no longer valuable to do it again?" |
| **Planning and Practice** | • Practice Cut It Short the same way as you would practice Do It Again, but with extra emphasis on the conclusion of the Do It Again. As you repeat the practice, try varying how quickly you perform the routine correctly so that the teacher learns to truly evaluate when it's time to stop the Do It Again. |
| **Real-Time Feedback** | • Nonverbal: signal to the teacher that it's time to stop repeating the Do It Again.<br><br>• Model: cut short the Do It Again. |

---

## Routines and Procedures 201

| Action Step | When to Use It | Probing Questions | Scenarios to Practice | Cues for Real-Time Feedback |
|---|---|---|---|---|
| **Revise routines** | Students are following the routine, but it is inefficient or ineffective. | • "What has been the challenge in implementing this routine?"<br><br>• "Where does the breakdown in this routine begin: When is the first moment that students don't follow the routine?"<br><br>• [Watch video of a better routine] "What can you draw from this routine to make your own more effective?" | • Focus practice at the point where the routine has been going wrong. Model any student errors you anticipate.<br><br>• Pay attention to teacher positioning (stand in ideal location), and incorporate Strong Voice (posture, register) and What to Do.<br><br>• Rehearse the first words to say to nonresponsive students. | Model: "This is my favorite routine. Can I show our students the new way to do it?" |
| **Do It Again** | The routine is effective, but students aren't following it. | • "What are the keys to running a Do It Again effectively?"<br><br>• "Why is it important to have students repeat this routine when they haven't done it correctly?" | • Plan each step of the Do It Again sequence:<br>  – Use Strong Voice (Square Up, Stand Still; formal register).<br>  – Deliver the What to Do (name the error, name the correct action). | Nonverbal: make a circle with your finger to cue the teacher to redo the routine.<br><br>Verbal: "Ms. Smith, I know the students can do that better. What would you like to see us do differently this time?"<br><br>Model: "Can I show our students what we'd like them to do?" Whisper to the teacher what you are modeling. |

PHASE 2

MANAGEMENT

| Action Step | When to Use It | Probing Questions | Scenarios to Practice | Cues for Real-Time Feedback |
|---|---|---|---|---|
| | | • [Watch video] "Where are the moments when students are incorrectly executing the routine? What would you like to see them do differently?"<br><br>• "What is challenging about noticing or stating what you want to see students change when they do it again?" | – Challenge students to do better.<br>– Give the signal to restart the routine.<br>• Role-play the revised routine: make the same student errors from class and have the teacher practice implementing Do It Again until the routine looks flawless. | |
| Cut It short | Teacher asks students to redo routines they have already performed sufficiently well. | • "Remember when you had students do it again for the third time? Did they perform it even better after that?"<br><br>• "What is the purpose of having your students do it again? When is it no longer valuable to do it again?" | • Practice Cut It Short the same way as you would practice Do It Again, but with extra emphasis on the conclusion of the Do It Again. As you repeat the practice, try varying how quickly you perform the routine correctly so that the teacher learns to truly evaluate when it's time to stop the Do It Again. | Nonverbal: signal to the teacher that it's time to stop repeating the Do It Again.<br><br>Model: cut short the Do It Again. |

## Teacher Radar

**Teacher Professional Development Goal**

**Teacher Radar:** Spot off-task behavior in its earliest stages so that you can treat it before it spreads.

My family and I once attended a party where a number of other families with young children were gathered. We adults were talking among ourselves while the kids played in the living room. All of a sudden, one mother bolted toward the couch. We had only a moment to wonder what she was doing before the couch began to topple over—with a two-year-old climbing on top of it. The mother caught the child just in time.

Every other adult in the room was astounded. It looked to us as if this woman had used X-ray vision or successfully predicted the future. But as we gaped at the scene of the narrowly averted disaster, we understood what had really happened: the mother had seen that the couch had no backing, and she predicted that as soon as the toddler clambered up on the headboard, it would tip. She was able to save him an injury, not because she saw him falling, but because she saw that he was on unstable ground. Her mother's instinct was the instinct of prevention: of stopping the catastrophe before it happened by spotting the right warning signs the moment they appeared.

A teacher's instinct—or, as we'll call it, Teacher Radar—is just the same. It often seems magical, even superhuman, to those who have never taught before; but in truth, great Teacher Radar comes from knowing how to spot the tipping couches of the classroom. Are students looking down at their independent writing assignments, or are their eyes casting about the room? Are their hands on their pencils, or are they busy passing something to a neighbor? Just as the backless couch became a threat to the children playing in the living room, so these small actions can quickly become a threat to children trying to learn: staring out the window becomes not writing; passing pencils becomes passing notes, which in turn becomes two students hitting each other. Teacher Radar prevents those small behaviors from causing the well-managed classroom from figuratively toppling to the floor.

In the pages that follow, we'll unpack the actions that make Teacher Radar look like magic, and show how to make them doable for a new teacher. Here are a few root causes of classroom management challenges that a new teacher can learn how to catch—thus preventing the chaos from actually occurring—with the action steps we'll summarize in this section:

- The teacher is not noticing the earliest actions of off-task behavior.

- The teacher is not scanning and watching the students; students veer off task as a result.

- The teacher is stationary, and his or her lack of movement makes it easier for students to go off task.

- When one student is speaking, the teacher stands very close to him or her while listening, and ignores other students, allowing them to become disengaged.

# TEACHER RADAR: SCAN HOT SPOTS

 Coaching Tips

## Teacher Context

### Challenge

The teacher is not noticing the earliest actions of student noncompliance and may wait until challenges have escalated before he or she does anything.

### Action Step

Choose three or four hot spots (places where you have students who often get off task) to scan constantly.

### Action Step Overview

Every classroom management challenge has a beginning: a moment when one or two students go off track before the rest follow. Just like the tipping couch we described earlier, though, this moment is very often predictable—which means it's preventable.

The first key to catching those first moments of disorder when they happen is to identify the places in the room where they usually spark. Often, one or more of these "hot spots" will be the seats of students whose "jumpy" actions often escalate into major disruptions. If there's one student who nearly always ends up whispering to peers when he or she shouldn't, for example, you need to notice when that student starts looking around the room.

Knowing where those hot spots are helps you scan more effectively. Developing this habit is the next step.

Teacher Radar is most effectively coached through real-time feedback, because it depends so much on the teacher's immediate response to student actions. Outside-of-class practice, in the case of these action steps, serves mostly to prepare the teacher as much as possible for the real-time feedback. Therefore, it's especially powerful when practicing this action step with a teacher to use video, so that the teacher can watch what's happening and have a strong sense of how scanning hot spots works before returning to class. From there, having someone in the room to point out right away any roadblocks the teacher is hitting is the best way to make sure the teacher will develop excellent Teacher Radar habits quickly.

**KEY LEADERSHIP MOVES**

| | |
|---|---|
| **Probing Questions** | • [Watch video of class] "At what moment do the first students begin to go off track?" |
| | • "Which of your students are most often off task?" |
| | • "If you know that these students are most likely to veer off track, where are your 'hot spots' that you want to scan continuously throughout the lesson?" |
| **Planning and Practice** | • Have the teacher identify hot spots and the moments in the lesson plan to scan those hot spots. |
| | • Position yourself in a hot spot and have the teacher begin teaching a portion of a lesson; role-play student behavior you want the teacher to be able to catch and correct by scanning hot spots. Repeat until the teacher is consistently scanning the hot spots and identifying off-task behavior. |
| **Real-Time Feedback** | • Nonverbal: hold up a sign that says "Scan." (See clip 7.) |
| | • Nonverbal: hold your hand out over a hot spot at the moment you want the teacher to notice and correct off-task behavior. (See clip 1.) |

Rewatch clip 7: Teacher Radar—Pause and Scan
(Key Leadership Move: Real-Time Feedback)

Rewatch clip 1: Teacher Radar—Scan
(Key Leadership Move: Plan/Practice)

These clips show us two examples of highly effective real-time feedback to help a teacher with his or her scanning. In clip 7, Ashley helps her teacher build the *habit* of scanning (making the decision to look around the room); in clip 1, Nikki focuses Jackson on noticing the areas of nonresponsiveness. Scanning is something very difficult to master outside of the actual teaching experience, so real-time feedback is particularly valuable here.

# TEACHER RADAR: BE SEEN LOOKING[3]

 Coaching Tips

## Teacher Context

### Challenge

The teacher does not appear to be scanning and watching the students; students veer off task as a result.

### Action Step

Be Seen Looking: crane your neck to appear to be seeing all corners of the room.

### Action Step Overview

As Doug Lemov mentions in *Teach Like a Champion*, students can sense right away if they need to pay attention in a certain class or not. Some teachers have an aura about them that immediately lets students know that listening is nonnegotiable. That aura is coachable, and in the case of Be Seen Looking, it requires actions as simple as craning your neck to visibly check all corners of the room.

These actions come naturally to an effective teacher. They explicitly communicate to every student: "I see you."

*Tip from a Teacher—Pause Enough to Look at What You're Scanning*
*Teacher Radar was absolutely key for me as a new teacher. I knew misbehavior was occurring in the room, but I just couldn't catch it quickly enough to do something about it. I thought to scan, I could just to crane my head and look quickly across the room, but I wasn't seeing anything. So my coach got me to really pause and look as I was scanning. There's sort of a blur or a daze that the new teacher has—a hazy vision in the classroom where you don't really see what's happening in front of you. But just by slowing down, I could tell even during practice that I was picking up on new things, like a part of my coach's office I hadn't noticed before. It made me realize that I really have to look at particular hot spots in the classroom if I want to scan effectively. I followed these steps from then on: crane your neck, pause at the hot spot, then look at the next hot spot.*
*—Adam Feiler, instructional coach, Newark, NJ*

## KEY LEADERSHIP MOVES

**Probing Questions**

- [Watch video of lesson and pick key moments] "Where are you looking right now? Where should you be looking?"
- [Model Be Seen Looking] "What did you notice about what I did when giving directions? What is the value of that body language?"

**Planning and Practice**

- Have the teacher practice scanning every row (for students' hands and eyes) of the classroom while teaching.
- Sit in a part of the classroom that's somewhat removed from the teacher as he or she launches into a lesson. Have the teacher practice being seen looking after every direction, and model some off-task behavior for the teacher to identify when scanning.

**Real-Time Feedback**

- Nonverbal: crane your neck to indicate that the teacher should do the same.
- Model: take over the routine and crane your neck/ scan with your finger while scanning students.

# TEACHER RADAR:
# CIRCULATE WITH PURPOSE (BREAK THE PLANE)

 *Coaching Tips*

## Teacher Context

### Challenge

The teacher is stationary, and his or her lack of movement makes it easier for students to go off task.

### Action Step

Circulate the room with purpose (break the plane):

- Move among the desks and around the perimeter.
- Stand at the corners: identify three spots on the perimeter of the room to which you can circulate to stand and monitor student work.

### Action Step Overview

Circulating the perimeter allows a teacher to listen to the one student who is speaking while simultaneously reminding the rest of the students that they need to be listening, too.

| | |
|---|---|
| **Probing Questions** | • "Where did the off-task behavior start? Where were you standing at that time?" "What is the challenge of not moving around during the lesson?"<br>• [Watch the video] "How much time do you spend away from the front of the room?" |
| **Planning and Practice** | • Have the teacher identify the hot spots in the room (that is, where off-task behaviors often occur).<br>• Create a pathway for walking around the classroom based on the hot spots, stopping at the corners to monitor the class.<br>• Practice moving along this pathway while teaching, stopping at hot spots to scan and giving off-task students a nonverbal redirect. |
| **Real-Time Feedback** | • Nonverbal: point to a corner of the room where the teacher should stand. |

 Watch clip 15: Teacher Radar—Break the Plane
(Key Leadership Move: Plan/Practice)

PHASE 2  MANAGEMENT

# TEACHER RADAR:
# MOVE AWAY FROM THE STUDENT WHO IS SPEAKING

 *Coaching Tips*

## Teacher Context

### Challenge
When one student is speaking, the teacher stands very close to him or her while listening, and ignores other students, allowing them to become disengaged.

### Action Step
Move away from the student who is speaking to monitor the whole room.

### Action Step Overview
Moving away from the student who is speaking allows a teacher to listen to the one student who is speaking while simultaneously reminding the rest of the students that they need to be listening, too.

### KEY LEADERSHIP MOVES

| | |
|---|---|
| **Probing Questions** | • "When did the off-task behavior start? Where were you in the classroom in relation to where the problem occurred?"<br>• "What is the value of moving away from the student who is speaking?" |
| **Planning and Practice** | • When it comes time for the teacher to practice moving away from a student who is speaking, have the teacher pretend to call on an imaginary student (or, if possible, recruit another adult to play the student). Then, while the imaginary student is responding, you can be playing the part of another student in another part of the room who is off task. The teacher can then practice moving around to remind the other student that he or she is still obligated to pay attention, and, if necessary, to give a silent redirect. |
| **Real-Time Feedback** | • Nonverbal: cue the teacher to move away from the student who is speaking. |

## Strategies for Coaching

### Teacher Radar

| Action Step | When to Use It | Probing Questions | Scenarios to Practice | Cues for Real-Time Feedback |
|---|---|---|---|---|
| **Scan hot spots** | Teacher is not noticing the earliest actions of off-task behavior. | • [Watch video of class] "At what moment do the first students begin to go off track?"<br>• "Which students are most often off task?"<br>• "If you know that these students are most likely to veer off track, where are your 'hot spots' that you want to scan continuously throughout the lesson?" | • Have the teacher identify hot spots and the moments in the lesson plan to scan those hot spots.<br>• Practice: role-play student behavior you want the teacher to be able to catch and correct by scanning. Repeat until the teacher is consistently scanning and identifying off-task behavior. | Nonverbal: hold up a sign that says "Scan."<br>Nonverbal: hold your hand out over a hot spot at the moment you want the teacher to notice and correct off-task behavior. |
| **Be Seen Looking** | Teacher is not scanning and watching the students; students veer off task as a result. | • [Watch video of lesson and pick key moments] "Where are you looking right now? Where should you be looking?"<br>• [Model Be Seen Looking] "What did you notice about what I did when giving directions? What is the value of that body language?" | • Practice scanning every row (for students' hands and eyes) of the classroom while teaching.<br>• Sit in the classroom far from the teacher. Model off-task behavior for the teacher to identify when scanning. | Nonverbal: crane your neck to indicate that the teacher should do the same.<br>Model: take over the routine and crane your neck/scan with your finger while scanning students. |

| Action Step | When to Use It | Probing Questions | Scenarios to Practice | Cues for Real-Time Feedback |
|---|---|---|---|---|
| Circulate with purpose (break the plane) | Teacher is stationary: lack of movement makes students go off task. | • "Where did the off-task behavior start? Where were you standing at that time? What is the challenge of not moving around during the lesson?"<br><br>• [Watch the video] "How much time do you spend away from the front of the room?" | • Identify the hot spots in the room (i.e., where off-task behaviors often occur).<br><br>• Create a pathway based on the hot spots.<br><br>• Practice moving along this pathway while teaching, stopping at hot spots to scan and giving students a nonverbal redirect. | Nonverbal: point to a corner of the room where the teacher should stand. |
| Move away from the student who is speaking | When one student is speaking, other students become disen-gaged. | • "When did the off-task behavior start? Where were you in the classroom in relation to where the problem occurred?"<br><br>• "What is the value of moving away from the student who is speaking?" | • Have the teacher pretend to call on an imaginary student. Then, while the imaginary student is responding, you can be playing the part of another student in another part of the room who is off task. The teacher can then practice moving around to remind the other student that he/she is still obligated to pay attention, and, if necessary, to give a silent redirect. | Nonverbal: cue the teacher to move away from the student who is speaking. |

## Whole-Class Reset

### Teacher Professional Development Goal

**Whole-Class Reset:** Stop and restart the class anytime they have begun to veer off task.

Do It Again (see earlier in this phase: Routines and Procedures 201) described how a new teacher can have students redo a routine when it's not done well. Sometimes, however, student nonresponsiveness doesn't begin with a broken routine but rather is a small building wave of student misbehavior. One student whispering turns into two, then a slow murmur arises, then loud talking throughout the room. In another case, the routine has been slightly weakening over the course of a few days. In each case, you don't need to revise the routine but reset the class, just as you might refresh a website that has frozen during a Google search. A whole-class reset reestablishes teacher expectations for student behavior in that moment.

## Findings from the Field: Prioritize the Top Three Things to Change

Often the best way to help our teachers plan for a whole-class reset is to get them to prioritize: If you had to really change three things in your classroom right now, what would they be? One teacher I remember was really struggling with a carpet transition. She had a number for each student to sit on, but the kids were still not moving efficiently to their carpet spots. It turned out the problem was that they weren't understanding which way to go when she told them all to move to the right—as five-year-olds they were still learning their right from their left, and moving in all different directions! Once we identified that this is where the confusion began, we had her clarify and simplify this first step in the transition: she told students to step toward the carpet, and got everyone moving in the same direction. Getting teachers to work through questions like "Why isn't this working? What part of it is causing the breakdown?" enables them to determine where modifications are needed, and then we can say, "OK, we're really going to focus on these first. We want you to spend this week on this one, and not move on until you get it right. Next week, we'll talk about other things that we still need to adjust."

—Christine Denison-Lipschitz, principal, Dallas, Texas

The following are the most common challenges of Phase 2 that can be solved with a whole-class reset:

- A class has slid into low engagement over a few days *or* within the same class period without the teacher realizing it:
  - Small talk is occurring during specific moments in the lesson.
  - Students are not on task during independent practice.
  - Turn and Talks are off task.

Although the two action steps that can both resolve these challenges are very similar, we address each of them separately.

# WHOLE-CLASS RESET: PLANNED WHOLE-CLASS RESET

 Coaching Tips

## Teacher Context

### Challenge

A class has slid into low engagement *over a few days* without the teacher realizing it:

- Small talk is occurring during specific moments in the lesson.
- Students are not on task during independent practice.
- Turn and Talks are off task.

### Action Step

Implement a whole-class reset to reestablish student behavioral expectations when a class has slowly weakened over previous classes.

### Action Step Overview

If students aren't following a routine, the teacher must reset, or reteach, that routine. The most reliably effective way the teacher can do this is to script a plan for the reset ahead of time.

*Quick Tip from a Coach—If You Don't Square Up, They're Not Going to Look at You*

*One of my teachers was struggling with whole-class resets, so we had to practice them a lot. We practiced in her classroom, right in front of the rug where she'd be when she was teaching. I'd go first, she'd go second, then she'd write down any revisions. I saw the impact of her writing down those steps on her plan. The hardest part for her was to stop teaching, square up, and give the What to Do with economy of language. We kept reducing the amount of language she used and squaring up and standing still. If you don't square up, they're not going to look up at you.*

—*Del Jones, principal, Philadelphia, Pennsylvania*

## KEY LEADERSHIP MOVES

| | |
|---|---|
| **Probing Questions** | • "How did you establish that routine so effectively the first time?"<br><br>• "What are the challenges in implementing the routine right now? Where does this routine break down?"<br><br>• "What are the root causes of the deterioration of this routine?"<br><br>• [Show a model: video or yourself modeling] "What did you notice: What were the key actions the teacher took to reengage the classroom?" |
| **Planning and Practice** | • Coach the teacher through the process of scripting the reset word by word. Keep the script to language as minimal as possible. Sample scripts could include best practices, such as the following:<br><br>  1. Pause.<br>  2. "Eyes on me."<br>  3. Narrate the problem.<br>  4. Give direction.<br>  5. Scan.<br>  6. Wait for 100 percent. If not there, give a second direction to off-task students.<br>  7. Continue the lesson.<br><br>• When practicing, really focus on incorporating all previous action steps, particularly:<br><br>  – Strong Voice (posture and register)<br>  – What to Do (using as few words as possible)<br>  – Teacher Radar (scan to make sure students are complying)<br><br>• Add complexity as you go:<br><br>  – Round 1: all students "comply" right away.<br>  – Round 2: a few students still don't comply, and the teacher has to get them on target. |
| **Real-Time Feedback** | • N/A (reset is planned in advance) |

# WHOLE-CLASS RESET: IN-THE-MOMENT RESET

 *Coaching Tips*

## Teacher Context

### Challenge

A class has slid into low engagement *within the same class period* without the teacher realizing it:

- Small talk is occurring during specific moments in the lesson.
- Students are not on task during independent practice.
- Turn and Talks are off task.

### Action Step

Implement an in-the-moment reset when a class veers off task during the class period.

- Example: Stop teaching. Square up. Give a clear What to Do: "Pencils down. Eyes on me. Hands folded in 3-2-1. Thank you: that's what Harvard looks like." Pick up tone and energy again.

### Action Step Overview

When you script a planned reset as described in the previous action step, you're planning to use that reset in your next class no matter what—you already know the problem that will occur. The in-the-moment reset is somewhat different: it can still be scripted in advance, but you'll need to use it only when students are having an "off" day, getting something wrong that they typically get right. What makes this type of reset such an effective way to redirect a class is that it works across a broad range of in-the-moment challenges. If the teacher has prepared a stock response like the one in the given example, rehearsing it diligently until both the words and the tone come automatically, most management challenges will result in only temporary, not permanent, disruption. In time, the students' improved behavior will come as quickly and naturally as the teacher's reset does.

Most of the same leadership moves in the planned reset work for the in-the-moment reset as well. The key difference will be in helping the teacher identify the moments when students need it.

**Probing Questions**

- "When are typical moments when your students go off track?" [If the teacher cannot answer, show him or her video footage of a part of the class when students frequently go off track, and use the video to guide the teacher in identifying the moment when a reset is needed.]

- "What are the key indicators in the class that you can look for that will tell you it is time to reset the class?"

- "When have you been most successful in resetting the classroom? How could you apply those same skills to this other context?"

**Planning and Practice**

- Ideally, watch video of the teacher's classroom, and have the teacher identify when the engagement is starting to drop and the signs that indicate the lower engagement.

- Coach the teacher through the process of scripting a generic in-the-moment reset that could be used in every situation:
  - Pause.
  - "Eyes on me."
  - Narrate the problem.
  - Give direction.
  - Scan.
  - Wait for 100 percent. If not there, give a second direction to students not on task.
  - Continue the lesson.

- Just as with planned resets, when practicing, really focus on incorporating all previous action steps, particularly
  - Strong Voice (posture and register)
  - What to Do (using as few words as possible)
  - Teacher Radar (scan to make sure students are complying)

- Just as with planned resets, add complexity as you go:
  - First role play: all students "comply" right away.
  - Second role play: a few students still don't comply, and the teacher has to get them on target.

**Real-Time Feedback**

- Nonverbal: create a cue for "reset" or hold up a sign.

- Model: "Students, we need to reset ourselves right now." Model a reset for the teacher.

## Strategies for Coaching

### Whole-Class Reset

| Action Step | When to Use It | Probing Questions | Scenarios to Practice | Cues for Real-Time Feedback |
|---|---|---|---|---|
| Planned whole-class reset | A class has slid into low engagement *over a few days* without the teacher realizing it. | • "How did you establish that routine so effectively the first time?"<br><br>• "What are the challenges in implementing the routine right now? Where does this routine break down?"<br><br>• "What are the root causes of the deterioration of this routine?"<br><br>• [Show a model: video or yourself modeling] "What did you notice: What were the key actions the teacher took to reengage the classroom?" | • Script the reset word by word: use as minimal language as possible; e.g.: Pause. "Eyes on me." Narrate the problem & give a direction. Scan. Wait for 100%. If not there, give a second direction to off-task students. Continue the lesson.<br><br>• Practice: incorporate all previous action steps, particularly Strong Voice (posture and register), What to Do, and Teacher Radar (scan).<br><br>• Rd 1: all students "comply" right away.<br><br>• Rd 2: a few students still don't comply, and teacher has to get them on target. | N/A (reset planned in advance) |

| Action Step | When to Use It | Probing Questions | Scenarios to Practice | Cues for Real-Time Feedback |
|---|---|---|---|---|
| In-the-moment whole-class reset | A class has slid into low engagement *within the same class period* without the teacher realizing it. | • "When are typical moments when your students go off track?" [If teacher cannot answer, show video footage of a part of the class when students frequently go off track, and use the video to guide the teacher in identifying the moment when a reset is needed.]<br><br>• "What are the key indicators in the class that you can look for that will tell you it is time to reset the class?"<br><br>• "When have you been most successful in resetting the classroom? How could you apply those same skills to this other context?" | • From video of the teacher's classroom, have the teacher identify the moment when engagement drops.<br><br>• Script a generic in-the-moment reset that could be used in every situation: Pause. "Eyes on me." Narrate the problem & give a direction. Scan. Wait for 100%. If not there, give a second direction to off-task students. Continue the lesson.<br><br>• Incorporate previous action steps.<br><br>• Rd 1: all students "comply" right away.<br><br>• Rd 2: a few students still don't comply, and teacher has to get them on target. | Nonverbal: create/use a cue for "reset" or hold up a sign.<br><br>Model: "Students, we need to reset ourselves right now." Model a reset for the teacher. |

---

## Stop and Jot

What are the three top coaching ideas you plan to use to train your teachers in these Phase 2 Management skills? Jot them down here.

_____

_____

_____

# PHASE 2 RIGOR—
# INDEPENDENT PRACTICE

## Quick Reference Guide

| If your teacher is struggling to . . . | Jump to . . . |
|---|---|
| **Write the Exemplar** ||
| Recognize a rigorous student response | Script the ideal written student response |
| Develop sufficiently rigorous independent practice assignments | Align independent practice to the assessment |
| **Independent Practice** ||
| Give students the opportunity to write before class discussion | Write first, talk second |
| Give students the opportunity to write before class starts | Do Now |
| Include at least ten minutes of independent practice in the lesson | Exit Ticket |
| **Monitor Aggressively** ||
| Monitor more than a few (or any) students during independent practice | Create a monitoring pathway |
| See patterns in student answers | Monitor the quality of student work |
| Give students explicit feedback during independent practice | Pen in Hand: mark up student work |

## Phase 2 Action Step Sequence

| Management Trajectory | Rigor Trajectory |
|---|---|
| **Roll Out and Monitor Routines** <br> 3. **What to Do:** Give clear, precise directions <br> • Economy of language: give crisp instructions with as few words as possible (e.g., 3-word directions). Check for understanding on complex instructions. | **Independent Practice** <br> 3. **Write the Exemplar:** Set the bar for excellence <br> • Script out the ideal written responses you want students to produce during independent practice. |

| Management Trajectory | Rigor Trajectory |
|---|---|
| **4. Routines & Procedures 201:** Revise and perfect them<br><br>• Revise any routine that needs more attention to detail or is inefficient, with particular emphasis on what students and teachers are doing at each moment.<br><br>• Do It Again: have students do the routine again if not done correctly the first time.<br><br>• Cut It Short: know when to stop the Do It Again.<br><br>**5. Teacher Radar:** Know when students are off task<br><br>• Deliberately scan the room for off-task behavior:<br><br>  – Choose 3–4 "hot spots" (places where you have students who often get off task) to scan constantly<br><br>  – Be Seen Looking: crane your neck to appear to be seeing all corners of the room.<br><br>• Circulate the room with purpose (break the plane):<br><br>  – Move among the desks and around the perimeter.<br><br>  – Stand at the corners: identify 3 spots on the perimeter of the room to which you can circulate to stand and monitor student work.<br><br>• Move away from the student who is speaking to monitor the whole room. | • Align independent practice to the rigor of the upcoming interim assessment. <br><br>**4. Independent Practice:** Set up daily routines that build opportunities for students to practice independently<br><br>• Write first, talk second: give students writing tasks to complete prior to class discussion, so that every student answers independently before hearing his/her peers' contributions.<br><br>• Implement a daily entry prompt (Do Now) to either introduce the day's objective or review material from the previous day.<br><br>• Implement and review a longer independent practice and/or a daily Exit Ticket (brief final mini-assessment aligned to your objective) to see how many students mastered the concept.<br><br>**5. Monitor Aggressively:** Check students' independent work to determine whether they're learning what you're teaching <br><br>• Create & implement a monitoring pathway:<br><br>  – Create a seating chart to monitor students most effectively.<br><br>  – Monitor the fastest writers first, then the students who need more support.<br><br>• Monitor the quality of student work: |

| Management Trajectory | Rigor Trajectory |
|---|---|
| 6. **Whole-Class Reset**<br><br>• Implement a planned whole-class reset to reestablish student behavioral expectations when a class routine has slowly weakened over previous classes.<br><br>• Implement an "in-the-moment reset" when a class veers off task during the class period.<br><br>   – Example: Stop teaching. Square up. Give a clear What to Do: "Pencils down. Eyes on me. Hands folded in 3-2-1. Thank you: that's what Harvard looks like." Pick up tone & energy again. |    – Check answers against your exemplar.<br><br>   – Track correct and incorrect answers to class questions.<br><br>• Pen in Hand: mark up student work as you circulate.<br><br>   – Use a coding system to affirm correct answers.<br><br>   – Cue students to revise answers, using minimal verbal intervention. (Name the error, ask them to fix it, tell them you'll follow up.) |

## Introduction to Phase 2 Rigor Skills: Independent Practice

Most of us in the field of education have a shared experience when it comes to the transition from high school to college—even if we haven't lived it ourselves, some of our students likely have. Here's how it goes: you leave your high school with enough honors, awards, and glowing recommendations from your teachers to feel confident in your skills as an intellectual. Yet when you arrive in your first college lecture hall, you find yourself overwhelmed and underprepared. Despite the rigor of your high school education, college is a different ball game. The expectations under which your new classmates have been working, and those your new professors are setting, are far higher than what you're used to.

The core problem here is that it's not enough to say that we have "high expectations" for our students. We have to define what we mean by high expectations, and we have to set our definitions in terms of concrete academic accomplishments, not abstract ideals. If we have high expectations already, we take them for granted—but high expectations are always made, not born. Who makes them? Teachers. If we were lucky enough to have had teachers and coaches who modeled high expectations for us, we may already have a reasonably good idea of what student achievements will reach the bar. But here's the good news for whether we were that fortunate or not: we can develop high expectations for our students at any time in our careers.

> ## Core Idea
>
> High expectations aren't born—they're made.
> And as teachers, we're the ones who get to make them.

> ### Findings from the Field: Build Capacity with Exemplars, and You Change Expectations
>
> The ten campuses I lead had been historically failing and underperforming for multiple years. With that struggle comes a huge number of students who are behind. We had so many trainings about raising expectations and believing in our children, but those didn't lead to change. Instead, as I watched my principals begin to coach teachers on the creation of exemplars, I started to see a shift in the capacity of my leaders—and they started to see faster growth in the capacity of their teachers. It makes a far greater difference to rally your teaching around an exemplar than to simply state what we believe kids can do. The use of exemplars has come at just the right time to propel us into success for our students, our system, and our community.
> —Billy Snow, principal manager, Caddo Parish, Louisiana

In the classroom, the most critical time to define expectations is the time students spend working independently. Too often, teacher development programs focus first on delivery of instructions, modeling, and leading discussion; but even though all of these are important, none of them can get to the heart of what we expect students to be able to do the way student independent work can.

Phase 2 Rigor starts there: with monitoring student independent practice and with giving students feedback as quickly and often as possible. No matter how well planned a lesson is, it's when students put their own pens to paper that they are learning most deeply and being formed as scholars most fundamentally. Those are the moments when they need their teacher's guidance the most, and this is the first area on which to focus when developing a teacher. The action steps in this section show how.

Focusing on independent practice first has another equally powerful consequence: you ensure that the teacher is setting the right bar for rigor. High expectations in a teacher are made, not born—and they have to be built with solidity and clarity to last. When you focus on what students must be able to *do* independently, you are helping the teacher define "high expectations" concretely, rather than as an abstract value or feeling.

The following teacher actions are the foundation for effective independent practice and, as such, for setting high academic expectations:

- **Writing the exemplar response** that the teacher wants students to be able to deliver by the end of the lesson

- Building **independent practice** into every lesson

- **Monitoring aggressively** when students do independent work, so that the teacher knows exactly where students are

Let's take a detailed look at each of these—and why they come first.

## Write the Exemplar

> ### Teacher Professional Development Goal
>
> **Write the Exemplar:** Script the ideal response you want students to be able to provide at the end of your lesson, so that you can plan how to get it from them and recognize it when they have given it.

Mark Twain famously wrote, "The difference between the right word and almost the right word is the difference between lightning and a lightning bug."[4] Doug Lemov makes the same distinction, cautioning: "The likelihood is strong that students will stop striving when they hear the word 'right,' so there's a real risk to naming as right that which is not truly and completely right."[5] Although a new teacher needn't perfect the basics of responding to an almost-right (or outright wrong) answer until Phase 4, *identifying* the right answer is a fundamental building block in this critical skill set that must be put in place during Phase 2.

Last year, my colleagues and I—along with countless other educators across the nation—faced the daunting task of raising the rigor of our writing instruction to match the demands of the Common Core. Together, we looked closely at exactly what our most successful teachers were doing to raise the bar for rigor higher than ever before while still meeting students at their level. The single biggest game-changer we discovered? The act of writing an exemplar. It's a practice that revolutionized how we taught not only English classes but also history, science, and even math.

The most successful teachers, we found, didn't stop at just writing a lesson objective—however precise and measurable—or even at defining how they would assess whether students had met that objective (both skills that were addressed in Phase 1 Rigor). They took it one step further and scripted *exactly what student responses would look like* when the students had learned what they needed to know. When teachers create a strong exemplar at the beginning of their lesson planning process, they don't just have an end goal for their lesson: they have an end goal in high definition.

> ## The Power of Exemplars, Take One
>
> When you create a strong exemplar, you don't just have an end goal:
> you have an end goal in high definition.

They can then "backwards-plan" with unparalleled clarity, creating exactly the lesson that will get students to be able to produce that exemplar themselves.

What does writing an exemplar look like? After designing an effective question (see Phase 1), the teacher's next step is to answer the question as an adult—not as a hypothetical student, the result of which would be a watered-down version of what the teacher thinks the students at the relevant grade level can accomplish. Too often, we prematurely lower our expectations for what students can do. Writing an adult exemplar prevents the teacher from falling into that trap. After doing so, the teacher can unpack all the steps he or she took in order to write that essay, considering, for example: "What was I thinking at each phase? How did I know to cite this evidence or write this transition?" The answers to these questions will get the teacher into the mind-set of the students, and they will help clarify what to look for and where the students will likely not have developed the same writing habits.

To be clear, when you look for student success in meeting an exemplar, you're not looking for a response that mimics the teacher's verbatim. On the contrary, you're looking for answers that reflect the analytical skill represented in the exemplar—so much the better if students are able to analyze texts with rigorous and independent thinking to reach, articulate, and support a rich array of valid conclusions. So how's a teacher to tell the difference between a limited student response and a response that simply voices a different, yet equally valid interpretation than the one the teacher captured in the exemplar? By *sparring with the exemplar*—just as one would want students to intellectually spar with each other in an animated class discussion—in advance of the lesson. The teacher can accomplish this by reading the critics who have written about the text his or her students are reading and comparing notes with other educators who are teaching the same literature. Then he or she can enhance the exemplar in response to any new findings, or change it, or note what evidence students would have to cite to adequately support other conclusions than the one the teacher wrote. Then, when the teacher checks students' responses, he or she will have a sense of whether varying responses are coming from way out in left field or just giving the teacher another chance to spar with his or her own reading of the text.

> ### The Power of Exemplars, Take Two
>
> If you want to be exemplary, spar with the exemplar.

Let's look at a couple of examples of the process of writing an exemplar. In the first, we'll build off of an example we used in the Principles of Coaching section of the book: that of a high school English teacher, Ashley, who is working with her students on Shakespeare's Sonnet 65.

Since brass, nor stone, nor earth, nor boundless sea,
But sad mortality o'er-sways their power,
How with this rage shall beauty hold a plea,
Whose action is no stronger than a flower?
O, how shall summer's honey breath hold out       5
Against the wreckful siege of battering days,
When rocks impregnable are not so stout,
Nor gates of steel so strong, but Time decays?
O fearful meditation! Where, alack,
Shall Time's best jewel from Time's chest lie hid?       10
Or what strong hand can hold his swift foot back?

Or who his spoil of beauty can forbid?
O, none, unless this miracle have might,
That in black ink my love may still shine bright.

Ashley generated an exemplar response to a final writing task: How does Shakespeare's use of figurative language help convey the theme of his sonnet? After doing do, she compared her answer to that of the head of her English Department, Steve Chiger:

> Shakespeare's Sonnet 65 is, in many ways, a poem about the transcendent power of writing. Through his use of imagery and metaphor, Shakespeare is ultimately able to underscore his poem's theme: that his writing, despite the entropic processes of the natural world, is ultimately what will sustain beauty. Here, time plays the role of the aggressor, devastating all in its path. Shakespeare develops an extended metaphor in lines 5–8 to highlight this notion, worrying that "summer's honey breath" cannot hold out against Time's "wreckful siege" (5–6). The diction of this metaphor suggests that Time is a conquering army with the power to destroy "rocks impregnable" and "gates of steel." The writer's choice amplifies the power of Time to destroy even a powerfully fortified city. Interestingly, beauty is not described as a fortified citadel, but rather simply as "honey breath" (5). Clearly, it is not long for the world. Shakespeare engineers a similar contrast during his first quatrain, where he offers up the concrete diction of "brass," "stone," and "boundless sea," only to remind the reader that they will be shuddered by time (1). When he compares beauty to a flower in line 4, the contrasting imagery signals that its doom is a foregone conclusion. With all of this in mind, it is perhaps the imagery at the poem's final couplet that is most compelling. When the speaker hopes the "miracle" of his writing "may still shine bright," his implied comparison to a star relies on a symbol that now outranks the earthly imagery used in the first two quatrains of his poem (13–14). That is, his writing is more powerful than an army, more powerful than a stone, more powerful than the earth itself. Time may be able to destroy Earth, but the speaker's poetry is of the heavens. By coding this hierarchy into the very level of his language, Shakespeare emphasizes the speaker's faith in the power of his writing.

She realized that she picked some different evidence (which was totally reasonable), but also that Steve's depth of analysis of particular diction used by

Shakespeare went beyond her own. As she unpacked the differences, she was able to start to identify the key areas where her students might overlook Shakespeare's power and where she should look when monitoring how students were doing during their writing.

Although math is a very different subject, generating an exemplar response to a complex word problem is just as valuable. Let's take a look at third-grade math, when students are learning to multiply. One of the core problems they will solve in class is as follows:

> Tajee had 14 cups of juice. Each cup of juice had 3 tablespoons of sugar. How many tablespoons of sugar did Tajee drink in all? Show all your work, write a number sentence, and explain your strategy.

On the surface, this is a basic question: $14 \times 3 = 42$. But for third graders who don't yet multiply numbers of this size with fluency or automaticity, there are a myriad of ways in which they might try to solve the problem. For a class where most students choose to add manually (14 +14, then add 14 more), the teacher might hope to get them to use more efficient strategies. So when asking the class why the answer is 42, the teacher is looking for the following response that she scripted:

> I broke down 14 into 10 and 4, and then made 3 groups of each. Since I know that $10 \times 3 = 30$ and $4 \times 3$ equals 12, $14 \times 3$ must equal 42, because $30 + 12 = 42$. This matches the problem because each of the 14 cups of juice is an equal group of 3 tablespoons, and so if you split up the 10 equal groups and the 4 equal groups, you can more efficiently solve.

Is this the only way to answer the question? By no means. But if this is a strategy that will help many students in the room, drafting this exemplar allows the teacher to look out for it while teaching, and it gives her clarity as to what additional strategies she will try to emphasize with students who are struggling. In short, it gives her a road map to rigor.

Once you have an exemplar in hand, the implementation of independent practice can fly (see upcoming action steps). Moreover, in the upcoming Phase 3 Rigor section, we'll dig more deeply into the process of planning the reset of the lesson to match an exemplar.

### Findings from the Field: Writing the Exemplar Is the First Step to Achievement

One of the biggest moments in my coaching most recently was around writing the exemplar: scripting out the ideal written responses you want students to produce during independent practice. Without an exemplar, teachers cannot monitor the quality of student work, because they haven't defined what they are monitoring for. This was a huge breakthrough with not only my teachers but also my fellow leaders. Doing this has helped us get to the precision in execution that we had yet to achieve. We talk about having to "increase the rigor," but what does that mean? Writing the exemplar has helped teachers unpack the standard and define the rigor. It defines the concrete action steps teachers need to take in their teaching, and more important, the reteaching so that we are hitting the mark and putting the right stuff in front of kids. What has been my greatest "aha" with this action step is the through line to data analysis meetings. Simply by focusing on three things—write the exemplar, plan what to teach based on student data, and observe/give feedback on the reteach—we can move mountains with our students. We are almost there.

—Monica Dilts Nurrenbern, principal manager, Denver, Colorado

What follows are the classroom challenges that a teacher will be able to meet most immediately by mastering the art of writing an exemplar:

- The teacher doesn't know what a rigorous student response looks like.
- The teacher's independent practice activities are not as rigorous as the final assessment that students are working toward.

Let's take a closer look at the action steps that will enable teachers to meet these challenges, as well as start them down the road to writing great exemplars.

# WRITE THE EXEMPLAR: SCRIPT THE IDEAL RESPONSE

**Coaching Tips**

## Teacher Context

**Challenge**
> The teacher doesn't know what a rigorous student response looks like.

**Action Step**
> Script out the ideal written responses you want students to produce during independent practice.

**Action Step Overview**
> A new teacher's first step to working with an exemplar successfully is scripting the exemplar word for word. The most important thing a teacher accomplishes by doing this is to define what "high expectations" means for every lesson. But scripting the exemplar also serves a secondary purpose: it subtly develops the teacher's own expertise. Writing and sparring with an exemplar serve to exponentially deepen the teacher's understanding of the topic he or she is teaching, because doing so forces him or her to think through what it really means to understand this topic.
>
> In working on exemplar responses with your new teacher, your probing questions will naturally blend into your planning and practice, as everything is centered around producing or revising the actual exemplar in your meeting. Here are the types of probing questions that you can ask throughout and the keys for practice.

## KEY LEADERSHIP MOVES

**Probing Questions**

- "Let's pull out an independent practice task. What do you want students to write when you give them this task? [If not yet written] Take a few minutes to write your exemplar."
- "What answers would be only partially correct?"
- "How do you want students to show or organize their work in answering this question?"
- "What are the advantages of writing an exemplar response? How is it different from writing objectives?"

**Planning and Practice**

- Write or revise exemplars for written-response questions in upcoming lessons. Make sure the teacher scripts the exact answers he or she is expecting. That way, the teacher will be able to recognize them when he or she hears them (or doesn't) from his or her students.
- Ideally, spar with another exemplar: either another teacher's exemplar or the analysis of the experts in the field (for example, the analysis that Shakespearean experts have done of the same sonnet or play).
- Break down the exemplar and identify the key actions the student will need to do to produce a response of the same quality. This will be critical for the execution of the rest of the teacher's lesson.

Watch clip 16: Write the Exemplar
(Key Leadership Moves: Leading PD, Practice)

# WRITE THE EXEMPLAR:
# ALIGN INDEPENDENT PRACTICE TO ASSESSMENT

 *Coaching Tips*

## Teacher Context

### Challenge

The teacher's independent practice activities are not as rigorous as the final assessment that students are working toward.

### Action Step

Align independent practice to the rigor of the upcoming interim assessment.

### Action Step Overview

During Phase 1, new teachers worked to develop lesson objectives that were aligned with the curriculum plan and upcoming assessment. But just as standards are meaningless until you determine how to assess them, a lesson objective doesn't have teeth until you decide how you'll know whether students have met it. This means that it's vital for every lesson objective to come paired with an independent practice assignment that matches the rigor of the upcoming assessment.

This action step will multiply in value during Phase 3, when new teachers will dive more fully into the skill area of using data to drive their lessons. To start, aligning independent practice to the rigor of the upcoming assessment is an essential building block—and one that will drive learning in the meantime as well.

## KEY LEADERSHIP MOVES

**Probing Questions**

- "Let's revisit what students will have to do on the upcoming assessment. Compare that to the independent practice in this lesson: What is the gap between the rigor of your independent practice and that of the assessment?"

- "What can we do to make the independent practice more aligned to the rigor of the end goal?"

- [If the teacher struggles to see the gap, use a model] "Here are two different independent practice activities, one of which is more aligned to the upcoming assessment. Why is activity 1 more aligned and more rigorous than activity 2?" [Teacher responds] "What, then, are your key takeaways for designing quality independent practice tasks?"

**Planning and Practice**

- Have the teacher pull up a lesson plan and the upcoming assessment, and find where the material being taught in the lesson is going to be addressed in the assessment. Then have the teacher write or revise the independent practice assignment in the lesson to match the rigor of the upcoming assessment.

- Have the teacher write scaffolded questions that ramp up to the rigor of the final assessment question. The students won't always be able to jump right into the most challenging way of applying the material they're learning; the teacher will need to guide them there, step-by-step.

## Write the Exemplar

| Action Step | When to Deliver It | Probing Questions | Scenarios to Practice | Cues for Real-Time Feedback |
|---|---|---|---|---|
| **Script the ideal written student response** | Teacher doesn't know what a rigorous student response to a question looks like. | • "Let's pull out an independent practice task. What do you want students to write when you give them this task? [If not yet written] Take a few minutes to write your exemplar."<br>• "What answers would be only partially correct?"<br>• "How do you want students to show or organize their work in answering this question?"<br>• "What are the advantages of writing an exemplar response? How is it different from writing objectives?" | • Write or revise exemplars for written-response questions in upcoming lessons.<br>• Spar with another exemplar: either another teacher's exemplar or the analysis of experts in the field (for example, Shakespearean critics).<br>• Break down the exemplar: ID key things the student will need to do to produce a response of the same quality. | N/A |
| **Align independent practice to the assessment** | Independent practice activities are not as rigorous as the final assessment students are working toward. | • "Let's look at the upcoming assessment. What is the gap between the rigor of your independent practice and that of the assessment?"<br>• "What can we do to make the independent practice more aligned to the rigor of the end goal?" | • Pull up a lesson plan and upcoming assessment: write or revise independent practice to match the rigor of the upcoming assessment.<br>• Write scaffolded questions that ramp up to the rigor of the final assessment question. | N/A |

RIGOR

PHASE 2

| Action Step | When to Deliver It | Probing Questions | Scenarios to Practice | Cues for Real-Time Feedback |
|---|---|---|---|---|
| | | • [If teacher struggles to see the gap, use a model] "Here are two different independent practice activities. Why is activity 1 more aligned and more rigorous than activity 2?" [Teacher responds] "What are your key takeaways for designing quality independent practice tasks?" | | |

## Independent Practice

> ### Teacher Professional Development Goal
>
> **Independent Practice:** Set up routines that build opportunities for students to practice independently into every lesson.

There are four key learning moments that make up a lesson (in whatever order you put them): times when the teacher is presenting information; times when the whole class is interacting with that information; small-group work time; and independent practice. Many leaders instinctively focus first on helping teachers perfect either the first or second of these categories—probably because they're the ones that are most visible when they're not going smoothly. Yet managing large- and small-group discussion is one of the most complex arts of teaching. In contrast, making independent practice go well is easier; and as counterintuitive as it may seem, ensuring that independent practice is a valuable learning opportunity for every student is one of the top priorities for teachers in the first weeks of school.

Starting with independent practice is valuable not only because it is easier. Independent practice is also the single one of these four moments when 100 percent of the class can engage in the heaviest work of learning. Even during whole-class discussion, when a skillful teacher can get to 90 percent engagement, still only one student can speak at a time. Independent practice is the time when all students are at work on a task that requires learning. Therefore, making time for it every day is the fastest way to get learning to begin for the greatest number of students.

Here, we'll look at several opportunities teachers can build in throughout the lesson for students to engage in independent work. These are a few challenges that may arise in a classroom if a new teacher is not providing sufficient opportunities for students to practice independently:

- Class discussion begins without students having the opportunity to write first.

- Class begins with a teacher presentation before students have had a chance to write/work independently.

- Lessons include less than ten minutes' worth of independent practice.

Let's take a look at the action steps that can address each of these.

# INDEPENDENT PRACTICE:
# WRITE FIRST, TALK SECOND

 Coaching Tips

## Teacher Context

### Challenge

Class discussion begins without students having the opportunity to write first.

### Action Steps

Write first, talk second: give students writing tasks to complete prior to class discussion, so that every student answers independently before hearing his or her peers' contributions.

### Action Step Overview

Few single actions can increase the rigor of the classroom more than having students respond in writing to key prompts before discussing those same prompts as a class: write first, talk second. During a discussion, you can never know for sure that the students who aren't speaking are doing the same heavy intellectual work as the ones who are actively speaking; and if you have students answer related prompts in writing after that discussion, you can't know whether students would have been able to respond as they did without listening to their peers' insights beforehand. When students respond in writing first, in contrast, you have documented evidence of the thinking they were able to do independently, and you can target the remainder of the lesson to their needs accordingly.

| | |
|---|---|
| **Probing Questions** | • "What is the value of having students write before beginning class discussion?"<br><br>• "What is the most important information you want to students to grapple with and write about before beginning the conversation?" |
| **Planning and Practice** | • Have teachers plan lessons that consistently place writing time before discussion time. They can most easily accomplish this by annotating their lesson plans with short moments to write before talking. You can likely make this annotation quickly over a full week's worth of lessons or more.<br><br>• Role-play practice is minimal: simply practice the launch of the writing task and bringing students back to discussion afterwards. |

RIGOR

PHASE 2

# INDEPENDENT PRACTICE:
# DO NOW

 *Coaching Tips*

**Challenge**

Teacher begins class before students have had a chance to write/work independently.

**Action Step**

Implement a daily entry prompt (Do Now) to either introduce the day's objective or review material from the previous day.

**Action Step Overview**

Many educators are aware of the immense advantages of having students begin each day's lesson with a writing prompt, or Do Now, that engages either the content they're about to learn or that they learned the previous day. Some of the benefits of Do Nows are related to management: getting students into the right mind-set for learning, giving them clear directions from the door, and so on. But the more valuable rewards are rigor rewards, and they're reaped by students and teacher alike. The students begin their day with the challenge of independent practice, and the teacher gains an instant means of checking student comprehension, which can then be used to inform the rest of the lesson (although, in the case of new teachers, it will be later in the year that they develop the skill of using the data from the Do Now to alter lesson plans).

## KEY LEADERSHIP MOVES

**Probing Questions**

- "What is the purpose of a Do Now?"
- Timing: "How long are students spending on the Do Now?" [If too long] "How can we reduce the Do Now so that students finish earlier?"
- Relevance: "What should be the purpose of your Do Now in this lesson: to tell you how well students learned the content from yesterday? Or to prepare them to learn the content you're teaching today?"

**Planning and Practice**

- For practice, have the new teacher write Do Now questions for upcoming lessons—questions that will take three to five minutes to complete and aligned to the objective. Have the teacher rehearse a start-of-class greeting that will prompt the students to begin working on the Do Now.
- As you review the Do Now, vet them for the following key characteristics:
  - Short: don't let the teacher create a Do Now that will last twenty minutes.
  - Easy to monitor: design a task so that in quickly looking over a student's shoulder, the teacher can see what progress the student is making. This doesn't mean just using multiple-choice questions: it can also be accomplished by giving students enough space to write easily so that the teacher can read it.

RIGOR

PHASE 2

# INDEPENDENT PRACTICE: EXIT TICKET

## Teacher Context

### Challenge

Lessons include less than ten minutes' worth of independent practice.

### Action Step

Implement and review a longer independent practice and/or a daily Exit Ticket (brief final mini-assessment aligned to your objective) to see how many students mastered the concept.[6]

### Action Step Overview

Practicing independently is essential for students to improve. Increasing the amount of independent practice in the lesson becomes the first step, via activities during the midst of the lesson and/or an Exit Ticket (an assignment that students complete and hand back to you at the very end of class that checks their understanding of the lesson objective). Exit Tickets came up in Phase 1 when we looked at early lesson planning skills, because they're so crucial that they should have been a daily lesson practice from the beginning. By this point in Phase 2, however, it may be necessary to ensure that Exit Tickets have been implemented properly and that new teachers are reviewing, as well as assigning, Exit Tickets.

Often what undermines the amount of time spent in independent practice is a teacher's pacing; that will be addressed more directly in Phase 3 Management.

PHASE 2

RIGOR

| | |
|---|---|
| **Probing Questions** | • "What is the purpose of daily independent practice/ Exit Tickets?" |
| | • Timing: "How long are students spending on independent practice/Exit Tickets?" |
| | • Relevance: "What do you need your Exit Ticket to tell about what students learned today?" |
| **Planning and Practice** | • Planning and practice will depend on where the teacher is struggling. If he or she just doesn't have quality independent practice/Exit Tickets, then most of the time can be spent in the design. If the teacher is struggling to execute, then you can spend time on the instructions he or she gives to students during the time and implementing the teacher's management action steps. Here are some possible activities, depending on your focus: |
| | – If the challenge is the quality of the Exit Tickets: write Exit Tickets that confirm student mastery. Look at IP and Exit Tickets side-by-side to make sure they align in level of rigor. |
| | – If the challenge is the delivery of the Exit Ticket part of the lesson: spend time on the instructions the teacher gives to students during the times, integrating management action steps: Strong Voice, What to Do, Teacher Radar. |

RIGOR

PHASE 2

## Strategies for Coaching

### Independent Practice

| Action Step | When to Use It | Probing Questions | Scenarios to Practice | Cues for Real-Time Feedback |
|---|---|---|---|---|
| **Write first, talk second** | Class discussion begins without students having the opportunity to write first. | • "What is the value of having students write before beginning class discussion?" <br> • "What is the most important information you want to students to grapple with/write about before beginning the conversation?" | • Plan lessons that consistently place writing time before discussion time: annotate a week's worth of lesson plans with short moments to write before talking. <br> • Minimal role play: practice the launch of the writing task and bringing students back to discussion afterwards. | N/A |
| **Do Now** | Teacher begins class before students have had a chance to write/work independently. | • "What is the purpose of a Do Now?" <br> • Timing: "How long are students spending on the Do Now?" [If too long] "How can we reduce the Do Now so that students finish earlier?" <br> • Relevance: "What should be the purpose of your Do Now in this lesson: to tell you how well students learned the content from yesterday? Or to prepare them to learn the content you're teaching today?" | • Write Do Now questions for upcoming lessons: short (3–5 minutes to complete), easy to monitor (teacher can check student work), and aligned to objective. <br> • Rehearse a start-of-class greeting that will prompt the students to begin working on the Do Now. | N/A |

| Action Step | When to Use It | Probing Questions | Scenarios to Practice | Cues for Real-Time Feedback |
|---|---|---|---|---|
| Exit Ticket and/or longer independent practice | Lessons include less than 10 minutes' worth of independent practice. | • "What is the purpose of daily independent practice/Exit Tickets?"<br><br>• Timing: "How long are students spending on independent practice/Exit Tickets?"<br><br>• Relevance: "What do you need your Exit Ticket to tell about what students learned today?" | Tailor practice to teacher need:<br><br>• If challenge is quality of Exit Ticket: write Exit Tickets that confirm student mastery. Look at IP and Exit Tickets side by side to make sure they align in their level of rigor/complexity.<br><br>• If challenge is delivery: spend time on the instructions the teacher gives to students, integrating management action steps: Strong Voice, What to Do, and Teacher Radar. | N/A |

## Monitor Aggressively

> ### Teacher Professional Development Goal
>
> **Monitor Aggressively:** Read students' independent work as they complete it to check understanding and give immediate feedback.

The coaching principle Make Feedback More Frequent showed how dramatically more quickly teachers improve when they receive frequent feedback in the moment, particularly as contrasted with annual or semiannual performance reviews. The same is true for our students: the teacher's five hours of grading papers in the evening may help them learn, but it won't do so nearly as quickly as will a few seconds of feedback delivered while students are in the act of writing. That's where aggressive monitoring during independent practice comes in.

Bring up the subject of monitoring independent practice, and the image that typically comes to mind is of a teacher standing at the front of the classroom, scanning simply to make sure that students are quiet and focused. But the limitation of this model is that it doesn't really show you whether students are doing quality work. Shift to aggressive monitoring, and independent practice becomes the rare opportunity to give students high-quality feedback in a large-group setting. Monitoring aggressively is about making independent practice the single most critical time for you as a teacher to change learning outcomes for your students. The keys are to

1. Create a monitoring pathway that enables you to get to as many students as possible during independent work (which means delivering feedback more swiftly).

2. Track student answers so that you can use them to inform your next teaching moves.

3. Give students immediate feedback.

If you have never seen effective monitoring in action, it can be difficult to visualize. To that end, we've included a brief teaching clip of Sari Fromson monitoring student work during a lesson on area. Watch how she executes all of these keys in just a few brief minutes (see clip 17).

 Watch clip 17: Monitor Aggressively—Mark Up Student Work and Cue Students (Note: this is a math teaching clip, not a leadership clip.)

On the surface, this looks similar to any class. Beneath the surface, however, a number of extraordinary things are happening. In the brief minutes of the clip, Sari has not only checked every student's work but also marked it correct or incorrect, prompted students to fix areas of growth (without giving them the answer!), and even gotten back to some of the students for a second round of feedback! Just as important, the monitoring sends a message to the students: I am watching your work, and I'm really happy to see your effort. That shows Sari's students she values their learning, making them even more on task during independent practice. No wonder Sari's students ended up in the top 1 percent of New York State. (She then replicated that success when she moved to Boston.)[7]

If you think this applies only to young students or to math, think again. In clip 18, Julia Goldenheim is working with her middle school students on a close reading task. They had to read two short, dense informational texts and state a common theme for the two of them. Watch how she uses the same principles of aggressive monitoring to greatly enhance the amount and quality of feedback that each student receives:

 Watch clip 18: Monitor Aggressively—Mark Up Student Work and Cue Students (Note: this is a reading teaching clip, not a leadership clip.)

Julia also does something that her peers have coined "name the lap": telling students what she will be monitoring each time around, which helps all students stay on task and keep pace.

### Findings from the Field: Don't Fixate Only on Management and Forgo Rigor

When I was a principal, my instinct was to coach my new teachers nearly entirely around classroom management: that's typically where they struggle! There was one moment that I remember distinctly that taught me the expense of this approach. I was engaged in a co-observation with my principal manager, Julie Jackson, and we walked into the classroom. My eyes immediately focused in on the two students who were off task. After a few minutes into the observation, Julie asked me what I noticed, and I told her about the two off-task students and what the teacher should have done differently. Julie listened and then shared that 50 percent of the students hadn't solved the math problem correctly. In the time that I spent fixated on the two off-task students, Julie had circulated the room to identify the trending error based on her review of student work. From that moment on, it became my mission to narrow in on student work within my first few minutes in the classroom. I focused on aggressive monitoring with my teachers. When I walked into the classroom, I would walk the same pathway that I expected my teachers to walk. I would then check in with the teacher and ask, "What do you notice? How will you respond?" These moves began to ensure that my teachers moved forward on the rigor trajectory alongside the management trajectory. In doing so, we lifted student mastery. New teachers can do this if as coaches we encourage it. To start, we need to train our own eyes during observations to focus on the learning and not just the management.

—Sultana Noormuhammad, principal manager, New York, New York

Replicating Sari's practices is very doable, but you must avoid some challenges a teacher may run into if aggressive monitoring isn't occurring:

- The teacher is monitoring only a handful of students—or none at all—during each round of independent practice.

- The teacher monitors only the work of the students who are struggling the most.

- The teacher does not see patterns in student answers and thus doesn't know how to adjust teaching in response.

- The teacher is not giving explicit feedback during independent practice to more than a handful of students, if any.

Let's examine the actions that will address these challenges.

# MONITOR AGGRESSIVELY: MONITORING PATHWAY

*Coaching Tips*

## Teacher Context

**Challenges**

- The teacher monitors only a handful of students—or none at all—during each round of independent practice.
- The teacher monitors only the work of the students who are struggling the most.

**Action Step**

Create and implement a monitoring pathway:

- Create a seating chart to monitor students most effectively.
- Monitor the fastest writers first, then the students who need more support.

**Action Step Overview**

One of the biggest differences between a teacher with strong results and one without (assuming both are starting with a quality lesson plan) is what the teacher does during independent practice.

Imagine attending a cooking class at your local community center. Would you prefer the chef to be walking around to see how you're doing or to be just standing in front as you try out his or her recipe? The traditional model of standing in the front of the room monitoring only for behavioral responsiveness is extremely limited in value. Monitoring each student and delivering feedback change the game.

Here are the steps that the highest-achieving teachers take to create an effective monitoring pathway.

1. **Choose the two or three students you will support first (hint: the fastest writers).** When monitoring independent work, most teachers go straight to the students who tend to have the most trouble with the content. But if the goal is to give *all* students powerful feedback, a better approach is to go first to the fastest writers, regardless of their learning level. Why? Because they'll have something for you to give them feedback on when you get to them. Then, by the time you

get to the slower writers, they'll have something written down as well. Identifying those two or three first quick writers to coach, and going straight to them when independent work time begins, enables a teacher to get to far more students than he or she could otherwise in the same amount of time. And giving as many students individual attention as possible maximizes both the instructional impact of the teacher's monitoring *and* the teacher's ability to keep everyone on task.

2. **Create a seating chart that will make getting to all students as easy as possible.** By creating a data-driven seating chart that places the students in an order that mirrors the order in which you need to reach students when you monitor, you can save yourself valuable steps and time when you need them the most. Here's a sample image that reflects how you might cluster the students you need to reach first. The students are numbered according to their achievement (1 is the highest achieving on the latest assessment; 30 is the lowest):

| 11 | 16 | 15 | 12 | 14 | 13 |
|----|----|----|----|----|----|
| 10 | 17 | 18 | 9 | 19 | 8 |
| 5 | 22 | 21 | 6 | 20 | 7 |
| 4 | 23 | 24 | 3 | 28 | 27 |
| 1 | 26 | 25 | 2 | 30 | 29 |

Teacher · · · Teacher

You could organize your students in any way you'd like. This particular arrangement pairs up the highest achievers with the most struggling students when they do pair work, and it puts those struggling students up front where the teacher can teach them most easily. Just as important, the teacher can quickly scan the first and fourth rows and see how the highest-achieving students are doing and quickly scan the right corner to see how the lowest-achieving students are doing. This makes it easier to identify patterns in student responses.

3. **Position yourself so you can still scan the remainder of the room for responsiveness.** From the right spot in the room, a teacher can tell whether all students are writing even at the same time as he or she is giving in-depth feedback to an individual student. The key is for the teacher to position himself or herself around the perimeter of the room as much as possible to make sure he or she is facing most of the students. This way, at any moment the teacher can poke his or her head up, see most of the students right away, and redirect any who aren't focused on the assignment.

---

### KEY LEADERSHIP MOVES

| | |
|---|---|
| **Probing Questions** | • [Watch a video of a master teacher monitoring independent practice] "What does the teacher do after launching independent practice?" |
| | • "What do you notice about this seating chart from your peer—what about it would make it easier to monitor your students' work?" |
| **Planning and Practice** | • Pull out seating charts from other teachers to use as guides, and build a seating chart for this teacher's class with data in hand. Then plan the monitoring pathway, starting with the fastest writers and then moving to the ones who need more time. Test out the seating chart and rearrange it if necessary. You'll need to have everyone seated in a way that doesn't disrupt classroom management (for example, by not putting multiple students who are often off task near each other). |
| **Real-Time Feedback** | • Nonverbal or whisper prompt: cue the teacher to monitor and/or to use tracking tools. |

---

 Watch clip 19: Monitoring Pathway and Collect Data
(Key Leadership Move: Plan/Practice)

---

# MONITOR AGGRESSIVELY: MONITOR FOR QUALITY

 Coaching Tips

## Teacher Context

### Challenge

The teacher does not see patterns in student answers and thus doesn't know how to adjust teaching in response.

### Action Step

Monitor the quality of student work:

- Check answers against your exemplar.
- Track correct and incorrect answers to class questions.

### Action Step Overview

A teacher's first priority when monitoring aggressively is to determine when students are struggling to complete their independent assignments correctly—not just who is having trouble and who isn't, but who is proving challenged by question 1 as opposed to question 4. From this level of awareness comes the ability to address those students specifically during the remainder of the lesson, dramatically increasing the likelihood that, by the end of it, those students will comprehend.

The act of swiftly checking over students' writing while they are working is greatly enhanced by the presence of an exemplar: this allows the teacher to know what he or she is looking for. There are two other steps that will increase a teacher's awareness of which students are struggling:

- **Annotate the exemplar for the key pieces to monitor.** The best way to use an exemplar while monitoring is to flag in advance specifically what you're going to look for as you circulate: key evidence, a thesis statement, an isolated variable, and so on. You cannot monitor all of students' work in five to ten minutes, but you can look for key pieces. Annotating your exemplar in advance allows you to do that.
- **Track the answers:** Remembering which students are struggling comes far more easily and reliably to a teacher of any experience level if he or she uses a formal tool to note incorrect responses. The teacher can use a "response tracker" to note when students answer incorrectly both during written work and class discussion, or when their responses improve over the course of the lesson. Figure 6 shows one example.

## Figure 6

## Daily Data Tracker–3rd Grade Math

| 3rd Grade Name | Monday | Tuesday | Wed | Thurday | Friday | Monday Q1.3.OA3 | Q2.3MD.7 | Q3.3NBT2 | Q4.3.OA3 | Q5.3MD.7 | Tuesday Q1.3.OA3 | Q2.3MD.7 | Q3.3NBT2 | Q4.3.OA3 | Q5.3MD.7 |
|---|---|---|---|---|---|---|---|---|---|---|---|---|---|---|---|
| NYU | 88% | 87% | 94% | 76% | 100% | | | | | | | | | | |
| Asad Rigging | 50% | 100% | 83% | 83% | 100% | | X | | | | | | | | |
| Alijah Dunnel | 83% | 100% | 83% | 67% | 100% | X | | | X | | | | | | |
| Robert Simpkins | 100% | 83% | 100% | 50% | 100% | | | | | | | X | | | |
| Mahki Johnson | 100% | 33% | 83% | 67% | 100% | | | X | | | | X | X | X | X |
| Moses Uzzell | 67% | 100% | 83% | 100% | 100% | | | X | X | | | | | | |
| Mazhe Juiston Freeman | 100% | 67% | 67% | 83% | 100% | | | | | | X | | | X | X |
| Adrianna Bankston | 100% | 83% | 100% | 50% | 100% | | | | | | | | | X | |
| Raaluchukwu M. | 100% | 100% | 100% | 100% | 100% | | | | | | | | | | |
| Nasir Glover | 67% | 67% | 100% | 83% | 100% | | X | | X | | X | | X | | |
| Ezekiel Bronson | 83% | 100% | 100% | 67% | 100% | | X | | | | | | | | |
| Kosiso | 83% | 100% | 100% | 100% | 100% | | X | | | | | | | | |
| Charif Harris | 100% | 83% | 100% | 83% | 100% | | | | | | | | X | | |
| Samani Ferrell | 100% | 100% | 100% | 100% | 100% | | | | | | | | | | |
| Taylor B. Malone | 100% | 83% | 83% | 67% | 100% | | | | | | X | | | | |
| Angel Johnson | 100% | 83% | 100% | 100% | 100% | | | | | | X | | | | |
| Miriam Tarraf | 100% | 67% | 100% | 67% | 100% | | | | | | X | | | X | |
| Destin Molina | 33% | 67% | 67% | 33% | 100% | | X | X | X | | | | X | X | |
| Aniyah Northover | 100% | 100% | 100% | 100% | 100% | | | | | | | | | | |
| Kayla Williams | 100% | 67% | 100% | 67% | 100% | | | | | | | | X | X | |
| Mikala Wilson | 83% | 83% | 100% | 50% | 100% | | | | | | | | X | X | |
| Joumee Williams | 67% | 100% | 100% | 83% | 100% | | | X | | | | | | | |
| Jahlil Gainer | 100% | 100% | 100% | 100% | 100% | | | | | | | | | | |
| Tristan Sexton | 100% | 100% | 100% | 50% | 100% | | | | | | | | | | |
| Adetinuke Adeyemi | 100% | 100% | 100% | 100% | 100% | | | | | | | | | | |
| Imani | 100% | 100% | 100% | 83% | 100% | | | | | | | | X | | |
| Kate | 83% | 83% | 83% | 50% | 100% | X | | | | | | | | | |
| | | | | | | 2 | 5 | 3 | 4 | 0 | 5 | 2 | 7 | 5 | 2 |
| | | | | | | 92% | 81% | 88% | 85% | 100% | 81% | 92% | 73% | 81% | 92% |

213

*Quick Tip from a Coach—Identify What You're Looking For*
*Aggressive monitoring has been huge for my teachers. I think the key is getting teachers to think about what they are looking for. Get them in the zone of, "Whose work is the best exemplar?" and "What question should I focus on during class discussion?" If a teacher can think through the purpose of monitoring, he or she can sort of get all the steps of aggressive monitoring right there: identify the gap, figure out what you're going to do to close the gap, and apply that to your work. You can course-correct on the spot based on the results.*

—Kathryn Orfuss, teacher and instructional leader, Newark, New Jersey

## KEY LEADERSHIP MOVES

| | |
|---|---|
| **Probing Questions** | • "What were the challenges for you as you monitored during independent practice? What made it difficult for you to remember all your students' answers?" |
| | • "If you cannot monitor everything a student writes, what are the key pieces based on the focus of today's lesson?" |
| | • "What trends did you notice as you aggressively monitored the independent work today? Who mastered it and who didn't?" |
| | • "What is the purpose of aggressive monitoring during independent practice? How can that help inform the rest of your lesson?" |
| **Planning and Practice** | • Have the teacher take out the exemplar and annotate for the keys to look for. In the humanities, that will often include the argument or thesis, evidence, or a writing technique. In STEM subjects, that will often be a certain formula or critical step in answering a problem. |
| | • Have the teacher set up a note-taking template for monitoring. |
| | • Lead the teacher in rehearsing aggressive monitoring by setting out papers with student writing on them on desks and giving the teacher a set amount of time to fill in the note-taking template and note the patterns in student responses—just as he or she will need to during independent practice in an upcoming lesson. |

| **Real-Time Feedback** | • Whisper prompt: cue the teacher to monitor student work. |
|---|---|
| | • Model: walk alongside the teacher and ask what trends he or she is noticing. Show the teacher how to use the exemplar to identify patterns and determine the trend. |

 Rewatch clip 19: Monitoring Pathway and Collect Data
(Key Leadership Move: Plan/Practice)

RIGOR

PHASE 2

# MONITOR AGGRESSIVELY:
# PEN IN HAND (MARK UP STUDENT WORK)

## Teacher Context

### Challenge

The teacher is not giving explicit feedback during independent practice to more than a handful of students, if any.

### Action Step

Pen in Hand: mark up student work as you circulate:

- Use a coding system to affirm correct answers.
- Cue students to revise answers, using minimal verbal intervention. (Name the error, ask them to fix it, tell them you'll follow up.)

### Action Step Overview

Once a teacher starts monitoring, the number one error is fixating on one or two students and spending most of his or her time with them. That might be good for those two students, but the rest of the class doesn't benefit from the teacher's feedback. Annotating student work takes feedback to the next level: it hugely increases the speed at which the teacher can deliver valuable feedback to students doing independent work and, therefore, the number of students who will get that type of feedback while independent work time is still occurring. Moreover, it's something teachers can do even at this early phase of this school year, when they likely have yet to master other ways of coaching students (such as responding to spoken student error during class discussion).

Because teachers are pressed for time, they cannot do the elaborate kind of feedback/annotating they might associate with grading papers: they need a much quicker and simpler system. An easy solution is simply to assign symbols to the most important feedback they could give students during independent writing time. A writing teacher could mark *A* if the argument is flawed, *E* if the evidence is missing or incorrect, and so on. A math teacher could write a check mark for correct answers and circle points of error or write *E* to indicate that the student needs to explain/justify his or her answer.

To understand why this is so powerful, think back to that cooking class analogy of the previous action step. Would you prefer the head chef to simply look at your attempt to master his or her cooking, or give you brief feedback on how to improve as you work? Clearly the latter. Annotating independent practice allows teachers to provide equally manageable feedback for content. If all that teachers need to do is write that single letter on a student's paper, they can get to ten students in a minute during which they might previously have reached only one or two.

Because giving feedback on literary analysis is one of the harder things to do briefly, we offer two examples of systems teachers can use to annotate student writing in literacy:

- Elementary school: RACCE—**R**estate answer, **A**nswer question with a complete inference, **C**ite evidence, give **C**ontext for that evidence, **E**xplain the new insight and its relevance to your argument.
- Middle and high school: ANEZZ—state your **A**rgument, **N**ame the technique the author uses to establish that argument, **E**xplain the use of the technique, **Z**oom in on particular words, **Z**oom out on the greater meaning (how this technique enhances the author's purpose).

*Quick Tip from a Coach—Learn from the Master Teacher*
*Last fall, I led a PD for our staff where we watched the video of Sari Fromson [clip 17], who had some of the highest math scores in the network. We saw her circulating around the room very intentionally, giving students very brief feedback that they could implement on their own, seating them in a very strategic way, and walking around to one student at a time. For my teachers it was hard at first, because they had a mentality of, "OK, it's independent practice time now, I've done my job by delivering the content. I've made it through the lesson." We saw a huge shift to a mind-set of "I need to be in the room right now collecting data and giving feedback to support the kids." The change was so empowering for them: they saw how they could help so many students rather than being stuck in a conversation with just one student. This action step has really been game-changing for our school.*

*—Dan Cosgrove, principal, Boston, Massachusetts*

## KEY LEADERSHIP MOVES

| | |
|---|---|
| **Probing Questions** | • "What is the student experiencing in the moment when you're monitoring? How many of them know if they are on the right track or not?" |
| | • [Present a coding technique/watch a video of a teacher marking up student work/look at a sample student work that has been marked up by a teacher] "How did the teacher give quick feedback to this student to help him or her get on track?" |
| | • "What is the power of a coding system for allowing you to give feedback to more students?" |
| **Planning and Practice** | • Create a feedback code: simple cues teachers can write on student work to spur self-correction. |
| | • Practice: put out a class set of student work on all the desks in the teacher's classroom; have the teacher try to monitor the room as quickly as possible and write feedback codes on as many papers as possible. |
| | • Debrief what was challenging about the immediate feedback. Identify ways to speed up, and then try again. |
| | • While practicing, make sure the teacher integrates the previous action steps: following a clear monitoring pathway and collecting data on the teacher's response tracker template. |
| **Real-Time Feedback** | • Model: walk alongside the teacher as he or she monitors, and whisper, for example, "I think you should put an E on this one" when you see him or her struggle to give the student feedback. |

 Rewatch clip 4: Mark Up Student Work and Cue Students
(Key Leadership Moves: Leading PD, Practice)

Strategies for Coaching

## Aggressively Monitor

| Action Step | When to Deliver It | Probing Questions | Scenarios to Practice | Cues for Real-Time Feedback |
|---|---|---|---|---|
| **Create a monitoring pathway** | Teacher monitors only a handful of students—or none at all—during independent practice. | • [Watch a model video] "What does the teacher do after launching independent practice?"<br><br>• "What do you notice about this seating chart from your peer—what about it would make it easier to monitor your students' work?" | • Pull out seating charts from other teachers to use as guides.<br><br>• Create a seating chart for this teacher's class with data in hand, & plan the monitoring pathway: start with fastest writers and then move to the ones who need more time.<br><br>• Practice: test out the seating chart walking around. Revise for anticipated management/off-task behavior. | Nonverbal or whisper prompt: cue teacher to follow his/her pathway. |
| **Aggressively monitor the quality of student work** | Teacher does not see patterns in student answers. | • "What were the challenges for you as you monitored during independent practice? What made it difficult for you to remember all your students' answers?"<br><br>• "If you cannot monitor everything a student writes, what are the key pieces based on the focus of today's lesson?" | • Planning: have the teacher take out the exemplar & annotate for the keys to look for:<br><br>– Humanities: the argument/thesis, evidence, or a writing technique<br><br>– STEM: a certain formula or critical step in answering a problem | Whisper prompt: Cue teacher to monitor student work.<br><br>Model: Walk alongside teacher and ask what trends s/he is noticing. Show teacher how to use exemplar to identify patterns and determine the trend. |

| Action Step | When to Deliver It | Probing Questions | Scenarios to Practice | Cues for Real-Time Feedback |
|---|---|---|---|---|
| | | • "What trends did you notice as you aggressively monitored the independent work today? Who mastered it and who didn't?" <br><br> • "What is the purpose of aggressive monitoring during independent practice? How can that help inform the rest of your lesson?" | • Set up a note-taking template for monitoring. <br><br> • Practice: set out papers with student writing on desks, and give the teacher a set amount of time to fill in the note-taking template and note the patterns in student responses. | |
| Pen in Hand (mark up student work) | Teacher is not giving explicit feedback during independent practice to more than a handful of students, if any. | • "What is the student experiencing in the moment when you're monitoring? How many of them know if they are on the right track or not?" <br><br> • [Present a coding technique/watch a video of a teacher marking up student work/look at a sample student work that has been marked up by a teacher] "How did the teacher give quick feedback to this student to help him/her get on track?" <br><br> • "What is the power of a coding system for allowing you to give feedback to more students?" | • Create a feedback code: simple cues to write on student work to spur self-correction. <br><br> • Practice: put out a class set of student work on all the desks. Have the teacher monitor the room and write feedback codes on as many papers as possible. <br><br> • Rd 2: ID ways to go faster. <br><br> • Integrate previous actions: monitoring pathway, collecting data. | Model: walk alongside the teacher as he/she monitors, and whisper, e.g., "I think you should put an E on this one" when you see him/her struggle to give the student feedback. |

## CONCLUSION

The very phrase *instant immersion* calls to mind the feeling of having leaped into deep waters. Whether you're surrounded by water, by voices speaking in a new language, or by twenty-five students with distinct learning needs, a time of instant immersion is a time of being surrounded by something unfamiliar, often disarming. Sometimes, it may be a time of anxiety: Are you really going to be able to keep your head above the water? But at its best, instant immersion also leads to something incredibly empowering: the experience of learning to stay afloat.

For a new teacher, this is an especially profound moment, because it's not just about treading water himself or herself. Rather, the new teacher who can navigate deeper waters is the teacher who's operating a seaworthy craft, gradually exploring deeper and deeper waters with every student on board. As we move on to Phase 3, we'll see what new teachers become capable of once teaching becomes not just about avoiding sinking but about sailing away on the learning adventure that everyone is there to embark upon.

# Getting into Gear

How often have you heard the cliché "It's like riding a bike"? The simile promotes the idea that when we have learned something deeply, we tend to remember it for many years to come. There is more to the simile than just that idea, however. Many bike riders begin and end their cycling development when they can stay balanced on the bicycle and ride around town. Competitive cyclists, however, go much further. They take that established learning and add a mastery of many other techniques, a notable one being the effective use of a bike's gears. They know how to shift into high gear when going downhill so as to greatly increase their speed (or as many like to say, "drop like a stone"). They also adeptly shift into low gear for uphill climbs. Each shift can be expertly timed to maximize efficiency and maintain a certain heart rate. When cyclists are at that stage, they no longer need to work on balance or starting and stopping—they can entirely focus on using the right gear at the right time.

Phase 3 of teaching is the gear-shifting phase: getting into gear. Teachers come to this phase when they've already learned to keep a class from toppling over, but they still need to learn to modify their technique to match the terrain at hand.

Let's take a first look at the leadership actions this entails.

# PHASE 3 COACHING BLUEPRINT: LOOKING AT STUDENT WORK

At this stage, you've now seen the three essential coaching skills play out in professional development settings and in feedback meetings:

- Go Granular

- Plan, Practice, Follow Up, Repeat

- Make Feedback More Frequent

How do these appear in your next phase of coaching? Precisely in the way you use student work to help your teacher grow.

## Weekly Data Meetings: Putting Student Learning First

In Phase 3, teachers begin tailoring their lessons to match student needs—the beginning of differentiated instruction. The highest-leverage way a leader can guide teachers is by implementing one of the cornerstones of successful data-driven instruction: a weekly data meeting.

The weekly data meeting has been called many things: a professional learning community (when focused on student work), a student work meeting, short-cycle analysis, and so forth. Whatever name you give these meetings, their impact for a new teacher is enormous. Multiple leading authors in education have demonstrated the impact of data-driven groups of teachers looking at student work, with Richard DuFour leading the way.[1] When done well, the weekly data meeting gives new teachers (and all teachers) clarity on how to monitor the learning in their classroom—but it also gives them the chance to interpret data themselves, building on the strength of their leaders and their peers. It both gives them the short-term ability to meet their students where they are and helps them build the strength to do so as a matter of second nature in the long run.

Despite all the best research, most teacher team meetings aren't as effective as they could be.[2] What we present here is a basic structure of an effective data meeting—the factors that separate an effective meeting from an ineffective one. You will note many similarities to a regular feedback meeting: prepare for the meeting by identifying the most urgent problem to solve (this time a student learning need rather than a teacher move), practice the skills that will be necessary to solve the problem, and follow up to ensure that the changes you've rehearsed during the meeting make their way into the classroom. Here are the key components that make this possible:

- **Start with the exemplar.** Look to the teacher exemplar and top student exemplar to identify what students must do to be successful.

- **Identify the gaps.** Find the most noteworthy ways in which students at varying achievement levels are struggling to create exemplar responses.

- **Plan the re-teach.** Pin down a strategy for reteaching the material and closing the gaps you identified.

Let's look at these in more detail, one by one.

### Start with the Exemplar

If starting with the exemplar looks familiar, you're right: this was the first rigor action step in Phase 2. In Phase 2 we discussed in detail the importance of starting from the end goal and planning backwards. Let's see in clip 20 how principal Nikki Bridges utilizes the exemplar to launch a weekly data meeting.

---

 Watch clip 20: Weekly Data Meetings—Unpack the Exemplar (Key Leadership Move: Looking at Student Work)

---

> ### Stop and Jot
>
> What actions did Nikki take to root data analysis in the exemplar?
>
> _____
> _____
> _____
> _____

Critically, Nikki's first action was to review the standard her teachers were teaching this week, so that everyone at the table was reminded of the central goal toward which he or she was working. From there, they unpacked the teacher-written exemplar and a top-tier student exemplar to get a clear idea of what an exemplar response needs to include. The combination of these two is critically important: without the assessment, your standard is undefined. Without the standard, you run the risk of figuring out a procedure to solve a problem without rooting it in the deeper conceptual understanding you want the student to grasp.

---

### Core Idea

Without the assessment, your standard is undefined.
Without the standard, you risk instruction not rooted in the deeper conceptual understanding.

---

When unpacking the teacher's exemplar, the following probing questions may be helpful for completing these tasks effectively:

- "What were the keys to an ideal answer?"

- "So the ideal is . . ."

- "So the exemplar needs to include what?"

- "How does that connect back to the standard?"

Once the teacher-created exemplar has been unpacked, Nikki has the teacher pull out the best student answer—which we'll call the "student exemplar." As counterintuitive as it might sound, starting with the top response allows teachers to make sure their instruction is high enough for every student, and it allows them to identify the gaps for even the strongest students in the class. When unpacking the student exemplar, prompts include the following:

- "How does your student exemplar compare to the teacher exemplar?"

- "What is the gap?"

- "Does the student exemplar offer something that your exemplar does not [sometimes student answers are even better than our own!]?"

### Findings from the Field: Get Every Student Doing What Your Best Students Are Doing

What really changed my thinking as a new teacher was thinking about the work of my best students and how to get all of my other students to reach their level. One of the best action steps from my coach was: "Look at the work your best students are able to do, and get everybody to be able to do that." Keeping this action step in mind, I constantly asked myself this question: What are the problems we want everyone to be able to do like my mathletes are doing? I started putting questions like those in my daily lesson plan, and that's how that became what all my students were working toward.

—Thomas O'Brien, principal, Brooklyn, New York

### Identify the Gaps

Once the teachers gathered at the analysis meeting have a clear vision of the specific student achievements they're aiming for and a sense of the highest performance in the class, Nikki and her teachers shift their focus to uncovering the gaps (clip 21).

 Watch clip 21: Weekly Data Meetings—Identify the Gaps
(Key Leadership Move: Looking at Student Work)

### Stop and Jot

What actions made it possible for Nikki's teachers to identify the gaps between the student responses and the exemplar?

_____

_____

_____

_____

Nikki began by having her teachers sort student work into four piles numbered by achievement level, 4 being the highest level of achievement and 1 the lowest. Why? Because then they could zero in on the 2s: the students who had almost mastered the standard, but still needed some additional support to make the rest of the climb. The gaps between the 2s and the student exemplar are the most important starting points, because closing them will get you to a place where you can focus on individual support for the final smaller group that still isn't there. Then you can repeat this cycle with your most struggling students.

During this process, teachers focused on naming as precisely as possible the error that the students in the 2 group were making, including the conceptual misunderstanding that the error reflected. From there, they could plan how to clarify the misunderstanding at hand.

---

## A Word on Struggling Students

One of the most frequent questions I get asked during workshops on data-driven instruction is how this applies to special education and English language learner (ELL) students. Too often we think special needs students don't benefit from this approach. I cannot overemphasize how wrong that assertion is! In reality, special educators and ELL teachers can repeat the same process focusing in on their students. In my experience interacting with high-achieving special educators across the country, they repeatedly tell me the same thing: data-driven instruction is at the heart of good teaching for students with special needs. The teaching techniques might end up being different (because these students have different learning needs), but rooting one's teaching in responding to student work is the foundation for differentiated instruction and for good special education instruction.

---

### Plan the Reteach

Gap analysis is important, but only effective reteaching will change outcomes. This step is often overlooked in some meetings that look at student work. Let's watch in clip 22 as Nikki makes sure the teachers build a reteaching plan based on the data.

 Watch clip 22: Weekly Data Meetings—Plan the Reteach
(Key Leadership Move: Looking at Student Work)

When you want to change results, you have to teach differently. Nikki's data meetings create a space where her teachers can practice and prepare those changes with her mentorship. Follow the protocol she uses, and you're prepared to bring a whole cohort of teachers—and, by extension, their students—up into high gear for learning.

### Findings from the Field: Move beyond the Simple Idea of Reteaching

A reteach is a reteach, right? Just tell the students what they should do next time. Not so for the best teachers. As I used the Get Better Faster sequence, I moved from having a teacher action step that was once: "reteach to address student misunderstanding" to a differentiated checklist of actions our teachers can use to effectively reteach anytime. Our teachers now think through: What are the elements of the reteach that target specific student gaps? What are the key questions or key phrases to use consistently in the reteach to make the reteach sticky for students? What is the structure of the reteach: Is it a think aloud/direct modeling, or is it discourse around exemplar work? What do students need to think about as they relearn the material? All of these questions have now been integrated into the Get Better Faster Scope and Sequence, and it's all about responding to the moment when students don't understand.

—Celestina De La Garza, principal, Brooklyn, New York

The following one-pager sums up the components of a successful data meeting looking at student work.

**Weekly/Daily Data Meetings: Leading Teacher Teams to Analyze Student Daily Work**

| 1<br>Affirm<br>1 min | **Praise—Narrate the Positive** |
|---|---|
| | Narrate academic goals already met:<br>• "Last week we were at ___% proficient on this standard, and now we've met our goal." |
| 2<br>Start with the Exemplar<br>7–10 min | **Analyze Teacher and Student Exemplars** |
| | Interpret the standard(s):<br>• "In your own words, what would a student have to know or be able to do to show mastery?"<br>**Unpack the teacher's written exemplar (only 2 min):**<br>• "What were the keys to an ideal answer?" "So the exemplar needs to include . . ."<br>• "How does this [part of the exemplar] align with the standard?"<br>**Analyze the student exemplar—acknowledge the connection between the exemplar and interpretation of the standard:**<br>• "How does your student exemplar compare to the teacher exemplar? What is the gap?"<br>• "Do students have different paths/evidence to demonstrate mastery of the standard?"<br>• "Does the student exemplar offer something that your exemplar does not?" |
| 3<br>Identify the Gaps<br>5–7 min | **Identify the Gaps in Student Work** |
| | **Focus on the 2s (almost mastered):**<br>• "What are the gaps that we see between the 2s and our student exemplar?"<br>• "What are the highest-leverage misconceptions to fix that will move them most quickly to a 3 or 4?"<br>• Analyze process and content: "What do we see students doing that led to this error?"<br>**Name the error (teachers first; leader stamps it or adds on if needed):**<br>• Describe the student error and name the conceptual misunderstanding evident in that error. |

| | |
|---|---|
| **4**<br><br>**Plan the Reteach**<br><br>8–10 min | **Plan Ahead—Design/Revise Upcoming Lesson Plans to Implement the Reteach** |
| | **Script the exemplar for the next applicable problem/ question/prompt:**<br><br>• "What would be the ideal we want to see?" Call on teachers to share exemplar and spar.<br><br>**Plan the structure:**<br><br>• "If this [exemplar] is what we want to see, how do we want to teach this?"<br><br>• Choose the reteach structure: model (think-aloud, modeling of the skill, mini-lesson) or inquiry (guided discourse, show-call, chart the error, and so on)<br><br>• Identify the conceptual impact: "What is the 'why' that students should be able to articulate?"<br><br>**Get specific:**<br><br>• [If one teacher's students were higher on the skill]: "How did you teach this skill?" [To peers] "What do you notice about the differences in how he or she taught the skill?"<br><br>• "Walk me through what steps you will take when reteaching this—what will be different?"<br><br>• "What will be the student materials? Of those, what will you monitor during class?"<br><br>• "Let's name those students/groups that need this reteaching."<br><br>• "Use your resources [for example, Guided Reading Prompting Guide]" |
| **5**<br><br>**Practice**<br><br>Remaining time | **Practice—Role-Play How the Teacher Will Reteach This Standard in an Upcoming Lesson** |
| | "Let's practice those new prompts now."<br><br>• [When applicable] Have teacher stand up/move around classroom to practice monitoring.<br><br>• Repeat until the practice is successful. CFU: "What made this more effective?" |
| **6**<br><br>**Follow Up**<br><br>2 min | **Set Timeline for Follow-Up** |
| | **Set the follow-up plan (when to teach, when to reassess, when to revisit this data):**<br><br>• Observe implementation within twenty-four hours of the meeting.<br><br>• Teacher sends reassessment data to instructional leader. |

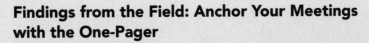

> ### Findings from the Field: Anchor Your Meetings with the One-Pager
>
> As a coach of principals, one of the smallest but most impactful things that has worked for me and the leaders who allow me to coach them is anchoring them back in the tools. For example, when you are trying to improve your weekly data meetings, having the weekly data meeting one-pager in hand always leads to the big "aha" of "It is all right there for me. I should start here when I plan this meeting."
>
> —Jesse Rector, dean, Relay National Principals Academy, New York, New York

The Phase 3 Rigor action steps directly build the skills teachers will use in looking at student work: Habits of Evidence, Check for Whole-Group Understanding, and Reteaching 101. (Phase 4 will continue that work and go deeper.) Let's dive into our closer look at each of the action steps of Phase 3.

## Teaching Skills Overview

Phase 3 marks a decided shift in focus for teachers. They move away from mostly whole-class techniques and start to differentiate their approach to reach individual students. Phase 3 Management moves toward pulling in the one or two students who still aren't acting in accordance with the expectations the teacher has set. The majority of the class is with the teacher already; now he or she is creating an environment where *all* students are engaged.

With this foundation, teachers turn with unprecedented focus to rigor: identifying student needs on a much more specific level, and planning instruction that targets those needs.

Here's the segment of the Get Better Faster Scope and Sequence that covers Phase 3 of the school year.

**Phase 3 Action Step Sequence**

| Management Trajectory | Rigor Trajectory |
|---|---|
| **Engage Every Student**<br><br>**7. Build the Momentum**<br><br>• Give the students a simple challenge to complete a task:<br><br>  – Example: "Now, I know you're only 4th graders, but I have a 5th-grade problem that I bet you could master!"<br><br>• Speak faster, walk faster, vary your voice, & smile (sparkle)!<br><br>**8. Pacing:** Create the illusion of speed so that students feel constantly engaged<br><br>• Use a handheld timer to stick to the times stamps in the lesson & give students an audio cue that it's time to move on.<br><br>• Increase rate of questioning: no more than 2 seconds between when a student responds and teacher picks back up instruction.<br><br>• Use countdowns to work the clock ("Do that in 5, 4, 3, 2, 1").<br><br>• Use call and response for key words.<br><br>**9. Engage All Students:** Make sure all students participate<br><br>• Make sure to call on all students.<br><br>• Cold-call students.<br><br>• Implement brief (15–30 second) Turn & Talks.<br><br>• Intentionally alternate among multiple methods in class discussion: cold calling, choral response, all hands, and Turn & Talks. | **Respond to Student Learning Needs**<br><br>**6. Habits of Evidence**<br><br>• Teach students to annotate with purpose: summarize, analyze, find the best evidence, etc.<br><br>• Teach and prompt students to cite key evidence in their responses.<br><br>**7. Check for Whole-Group Understanding:** Gather evidence on whole-group learning:<br><br>• Poll the room to determine how students are answering a certain question.<br><br>  – "How many chose letter A? B? C? D?"<br><br>  – Students answer the question on whiteboards: "Hold up your whiteboards on the count of three . . ."<br><br>• Target the error: focus class discussion on the questions where students most struggle to answer correctly.<br><br>**8. Reteaching 101—Model:** Model for the students how to think/solve/write<br><br>• Give students a clear listening/note-taking task that fosters active listening to the model, and then debrief the model:<br><br>  – "What did I do in my model?"<br><br>  – "What are the key things to remember when you are doing the same in your own work?" |

| Management Trajectory | Rigor Trajectory |
|---|---|
| **10. Narrate the Positive**<br><br>• Narrate what students do well, not what they do wrong.<br>  – "I like how Javon has gotten straight to work on his writing assignment."<br>  – "The second row is ready to go: their pencils are in the well, and their eyes are on me."<br><br>• While narrating the positive and/or while scanning during a redirect, look at the student(s) who are off task.<br><br>• Use language that reinforces students' getting smarter:<br>  – Praise answers that are above and beyond, or strong effort.<br><br>**11. Individual Student Corrections**<br><br>• Anticipate student off-task behavior and rehearse the next two things you will do when that behavior occurs. Redirect students using the least invasive intervention necessary:<br>  – Proximity<br>  – Eye contact<br>  – Use a nonverbal<br>  – Say student's name quickly<br>  – Small consequence | • Model the thinking, not just a procedure:<br>  – Narrow the focus to the thinking students are struggling with.<br>  – Model replicable thinking steps that students can follow.<br>  – Model how to activate one's own content knowledge and skills that have been learned in previous lessons.<br>  – Vary the think-aloud in tone and cadence from the normal "teacher" voice to highlight the thinking skills.<br><br>• We Do and You Do: give students opportunities to practice with your guidance. |

# PHASE 3 MANAGEMENT—ENGAGE EVERY STUDENT

## Quick Reference Guide

| If your teacher is struggling to . . . | Jump to . . . |
|---|---|
| **Build the Momentum** ||
| Present content in a way that doesn't seem dull but grabs student attention | Create a challenge |
| Convey the joy and excitement that should infuse the classroom | Speak faster, walk faster, vary your voice, and smile |
| **Pacing** ||
| Keep up with the planned pacing of his or her lesson plan | Time yourself |
| Keep up the pace of instruction when asking students questions | Increase the rate of questioning |
| Get students to move quickly during whole-class transitions | Countdown to work the clock |
| Hold students' focus and engagement while he or she is modeling or talking | Call and response |
| **Engage All Students** ||
| Call on a variety of students | Call on all students |
| Keep students engaged when he or she asks a question | Cold Call |
| Keep students engaged during a lengthy I Do or class discussion | Turn and Talk |
| Use a variety of techniques for engaging all students | Use multiple methods to call on students |
| **Narrate the Positive** ||
| Maintain a positive tone when addressing management problems | Narrate what students do well |
| Get students who are off task to respond to positive narration | Look at students who are off task |

## Introduction to Phase 3 Management Skills: Engage Every Student

What makes a two-hour action movie seem to fly by more quickly than a painstaking twenty-minute silent short film? Why is it possible to feel as though you're driving at a normal speed in a sports car going eighty miles per hour on a six-lane highway, whereas you fear for your life in a taxi driving forty-five miles per hour on a narrow side street? Why does an airplane ride seem interminable, while a roller-coaster ride gives you an incredible rush of adrenaline?

The answers come down to one principle: the illusion of speed. What makes us feel as though we are going fast or slow are the markers in the environment around us: buildings, sound, perspective, and sudden motion, to name a few. When we are on a highway, and buildings are at least a hundred yards away on either side, we lose a sense of our distance from those buildings—they seem to be moving past so slowly that we feel we must not be moving very quickly. In the taxi on a narrow street, in contrast, the buildings are only fifteen feet away, and everything feels as if it's moving faster. Sound is the same: an elegant sports car hums softly at eighty miles an hour, creating the sense that everything is happening at a steady, comfortable pace, while the engine of an old Volkswagen bug will scream for its life at sixty. All these factors can transform our sense of speed. They have the power to make potentially ho-hum experiences into wild rides so exciting we can't believe our watches when they're over.

As anyone who's ever attended either an extraordinarily poor or an exceptionally good class or workshop can attest, the same concept applies to the classroom. A poor speaker can make one hour of listening and learning feel like three, but a skilled one engages the audience so fully that a two-day workshop doesn't seem long enough. It's not about going faster, but *appearing* to go faster: creating the illusion of speed.

When it comes to our children's education in the modern era, the illusion of speed is a powerful tool. Students' time in the classroom is too precious for them to spend it checked out. Phase 3 Management looks at the techniques a teacher can use to draw students in. Some of them, such as teaching with a timer in hand, are specific to the teaching profession; others, such as physically moving and speaking quickly and loudly, aren't so different from the tricks of the action movie trade. All of them, though, when deployed properly, can make a lesson as riveting as a high-speed car chase.

> ## Core Idea
>
> Students' time in the classroom is too precious
> for them to spend it checked out.
> Phase 3 Management is about drawing students in.

In this section, we'll focus on increasing engagement for every child in three key ways: picking up the pace of the lesson without sacrificing students' thinking time; increasing the teacher's (and thus the students') enthusiasm; and getting individual off-task students involved in the class. Let's dive in.

## Build the Momentum

> ### Teacher Professional Development Goal
>
> **Build the Momentum:** Transform the simplest tasks into exciting challenges that bring all students to the edges of their seats.

Teachers often make statements like "This is a little boring, but . . ." or "This next part is going to be pretty hard, so . . ." The intention behind such disclaimers is usually to prepare students for what's coming and to remind them that the challenge they're about to take on will reap long-term rewards. Unfortunately, however, the real impact of these words is usually to undermine the lesson. In short, they increase drag.

The trick to creating momentum where a lesson might otherwise drag is to reframe challenges so that they are exciting, not dull. Change "This is going to be pretty hard" to "OK, fourth graders, here's a sixth-grade problem I bet you can solve!" and you transform your classroom from a place of drudgery to a place of motivation. Students will treat the challenge with enthusiasm if you do, becoming eager to show how prepared they are to meet the challenge. Building the momentum doesn't just engage students: it keeps them riveted.

Building the momentum will help a new teacher overcome the following core challenges:

- The teacher states or acknowledges the boring/hard nature of the content he or she is teaching.

- The teacher's tone is flat: it doesn't convey joy and excitement about the lesson.

# BUILD THE MOMENTUM: CREATE A CHALLENGE

## Teacher Context

### Challenge

The teacher states or acknowledges the boring/hard nature of the content he or she is teaching.

### Action Step

Give the students a simple challenge to complete a task—for example, "Now, I know you're only fourth graders, but I have a fifth-grade problem that I bet you could master!"

### Action Step Overview

If you've ever struggled to keep students focused in your classroom, you may have felt a twinge of frustration on noticing the same students rush as one enthusiastic mass into a ball game during P.E. or recess a few moments later. But here's the good news for new teachers: any teacher can channel into his or her lessons the same qualities that make handball and basketball so exciting. A huge part of the appeal of playground games is that they set up something for students to beat, making students eager to show they can do it. There's no reason a math problem or close reading exercise can't be framed as a suspenseful game—and the difference in student engagement when a teacher does so is stunning.

*Tip from a Teacher—Start Simple*

*I was an intensely struggling kindergarten teacher in my first year. I'm not being modest or exaggerating: my classroom was truly "on fire"—and not in a good way! After addressing the action steps in Phases 1 and 2, my coach focused me in on creating a challenge. We started simple with in-class transitions. My job became to say, "I'm looking to see who can be fast and silent when they stand up." That way, the kids would be more motivated to comply and exhibit the behavior I was looking for. Monday of that week, I stood in the back and watched my coach model it with my kids. Then we practiced some more and debriefed what she'd done. Wednesday, I led the transition with her jumping in as necessary, and we practiced more after that. On Thursday, I led it myself and she watched in the back. It was the first time that something in my classroom went well, which is why I've become so passionate about the way to coach. I am obsessed with challenge now, and in my current role as coach, I always try to make sure that we're planning our practice with three or four lines that the teacher can just memorize, and running the practice three or four times. Trying to do it for the first time in front of the kids doesn't work.*

—Andrea Palmer Kleinbard, coach, Brooklyn, New York

---

### KEY LEADERSHIP MOVES

| | |
|---|---|
| **Probing Questions** | • [Watch model video] "What does this teacher say to get her students so excited to complete the task?"<br>• "What is the value of providing a challenge to build momentum in the class?"<br>• "Where in your lesson did you miss an opportunity to create a challenge? What could you do differently next time?" |
| **Planning and Practice** | • Have the teacher script challenges into the lesson plan and practice delivering them. |
| **Real-Time Feedback** | • Nonverbal: pump your hands in the air like a cheerleader.<br>• Model: model creating a challenge. |

---

PHASE 3 MANAGEMENT

# BUILD THE MOMENTUM:
# SPEAK FASTER, WALK FASTER, VARY YOUR VOI
# AND SMILE

 Coaching Tips

## Teacher Context

### Challenge

The teacher's tone is flat: it doesn't convey joy and excitement about the lesson.

### Action Step

Speak faster, walk faster, vary your voice, and smile (sparkle)!

### Action Step Overview

Think of a classic storyteller, one whose energy is contagious and who can entrance you completely with words alone. Just by speaking animatedly, smiling, and varying the tone and energy of one's delivery (lowering the voice to build suspense or increase tension, for example, can be just as powerful as speaking more loudly to emphasize a climax), any speaker can accomplish this. For a teacher, this is incredibly valuable: it makes your students not just engaged but riveted on the lesson. Some of my colleagues call this deceptively simple technique "sparkle."

*Tip from a Teacher—Go Slow and Low*
*My principal tried to model for me what it looked like to vary your voice. In talking with the students, she really built up to something with anticipation, and when she finally got to the big announcement, she dropped her voice almost to a whisper. In hindsight, she probably overdid it to show me the difference, but I remember hearing the room freeze because they were so fixed on what she was saying. This was really hard for me to replicate at the time, so she practiced it with me a lot after modeling. We actually picked one time in the lesson for me to use it every day for a couple of days. We called it "go slow and low": when you hit the climax, slow down your words and lower your volume. Then we just did more and more practice. I can still hear her words in my head: "At the peak, adjust your voice to go slow and low."*

*—Kathryn Orfuss, teacher and instructional leader, Newark, New Jersey*

## KEY LEADERSHIP MOVES

**Probing Questions**

- [Show model video] "What do you notice about Ms. Smith's tone in this clip? What does she do to make her delivery sparkle?"
- "Now think about your own classroom. What's creating the gap between this teacher's tone and yours?"

**Planning and Practice**

- Have the teacher teach part of an upcoming lesson while speaking faster and smiling.
- If necessary, stop the teacher and repeat what he or she has just said, while smiling and speaking more quickly.
- Have the teacher vary his or her voice, dropping lower to create tension rather than always remaining at high or low volume.
- Your feedback will be critical here: modulating the voice is very hard for teachers to develop on their own. In some cases, you'll be changing the way they've spoken for years! Make sure you create a safe space where they don't get discouraged while they practice.

**Real-Time Feedback**

- Nonverbal: point to the corners of your mouth to remind the teacher to smile, or gesture with your hand to remind him or her to speak more quickly.
- Whisper prompt: "Sparkle! Smile! Jump back into teaching!"

PHASE 3

MANAGEMENT

Strategies for Coaching

## Build the Momentum

| Action Step | When to Use It | Probing Questions | Scenarios to Practice | Cues for Real-Time Feedback |
|---|---|---|---|---|
| **Create a challenge** | • Teacher states or acknowledges the boring/hard nature of the content he/she is teaching. | • [Watch model video] "What does this teacher say to get her students so excited to complete the task?"<br><br>• "What is the value of providing a challenge to build momentum in the class?"<br><br>• "Where in your lesson did you miss an opportunity to create a challenge? What could you do differently next time?" | • Have teacher script challenges into the lesson plan and practice delivering them. | • Nonverbal: pump your hands in the air like a cheerleader.<br><br>• Model: model creating a challenge. |
| **Speak faster, walk faster, vary your voice, and smile** | • Teacher's tone doesn't convey the joy and excitement that should infuse the classroom. | • [Show model video] "What do you notice about Ms. Smith's tone in this clip? What does she do to make her delivery sparkle?"<br><br>• "Now think about your own classroom. What's creating the gap between this teacher's tone and yours?" | • Have teacher teach part of an upcoming lesson while speaking faster and smiling.<br><br>• Stop teacher and repeat what he/she has just said, while smiling and speaking more quickly.<br><br>• Have the teacher vary his/her voice, dropping lower to create tension rather than always remaining at high or low volume. | • Nonverbal: point to the corners of your mouth to remind teacher to smile, or gesture with your hand to remind him/her to speak more quickly.<br><br>• Whisper prompt: "Sparkle! Smile! Jump back into teaching!" |

## Pacing

In *Teach Like a Champion,* Doug Lemov explains that the pace of the lesson "isn't the rate at which material is presented, but rather the rate at which the lesson makes the material appear to unfold."[3] Rushing through your presentation of a new math concept, for example, won't help students learn it better; it may do just the opposite. But if you dive into that concept with great gusto, building suspense and energy, students can process vital information at a reasonable pace—all while feeling as though they're flying at lightning speed that will keep them on the edge of their seats.

Here are three challenges that Pacing can typically address during this phase:

- The teacher falls way behind the planned pacing of his or her lesson plan. (For example, thirty minutes into the lesson, the class is still reviewing the Do Now.)

- The teacher pauses too long between questions, resulting in losing the students' engagement.

- Students are slow to get started with shifting from one part of the lesson to the next: whole-group discussion to pair-share to independent practice, and so on.

- Students lose focus and engagement while the teacher is modeling or talking.

# PACING: USE A TIMER

**Coaching Tips**

## Teacher Context

### Challenge

The teacher falls way behind the planned pacing of his or her lesson plan. (For example, thirty minutes into the lesson, the class is still reviewing the Do Now.)

### Action Step

Use a handheld timer to stick to the time stamps in the lesson and give students an audio cue that it's time to move on.

### Action Step Overview

If the teacher's lesson doesn't keep to its time stamps, students are probably running out of time for end-of-lesson independent work—the most important step in their learning. To keep the lesson moving as planned and to keep students attentive and eager to learn, have the teacher use a timer to make sure that an activity that ought to last for only, say, fifteen minutes really does conclude after fifteen minutes.

*Tip from a Teacher—Know the Minute, Not Just the Hour*
*I always struggled with pacing. Sometimes I would check for understanding too much, and students would never get to independent practice, which is where they need to go to show mastery. So the timer came out. I would time specific chunks of my lesson, and I knew 2:35 is when we have to start something new. I never knew the hour, but I always knew the minute, and it was observable to my coach and co-teacher, who could give me the move-on signal when the timer went off.*
—Nikki Bowen, principal, Brooklyn, New York

## KEY LEADERSHIP MOVES

**Probing Questions**

- "How much time did you want to spend on the I Do part of the lesson? What kept you from sticking to that amount of time?"
- "How much time had you planned to have left for independent work at the end of the lesson? What kept you from having enough time?"

**Planning and Practice**

- With lesson plan in hand, have the teacher look at the time stamps for each part of the lesson. Plan together what to do when the timer goes off and the teacher hasn't finished that section. Make decisions as to what can be cut from that part of the lesson and the language the teacher can use to transition to the next section.
- Plan ahead where the teacher can cut certain questions or small-group work when falling behind to make sure the core parts of the lesson are protected.
- Have the teacher practice teaching the parts of the lesson with a timer set. Practice what to do when the timer goes off and the teacher isn't finished with that section.

**Real-Time Feedback**

- Nonverbal: point at watch/wrist when it's time to move on.
- Nonverbal: give a hand signal indicating how many more minutes to stay on this activity.

# PACING:
# INCREASE THE RATE OF QUESTIONING

## Teacher Context

### Challenge
The teacher pauses too long between questions during class discussion, resulting in losing the students' engagement.

### Action Step
Increase the rate of questioning: there should be no more than two seconds between when a student responds and when a teacher picks back up instruction.

### Action Step Overview
In casual conversation, the occasional pause between one person speaking and the other responding isn't necessarily awkward or harmful. But in the classroom, too many long pauses can drag down the pace of instruction. A teacher can avoid this by intentionally waiting no more than two seconds after a student finishes speaking before continuing instruction.

The heart of increasing the response rate for a teacher is knowing what to do next after a student responds. Although a teacher won't yet know what to do with a wrong answer (see Phase 4), he or she can pick up instruction with the prewritten questions or instructions that he or she has in the lesson plan. Thus, much of mastering this skill is internalizing the lesson plan.

| | |
|---|---|
| **Probing Questions** | • "What is the key to pacing? Given that principle, what do you think is the ideal amount of time after each student answer before you ask another question?"<br><br>• "Do you recall what happened after you called on _____ yesterday? What would you need in order to keep instruction moving more immediately after calling on a student?" |
| **Planning and Practice** | • Role-play a questioning sequence from an upcoming lesson, keeping track of the rate of questioning. Note specifically moments where the rate slows due to pauses in between questions and lack of teacher preparation. Key teacher actions to look for: knowing the questions cold and knowing which student to call on. |
| **Real-Time Feedback** | • Model: model the questioning pace for the teacher. |

# PACING:
# WORK THE CLOCK

 Coaching Tips

## Teacher Context

### Challenge

Students are slow to get started with shifting from one part of the lesson to the next: whole-group discussion to pair-share to independent practice, and so on.

### Action Step

Use countdowns to work the clock ("Do that in 5 . . . 4 . . . 3 . . . 2 . . .1").

### Action Step Overview

When the teacher has gotten the hang of using the timer to keep the lesson moving, the next step is to bring the students on board. Teachers can accomplish this by making the students aware of the time stamps they are trying to stick to. Activities can begin with a statement like "You have five minutes to complete your Do Now," be punctuated by reminders like "We're halfway done" and "Thirty seconds to go," and end with a final countdown. Work that students once approached listlessly becomes an exciting challenge that they focus on intently and complete as quickly as possible.

| KEY LEADERSHIP MOVES | |
|---|---|
| **Probing Questions** | • "How much time did you want to take in this transition?" |
| | • [Watch model video] "What actions does the teacher take to go faster? How could you apply them to your lesson?" |
| | • "How could you challenge your students to work with greater purpose?" |
| **Planning and Practice** | • Script and practice Bright Lines—cues to signal a significant shift from one activity to the next: claps, hand gestures, and so on. |
| | • Play the part of students and have the teacher transition from one activity to the next using a countdown to work the clock. |
| **Real-Time Feedback** | • Nonverbal: signal "5-4-3-2-1" to the teacher with your fingers when it's time for a countdown. |

# PACING:
# CALL AND RESPONSE

 Coaching Tips

## Teacher Context

### Challenge

Students lose focus and engagement while the teacher is modeling or talking.

### Action Step

Use call and response for key words.

### Action Step Overview

Asking students to answer questions in unison reaps untold benefits. Students pay close attention, knowing they might be asked to speak up at any moment; and the teacher is automatically checking the understanding of everyone in the room.

| KEY LEADERSHIP MOVES | |
| --- | --- |
| **Probing Questions** | • "What is the purpose of a choral response? How does it add value to engagement both behaviorally and academically?" |
| | • "Here's a video clip from your lesson yesterday. Where could you have used a choral response to increase engagement?" |
| **Planning and Practice** | • Identify moments when it would be most useful to implement a choral response. Role-play that part of the lesson while you, in the role of student, provide the choral responses. Provide occasional lackluster responses so that the teacher can practice having students Do It Again for choral response. |
| **Real-Time Feedback** | • Nonverbal: create/use a cue for choral response. |

## Pacing

| Action Step | When to Use It | Probing Questions | Scenarios to Practice | Cues for Real-Time Feedback |
|---|---|---|---|---|
| Use a timer | Teacher falls way behind the planned pacing of his/her lesson plan | • "How much time did you want to spend on the I Do part of the lesson? What kept you from sticking to that amount of time?"<br><br>• "How much time had you planned to have left for independent work at the end of the lesson? What kept you from having enough time?" | • Plan: review time stamps for each part of the lesson. Script how to move on when the timer goes off and the teacher hasn't finished that section. Plan where teacher can cut certain parts of the lesson when falling behind.<br><br>• Practice a lesson with a timer. Rehearse what to do when the timer goes off & teacher isn't finished with that section. | Nonverbal: point at watch/wrist when it's time to move on.<br><br>Nonverbal: give a hand signal of how many more minutes to stay on this activity. |
| Increase the rate of questioning | Teacher pauses too long between questions, losing the students' engagement. | • "What is the key to pacing? Given that principle, what do you think is the ideal amount of time after each student answer before you ask another question?"<br><br>• "Do you recall what happened after you called on ____ yesterday? What would you need in order to keep instruction moving more immediately after calling on a student?" | • Role-play a questioning sequence from an upcoming lesson, keeping track of the rate of questioning. Note specifically moments where the rate slows due to pauses in between questions and lack of teacher preparation.<br><br>• Key teacher actions to look for: knowing the questions cold and knowing which student to call on. | Model: model the questioning pace for the teacher. |

| Action Step | When to Use It | Probing Questions | Scenarios to Practice | Cues for Real-Time Feedback |
|---|---|---|---|---|
| Use count-downs to work the clock | Students are slow to move during lesson transitions: whole-class to pairs to IP, etc. | • "How much time did you want to take in this transition?"<br>• [Watch model video] "What actions does the teacher take to go faster? How could you apply them to your lesson?"<br>• "How could you challenge your students to work with greater purpose?" | • Script and practice Bright Lines—cues to signal switching between activities: claps, hand gestures, etc.<br>• Play the part of students and have the teacher transition from one activity to the next using a countdown to work the clock. | Nonverbal: signal "5-4-3-2-1" with your fingers when it's time for a countdown. |
| Call & response | Students lose focus & engagement while teacher is modeling or talking. | • "What is the purpose of a choral response? How does it add value to engagement both behaviorally and academically?"<br>• "Here's a video clip from your lesson yesterday. Where could you have used a choral response to increase engagement?" | • ID moments when it would be most useful to implement a choral response.<br>• Role-play: provide occasional lackluster responses so that the teacher can practice having students Do It Again for choral response. | Nonverbal: create/use a cue for choral response. |

## Engage All Students

> ### Teacher Professional Development Goal
>
> **Engage All Students:** Keep every student listening and learning at every moment—even when you're calling on just one of them at a time.

The guiding belief behind each course of action we've recommended teachers take within the first ninety days of the school year is that *every* student can and must be learning on target at all times throughout the year. Phases 1 and 2 focused on whole-class actions; Phase 3 engages students as individuals: contributing to the discussion at hand and doing the work of learning.

The next step in that direction is to make sure that every student is actively engaged in the learning. Too often our students "we love the most" are allowed to opt out of class instruction: sitting back and not participating in the learning. The action steps in this section focus on calling techniques that get students involved in class discussion. These help avoid the tendency for a few students to dominate and others to remain largely silent.

---

### Findings from the Field: Use the LeMar Strategy

As a first-year fifth-grade teacher, I was rigid, and I struggled to engage the most challenging students in my class. One thing that helped was to observe other teachers who also taught my students. I remember watching Emily teach, and we both had this student LeMar. In my class, he was constantly off task and disengaged. But in Emily's class, he was highly engaged and was excited to learn. She would make an extra effort to cold-call him consistently throughout the lesson, give him a job, and praise his effort. I started to do this with my most difficult students too by incorporating them more fully into my lessons and building relationships with them. If you get to know them as people and also preview the content to build their intellectual curiosity, you can build their confidence in the content and demonstrate respect for them as learners. I called it the LeMar strategy.

—Jody-Anne Jones, principal, Newark, New Jersey

---

These actions steps for engaging all students will overcome the following specific challenges:

- The teacher tends to call on the same few students over and over.

- Some students disengage when the teacher asks a question, assuming that if they don't raise their hands, they won't have to answer.

- Students become restless during a lengthy I Do or other teacher presentation of material.

- Students become restless during a lengthy class discussion.

- The teacher overrelies on just one technique for engaging all students.

# ENGAGE ALL STUDENTS: CALL ON ALL STUDENTS

**Coaching Tips**

## Teacher Context

**Challenge**

The teacher tends to call on the same few students over and over.

**Action Step**

Make sure to call on all students.

**Action Step Overview**

It's a common pattern among teachers to have a few specific students they tend to call on frequently, meaning that the rest of the students are only much more rarely required to speak. This could be because there are students eager to participate or because the teacher is overrelying on calling on the strongest students to keep a conversation going. The first step to engaging every student, then, is to consciously avoid these pitfalls by tracking which students are being called on and deliberately calling on those who have not.

| | KEY LEADERSHIP MOVES |
|---|---|
| **Probing Questions** | • "Let's look at this footage from some of your questioning sequences in the past week. Which students are you calling on, and which aren't getting called?" |
| | • "What could you do to make sure you call on all students? How will you remember to do so in the moment?" |
| **Planning and Practice** | • Option 1: embed in the lesson plan: plan which specific students to call on with each question in the lesson plan, ensuring that students at different levels of mastery of the content are getting called on and that everyone gets to speak frequently. Guide the teacher to write the students' names right into his or her lesson plan. |
| | • Option 2: use the class attendance list: pull out the teacher's class attendance list and have the teacher check students off as they are called on. Set a goal to call on every student before any student responds more than twice. |
| **Real-Time Feedback** | • Nonverbal: point to the student who would be ideal for the teacher to call on. |

# ENGAGE ALL STUDENTS: COLD CALL[4]

**Coaching Tips**

## Teacher Context

### Challenge

Some students disengage when the teacher asks a question, assuming that if they don't raise their hands, they won't have to answer.

### Action Step

Cold-call students.

### Action Step Overview

In some cases, it makes sense for a teacher to choose which student to call on from among those who have volunteered to answer the question—but not always. To limit yourself to calling only on students with their hands raised is to give some of your students the ability to opt out of participation. That cedes control of who engages and who doesn't to the students rather than the teacher. One solution is cold calling, a practice whose many powerful benefits Doug Lemov discusses in detail in *Teach Like a Champion*: by letting students know that they could be called on at any moment, the teacher holds students accountable for their learning at all times, improving both management and rigor.

| | KEY LEADERSHIP MOVES |
|---|---|
| **Probing Questions** | • "What is the purpose of cold calling?" |
| | • "Where in your lesson today could a cold call have increased engagement?" |
| | • "Who are the students who would benefit the most from a cold call?" |
| **Planning and Practice** | • Have the teacher choose students to cold-call in advance. |
| | • Rehearse a questioning sequence from an upcoming lesson, with you playing the part of various students and the teacher strategically cold-calling these students depending on their achievement level and the difficulty of the question. |
| **Real-Time Feedback** | • Nonverbal: point at the ideal student for the teacher to cold-call. |

PHASE 3  MANAGEMENT

# ENGAGE ALL STUDENTS: TURN AND TALK

 Coaching Tips

## Teacher Context

### Challenges

- Students become restless during a lengthy I Do or other teacher presentation of material.
- Students become restless during a lengthy class discussion.

### Action Step

Implement brief (fifteen- to thirty-second) Turn and Talks.

### Action Step Overview

Keeping students engaged and moving quickly is just one of the benefits of the quick Turn and Talk. Having students turn and talk with a partner at the right instant also ensures 100 percent participation, creates a forum for cooperative learning, and provides the teacher with an immediate whole-class check for understanding. All of this is optimized when the Turn and Talk lasts no longer than thirty seconds—long enough for all students to address the question adequately, but not so long that their focus has the opportunity to wane.

*Quick Tip from a Coach—It's About the "When"*
*Turn and Talk is easy to execute in and of itself, but it's all about the when. Timing a Turn and Talk right is everything. What really makes it sticky is to use your lesson plan, preselect the right moments, and then stick to the plan. Planning the "when" is the key to making Turn and Talk something teachers can do successfully without your help.*
—Ramy Abdel-Nabi, teacher and coach, Brooklyn, New York

### KEY LEADERSHIP MOVES

**Probing Questions**
- "What are the benefits of having students do a Turn and Talk?"
- "What are the keys to an effective Turn and Talk?"
- "How will you know the Turn and Talk is effective?"

**Planning and Practice**
- Identify moments in an upcoming lesson to do a quick Turn and Talk based on the content of the lesson, pace, and momentum.
- Create Bright Lines to make the Turn and Talk entry and exit unmistakably crisp:
  - Preestablish whom students will turn toward so that there is no confusion. Give clear What to Do instructions: "Turn your body toward your partner. Make eye contact."
  - Use brisk signal: "Go!"
- Incorporate actions from previous action steps: scan the room and redirect off-task students.

**Real-Time Feedback**
- Nonverbal: turn forefingers toward each other.
- Model: lead a Turn and Talk and then explain the rationale to the teacher during the Turn and Talk.

 Watch clip 23: Turn and Talk, Middle School
(Key Leadership Move: Plan/Practice)

 Watch clip 24: Turn and Talk, Elementary School
(Key Leadership Move: Real-Time Feedback)

# ENGAGE ALL STUDENTS: USE MULTIPLE METHODS TO CALL ON STUDENTS

 *Coaching Tips*

## Teacher Context

### Challenge
The teacher overrelies on just one technique for engaging all students.

### Action Step
Intentionally alternate among multiple methods in class discussion: cold calling, choral response, all hands (having all students raise their hands when it is a question to which everyone should know the answer), and Turn and Talks.

### Action Step Overview
Once new teachers learn certain techniques for calling on students, they have the tendency to overrely on them. They will always cold-call, and no students raise their hands; or they will always call on one student at a time, and students figure out that they won't be called on again for a long time. To engage all students to the fullest possible extent, teachers are best served by being mindful of not only which student would be best to call on but also what method would be the most effective for choosing the right student to call on. There's no one-size-fits-all here: the magic is in the variation.

*Quick Tip from a Coach—Not Just Balance, but Purpose*
*The key to the rule of fourths is not just alternating but choosing the method that most meets the purpose of that moment. Does nearly everyone know the answer? Then choose call and response or all hands. Do you want everyone to have a chance to grapple out loud with the question? Choose Turn and Talk. Using a variety of methods to call on students is not just about the balance: it's about the purpose. Finding the purpose is most easy to do with the lesson plan in hand. Then you can ask, "OK, which questions are we going to cold-call? Which students will we call on, and why? Where are we going to use call and response, and why?" This builds [the teacher's] understanding of that rationale.*
—Ramy Abdel-Nabi, teacher and coach, Brooklyn, New York

PHASE 3

MANAGEMENT

**Probing Questions**

- "We've discussed multiple ways to call on students: cold calling, all hands, Turn and Talks, and choral response. Which ones do you use the most? Which ones could you use more frequently in your lesson?"
- "What are the times in which each technique would be best to use in your class?"

**Planning and Practice**

- Plan a whole-group discussion: note which questions are best suited for cold call, all hands, choral response, or Turn and Talk.
- Role-play the discussion following the script the teacher created.

**Real-Time Feedback**

- Nonverbal: create/use cue for cold calling, Turn and Talk, choral response, or all hands.
- Whisper prompt: "When you call the group back together, start with a choral response followed by a cold call." Model (if needed).

## Engage All Students

| Action Step | When to Use It | Probing Questions | Scenarios to Practice | Cues for Real-Time Feedback |
|---|---|---|---|---|
| **Call on all students** | Teacher tends to call on the same few students over and over. | • "Let's look at this footage from some of your questioning sequences in the past week. Which students are you calling on, and which aren't getting called?"<br><br>• "What could you do to make sure you call on all students? How will you remember to do so in the moment?" | • Option 1—embed in lesson plan: write into plan which specific students to call on during plan, ensuring that students at different levels of mastery of the content are getting called on and that everyone gets to speak frequently.<br><br>• Option 2—use attendance list: pull out teacher's attendance list and have teacher check students off as they are called on. | Nonverbal: point to the student who would be ideal for the teacher to call on. |
| **Cold call** | Some students disengage when the teacher asks a question. | • "What is the purpose of cold calling?"<br><br>• "Where in your lesson today could a cold call have increased engagement?"<br><br>• "Who are the students who would benefit the most from a cold call?" | • Have teacher choose students to cold-call in advance.<br><br>• Practice: run through a questioning sequence, with teacher strategically cold-calling various students. | Nonverbal: point at the ideal student for the teacher to cold-call. |

| Action Step | When to Use It | Probing Questions | Scenarios to Practice | Cues for Real-Time Feedback |
|---|---|---|---|---|
| **Turn & Talk** | Students become restless during a lengthy I Do or class discussion. | • "What are the benefits of having students do a Turn & Talk?"<br>• "What are the keys to an effective Turn & Talk?"<br>• "How will you know the Turn & Talk is effective?" | • Planning: ID moments in an upcoming lesson to do a quick Turn & Talk.<br>• Create Bright Lines—make Turn & Talk entry and exit unmistakably crisp: preestablish whom students turn toward; give clear What to Do instructions and brisk signal: "Go!"<br>• Scan the room and redirect off-task students. | Nonverbal: turn forefingers toward each other.<br>Model: lead a Turn & Talk and then explain rationale to teacher during the Turn & Talk. |
| **Use multiple methods to call on students** | Teacher overrelies on just one technique for engaging all students. | • "We've discussed multiple ways to call on students: cold calling, all hands, Turn & Talks, and choral response. Which ones do you use the most? Which ones could you use more frequently in your lesson?"<br>• "What are the times in which each technique would be best to use in your class?" | • Plan a whole-group discussion: note which questions are best suited for cold call, all hands, choral response, or Turn & Talk.<br>• Role-play the discussion following the script the teacher created. | Nonverbal: create/use cue for cold call, Turn & Talk, choral response, and all hands.<br>Whisper prompt: "When you call the group back together, start with a choral response followed by a cold call."<br>Model (if needed). |

## Narrate the Positive[5]

> ### Teacher Professional Development Goal
>
> **Narrate the Positive:** Narrate what students do well, not what they do wrong.

As the popular Johnny Mercer song says, the best way to eliminate the negative is to accentuate the positive. In the classroom, that means narrating the positive: drawing attention to what students are doing well, rather than what they are doing poorly. In contrast with the common misconception that maintaining a well-managed classroom will eliminate joy from the classroom, narrating the positive reveals that keeping students on task can be a joyful action in itself. Narrating the positive is an extremely powerful step toward making joy something that great management doesn't deplete, but rather reinforces.

Two great benefits result from narrating the positive. The joy it will bring to the classroom is the first. The second is that you're positively reinforcing the actions you want to see in the classroom. Praising students for doing something well stacks the odds significantly in favor of their doing it again next time. Thus, by narrating the positive, you create the classroom of your dreams both in the tone you strike and in the practical actions that are accomplished each day.

### Findings from the Field: Don't Stop Narrating

One day I walked into the classroom of one of my teachers who generally had great classroom management, and noticed that the room wasn't tightly managed as it had been. I pulled out the Get Better Faster Scope and Sequence and started from the top. I stopped at Narrate the Positive because I noticed the teacher just gave directions and moved on—she didn't stop or slow down to recognize the behaviors she wanted to see. During our check-in, I showed her the video of the session I observed, and right away she noticed that half of her students weren't meeting her expectations after receiving a clear direction. Then I pulled up another video of her from the beginning of the year to help her identify the gap—that was her "aha" moment! "Oh my god," she proclaimed, "I no longer narrate the positive!" After the practice she said, "Wow, that felt so good. The little things we forget to do have the biggest impact!" Even if this tool is used for a "cleanup" action step with veteran teachers, it still works! The tool will never steer you wrong when used correctly.

—Natalie Catin-St. Louis, principal, Philadelphia, Pennsylvania

Here are a few common challenges that a teacher can mitigate by narrating the positive:

- The teacher's tone when addressing management problems is overly negative.
- Students who are off task don't respond to positive narration.
- The teacher tends to praise behavior rather than academic effort or achievement.

# NARRATE THE POSITIVE: NARRATE WHAT STUDENTS DO WELL

 *Coaching Tips*

## Teacher Context

### Challenge

The teacher's tone when addressing management problems is overly negative.

### Action Step

Narrate what students do well, not what they do wrong.

- "I like how Javon has gotten straight to work on his writing assignment."
- "The second row is ready to go: their pencils are in the well, and their eyes are on me."

*Quick Tip from a Coach—Focus on the "Swing Kids"*
*I think the most valuable tip I've been given was this idea that every classroom has "swing kids." You've got the kids who are already there with you, you've got your three or four outliers who you can narrate the positive to all day and they'll still be slow to respond, and then there's this sweet spot of six or eight kids in the middle in each class who can go either way. Those are the kids that you need to get on your side and be narrating the positive all the time.*
—*Lauren Moyle, principal, Newark, New Jersey*

## KEY LEADERSHIP MOVES

| | |
|---|---|
| **Probing Questions** | • [Watch model video] "How did the teacher get students to correct misbehaviors without being negative?"<br>• [Watch video of the teacher] "What could you have done in this particular moment to increase the positivity of your tone?"<br>• "What negative phrases do you find yourself using most often?" |
| **Planning and Practice** | • Planning: rewrite teacher's most frequent negative comments into positive statements.<br>• Practice: role-play keeping students on track through positive narration.<br>• While practicing, focus not only on the words but also on the positive tone in which the teacher delivers them. Practice the tone until it feels authentic: not exaggeratedly positive or too flat/negative. |
| **Real-Time Feedback** | • Nonverbal: hold up an index card with a plus sign written on it or sign that says "Narrate the positive."<br>• Whisper prompt: "Narrate the positive." |

# NARRATE THE POSITIVE: LOOK AT STUDENTS WHO ARE OFF TASK

 *Coaching Tips*

## Teacher Context

### Challenge
Students who are off task don't respond to positive narration.

### Action Step
While narrating the positive and/or while scanning during a redirect, look at the student(s) who are off task.

### Action Step Overview
Some students may not realize right away that their teacher is still paying attention to them while he or she is narrating the positive behavior of other students. Often as not, however, all it will take to correct this is a firm look at the student or students who are off task while narrating what other students are doing correctly.

*Tip from a Teacher: The Simplest Idea Can Be the Most Effective*
*When I was doing my new teacher training, narrating the positive seemed like such a silly idea. I can say what one kid's doing and another kid's going to do it? Now I think of it as teacher magic, because it works. It's a teacher magic trick. That was the most important step my first year. That was big.*
—Jamie Gumpper, teacher and coach, Boston, Massachusetts

---

### KEY LEADERSHIP MOVES

| | |
|---|---|
| **Probing Questions** | • [Watch model video] "Where is the teacher looking while narrating the positive? How does that affect student responsiveness?" |
| **Planning and Practice** | • Role-play: you play the role of a student and model off-task behavior while the teacher looks at you and narrates the positive actions of another (imaginary) student. |
| **Real-Time Feedback** | • Whisper prompt: "Look at off-task students while narrating positive." |

---

 Watch clip 25: Narrate the Positive (Key Leadership Move: Plan)

PHASE 3 MANAGEMENT

# NARRATE THE POSITIVE: SCRIPT LANGUAGE THAT REINFORCES STUDENTS' GETTING SMARTER

 *Coaching Tips*

## Teacher Context

### Challenge

The teacher tends to praise behavior rather than academic effort or achievement.

### Action Step

- Use language that reinforces students' getting smarter:
  - Praise answers that are above and beyond, or strong effort.

### Action Step Overview

The independent thinker is not the person who knows the right answer but the person who knows how to find the right answer. Many of the best academic habits we strive to teach students, from showing their work in math class to citing their evidence in English, reflect this. For this reason, it is essential to praise students for more than the answers they deliver, emphasizing instead the processes they use to get there. If you don't reward this part of their learning, they will make a habit of focusing on the answer rather than the work of finding it, which is detrimental to their development as learners.

| | KEY LEADERSHIP MOVES |
|---|---|
| **Probing Questions** | • [Watch model video] "What does this teacher say when her students are responding? What behavior is she reinforcing?"<br>• "When do you find yourself giving positive feedback to students?"<br>• "What are the classroom culture benefits of praising academics over behavior?" |
| **Planning and Practice** | • Plan: with an upcoming lesson plan, script moments when the teacher could give precise academic praise that would reinforce students' effort.<br>• Practice students giving a response and the teacher giving precise praise. |
| **Real-Time Feedback** | • Model: praise student thinking if an opportunity is missed.<br>• Whisper to teacher to give precise praise after another positive academic behavior. |

Strategies for Coaching

## Narrate the Positive

| Action Step | When to Use It | Probing Questions | Scenarios to Practice | Cues for Real-Time Feedback |
|---|---|---|---|---|
| Narrate what students do well | Teacher's tone when addressing management problems is overly negative. | • [Watch model video] "How did the teacher get students to correct misbehaviors without being negative?"<br><br>• [Watch video of the teacher] "What could you have done in this particular moment to increase the positivity of your tone?"<br><br>• "What negative phrases do you find yourself using most often?" | • Planning: rewrite teacher's most frequent negative comments into positive statements.<br><br>• Practice: role-play keeping students on track through positive narration.<br><br>• Focus on positive tone: practice tone until it feels authentic: not overly positive or too flat/negative. | Nonverbal: hold up an index card with a plus sign written on it or a sign that says "Narrate the positive."<br><br>Whisper prompt: "Narrate the positive." |
| While narrating the positive, look at off-task students | Students who are off task don't respond to positive narration. | • [Watch model video] "Where is the teacher looking while narrating the positive? How does that affect student responsiveness?" | • Practice: you play the role of a student and model off-task behavior while the teacher looks at you and narrates the positive actions of another (imaginary) student. | Whisper prompt: "Look at off-task students while narrating positive." |
| Use language that reinforces students' getting smarter | Teacher tends to praise behavior rather than academic effort or achievement. | • [Watch model video] "What does this teacher say when her students are responding? What behavior is she reinforcing?"<br><br>• "When do you find yourself giving positive feedback to students?"<br><br>• "What are the classroom culture benefits of praising academics over behavior?" | • Plan: with an upcoming lesson plan, script moments when the teacher could give precise academic praise that would reinforce students' effort.<br><br>• Practice students giving a response and the teacher giving precise praise. | Model: praise student thinking if an opportunity is missed.<br><br>Whisper to teacher to give precise praise after another positive academic behavior. |

## Individual Student Corrections

> ### Teacher Professional Development Goal
>
> **Individual Student Corrections:** Deliver corrections to individual off-task students, not to the entire class.

The management skills of Phases 1 and 2 focus on general whole-class techniques. Here in Phase 3, a teacher can dive more deeply into correcting the off-task behavior of individual students.

Initial challenges of correcting individual students may include the following:

- The teacher sees the problem, but the basic strategies of What to Do and Narrate the Positive aren't working for a few students.

- The teacher does not consistently or effectively provide consequences when students show minor misbehaviors.

- The teacher uses corrections that draw more attention than necessary to the student who has been off task.

- Students consistently exhibit certain off-task behaviors that the teacher struggles to manage.

### Findings from the Field: Change the Weather to Make It Stick

At my school, the last two years I've given a mini-PD on Control the Weather. In it I teach that the teacher "controls the weather" in his or her class. When it's sunny (most of the time) the teacher is upbeat, warm, and smiling, and when there needs to be a lightning-quick correction, the weather changes quickly and dramatically, then immediately gets back to warm and upbeat. I've coached teachers to stop moving during any moment where they have to reset the class or an individual student. Then move slightly (step a little to the side) and raise their voice to bring the weather back to warm and sunny.

—Rebecca Utton, principal manager, Denver, Colorado

# INDIVIDUAL STUDENT CORRECTIONS: LEAST INVASIVE INTERVENTION

 Coaching Tips

## Teacher Context

### Challenges

- The teacher sees the problem, but the basic strategies of What to Do and Narrate the Positive aren't working for a few students.
- The teacher does not consistently or effectively provide consequences when students show minor misbehaviors.
- The teacher uses corrections that draw more attention than necessary to the student who has been off task.
- Students consistently exhibit certain off-task behaviors that the teacher struggles to manage.

### Action Step

Anticipate student off-task behavior and rehearse the next two things you will do when that behavior occurs. Redirect students using the least invasive intervention necessary:

- Proximity
- Eye contact
- Use a nonverbal (use a gesture to guide a student to follow a certain action: write in the air to get him to write, palms open to tell her to open her book, and so on)
- Say the student's name quickly, give What to Do, and scan
- Small consequence

### Action Step Overview

To deliver corrections while maintaining a joyful classroom and a respectful attitude toward students, a teacher can communicate the correction in a way that draws minimal attention to the student. Having a hierarchy of least to most invasive interventions to use when a student is off task equips a teacher with a tool box of actions he or she can take to redirect individual students.

*Tip from a Teacher—Fix the Stare*

*My coach would pretend to be specific students and would role-play the specific behaviors they were displaying. What made that particularly effective is that we'd watch video of my classroom together and really see what would happen when I implemented what we used. The pattern that ended up working the best was square up in the corner, give the small consequence, quick stare, then continue the lesson. It was the fixing the stare that transformed my implementation.*

—*Christine Mariani, teacher and coach, Newark, New Jersey*

---

### KEY LEADERSHIP MOVES

| | |
|---|---|
| **Probing Questions** | • "When a student shows ___ [insert low-level misbehavior, such as calling out, repeated head down, being off task, and the like], what is your ideal response?" |
| | • "What is the challenge when you try to redirect an off-task student?" |
| | • "Look at this list of interventions from least to most invasive. What is the advantage of starting with the least invasive intervention?" |
| | • "When you are intervening with off-task students, which of these interventions are you using? Which ones could you add to your repertoire?" [Watch video of teaching if needed] |
| | • "Which intervention is most appropriate given the behavior and the part of the lesson in which it occurs?" |
| **Planning and Practice** | • You really cannot overplan or overpractice this action step. The more at-bats the better! |
| | • Script the precise language of administering the consequence. This is often the hardest part for a struggling teacher. Don't practice until the language is fully scripted. |
| | • After scripting the words, practice the tone and timing until the teacher has mastered a formal tone. Then move to full role-play practice. |
| | • Role-play as a student with different types of off-task behavior. Have the teacher redirect you with least invasive interventions. Slowly progress up to persisting in the off-task behavior so that the teacher has a chance to escalate to every type of intervention. |
| **Real-Time Feedback** | • Nonverbal: point to the off-task student and give a redirect signal. |
| | • Whisper prompt: "This student is off task. Use ___ intervention." |
| | • Model: redirect an off-task student and wait for the teacher to repeat the action with the next off-task student. |

## Strategies for Coaching

### Individual Student Corrections

| Action Step | When to Use It | Probing Questions | Scenarios to Practice | Cues for Real-Time Feedback |
|---|---|---|---|---|
| Least invasive intervention | Teacher sees the problem, but What to Do and Narrate the Positive aren't working for a few students, or teacher does not consistently or effectively provide consequences for minor misbehaviors.<br><br>Teacher uses corrections that draw unnecessary attention to the student who has been off task. | • "When a student shows ___ [insert low-level misbehavior, such as calling out, repeated head down, being off task, etc.], what is your ideal response?"<br>• "What is the challenge when you try to redirect an off-task student?"<br>• "Look at this list of interventions from least to most invasive. What is the advantage of starting with the least invasive intervention?"<br>• "When you are intervening with off-task students, which of these interventions are you using? Which ones could you add to your repertoire?" [Watch video of teaching if needed]<br>• "Which intervention is most appropriate given the behavior and the part of the lesson in which it occurs?" | You really cannot overplan or overpractice this action step. The more at-bats the better!<br><br>• Script the precise language of administering the consequence.<br>• Practice the tone and timing until teacher has mastered a formal tone.<br>• Role-play as a student with different types of off-task behavior. Have teacher redirect you with the least invasive interventions. Slowly progress up to persisting in off-task behavior so that teacher has a chance to escalate to every type of intervention. | Nonverbal: point to the off-task student and give a redirect signal.<br><br>Whisper prompt: "This student is off task. Use ___ intervention."<br><br>Model: redirect an off-task student and wait for the teacher to repeat the action with the next off-task student. |

---

### Stop and Jot

What are the three top coaching ideas you plan to use to train your teachers in these Phase 3 Management skills? Jot them down here.

_____

_____

_____

# PHASE 3 RIGOR—RESPOND TO STUDENT LEARNING NEEDS

## Quick Reference Guide

| If your teacher is struggling to . . . | Jump to . . . |
|---|---|
| **Habits of Evidence** | |
| Get students to annotate texts when reading | Teach students to annotate with purpose |
| Get students to cite evidence from the text | Teach students to cite key evidence |
| **Check for Whole-Group Understanding** | |
| Pin down a clear vision of which (or how many) students comprehend | Poll the room |
| Respond to student data after collecting it | Target the error |
| **Reteaching 101: Model** | |
| Keep students intellectually engaged while modeling | Give students a clear listening/note-taking task |
| Provide a clear model or unpack the thinking behind the model | Model the thinking, not just the procedure |
| Get students to practice after completing the model | Give students opportunities to practice |

**Phase 3 Action Step Sequence**

| Management Trajectory | Rigor Trajectory |
|---|---|
| **Engage Every Student**<br>**7. Build the Momentum**<br><br>• Give the students a simple challenge to complete a task:<br><br>– Example: "Now, I know you're only 4th graders, but I have a 5th-grade problem that I bet you could master!!"<br><br>• Speak faster, walk faster, vary your voice, & smile (sparkle)!<br><br>**8. Pacing:** Create the illusion of speed so that students feel constantly engaged<br><br>• Use a handheld timer to stick to the times stamps in the lesson & give students an audio cue that it's time to move on.<br><br>• Increase rate of questioning: no more than 2 seconds between when a student responds and teacher picks back up instruction.<br><br>• Use countdowns to work the clock ("Do that in 5, 4, 3, 2, 1").<br><br>• Use call and response for key words.<br><br>**9. Engage All Students:** Make sure all students participate<br><br>• Make sure to call on all students.<br><br>• Cold-call students.<br><br>• Implement brief (15–30 second) Turn & Talks.<br><br>• Intentionally alternate among multiple methods in class discussion: cold calling, choral response, all hands, and Turn & Talks. | **Respond to Student Learning Needs**<br>**6. Habits of Evidence** <br><br>• Teach students to annotate with purpose: summarize, analyze, find the best evidence, etc.<br><br>• Teach and prompt students to cite key evidence in their responses.<br><br>**7. Check for Whole-Group Understanding:** Gather evidence on whole-group learning:<br><br>• Poll the room to determine how students are answering a certain question.<br><br>– "How many chose letter A? B? C? D?"<br><br>– Students answer the question on whiteboards: "Hold up your whiteboards on the count of three . . ."<br><br>• Target the error: focus class discussion on the questions where students most struggle to answer correctly.<br><br>**8. Reteaching 101—Model:** Model for the students how to think/solve/write<br><br>• Give students a clear listening/note-taking task that fosters active listening to the model, and then debrief the model:<br><br>– "What did I do in my model?"<br><br>– "What are the key things to remember when you are doing the same in your own work?" |

RIGOR

| Management Trajectory | Rigor Trajectory |
|---|---|
| **10. Narrate the Positive**<br><br>• Narrate what students do well, not what they do wrong.<br><br>  – "I like how Javon has gotten straight to work on his writing assignment."<br><br>  – "The second row is ready to go: their pencils are in the well, and their eyes are on me."<br><br>• While narrating the positive and/or while scanning during a redirect, look at the student(s) who are off task.<br><br>• Use language that reinforces students' getting smarter:<br><br>  – Praise answers that are above and beyond, or strong effort.<br><br>**11. Individual Student Corrections**<br><br>• Anticipate student off-task behavior and rehearse the next two things you will do when that behavior occurs. Redirect students using the least invasive intervention necessary:<br><br>  – Proximity<br><br>  – Eye contact<br><br>  – Use a nonverbal<br><br>  – Say student's name quickly<br><br>  – Small consequence | • Model the thinking, not just a procedure:<br><br>  – Narrow the focus to the thinking students are struggling with.<br><br>  – Model replicable thinking steps that students can follow.<br><br>  – Model how to activate one's own content knowledge and skills that have been learned in previous lessons.<br><br>  – Vary the think-aloud in tone and cadence from the normal "teacher" voice to highlight the thinking skills.<br><br>• We Do and You Do: give students opportunities to practice with your guidance. |

## Introduction to Phase 3 Rigor Skills: Respond to Student Learning Needs

By Phase 3, a teacher has all the skills he or she needs to teach a lesson that looks completely superb. The lesson plan is polished, curriculum driven, and well rehearsed. The routines go smoothly without the need for additional prompting. The students are engaged, rarely veering off task; and a number of individuals offer accurate, insightful responses when called on to do so. At first glance, everything is going extremely well.

Yet often you can teach a lesson this competent only to realize, when you review student work, that the students didn't truly learn the material. Their written responses are less precise overall than the comments of the students who spoke up in class (often, the students who commented during class may have been the highest-achieving ones). Moreover, the following day's lesson, which builds on the material from this lesson, proves too challenging for the students to manage. The outstanding lesson plan, tight routines, and high level of student achievement were all necessary for learning to happen—but they didn't guarantee learning in and of themselves.

What's the missing piece? Responding to student learning needs. Looking at student learning closes the gap between teaching that looks incredible and teaching that teaches. After all, if you teach and students don't learn, is it really teaching? Phase 3 Rigor shows how to make sure teaching = learning.

---

### Core Idea

Looking at student work closes the gap between teaching that appears credible and teaching that approaches the incredible.

---

Some of the action steps we present in Phase 3 Rigor will take place outside the classroom, as teachers analyze data from independent practice or interim assessments and weave their insights into upcoming classes. But all these actions end up influencing instruction in the midst of the lesson itself: they don't leave the true learning to chance. They zero in on where students are, and they set the class up to climb from there.

### Findings from the Field: Break Down Resistance by Responding to Data

One of my teachers was very resistant to feedback. She felt stronger in her delivery than many of her peers and thought her students' struggles on assessments were just an anomaly. I realized that she wasn't able to visualize what students were thinking when answering a question. I shifted my coaching to the area of Phase 3—respond to student learning. We planned specific questions she would ask at specific moments of the lesson to check for understanding. While she was skeptical at first, it was as if a lightbulb went off: the teacher was shocked by what students were not able to do initially. She started focusing on making student thinking visible to her to help her teaching, and the

> results were immediate. Students performed much better on her next assessment, and seeing that result changed the teacher's mind-set about her teaching. Now she checks for understanding all the time. All it took was that one small action, and the resistance disappeared.
>
> —Hilda Abarca Muñoz, coach, Santiago, Chile

For teachers who are hungry to be able to see for themselves what their students need the most, Phase 3 is an exciting time. In this phase of the rigor trajectory, when teachers first begin analyzing and planning with data, they're preparing for the time when they won't need someone else to show them how to do it. They can find out how well students are understanding, analyze why, and plan every part of how to improve instruction. They're learning not only how to get up to speed but how to evaluate the best course to follow.

## Habits of Evidence

The first action step of Phase 3 Rigor is a general tactic that comes in handy with all parts of student learning. Building the habit in students of citing key text evidence in their answers directly connects to helping students correct their own errors. Using evidence benefits both the teacher and the student. For the teacher, hearing the students' evidence that underlies their answers is one of the fastest ways to diagnose where their thinking broke down if they have incorrect answers. For students, when they understand and debate the proper evidence, they start to be able to identify stronger and weaker arguments as well. This habit of mind becomes particularly important today when nearly every form of assessment is asking students to justify their answers with solid evidence. These action steps ensure that teachers have the opportunity to enable them to do so.

---

### Teacher Professional Development Goal

**Habits of Evidence:** Teach and prompt students to cite text evidence as they read and when responding to questions.

---

Teachers are likely at this time to be facing these three challenges that will be mitigated by improving their use of evidence:

- Students don't annotate texts effectively when reading, making it difficult for them to go back and cite the best evidence.
- Students don't cite evidence from the text when answering questions.

# HABITS OF EVIDENCE:
# TEACH STUDENTS TO ANNOTATE WITH PURPOSE

 Coaching Tips

## Teacher Context

### Challenge

Students don't annotate texts effectively when reading, making it difficult for them to go back and cite the best evidence.

### Action Step

Teach students to annotate with purpose: summarize, analyze, find the best evidence, and so on.

### Action Step Overview

In effect, what you're doing when you ask students to annotate evidence when reading a text is training them to be good writers and speakers. Just as important, you make it much easier for you as the teacher to see their thinking while they're reading. Prompting students to identify the most important evidence even before they're asked to generate a response is teaching them argumentation skills and essentially teaching them to be better critical readers. Building the habit of annotating key evidence as they read a text will get students to the point where they are able to identify key evidence automatically whenever they read.

## KEY LEADERSHIP MOVES

**Probing Questions**

- "What is the purpose of annotating a text? Based on your prompt/task, what would be the best focus for students' annotation?"
- "How many students are annotating the text while reading?"
- "For the students who are annotating, what are the biggest gaps in their ability to annotate for the best evidence?"

**Planning and Practice**

- Review text the students will be reading in the upcoming week. Have the teacher create an exemplar annotation: What are the key pieces of evidence you would like them to highlight?
- Place this annotated exemplar on a clipboard for the teacher to carry around with him or her as he or she monitors independent practice.
- Set up a simple written feedback/cue to give to students while monitoring their annotation:
- Example: a check mark means "good evidence annotated"; a circle means "look for better evidence."

**Real-Time Feedback**

- Walk alongside the teacher when monitoring student annotation of their reading. Look for patterns of good and weak annotations. Whisper prompt: "Prompt [x student] to improve his or her annotations."

# HABITS OF EVIDENCE:
# TEACH STUDENTS TO CITE KEY EVIDENCE

 Coaching Tips

## Teacher Context

### Challenge

Students don't cite evidence from the text when answering questions.

### Action Step

Teach and prompt students to cite key text evidence in their responses.

### Action Step Overview

Once students are looking for the best evidence while reading, the next step is to cite that evidence when talking in class. This is an essential step for students and teachers alike: for the students, it's an academic habit that will serve them well throughout their careers; for the teacher, it reveals a great deal about student comprehension. It is much easier to help students improve their argument when you understand the evidence on which they built it. For this habit to be cemented, the teacher has to prompt the students to do it any time that they don't do so automatically.

| KEY LEADERSHIP MOVES | |
|---|---|
| **Probing Questions** | • "What is the importance of citing evidence in answering a question?"<br>• "Where in your last lesson could students have been asked to cite their evidence more clearly/effectively?" |
| **Planning and Practice** | • With the teacher, name key evidence from the exemplar, identify additional valid evidence, and predict wrong evidence.<br>• Role-play the teacher prompting students when they don't cite evidence or when the evidence is weak. |
| **Real-Time Feedback** | • Nonverbal: give a cue for the teacher to ask the students for evidence—for example, by holding up a card with "E" printed on it.<br>• Whisper prompt: "Ask for evidence." Model if needed. |

Strategies for Coaching

## Habits of Evidence

| Action Step | When to Use It | Probing Questions | Scenarios to Practice | Cues for Real-Time Feedback |
|---|---|---|---|---|
| **Teach students to annotate with purpose** | Students don't annotate texts effectively when reading, making it difficult for them to go back and cite the best evidence. | • "What is the purpose of annotating a text? Based on your prompt/task, what would be the best focus for students' annotation?"<br>• "How many students are annotating the text while reading?"<br>• "For the students who are annotating, what are the biggest gaps in their ability to annotate for the best evidence?" | • Review text the students will be reading in the upcoming week. Have teacher create an exemplar annotation: What are the key pieces of evidence you would like them to highlight?<br>• Practice: monitor student work with annotated exemplar on a clipboard.<br>• Set up a simple written feedback/cue to give to students while monitoring their annotation (e.g., circle = look for better evidence). | Walk alongside the teacher when monitoring student annotation of their reading. Look for patterns of good and weak annotations. Whisper prompt: "Prompt [x student] to improve his/her annotations." |
| **Teach & prompt students to cite key evidence** | Students don't cite evidence from the text when answering questions. | • "What is the importance of citing evidence in answering a question?"<br>• "Where in your last lesson could students have been asked to cite their evidence more clearly/ effectively?" | • Name key evidence from exemplar, identify additional valid evidence, and predict wrong evidence.<br>• Practice: prompt students when they don't cite best evidence. | Nonverbal: cue teacher to ask for evidence (e.g., hold up card with "E" printed on it). Whisper prompt: "Ask for evidence." Model if needed. |

## Check for Whole-Group Understanding

Planning with data comes in two flavors: the planning teachers do outside the classroom based on written assessment results, and the lightning-fast adjustments they make during the lesson to meet students' learning needs in the moment. They began to develop this skill in Phase 2 by monitoring independent practice—that's the easiest form, because the teacher has a moment to think before intervening. Now teachers begin doing this same thing with spoken error by checking for whole-group understanding.

**Findings from the Field: Brain Breaks—Check for Understanding *and* Engage**

Checking for understanding is such a valuable action step, because you not only gather data but also engage students at multiple levels. By including a physical activity with the check for understanding, students remain engaged. We call these "Brain Breaks": for example, thumbs up/down for whether you think the answer is right/wrong, holding up cards to share the answer to a multiple-choice question (different colored cards labeled A, B, C, D), or using whiteboards to write and reveal your answer. Each of these gives you instant data on the whole class, but you have also gotten students kinesthetically involved. That helps all students, especially those we love the most.

—Savanna Flakes, coach, Alexandria City, Virginia

The challenges teachers will overcome by checking for whole-group understanding are as follows:

- The teacher moves ahead without a clear vision of which (or how many) students comprehend.

- Class discussion does not focus on common misconceptions with which many students are struggling.

# CHECK FOR WHOLE-GROUP UNDERSTANDING: POLL THE ROOM

 Coaching Tips

## Teacher Context

### Challenge

The teacher moves ahead without a clear vision of which (or how many) students comprehend.

### Action Step

Poll the room to determine how students are answering a certain question:

- "How many chose letter A? B? C? D?"
- [Students answer the question on whiteboards] "Hold up your whiteboards on the count of three . . ."

### Action Step Overview

Class discussions can be some of the richest parts of a class. Yet they are also where students who are struggling can often hide behind the comments of their peers. The long way to solve that is to wait until every student has participated in the discussion, but even then they might just be building off of what other students said. The quicker way to collect data is by polling the room. Polling the room is a simple yet profoundly powerful tool: by as little as a show of hands, you can find out in no more than a few seconds what level of understanding every student has reached. For multiple-choice or true-false questions, you need only list the choices and have students raise a hand to show which answer they selected; for non-multiple-choice questions, you can poll the room by providing each student with a small whiteboard and dry-erase marker, and asking students to show what they have written on their whiteboards (an even more cost-effective version of this is to have students write on sheet protectors: they can quickly erase and use them again).

Collecting this data is the difference between a discussion that merely looks good and one that is advancing learning. You cannot advance the learning, however, until you know the data: what proportion of students are comprehending the material? Which students specifically are not?

(How to act on that data comes in the upcoming Phase 3 and Phase 4 Rigor action steps.)

*Quick Tip from a Coach—Think Whiteboards*

*I was struggling for a while to coach teachers to check for understanding effectively after independent practice. Then I ran into a teacher who was an early adopter of the individual whiteboards approach. His practice time in math demanded that students work through tough problems on their own whiteboards and then hold up the whiteboard for his assessment at every step, not just at the end with the answer. He would chant things like, "Nope, check your signs," "Go back and label your variables," or "Good, but move faster." All kids got what they needed, behavior and focus were observable, and he got consistent data about the quality of work. And all by just standing in one place and knowing what he was looking for.*

*I began to use "Think whiteboards" as a metaphor for effective independent practice with new teachers, because it rolled up into a single move all the complex variables that seemed just too tough to run simultaneously in their brains. For many (even in ELA, science, and electives), this meant using the same literal approach with whiteboards themselves. For others, simply thinking about the whiteboards move while planning their practice allowed them to account for all the variables in one pass. It allowed them—among other things—to catch a key move they'd miss otherwise. (For example, I planned an essay, but when I "thought whiteboards," I realized there wasn't enough work visibility for the teacher, so I switched the essay to Google docs so I could follow along on my screen.)*

—Benjamin Marcovitz, principal manager, New Orleans, Louisiana

| | |
|---|---|
| **Probing Questions** | • [Debrief your own intervention] "I intervened in your class and polled the room. What was the purpose of doing so? How did that help guide the rest of your lesson?"<br><br>• "What is the purpose of polling the room? Taking that into account, what would be the best moments in your upcoming lesson to poll the room?"<br><br>• "What are the advantages of these polling techniques (for example, whiteboards) versus self-report thumbs up/thumbs down?" |
| **Planning and Practice** | • Script into the lesson plan key moments to conduct a poll of the room. Plan how the teacher will capture that data.<br><br>• Plan the rollout of the polling routine: use the lessons learned in rolling out other procedures (see Phase 1 and 2 Management action steps):<br><br>    – Script out the instructions<br><br>    – Practice<br><br>    – Do It Again<br><br>• Predict the outcome for the polling of upcoming classes to help a teacher start to anticipate student error. |
| **Real-Time Feedback** | • Nonverbal: hold up a sign that says "Poll."<br><br>• Model: poll the room yourself. |

 Watch clip 26: Check for Understanding
(Key Leadership Move: Real-Time Feedback)

# CHECK FOR WHOLE-GROUP UNDERSTANDING: TARGET THE ERROR

 **Coaching Tips**

## Teacher Context

### Challenges
- The teacher collects data, but then moves on with his or her lesson without responding to it.
- Class discussion does not focus on common misconceptions with which many students are struggling.

### Action Step
Target the error: focus class discussion on the questions where students most struggle to answer correctly.

### Action Step Overview
Once you've collected data about student performance, the key is to act on it. There are more comprehensive and sophisticated techniques that will be pursued in upcoming steps. A simple starting point is to target the error: simply focus on the part where students are struggling. Often a teacher will fall into the trap of reviewing all questions on a homework assignment or quiz. If you've collected data, however, and you see that nearly everyone answered questions 1–4 correctly and struggled with question 5, then spend your review time on question 5. Simple? Yes. An automatic response by every teacher? No. If we build this habit early, it can quickly make each class review more effective. Watch high school history teacher Ryan Miller do this as he discusses the impact of certain laws in the aftermath of a revolution:

 Watch clip 27: Target the Error and Close the Loop (teaching clip)

PHASE 3

RIGOR

## KEY LEADERSHIP MOVES

**Probing Questions**

- "What challenges do you anticipate during independent practice?"
- "When you plan your review of the homework/quiz/independent practice, where is the most important area to focus?"
- [Watch video of a master teacher responding to student errors in independent practice] "What actions does this teacher take to respond to students' written errors?"

**Planning and Practice**

- A quick way to make it easier for a teacher to develop this habit is to anticipate the errors students will make in an upcoming lesson. Then the teacher is prepared to target these questions in advance.
- Practice: review student work (Exit Tickets, Do Nows) and name the error.

**Real-Time Feedback**

- Whisper prompt during independent practice: "What patterns of error are you noticing? Plan to review only the areas of error."

## Check for Whole-Group Understanding

| Action Step | When to Use It | Probing Questions | Scenarios to Practice | Cues for Real-Time Feedback |
|---|---|---|---|---|
| **Poll the room** | Teacher moves ahead without a clear vision of which (or how many) students comprehend. | • [Debrief your own intervention] "I intervened in your class and polled the room. What was the purpose of doing so? How did that help guide the rest of your lesson?"<br><br>• "What would be the best moments in your upcoming lesson to poll the room?"<br><br>• "What are the advantages of these polling techniques versus self-report thumbs up/ thumbs down?" | • Script into the lesson plan key moments to conduct a poll of the room.<br><br>• Plan the rollout of the polling routine: integrate Phase 1 & 2 actions for rollouts.<br><br>• Predict the outcome for the polling of upcoming classes to help teacher start to anticipate student error. | Nonverbal: hold up a sign that says "Poll."<br><br>Model: poll the room yourself. |
| **Target the error** | Teacher collects data, but then moves on with his or her lesson without responding to it. Class discussion does not focus on students' common misconceptions. | • "What challenges do you anticipate during independent practice? Where is the most important area to review?"<br><br>• [Watch model video] "What actions does this teacher take to respond to students' written errors?" | • Planning: anticipate the errors students will make in an upcoming lesson.<br><br>• Practice: review student work and name the error. | Whisper prompt during IP: "What patterns of error are you noticing? Plan to review only the areas of error." |

## Reteaching 101—Model

The heart of great instruction is reteaching something when students struggle (and then giving them a chance to try it again). Although there are many ways to reteach, they essentially form two types of lessons: the teacher models for the student what to do (think aloud, mini-lesson), or the teacher guides the students to figure it out through their discussion of the error (guided discourse, partner work, and the like). We link these together as Reteaching 101 and Reteaching 201. The first one is slightly easier; the second one, which we discuss in Phase 4, is a hallmark of great teachers.

> ### Teacher Professional Development Goal
>
> **Reteaching 101—Model:** Model for the students the thinking required to answer a question or perform a task effectively.

Until a teacher masters facilitating class discussion, Reteaching 101 is a quick, effective way to remediate error. Here are some common challenges new teachers may run into as they try to model for students how to accomplish a task, write an essay, or solve a problem:

- The teacher gives a clear model, but the students don't have a task to do while listening to the model.

- The teacher's model is blurry, blending right in with everything else the teacher says (for example, delivered in a monotone or without emphasis on key points), making it difficult for students to know which parts are most important.

- The teacher tells the students about a process or procedure, but doesn't unpack the thinking or conceptual understanding that helped him or her arrive at that procedure.

- The teacher gives a clear model, but the students don't have the opportunity to try to replicate it after the model is done.

# RETEACHING 101:
# GIVE STUDENTS A CLEAR LISTENING TASK

 Coaching Tips

## Teacher Context

### Challenge

The teacher gives a clear model, but the students don't have a task to do while listening to the model.

### Action Step

Give students a clear listening/note-taking task that fosters active listening to the model, and then debrief the model:

- "What did I do in my model?"
- "What are the key things to remember when you are doing the same in your own work?"

### Action Step Overview

Before a teacher's model can have impact, he or she needs to make sure that students are actively listening. Here is an example from high school history teacher Art Worrell (clip 28). He is modeling for his students how to unpack the prompt for a document-based question, a staple of history assessments. On the previous assessment, his students struggled to identify all the background knowledge they had that was embedded in the prompt that would help them answer the question more effectively. Watch as Art sets up his model:

 Watch clip 28: Think-Aloud—Set Listening Task (teaching clip)

By giving them a listening and note-taking task, he makes them more active learners or more likely to be able to retain what he models.

*Quick Tip from a Coach—Have Students "Mirror" Your Work*
*Modeling the thinking, not just the procedure, is really helpful for any type of question. But sometimes the students are just passive observers and don't actively engage in absorbing the model. One of the most*

PHASE 3

RIGOR

*powerful strategies that I've seen to prevent this is to "mirror." We give students a task that is different than the teacher's model but requires the same thinking. Then after each thinking process that the teacher models, we ask the students to replicate that thinking with the new problem in front of them. This gives them an immediate opportunity to practice the thinking of the model. Mirroring has completely transformed the quality of our modeling.*

—Whitney Hurwitz, principal, Dallas, Texas

---

### KEY LEADERSHIP MOVES

| | |
|---|---|
| **Probing Questions** | • [Watch a model video] "What were the key actions the teacher took to make sure the students were listening?" |
| **Planning and Practice** | • This action is dependent on already developing the model and the key skills that students need to see. Once that is complete, identify the note-taking/ listening task that will get students thinking and not just copying. Then check for understanding. |
| **Real-Time Feedback** | • Verbal prompt: "Ms. Smith, before you begin your model, I want to make sure the students have their notebooks out to take notes: this is too valuable not to write anything down!" |

# RETEACHING 101:
# MODEL THE THINKING, NOT JUST THE PROCEDURE

 *Coaching Tips*

## Teacher Context

### Challenges

- The teacher's model is blurry, blending right in with everything else the teacher says (for example, delivered in a monotone or without emphasis on key points), making it difficult for students to know which parts are most important.
- The teacher tells the students about a process or procedure, but doesn't unpack the thinking and conceptual understanding that helped him or her arrive at that procedure.

### Action Step

Model the thinking, not just a procedure:

- Narrow the focus to the thinking students are struggling with.
- Model replicable thinking steps that students can follow.
- Model how to activate one's own content knowledge and skills that have been learned in previous lessons.
- Vary the think-aloud in tone and cadence from the normal "teacher" voice to highlight the thinking skills.

### Action Step Overview

When students struggle to master something the first time, an effective teacher will try a way of teaching it differently. Modeling their own thinking for the students—often called a think-aloud—is one of those core teaching and re-teaching strategies.

The difference between an effective and ineffective model can be subtle for a newer teacher. The first factor is as simple as the intonation of the teacher's voice. What makes a think-aloud effective is the change in the teacher's tone at key points: the teacher's "think-aloud" voice is different than his or her "teacher" voice, giving students a bright line as to when the thinking is being modeled. (If this sounds like the bright lines in pacing, you are absolutely right!) Watch the continuation of high school history teacher Art Worrell's model lesson:

Rewatch clip 28: Think-Aloud—Set Listening Task and watch clip 29: Model the Thinking (teaching clips)

Yet you cannot know where to vary your tone if you have not unpacked precisely what you want to model. The key is to narrow the focus of the model to what students struggled with when answering the question. If they misunderstood the writing prompt, don't show them how to write a body paragraph: show them how to unpack and understand the prompt itself. What follows are the moves that can make that possible.

*Quick Tip from a Coach—Create an Image to Accompany the Words*
*As a math coach, I would lead a PD on how to model any type of mathematical problem, going through a series of problems that are eighth-grade-level problems. One of the big takeaways was that most mathematical concepts can be articulated using a picture—sometimes this can do it better than our words can. So instead of just words, also include a picture or image to summarize the key ideas. When a teacher doesn't know the standard, sit down with it and try to draw a picture. As a teacher does so, it helps him or her understand the key components. Then you can plan the lesson.*
—Katie McNickle, math coach, Newark, New Jersey

---

### KEY LEADERSHIP MOVES

**Probing Questions**

- "Let's look over your exemplar for the independent practice. Talk aloud about how you would solve this problem/write this essay." [After the teacher answers] "What are students struggling to do to match the quality of your exemplar? Where is their thinking or understanding breaking down?"

- "Given those gaps, what is the most important thing for you to model for them? What error do you need to name for them, and how will you emphasize the key skills/strategies for them to use?"

- [Watch a model video] "What were the key actions the teacher took to model the skill effectively? What tone did he or she use in delivering the think-aloud? How do those differ from what you have been doing in class?"

| | |
|---|---|
| **Planning and Practice** | • None of the practice will be effective if you don't spend enough time unpacking the key errors that students are making. Start by going back to the key actions listed in the "Phase 3 Coaching Blueprint: Looking at Student Work" section:<br><br>  – Start with the exemplar: look to the teacher exemplar and top student exemplar to identify what students must do to be successful.<br><br>  – Identify the gaps: find the key ways in which students at varying achievement levels are struggling to create exemplar responses.<br><br>  – Plan the reteach (see upcoming section).<br><br>• With an effective analysis in place, the key is to design an effective think-aloud. Here are the keys to delivery:<br><br>  – Target the error: narrow the focus to the thinking students are struggling with.<br><br>  – Model replicable thinking steps that students can follow.<br><br>    For example, model how to activate one's own content knowledge and skills that have been learned in previous lessons. ("When I see the 'Era of Good Feelings,' I know we're talking about the 1800s and the time period of the Monroe Doctrine.")<br><br>  – Check for understanding.<br><br>  – Vary the tone and cadence of the think aloud/model to emphasize key points and be as clear as possible. |
| **Real-Time Feedback** | • Verbal prompt: "Ms. Smith, that was very interesting. Can you tell me again what you were thinking when you took that step? I want to make sure I understand."<br><br>• Model: do a think-aloud yourself. |

 Watch clip 30: Think-Aloud—Model the Thinking
(Key Leadership Move: Plan)

# RETEACHING 101:
# GIVE STUDENTS OPPORTUNITIES TO PRACTICE

 *Coaching Tips*

## Teacher Context

### Challenge

The teacher gives a clear model, but the students don't have the opportunity to try to replicate it after the model is done.

### Action Step

We Do and You Do: give students opportunities to practice with your guidance.

### Action Step Overview

Once a teacher models effectively and students have listened (see previous action steps), the key is to make sure that students have a chance to practice. Without that, the experience of watching an effective model will quickly be lost.

---

### KEY LEADERSHIP MOVES

| | |
|---|---|
| Probing Questions | • "What is the best way for students to practice after they have listened to your model?" |
| Planning and Practice | • Planning is the most important move here: you have to make sure the students' at-bat genuinely practices what the teacher just modeled. Be careful to create an activity in which students will practice the thinking involved and not just a procedure. |
| Real-Time Feedback | • Nonverbal: give a cue that it's time for students to practice. |

---

## Strategies for Coaching

### Reteaching 101—Model

| Action Step | When to Use It | Probing Questions | Scenarios to Practice | Cues for Real-Time Feedback |
|---|---|---|---|---|
| Give students a clear listening/note-taking task | Teacher gives a clear model, but the students don't have a task to do while listening to the model. | • [Watch a model video] "What were the key actions the teacher took to make sure the students were listening?" | • Focus on planning: include a note-taking task and a check for understanding. | Verbal prompt: "Ms. Smith, before you begin your model, I want to make sure the students have their notebooks out to take notes: this is too valuable not to write anything down!" |
| Model the thinking, not just the procedure | Teacher's model is confusing or unclear.<br><br>Teacher tells the students a procedure, but doesn't unpack the thinking behind it. | • "Let's look over your exemplar for the independent practice. Talk aloud how you would solve this problem/write this essay." [After teacher answers] "What are students struggling to do to match the quality of your exemplar. Where is their thinking or understanding breaking down?"<br><br>• "Given those gaps, what is the most important thing for you to model for them?"<br><br>• [Watch a model video] "What were the key actions the teacher took to model the skill effectively? How do those differ from what you have been doing in class?" | • Preparation: unpack the key errors that students are making. (Phase 3 Coaching Blueprint: 1. Start with the exemplar. 2. Identify the gaps. 3. Plan the reteach.)<br><br>• Plan: design an effective think-aloud. (1. Target the error. 2. Model replicable thinking. 3. Check for understanding.)<br><br>• Practice: vary tone and cadence of the think-aloud/model to emphasize key points and be as clear as possible. | Verbal prompt: "Ms. Smith, that was very interesting. Can you tell me again what you were thinking when you took that step? I want to make sure I understand."<br><br>Model: do a think-aloud yourself. |

| Action Step | When to Use It | Probing Questions | Scenarios to Practice | Cues for Real-Time Feedback |
|---|---|---|---|---|
| Give students opportunities to practice | Teacher gives a clear model, but students don't have the opportunity to try to replicate it after the model is done. | • "What is the best way for students to practice after they have listened to your model?" | • Plan: create an at-bat where students genuinely practice what teacher just modeled. Make sure they practice the thinking involved and not just a procedure. | Nonverbal: give a cue that it's time for students to practice. |

---

### Stop and Jot

What are the three top coaching ideas you plan to use to train your teachers in these Phase 3 Rigor skills? Jot them down here.

_____

_____

_____

## CONCLUSION

Congratulations! You have just taken a great step forward in your teacher's development. Completing Phase 3 is a major milestone: the teacher has not only mastered the most basic skills of teaching but gotten to the heart of teaching what students most need to learn. What comes next starts to enter the terrain of a truly strong teacher. Onward!

Phase 4

# The Power of Discourse

As legend has it, the original eureka moment took place in a very private space: the bathtub of the renowned mathematician Archimedes. Sinking into the bath after a long day of work, Archimedes thought he was about to take a break from the problems that had been puzzling him. Instead, he noticed the way the water rose when he sank into the tub, and instead of relaxing, he was struck by inspiration. Supposedly, Archimedes was so excited by his discovery that he cried "Eureka," the Greek for "I have found it!" It was in this way that Archimedes became the first to articulate the law of motion that explains why some objects float in water and others sink.

This story is so ingrained in our culture that we often describe the moment when inspiration strikes as a eureka moment. We have a tendency to think of that moment when inspiration strikes as an individual experience, forged by solitude and deep thinking.

Yet modern research has begun to debunk this theory of creativity. A few of the thinkers leading the way are Kevin Dunbar and Steven Johnson, the latter the author of *Where Good Ideas Come From: The Natural History of Innovation*. In Johnson's study of people who are considered great innovators—from Enlightenment thinkers to researchers in modern-day science laboratories—he discovered that the real innovations happened when groups of people came together, sharing their ideas and their errors, and putting previous ideas together in new ways. Even though one person was often credited for the innovation, the network of people and ideas made the difference. In Johnson's own words, "Innovation didn't happen alone at the lab in front of the microscope, but at the conference table during the weekly lab meeting."[1] In other words, eureka moments are not "I have found it!" but "*We* have found it!"

Nowhere does this play out more in the classroom than in class discussion and small-group work. Now that a teacher has established clear classroom routines and procedures, and processes for managing independent practice and teacher-centered parts of the lesson, you can start to work on some of the real "magic" of great instruction: high-quality intellectual discussions during which students grapple with difficult tasks.

> ## Core Idea
>
> Student thinking grows sharper on the whetstone
> of peer-to-peer discourse than it ever could in isolation.

How do you guide your teacher to create an environment where class discussion isn't off-track banter but intellectual discourse? The next steps tell you how.

# PHASE 4 COACHING BLUEPRINT: RESPOND TO IN-THE-MOMENT DATA

The coaching blueprint for Phase 4 builds perfectly on the blueprint from Phase 3. Where Phase 3 focuses on weekly data meetings—looking at student work once the class has finished—Phase 4 focuses on using data collected in the moment of class to drive learning. A masterful coach becomes a coparticipant in analyzing student learning with the teacher while observing. We'll look at two ways a leader can accomplish this: monitoring the learning in the classroom and targeting real-time feedback toward rigor.

## Monitor for Learning While Observing

After a certain point, you can't give a teacher feedback for rigor unless you're making in-the-moment observations about what his or her students are learning. Just like the teacher, you shift your focus from checking whether students are behaving well to whether they're mastering the material. In the beginning of this video (clip 31), Nikki Bridges shows what becomes possible when you make that leap. Her teacher Sarah Engle is working with her students on the skill of adding tens and ones. Both leader and teacher notice and discuss that the students are either misapplying the tens and ones strategy or not using the strategy at all. After discussing with Nikki, Sarah decides she is going to try to facilitate the discussion using Show Call, putting up the correct student work from a student named Camiah and asking students to describe "what Camiah did." When deeper questioning becomes necessary, Nikki jumps in.

 Watch clip 31: Strategic Prompting—Call on Students Based on Their Learning Needs (Key Leadership Move: Real-Time Feedback)

For reference, here's the questioning sequence Nikki follows as she addresses the class:

- Asks Camiah, who has the right answer: "What did you do?"

- Asks Aniyah, a top-scoring student: "She did what first?"

- Asks Jehavani, a low-scoring student: "What sum did she get when she added the tens?"

- Asks Mohammed, a high-scoring student: "What sum did she get when she added ones?"

- Turn and Talk: "What is the rule we can use?"

- Asks Aaliyah, one of the highest-achieving students in the class, to articulate the process after the Turn and Talk.

As you can see, Nikki has shifted the entire focus of her monitoring from watching the teacher to observing the students' learning. Her biggest observation is looking directly at student work during independent practice. Here we come to a very important idea: to identify the right action step for rigor, you need to see the learning for yourself.

> ## Core Idea
>
> To identify the right action step for rigor,
> you need to see the learning for yourself.

In Phase 4, your teachers have the tools: they just need to know when and how to use them. Your feedback won't have the same impact without your looking over students' shoulders in the moment to see their work.

This action is what enables Nikki to consult with the teacher and hear what reteaching plan she has to address student error. It will also allow her to intervene a bit later in class. For that, let's turn to real-time feedback for rigor.

## Give Real-Time Feedback for Rigor

It's when Nikki begins giving real-time feedback around what she has just observed that we truly begin to see the power of what she and the teacher just accomplished during monitoring. Rewatch clip 31 to see the impact that came when she was able to respond to student data.

 Rewatch clip 31: Strategic Prompting—Call on Students Based on Their Learning Needs (Key Leadership Move: Real-Time Feedback)

Utterly seamlessly, Nikki becomes a part of the conversation that gets the students to a higher level of understanding. If she had waited to debrief what she saw until after the lesson, the students would not have unpacked their confusion, and the teacher wouldn't have gotten a clear sense of what to do next time. Here we see the art of real-time feedback for rigor: the students just see Nikki as a fellow teacher in the room. By making her feedback immediate, Nikki increases student learning immediately, and the teacher learns something irreplaceable about leading a rigorous discussion. The students never notice a change in the way the class is being run; they simply have two different adults asking them questions instead of just their teacher.

What makes Nikki's feedback effective is not just that she intervened; it is *how* she intervened. If you closely rewatch her questioning, she has an end goal in mind, and it's not a procedure. She wants students to understand the deeper concept beneath the procedure: in this case, the value of grouping tens and ones separately before adding them together. This is driving home base-ten understanding—a critical foundation for later math. In short, Nikki focused on the longer-term foundational understanding, not just the quick fix.

> ## Core Idea
> Lock in long-term learning, not short-term shortcuts.
> Root your actions in mastering the *deeper understanding*,
> not just the process.

What we see here is that real-time feedback doesn't have to decline when teachers get better; in fact, you can become even more of a colleague with them in the work. If you participate to increase rigor, teachers will be excited to have you as a companion on the journey. And there is no better way to practice student discourse than doing so in the moment. Student discussion is a fluid phenomenon, and it's difficult to simulate as effectively in a practice session. By giving the teacher as much immediate feedback around this as possible, you increase the rate of progress exponentially—and with it, the number of high-quality conversations that will contribute to student learning over the course of the year.

## Teaching Skills Overview
In Phase 4, management issues transition to the teacher's periphery. The only necessary steps now are developing quality routines for class discussion that will allow the teacher to focus more on the rigor: namely, a quality pace of questioning and the routines of small-group work.

The rigor action steps move completely into leading quality discourse—much harder than it seems! Teachers will learn to leverage their monitoring of student work to target the discussion on what will most push forward the learning, and then they will learn universal prompts to keep the conversation going. These are then solidified even further by developing habits of discussion in the students so that they can take even more control of the quality and rigor of the discourse.

This section of the Get Better Faster Scope and Sequence shows the skills that teachers will develop during Phase 4.

**Phase 4 Action Steps Sequence**

| Management Trajectory | Rigor Trajectory |
|---|---|
| **Set Routines for Discourse** | **Lead Student Discourse 101** |
| **12. Engaged Small-Group Work:** Maximize the learning for every student during small-group work | **9. Reteaching 201—Guided Discourse:** Let students unpack their own errors & build a solution |
| • Deliver explicit step-by-step instructions for group work: | • Show Call: post student work (either an exemplar or incorrect response) & ask students to identify why that answer is correct/incorrect. |
| – Make the group tasks visible/easily observable (e.g., a handout to fill in, notes to take, product to build, etc.). | • Stamp the understanding: |
| – Create a role for every person (with each group no larger than the number of roles needed to accomplish the tasks at hand). | – "What are the keys to remember when solving problems like these?" or "Can someone give me a rule?" (Students use their own words.) |
| – Give timed instructions, with benchmarks for where the group should be after each time window. | • Give them at-bats: give students opportunities to practice with your guidance. |
| • Monitor the visual evidence of group progress: | **10. Universal Prompts:** Push the thinking back on the students through universal prompts that could be used at any point |
| – Check in on each group every 5–10 minutes to monitor progress. | • Provide wait time after posing challenging questions. |

| Management Trajectory | Rigor Trajectory |
|---|---|
| • Verbally enforce individual & group accountability:<br>  – "You are five minutes behind; get on track."<br>  – "Brandon: focus." | • Precall: let a student who needs more time know you're calling on him/her next.<br>• Roll back the answer: repeat the wrong answer back to the student. (Give the student time to think and you time to build a plan!)<br>• Ask universal prompts to push the student to elaborate:<br>  – "Tell me more."<br>  – "What makes you think that?"<br>  – "How do you know?"<br>  – "Why is that important?"<br>• Close the loop: after correcting their error, go back to students with wrong answers to have them revise their answers.<br>**11. Habits of Discussion:** Teach and model for students the habits that strengthen class conversation<br>• Keep neutral/manage your tell: don't reveal the right/wrong answer through your reaction to the student response.<br>• Agree and build off: "I agree with _____, and I'd like to add . . ."<br>• Disagree respectfully: "While I agree with [this part of your argument], I disagree with _____. I would argue . . ." |

# PHASE 4 MANAGEMENT—SET ROUTINES FOR DISCOURSE

## Quick Reference Guide

| If your teacher is struggling to . . . | Jump to . . . |
|---|---|
| **Engaged Small-Group Work** | |
| Set clear guidelines for group work | Create explicit instructions for group work |
| Keep student groups on task despite clear instructions | Monitor progress and verbally enforce group accountability |

## Phase 4 Action Steps Sequence

| Management Trajectory | Rigor Trajectory |
|---|---|
| **Set Routines for Discourse** | **Lead Student Discourse 101** |
| 12. **Engaged Small-Group Work:** Maximize the learning for every student during small-group work <br><br> • Deliver explicit step-by-step instructions for group work: <br><br> – Make the group tasks visible/easily observable (e.g., a handout to fill in, notes to take, product to build, etc.). <br><br> – Create a role for every person (with each group no larger than the number of roles needed to accomplish the tasks at hand). <br><br> – Give timed instructions, with benchmarks for where the group should be after each time window. <br><br> • Monitor the visual evidence of group progress: <br><br> – Check in on each group every 5–10 minutes to monitor progress. | 9. **Reteaching 201—Guided Discourse:** Let students unpack their own errors & build a solution <br><br> • Show Call: post student work (either an exemplar or incorrect response) & ask students to identify why that answer is correct/incorrect. <br><br> • Stamp the understanding: <br><br> – "What are the keys to remember when solving problems like these?" or "Can someone give me a rule?" (Students use their own words.) <br><br> • Give them at-bats: give students opportunities to practice with your guidance. <br><br> 10. **Universal Prompts:** Push the thinking back on the students through universal prompts that could be used at any point <br><br> • Provide wait time after posing challenging questions. |

| Management Trajectory | Rigor Trajectory |
|---|---|
| • Verbally enforce individual & group accountability:<br>  – "You are five minutes behind; get on track."<br>  – "Brandon: focus." | • Precall: let a student who needs more time know you're calling on him/her next.<br>• Roll back the answer: repeat the wrong answer back to the student. (Give the student time to think and you time to build a plan!)<br>• Ask universal prompts to push the student to elaborate:<br>  – "Tell me more."<br>  – "What makes you think that?"<br>  – "How do you know?"<br>  – "Why is that important?"<br>• Close the loop: after correcting their error, go back to students with wrong answers to have them revise their answers.<br>11. **Habits of Discussion:** Teach and model for students the habits that strengthen class conversation<br>  • Keep neutral/manage your tell: don't reveal the right/wrong answer through your reaction to the student response.<br>  • Agree and build off: "I agree with ____, and I'd like to add . . ."<br>  • Disagree respectfully: "While I agree with [this part of your argument], I disagree with ____. I would argue . . ." |

## Introduction to Phase 4 Management Skills: Set Routines for Discourse

Managing small-group work and whole-class discussion can be challenging even for the most experienced teacher. The very nature of group work implies that students will be working simultaneously on all sorts of different projects. When this work is not managed well, the outcomes are mixed. Certain groups will work very well together and produce high-quality work; other groups will be largely off task, or one team member will carry the weight of all the others. The same can happen in whole-class discussion: a few students are actively learning, and the rest are passively observing or totally checked out. Thus whole-class discussions can create great learning experiences for some at the expense of wasted learning time for the rest.

> ### Core Idea
>
> Great small-group work must be time well spent for *all* students—not active learning time for a few and wasted learning time for the rest.

The heart of maximizing the learning time is to design solid routines that establish clear expectations for each individual so that everyone benefits from the networking of ideas. When we build these routines, the collective eureka moments have every possible second to sprout, take root, and blossom.

## Engaged Small-Group Work

> ### Teacher Professional Development Goal
>
> **Engaged Small-Group Work:** Maximize the learning for every student during small-group work.

The power of small-group work is similar to that of Turn and Talks: more students are able to directly engage in learning at the same time than in a whole-class discussion. The challenge? Creating routines that make small-group work time productive. Small-group work is the most difficult type of classroom activity to manage because of how challenging it is to move from group to group and discover whether each discussion is going well—more difficult than either monitoring individual students or directing a whole-class discussion.

Here are two difficulties that many teachers encounter along the way to making the most of small-group work:

- Groups are off task because they're confused about what to do or because not every student has something to do.

- Some groups are off task despite clear instructions.

# ENGAGED SMALL-GROUP WORK: DELIVER EXPLICIT INSTRUCTIONS

 *Coaching Tips*

## Teacher Context

### Challenge

Groups are off task because they're confused about what to do or because not every student has something to do.

### Action Step

Create and deliver explicit step-by-step instructions for group work:

- Make the group tasks visible and easily observable (a handout to fill in, notes to take, product to build, and the like).
- Create a role for every person (with each group no larger than the number of roles needed to accomplish the tasks at hand).
- Give timed instructions, with benchmarks for where the group should be after each time window.

### Action Step Overview

When students split off into small-group work, what they should be doing needs to be clearer than ever, so that they both can and will do it even without constant teacher supervision (and so that the teacher can see the trouble quickly if they don't). The best way to ensure this is through explicit step-by-step instructions for group work: they will make it easier for students to follow them and for the teacher to monitor whether or not the students are on track.

| | KEY LEADERSHIP MOVES |
|---|---|
| **Probing Questions** | • "What do you want students doing during group work? What will they have produced if they are successful?" |
| | • "How many student roles do you need in order for your students to complete their group work task? Based on that, what size should the groups be?" |
| | • "What will be the hardest part to enforce? What visual evidence can you create to make it easier for you to make sure they're on track?" |
| **Planning and Practice** | • Guide the teacher through the process of scripting out explicit directions for group work. |
| | • Think particularly about the visual evidence. For example, if the students are discussing a rich part of the text to understand characterization, have them chart their thoughts on the whiteboard/blackboard. If they do that, the teacher can quickly scan the room and see where each group is in its work. It creates "visual" accountability, which is much more effective than if they only talk. |
| | • Have the teacher practice delivery. |
| **Real-Time Feedback** | • Model: model delivering explicit small-group work instructions. |

# ENGAGED SMALL-GROUP WORK: MONITOR GROUP PROGRESS AND VERBALLY ENFORCE ACCOUNTABILITY

 *Coaching Tips*

## Teacher Context

### Challenge
Some groups are off task despite clear instructions.

### Action Step
- Monitor the visual evidence of group progress:
  - Check in on each group every five to ten minutes to monitor progress.
- Verbally enforce individual and group accountability:
  - "You are five minutes behind; get on track."
  - "Brandon: focus."

### Action Step Overview
Sometimes small groups of students will go off task despite clear instructions. The first step is to have the radar to notice it: that is accomplished by the visual evidence in the previous action step. The second step is to actually monitor that evidence and pull groups/ students back on track. The key in coaching is to develop in the teacher the habit of scanning all groups every five minutes (not getting stuck too long in helping one group) and to have a quick response ready to reset or individually correct an off-task group or student.

*Quick Tip from a Coach—"You Should Now Be on This Question"*
*How to manage small-group work is something we have to coach our teachers on a lot. When you just say, "Do the guided practice with your partner" and leave students to pace themselves, you walk around a bit later to discover they're only on number one. Instead, think about how many questions you want them to do, and chunk the guided practice into smaller parts. When you circulate, say, "You should now be on this question. If you're not there yet, pick up the pace."*

*—Whitney Hurwitz, principal, Dallas, Texas*

## KEY LEADERSHIP MOVES

**Probing Questions**

- "Despite your quality instructions, you had a few groups who weren't on task today. Did you notice when they started to get off track?"
- "Looking back on your previously learned action steps, what sort of small-group reset or individual correction could you deliver to get the group/individual back on track?"
- "In which groups were some students shouldering more of the work? What steps can you take to remedy this?"

**Planning and Practice**

- The practice for this is really about incorporating previously learned skills. From Phase 2, the teacher can incorporate monitoring effectively (Teacher Radar and aggressive monitoring, but this time for group work), and from Phases 2 and 3, he or she can incorporate a whole-class reset (but this time for just a small group) or individual student corrections.
- For monitoring, plan out exactly what the teacher will want to see—on chart paper, in student notebooks, and/or as work product—at each stage of the class period. That will enable the teacher to monitor.
- For resetting, script out the language for an effective reset or individual correction. The teacher is likely to have already mastered this and just needs to be prompted to utilize those skills for small-group work. Incorporate all the keys from those action steps:
- Practice: monitor group work, and practice individual student corrections and whole-class reset.

**Real-Time Feedback**

- Nonverbal or whisper prompt: identify the off-task groups.

## Engaged Small-Group Work

| Action Step | When to Use It | Probing Questions | Scenarios to Practice | Cues for Real-Time Feedback |
|---|---|---|---|---|
| **Deliver explicit instructions for group work** | Groups are off task because they're confused about what to do or because not every student has something to do. | • "What do you want students doing during group work? What will they have produced if they are successful?"<br><br>• "How many student roles do you need in order for your students to complete their group work task? Based on that, what size should the groups be?"<br><br>• "What will be the hardest part to enforce? What visual evidence can you create to make it easier for you to make sure they're on track?" | • Planning: script out explicit directions for group work.<br><br>• Focus on visual evidence of on-task behavior to make group work easier to monitor (e.g., students chart their thoughts on whiteboards).<br><br>• Practice delivery. | Model: model delivering explicit small-group work instructions. |
| **Monitor group progress and verbally enforce accountability** | Some groups are off task despite clear instructions. | • "Despite your quality instructions, you had a few groups who weren't on task today. Did you notice when they started to get off track?"<br><br>• "Looking back on your previously learned action steps, what sort of small-group reset or individual correction could you deliver to get the group/individual back on track?"<br><br>• "In which groups were some students shouldering more of the work? What steps can you take to remedy this?" | • Plan out what teacher will want to see on chart paper/student notebooks during group work.<br><br>• For resetting, script out the language for an effective reset or individual correction. Incorporate all the keys from previous action steps.<br><br>• Practice: monitor group work, and practice individual student corrections and whole-class reset. | Nonverbal or whisper prompt: ID the off-task groups. |

## Stop and Jot

What are the three top coaching ideas you plan to use to train your teachers in these Phase 4 Management skills? Jot them down here.

_____

_____

_____

# PHASE 4 RIGOR—LEAD STUDENT DISCOURSE 101

## Quick Reference Guide

| If your teacher is struggling to . . . | Jump to . . . |
|---|---|
| **Reteaching 201—Guided Discourse** ||
| Focus class discussion on students' common misconceptions | Show Call |
| Ensure that students know what to do differently once they recognize their error | Stamp the understanding and give them at-bats |
| **Universal Prompts** ||
| Give students sufficient time to respond after a challenging question | Wait time, precall, roll back |
| Identify why a student got an answer wrong | Ask universal prompts |
| Get the student who originally gave an incorrect answer to deliver the correct answer | Close the loop |
| **Habits of Discussion** ||
| Avoid revealing whether student responses are correct before the students can figure it out on their own | Keep neutral |
| Get students to deliver answers that are connected to each other even when they agree | Agree and build off |
| Get students to disagree with their peers in a respectful manner | Disagree respectfully |

## Phase 4 Action Steps Sequence

| Management Trajectory | Rigor Trajectory |
|---|---|
| **Set Routines for Discourse** | **Lead Student Discourse 101** |
| 12. **Engaged Small-Group Work:** Maximize the learning for every student during small-group work | 9. **Reteaching 201—Guided Discourse:** Let students unpack their own errors & build a solution |
| • Deliver explicit step-by-step instructions for group work: | • Show Call: post student work (either an exemplar or incorrect response) & ask students to identify why that answer is correct/incorrect. |
| – Make the group tasks visible/easily observable (e.g., a handout to fill in, notes to take, product to build, etc.). | • Stamp the understanding: |
| – Create a role for every person (with each group no larger than the number of roles needed to accomplish the tasks at hand). | – "What are the keys to remember when solving problems like these?" or "Can someone give me a rule?" (Students use their own words.) |
| | • Give them at-bats: give students opportunities to practice with your guidance. |
| – Give timed instructions, with benchmarks for where the group should be after each time window. | 10. **Universal Prompts:** Push the thinking back on the students through universal prompts that could be used at any point |
| • Monitor the visual evidence of group progress: | • Provide wait time after posing challenging questions. |
| – Check in on each group every 5–10 minutes to monitor progress. | • Precall: let a student who needs more time know you're calling on him/her next. |
| • Verbally enforce individual & group accountability: | • Roll back the answer: repeat the wrong answer back to the student. (Give the student time to think and you time to build a plan!) |
| – "You are five minutes behind; get on track." | • Ask universal prompts to push the student to elaborate: |
| – "Brandon: focus." | – "Tell me more." |
| | – "What makes you think that?" |
| | – "How do you know?" |
| | – "Why is that important?" |
| | • Close the loop: after correcting their error, go back to students with wrong answers to have them revise their answers. |
| | 11. **Habits of Discussion:** Teach and model for students the habits that strengthen class conversation |
| | • Keep neutral/manage your tell: don't reveal the right/wrong answer through your reaction to the student response. |
| | • Agree and build off: "I agree with ____, and I'd like to add . . ." |
| | • Disagree respectfully: "While I agree with [this part of your argument], I disagree with ____. I would argue . . ." |

## Introduction to Phase 4 Rigor Skills: Lead Student Discourse 101

During every presidential election cycle in the United States, we are able to watch a large number of presidential debates—from the primaries all the way up to the days before the election. Those debates give us the opportunity to see how various candidates answer important questions about what they would do if elected president.

What most of us value about the debate format is the ability to see candidates spar with each other, critiquing the other's position and attempting to offer a better alternative. The better the debater, the more deftly he or she turns the debate in his or her favor.

This sort of rigorous discourse not only is beneficial to watch as an observer but also sharpens the intellect of the debater. We have to think harder to learn about the world in this way, putting our own opinions to the test by considering other points of view. We don't learn from one-sided explanations of the barest facts at hand: we learn from discourse.

An often overlooked component of a presidential debate is the role of the moderator. With a poor moderator, the debaters engage in too much unnecessary back-and-forth, and the debate quality sinks. When a quality moderator manages a debate, however, you rarely notice the adept way in which he or she interrupts the speakers, calls on others, and pushes the debate forward by asking critical questions at key times. When a debate goes well, you don't notice the moderator: you notice the debate.

Quality student discourse is similar. A class discussion can become so strong that you might be tempted to think it happened by circumstance, but it didn't. Without effective moderation by the teacher, students might have talked at a very superficial level, not used effective evidence, or rarely pushed each other on certain opinions. A skilled facilitator will elevate the rigor of the discourse in ways that might not even be noticed by the untrained eye. That is the goal of Phase 4 Rigor: learn the skills to increase the quality of the discourse.

---

### Core Idea

Change the way students talk, and you change the way they think.
The quality of student discourse is measured by the caliber of what
students—not teachers—say.

---

In Phase 4 Rigor, teachers take on the task of being a skilled moderator of student discourse. By starting our students on discourse at a young age, we give them the lifelong ability to question, to listen, and to form their own images of the world with a balance of thoughtfulness and independence.

## Reteaching 201—Guided Discourse

> ### Teacher Professional Development Goal
>
> **Reteaching 201—Guided Discourse:** Let students unpack their own errors and build a solution.

If Reteaching 101 focused on the first go-to strategy for reteaching (modeling), Reteaching 201 is a notable step forward. Here is a beautiful moment when a teacher starts to leverage the students' own expertise to help build understanding in the class. This is incredibly empowering for the teacher and students alike. The easiest entry into this is Show Call—showing individual student work to the rest of the class and using it to drive discussion. It is a natural next step after aggressive monitoring: showing targeted student work enables the student discussion to be focused on remediating error and deepening understanding. This is coupled with stamping that understanding and giving students a chance to practice. The result is discussion and learning in which students guide each other at an unprecedented level over particular hurdles in the learning process.

Here are the challenges that can be mitigated by guided discourse:

- Many students are struggling to identify the error in their understanding.

- Students are able to produce limited answers to questions, but struggle to generate an exemplar response.

- The teacher is trying to use student work, but struggles to lead discussion around it.

- Students can figure out their error, but they do not articulate clearly what they have to do to prevent those errors in the future.

- Students are not given time to practice their new understanding after identifying the error or learning something new.

# GUIDED DISCOURSE: SHOW CALL

 Coaching Tips

## Teacher Context

### Challenges
- Many students are struggling to identify the error in their understanding.
- Students are able to produce limited answers to questions, but struggle to generate an exemplar response.
- The teacher is trying to use student work, but struggles to lead discussion around it.

### Action Step
- Show Call: post student work (either an exemplar or incorrect response) and ask students to identify why that answer is correct/incorrect.

### Action Step Overview
The heart of using student work is to allow students to diagnose their own errors or the effective strategies their peers are using, in order to help their own practice. There are two keys to Show Call, aptly divided by the name itself: the "Show" and the "Call." "Show" is picking the right piece of student work to show to the class (it all depends on your focus). "Call" is asking the right questions and calling on the appropriate student to start the conversation. Clip 32 is an example from principal and teacher Andrew Shaefer. He is working with fourth-grade students to understand the importance of the denominator in writing a fraction. Students are working with the following image of a flag:

They are asked the question: "What fraction of the flag is each color?" In their independent practice, about half of the students say "1/3," and the other half say "1." Watch how Andrew uses Show Call to allow the students to do the thinking in unpacking the error:

 Watch clip 32: Guided Discourse—Show Call (Math) (teaching clip)

The act of letting the students see correct and incorrect answers gave them the opportunity to identify the error themselves. If you think it works only for math, here is an example in literacy, where students are trying to get better at citing strong evidence to justify their inference:

 Watch clip 33: Guided Discourse—Show Call (Literacy) (teaching clip)

*Quick Tip from a Coach—Make Student Work Visible*
*The three action steps I give my teachers most often are to place student work on the board/document camera so it's visible to all students, to ask students what they think, and to name the skill. It has hugely moved the needle with regard to rigor. I stress that they should have students comment on Show Call work "as a good reader." "What did so-and-so do as a good reader? What does so-and-so need to do as a good reader?"*

—Andrea Palmer Kleinbard, coach, Brooklyn, New York

| KEY LEADERSHIP MOVES | |
|---|---|
| **Probing Questions** | • [Watch video of Show Call] "What was the value of the teacher showing a piece of student work to jump-start the conversation? How did the teacher do this effectively?"<br><br>• "What common errors are your students making when solving these problems/completing these types of tasks?"<br><br>• "When looking at student work, what do they need to see more: an exemplar response from their peer, or the error that they are making?"<br><br>• "What would an ideal answer from a student look like?" |

| | |
|---|---|
| **Planning and Practice** | • Planning: follow the weekly data meeting protocol (see Phase 3 Coaching Blueprint). |
| | • Planning: identify the best work samples to show-call: look at Exit Tickets and select a strong student exemplar and a representative incorrect/incomplete student response that is indicative of an error that many students are making. |
| | • Script out the steps to Show Call: (1) post the work (either exemplar, incorrect answer, or both); (2) Turn and Talk: ask students to evaluate; (3) lead whole-class discussion: name the error and the best practice. |
| | • Script and rehearse the language the teacher will use: |
| |   – "As I looked at your work, I noticed the following strategy [show-call the work]. What did [student] do to solve the problem? Why do you think she used this strategy?" |
| **Real-Time Feedback** | • Whisper prompt: during independent practice, identify one or more student work samples that would be valuable for the teacher to use during Show Call. Ask the teacher which ones he or she would show-call; if the teacher makes a weak choice, show him or her the ones you selected and briefly explain why. |

# GUIDED DISCOURSE: STAMP THE UNDERSTANDING AND GIVE THEM AT-BATS

 Coaching Tips

## Teacher Context

### Challenges
- Students can figure out their error, but they do not articulate clearly what they have to do to prevent those errors in the future.
- Students are not given time to practice their new understanding after identifying the error or learning something new.

### Action Step
- Stamp the understanding:
  - "What are the keys to remember when solving problems like these?" or "Can someone give me a rule?" (Students use their own words.)
- Give them at-bats: give students opportunities to practice with your guidance.

### Action Step Overview
Once you have picked appropriate student work and begun the discourse, the key is to nail down the key understanding you want to pull from the students: we call that "stamping." After that is done, give them time to practice: it's that simple!

## KEY LEADERSHIP MOVES

**Probing Questions**

- "Once the students identify the error or strategies in the exemplar, what is the key understanding you want them to stamp? What would the ideal answer look like?"
- "What would be the best form of practice for the students to get a chance to master this new strategy/understanding?"

**Planning and Practice**

- For stamping the understanding, the most important thing to do is to articulate exactly what the teacher will look for. (Start from the exemplar.) Then simply plan for the teacher to write down that key understanding on the board so that students can see it.
- Giving students more at-bats is simply accomplished in the lesson planning process. Make sure there is enough time in the lesson to practice.

**Real-Time Feedback**

- Model: if the teacher doesn't stamp the understanding, intervene to make sure students grasp the concept.
- Nonverbal: give a cue that it's time for students to practice.

Strategies for Coaching

## Reteaching 201—Guided Discourse

| Action Step | When to Use It | Probing Questions | Scenarios to Practice | Cues for Real-Time Feedback |
|---|---|---|---|---|
| Show Call | Many students are struggling to identify the error in their understanding. The teacher is trying to use student work, but struggles to lead discussion around it. | • [Watch video of Show Call] "What was the value of the teacher showing a piece of student work to jump-start the conversation? How did the teacher do this effectively?"<br><br>• "What common errors are your students making when solving these problems/ completing these types of tasks?"<br><br>• "When looking at student work, what do they need to see more: an exemplar response from their peer, or the error that they are making?"<br><br>• "What would an ideal answer from a student look like?" | • Planning: look at Exit Tickets and select a strong student exemplar and a representative incorrect/ incomplete student response that is indicative of an error that many students are making.<br><br>• Script out the steps: (1) post the work (either exemplar, incorrect answer, or both); (2) Turn & Talk: ask students to evaluate; (3) as a whole class: name the error and the best practice.<br><br>• Practice: rehearse the script. Focus on economy of language. | Whisper prompt: during independent practice, identify one or more student work samples that would be valuable for teacher to use during Show Call. Ask teacher which ones he/she would show-call; if teacher makes a weak choice, show him/her the ones you selected and briefly explain why. |
| Stamp the under-standing and give them at-bats | Students can figure out their error, but they do not articulate clearly what they have to do to prevent those errors in the future and don't have time to practice. | • "Once the students identify the error or strategies in the exemplar, what is the key understand-ing you want them to stamp? What would the ideal answer look like?"<br><br>• "What would be the best form of practice for the students to get a chance to master this new strategy/ understanding?" | • Practice stamping the understand-ing: articulate exactly what the teacher will look for in student answers. Write down that key understanding on the board.<br><br>• Plan: incorporate into lesson plan more at-bats to practice the new skill. | Model: if teacher doesn't stamp the understanding, intervene to make sure students grasp the concept.<br><br>Nonverbal: give cue that it's time for students to practice. |

## Universal Prompts

> ### Teacher Professional Development Goal
>
> **Universal Prompts:** Push the thinking back on the students through universal prompts that could be used at any point.

In any society, there are certain social graces that its citizens know so automatically that they become collective habits. Saying "please" and "thank you," shaking hands, waiting to begin a meal until everyone has been served—we repeat all of these actions without a second thought. By having these habits, we can focus more on the quality of the interaction and conversation and don't need to spend mental energy on how to behave. (If you have ever been in a setting where you don't know the proper etiquette, think about how difficult it was to track the conversation because of simply trying not to mess up!)

Universal prompts are the "please" and "thank you" of facilitating quality discourse. They are habits teachers can build to give them time to diagnose what is going on in the conversation. After the students master these habits, the teacher can move on to more sophisticated prompting (see the discussion of strategic prompting in the Stretch It section). Yet it's nothing short of miraculous how far the most basic prompts can take you, and you'll keep using them no matter how far you advance. The prompts described in this section are powerful in any subject area, and continue to be so even for teachers who are also able to prompt much more specifically within their particular subject.

Universal prompts address the following challenges during class discussion:

- After asking a challenging question, the teacher moves on too quickly, not giving a student enough time to answer the question.

- The teacher doesn't know why a student got an answer wrong.

- After a student gives an incorrect answer, the teacher moves on to a different student without first correcting the original student's error.

# UNIVERSAL PROMPTS: PROVIDE WAIT TIME, PRECALL, ROLL BACK

 *Coaching Tips*

## Teacher Context

**Challenge**

After asking a challenging question, the teacher moves on too quickly, not giving a student enough time to answer the question.

**Action Step**

- Provide wait time after posing challenging questions.
- Precall: let a student who needs more time know you're calling him or her next.
  - Example: "There are two questions on the board. Jared's going to answer the first question. Alyssa, I'm coming to you with the second one, so get ready!"
- Roll back the answer: repeat the wrong answer back to the student. (Give the student time to think and you time to build a plan!)
  - Example: "You said the square root of 16 is 5." (Give time to see if student can recognize his or her own error.)

**Action Step Overview**

Sometimes the most powerful prompt is the nonprompt: just giving someone time to think. Like adults, students need time to get their thoughts in order before tackling particularly challenging problems. Each of the three action step strategies does just that: ensure that students have enough time to think. Wait time is the simplest (just wait!). Precall—giving students notice that you're going to call on them—is very helpful for students who just need a little extra processing time. Rolling back—repeating a student's response in a neutral tone of voice—is equal parts power and simplicity. It allows the teacher, the student who just spoke, and every other child in the room to assess the answer and collect their thoughts before pushing the discussion forward. (It won't solve every problem, but it's a start. Subsequent action steps in this phase will close the gap.) The key is to plan how to use these three strategies together.

*Quick Tip from a Coach—Use "Warm Call" with Wait Time*
*One of my teachers would often avoid wait time with scholars who she knew struggled academically—particularly scholars with IEPs. Over time in her class,*

*she had unwittingly taught them that if after asking a question, they would just be silent and not respond, she would rush in to fill the air with her own answer. We practiced in my office asking a question and not rushing in with the answer. We practiced reframing the question positively, stating that she knew the student could do it and asking the question again. We varied with giving the whole class a Turn and Talk and then going to the student to help them prepare their answer (warm call) and telling the class to write down some ideas to prep the student to answer. When we practiced, I assumed the role of a student whom we both knew and loved and who was also the master of silently avoiding the work. There was a moment when the teacher caught herself with me rushing in to give the answer, and she realized what she was doing. After that, the teacher was ready when a student was avoiding answering to hold them accountable and set the student up to be successful when they answered.*

—Rebecca Utton, principal manager, Denver, Colorado

| | KEY LEADERSHIP MOVES |
|---|---|
| **Probing Questions** | • "What are the possible reasons a student might not be able to answer a question you ask on the spot—beyond just not knowing the answer"? |
| | • [Watch a video or model for the teacher] "What actions did the teacher take? Why were these beneficial?" |
| | • "What is the purpose of repeating the student's answer back to him or her? Why not just correct the error?" |
| | • "Which students need more time than others to formulate an answer? Which ones would benefit from a precall to give them enough thinking time?" |
| **Planning and Practice** | • Integrate your practice of all three skills. |
| | • To practice wait time: have the teacher identify higher-order questions that might require more think time. Script concise directions that the teacher will narrate during wait time. ("This answer requires strong evidence. Everyone can be looking as we wait.") |
| | • To practice precall: have the teacher identify the students who would benefit from a precall—normally, it's not every student. Pick the questions in the lesson plan that would be ideal to ask those students during the discussion, and script the language the teacher will use to precall the student. Have the teacher practice the precall questions and then the precall itself, so that the teacher gets a feel for incorporating precalls into his or her questioning sequence. |

- To practice rollback: have the teacher role-play a questioning sequence from an upcoming lesson, with you playing the student. Provide answers to which the teacher could helpfully respond by rolling back, and have him or her continue the lesson after rolling back as well.

**Real-Time Feedback**
- Nonverbal: create and use a cue for wait time (for example, hold up a hand as a stop sign).
- Intervene: roll back the answer to the original student, modeling for the teacher.

 Watch clip 34: Prompting: Universal (Roll Back) and Strategic (Provide a Resource) (Key Leadership Move: Plan)

# UNIVERSAL PROMPTS:
# ASK UNIVERSAL PROMPTS TO PUSH STUDENTS
# TO ELABORATE

 Coaching Tips

## Teacher Context

### Challenge

The teacher doesn't know why a student got an answer wrong.

### Action Step

Ask universal prompts to push the student to elaborate:

- "Tell me more."
- "What makes you think that?"
- "How do you know?"
- "Why is that important?"

### Action Step Overview

When a student gets an answer wrong, often a teacher will move on. He or she will correct the wrong answer himself or herself or just go on to another student to get the answer. Doing so, however, is a critical lost opportunity. If we don't know why the student got the answer wrong, we cannot help him or her correct the misunderstanding. The same error occurs when a teacher accepts a correct answer without explanation. That student might have gotten lucky and might not be able to replicate his or her success. Using universal prompts helps a teacher unpack the student's thinking. These prompts are triply beneficial: they give the teacher more time to diagnose the error, and they allow students to understand their peers more effectively as well. They also keep a teacher from "rounding up"—adding his or her own thoughts as to what a student meant—and keep the thinking on the students. Although there are certainly more content-specific ways to respond to error, the universal prompts work well in any content area and are as powerful as they are simple.

*Quick Tip from a Coach—Script the Prompts into Your Plans*
*At our schools, we were struggling with how to engage our students thoughtfully in difficult academic content. We posted these prompts on the wall in the classrooms, but what really ended up being most effective*

*was picking three of the universal prompts and strategically scripting them into their plans. Then we practiced those precise moments when they would use them. Even if the discussion didn't go quite like you imagined, the teacher developed the instinct to use the prompts. In doing so, our students quickly became better listeners, and our teachers were leading significantly more thoughtful discussions.*

—Stacey Shells, principal manager, Chicago, Illinois

---

### KEY LEADERSHIP MOVES

| | |
|---|---|
| **Probing Questions** | • "When the student delivered the incorrect answer, what happened next? How do you know if that student now understands at the end of the class?" |
| | • "Let's look at this list of universal prompts. What is the value of using prompts like these?" |
| | • "Where in your lesson could you have used one or more of these prompts?" |
| **Planning and Practice** | • Work with the teacher to pick the very next lesson where class discussion will occur. Predict the types of student responses that will benefit from these prompts: potential wrong answers and correct answers with limited explanation. |
| | • As the leader, play the roles of three different students: one with a wrong answer, two more with limited answers. Role-play a discussion where the teacher practices using each of the prompts. At the end, ask the teacher what he or she learned about the student's understanding to see how well the teacher diagnosed the error. |

---

# UNIVERSAL PROMPTS: CLOSE THE LOOP

**Coaching Tips**

## Teacher Context

### Challenge

After a student gives an incorrect answer, the teacher moves on to a different student without correcting the original student's error.

### Action Step

Close the loop: after correcting their error, go back to students with wrong answers to have them revise their answers.

### Action Step Overview

Sometimes a teacher may need to move on from a struggling student before this student can get to the right answer in the moment. When this happens, however, the student's learning will be most benefited if the teacher still goes back to him or her after the other students have worked to determine the right answer, to make sure that the first student has successfully followed along and learned how to solve the problem himself or herself. This is a highly underrated and underused action, but so valuable for student learning. Recall the video clip of high school history teacher Ryan Miller. After targeting the discussion on the point of error, he went back to the students and made sure they revised their answer with their new understanding.

 Rewatch clip 27: Target the Error and Close the Loop (teaching clip)

---

**KEY LEADERSHIP MOVES**

| | |
|---|---|
| **Probing Questions** | • "When [student] delivered that incorrect answer yesterday, what did you do next? How did you know if [student] understood why he or she was wrong? What could you do next time?"<br><br>• [Watch model video] "How does this teacher guarantee that the student has learned after his original misconception?" |
| **Planning and Practice** | • Role-play a questioning sequence from an upcoming lesson, with you playing different students so that the teacher has a chance to play out the process of coming back to the first student he or she has called on. |
| **Real-Time Feedback** | • Whisper prompt: "Come back to [x student] to make sure he understands."<br><br>• Model: "Jared, why is that answer right?" |

---

 Rewatch clip 26: Check for Understanding
(Key Leadership Move: Real-Time Feedback)

---

 Watch clip 35: Close the Loop
(Key Leadership Move: Plan)

---

## Universal Prompts

| Action Step | When to Use It | Probing Questions | Scenarios to Practice | Cues for Real-Time Feedback |
|---|---|---|---|---|
| Provide wait time, precall, roll back | The teacher moves on too quickly after asking a challenging question. | • "What are the possible reasons a student might not be able to answer a question you ask on the spot—beyond just not knowing the answer?"<br><br>• [Watch a video or model for the teacher] "What actions did the teacher take? Why were these beneficial?"<br><br>• "What is the purpose of repeating the student's answer back to him/her? Why not just correct the error?"<br><br>• "Which students need more time than others to formulate an answer? Which ones would benefit from a precall to give them enough thinking time?" | Integrate the practice of all three skills:<br><br>• Wait time: ID higher-order questions that might require more think time. Script concise directions that teacher will narrate during wait time ("This answer requires strong evidence. Everyone can be looking as we wait.").<br><br>• Precall: ID the students who would benefit from a precall. Pick the questions in the lesson plan that would be ideal to ask those students.<br><br>• Rollback: role-play a questioning sequence from an upcoming lesson, providing student answers that would benefit from rolling back. Continue the lesson after rolling back as well. | Nonverbal: create/use a cue for wait time (e.g., hold up a hand as a stop sign).<br><br>Model: roll back answer to the original student, modeling for the teacher. |
| Ask universal prompts | The teacher doesn't know why a student got an answer wrong. | • "When the student delivered the incorrect answer, what happened next? How do you know if that student now understands at the end of the class?"<br><br>• "Let's look at this list of universal prompts. What is the value of using prompts like these?"<br><br>• "Where in your lesson could you have used one or more of these prompts?" | • Plan next lesson: predict the types of student responses that will benefit from these prompts.<br><br>• Practice: play the roles of 3 different students: 1 with a wrong answer, 2 more with limited answers. Role-play using each of the prompts. | N/A |

| Action Step | When to Use It | Probing Questions | Scenarios to Practice | Cues for Real-Time Feedback |
|---|---|---|---|---|
| Close the loop | After an incorrect answer, the teacher moves on without correcting the error with that student. | • "When [student] delivered that incorrect answer yesterday, what did you do next? How did you know if [student] understood why he/she was wrong? What could you do next time?" <br><br> • [Watch model video] "How does this teacher guarantee that the student has learned after his original misconception?" | • Role-play a questioning sequence from an upcoming lesson, with you playing different students so that teacher has a chance to play out the process of coming back to the first student he/she has called on. | Whisper prompt: "Come back to [x student] to make sure he understands." <br><br> Model: "Jared, why is that answer right?" |

## Habits of Discussion

> ### Teacher Professional Development Goal
>
> **Habits of Discussion:** Teach and model for students the habits that strengthen class conversation.

In schools throughout the country, the area in which students are graded least meaningfully is classroom discussion. Far too often, educators presume that simply "participating" in a discussion by speaking at all is sufficient for a satisfactory grade, despite the discussion's being redundant or anemic. One student may follow another's comment with a comment that essentially repeats what the first student said; another might bring up an insightful or relevant comment, but not one which indicates that he or she heard or comprehended what the previous student said; and the conversation never goes further because the students lack the skills to push each other.

How can teachers ensure that students *contribute* rather than merely participate? By training students in the habits of discussion. That's the name my colleagues and I use to describe skills that come naturally in high-level dialogue and discourse: agreeing with someone meaningfully; disagreeing with someone respectfully; pushing an academic conversation to a deeper level. All of these are teachable skills that even our youngest students can master.

*Great Habits, Great Readers* provides a complete taxonomy of habits of discussion for K–8 students and the ideal learning levels at which to introduce them to students. (For more advanced habits of discussion, we have included on the DVD the High School Habits of Academic Discourse Guide built by high school teachers Sean Gavin, Matthew McCluskey, Laura Palumbo, and Rose Bierce—this is a fantastic resource for high school classrooms!)

## Findings from the Field: Build in Student Reflection Time to Internalize the Habits

It has taken time and practice, but our teachers have trained our students to consistently use discussion prompts, build off one another, and disagree respectfully. We have schoolwide discussion protocols, and our teachers consistently reinforce habits of discussion before and during the discussion, but it was not until we built in student reflection time after whole-class discussions that our students internalized the process. After a whole-class discussion, our teachers ask students to reflect on their discussion and to compare the discussion habits of themselves and their classmates with our schoolwide habits of discussion. Students are quick to provide feedback and identify areas in which their class needs to improve the following day. When students take this time to reflect, they hold themselves and their peers accountable, and the quality of whole-class discussions improves at a rapid rate.

—Greg Dutton, principal, Queens, New York

Regardless of the grade level of the students, the following three challenges are the most significant roadblocks to great conversations that teachers will encounter early in their work as facilitators of discussion:

- The teacher's reaction to student responses reveals whether those responses are correct before the students have the opportunity to get there on their own as a group ("Are you *sure* the answer is *really* right? Have you checked your work?").

- Student answers are disconnected from each other, even when the students agree.

- Students either don't express disagreement with their peers or don't do so in a respectful manner.

The habits of discussion presented here are the ones that will dispel these challenges, setting in place the most important parts of the foundation for great academic discourse.

# HABITS OF DISCUSSION—KEEP NEUTRAL

 **Coaching Tips**

## Teacher Context

### Challenge
The teacher's reactions to student responses reveal whether those responses are correct before the students have the opportunity to get there on their own as a group.

### Action Step
Keep neutral/manage your tell: don't reveal the right/wrong answer through your reaction to the student response.

### Action Step Overview
Teachers often inadvertently reduce rigor in their classrooms by giving away the correct answer before the students get to it on their own. They may nod or smile when the answer is correct, ask leading questions ("Two plus two equals *five*? Are you *sure*?"), or consistently say "Yes" when the answer is correct and probe when it's incorrect (leading students to recognize probing as a sign that the answer is incorrect). By keeping your expression neutral, you allow your students to reach a conceptual understanding of material on their own, rather than simply reading your reaction.

*Quick Tip from a Coach—Temporarily Hide Your Excitement*
*When we rolled out the habits of discussion, a key push for our teachers was to ensure they were remaining neutral with their own reactions to student responses—a great answer would often generate excitement from the teacher, but the push was for scholars to be able to evaluate the quality of a response, not the teacher. To execute on this action step, we delivered a PD and practiced remaining neutral when one of their peers gave a perfect response. It was harder than we realized!*
—Shara Hegde, principal manager, San Jose, California

## KEY LEADERSHIP MOVES

**Probing Questions**

- "Recall our recent PD on habits of discussion. What is the goal of getting students to use the habits of discussion?"

- [Watch video of the teacher] "I want you to watch your responses—both verbal and nonverbal—to students' correct answers and compare those to your responses to incorrect answers. What are the differences? How do your different responses limit the rigor of the discussion?"

- "What would be the key actions for you to take to make sure your responses to correct and incorrect answers are the same?"

**Planning and Practice**

- Have the teacher think about how to keep his or her response neutral when students give answers. The following are key components to a neutral response:

  - Keep your eyebrows neutral. (We often raise our eyebrows or scrunch them up when having a positive or negative response. Keep them from moving, and you neutralize your face![2])

  - Nod either after every response or after none of them.

  - Speak the same number of words after each response (none or few).

  - Provide wait time: make it clear that you want the students, not you, to evaluate the answer.

- After practicing each part of a neutral response, role-play a questioning sequence with you playing the part of the student. Give a series of wrong answers, and have the teacher practice staying neutral. Have the teacher prompt students to use the habits of discussion to push each other further: "Do you agree or disagree with Julia's answer?"

# HABITS OF DISCUSSION: AGREE AND BUILD OFF

 *Coaching Tips*

## Teacher Context

### Challenge
Student answers are disconnected from each other, even when the students agree.

### Action Step
Teach students to agree and build off of one another's responses: "I agree with ____, and I'd like to add . . ."

### Action Step Overview
As adults, most of us automatically express agreement with a peer where appropriate in the midst of a conversation. Many students, however, especially our youngest ones, have not yet learned this habit; and even for those who have done so, it may be challenging (as it is even for many adults!) to add to or build off of the statement they agree with. Getting students to master this skill is an essential building block to facilitating meaningful class discussions. For younger students, this generally means teaching them to use "I agree with ____ because . . ." when responding to a peer they agree with; for students who already know that this type of statement is expected when they respond to a peer's comment, it may simply mean asking them, "Do you agree with [name of student who last spoke]?" if they begin to make a comment that does not relate to what was said previously.

| | KEY LEADERSHIP MOVES |
|---|---|
| **Probing Questions** | • "What do you ideally want students to do when they agree with what a peer is saying? How could you get them to do it in the moment?"<br><br>• "Let's think about that moment during your lesson when [x student] shared his answer and the next student just repeated it. What training do the students need in how to build off of another student's answer?" |
| **Planning and Practice** | • Script prompts to get students to build off of one another's arguments: "I agree with _____, and I would like to add that . . ." Then role-play a class discussion in which you play the students, and the teacher prompts you to build off of one another's comments.<br><br>• Practice: role-play a class discussion. Prompt the students to build off of one another's answers. |
| **Real-Time Feedback** | • Nonverbal: post the habits of discussion in the classroom; when students aren't using them, point to the posted habits.<br><br>• Model: "David [student], can you restate your answer using one of the habits of discussion posted on the wall?" |

Rewatch clip 3: Habits of Discussion
(Key Leadership Move: Plan/Practice)

# HABITS OF DISCUSSION: DISAGREE RESPECTFULLY

 Coaching Tips

## Teacher Context

### Challenge
Students either don't express disagreement with their peers or don't do so in a respectful manner.

### Action Step
Teach students to disagree respectfully: "While I agree with [this part of your argument], I disagree with _____. I would argue . . ."

---

| | **KEY LEADERSHIP MOVES** |
|---|---|
| **Probing Questions** | • "What do you ideally want students to do when they disagree with what a peer is saying?"<br>• "What is the gap between that ideal response and what they are doing in class?"<br>• "How could you get them to do those ideal actions in the moment?" |
| **Planning and Practice** | • Script prompts to get students to respectfully disagree with one another's arguments, include the following: "I disagree with you, [peer], because . . ." or "I agree that _____, but I disagree that _____. I would argue that . . ." Role-play a class discussion in which you play the students, and the teacher prompts the students to express respectful disagreement. |
| **Real-Time Feedback** | • Nonverbal: point to prompts posted on the classroom walls.<br>• Model: "Laura, can you restate your disagreement using one of the habits of discussion prompts posted on the wall?" |

Strategies for Coaching

## Habits of Discussion

| Action Step | When to Use It | Probing Questions | Scenarios to Practice | Cues for Real-Time Feedback |
|---|---|---|---|---|
| Keep neutral | The teacher's reactions reveal whether student responses are correct before the students can figure it out on their own. | • "Recall our recent PD on habits of discussion. What is the goal of getting students to use the habits?" <br><br> • [Watch video of the teacher] "Compare your responses to correct and incorrect answers. What are the differences? How do your different responses limit the rigor of the discussion?" <br><br> • "What actions can you take to ensure that your responses to correct and incorrect responses are the same?" | • Practice: role-play correct and incorrect responses. Focus teacher on staying neutral: eyebrows neutral, consistent nodding or not, same number of words after each response. <br><br> • Incorporate the use of habits of discussion and wait time. | N/A |
| Agree and build off | Student answers are disconnected from each other, even when students agree. | • "What do you ideally want students to do when they agree with what a peer is saying? How could you get them to do it in the moment?" <br><br> • "Let's think about that moment during your lesson when [x student] shared his answer and the next student just repeated it. What training do the students need in how to build off of another student's answer?" | • Script prompts to get students to build off of one another's arguments: "I agree with ____, and I would like to add that . . ." <br><br> • Practice: role-play a class discussion. Prompt the students to build off. | Nonverbal: post the habits of discussion in the classroom; point to the posted habits when needed. <br><br> Model: "David [student], can you restate your answer using one of the habits posted on the wall?" |

| Action Step | When to Use It | Probing Questions | Scenarios to Practice | Cues for Real-Time Feedback |
|---|---|---|---|---|
| Disagree respectfully | Students either don't disagree with their peers or don't do so in a respectful manner. | • "What do you ideally want students to do when they disagree with what a peer is saying?" <br> • "What is the gap between that ideal response and what they are doing in class?" <br> • "How could you get them to do those ideal actions in the moment?" | • Script prompts to get students to respectfully disagree with one another's arguments. <br> • Practice: role-play a class discussion: prompt the students to express respectful disagreement. | Nonverbal: point to prompts posted on the classroom walls. <br><br> Model: "Laura, can you disagree using one of the habits posted on the wall?" |

---

### Stop and Jot

What are the three top coaching ideas you plan to use to train your teachers in these Phase 4 Rigor skills? Jot them down here.

_____

_____

_____

## CONCLUSION

Think back to the presidential debate we envisioned at the beginning of this section. When we train our teachers to be to student discussions what facilitators are to debates like these, we are preparing our students to succeed in the debates they will face in their own lives. For some of them, this might even be a presidential debate. For others, it will be medical research they have to defend, a new policy they choose to propose for a company they run, or, should they become teachers themselves, a future student they must convince to persevere during a difficult time. Whatever paths our students choose, the skills of leading thoughtful discourse will not only serve them well but also empower them to build a better future. By prioritizing discourse when we think about the skills our teachers need, we are putting our students in a position to become the leaders we need.

# Stretch It: Ready to Paint

Teaching is an incredibly complex craft. It requires you to make hundreds of small decisions on the fly every day, and each one has an impact on what children will learn. That being the case, it's all too easy, when we're on the ground doing the daily work of teaching and leading, to undermine the value of mastering the sheer quantity of Get Better Faster action steps that have gotten you to this phase. So if you, or your teachers, have made it so far along on the Scope and Sequence that they're making daily habits of the actions in Phases 1 through 4, take a moment to sincerely congratulate yourself. The impact of those particular habits is multiplied by the weight they carry—and by the way they affect every individual student who learns more because they have been set in place.

Teachers who have mastered all of this can say, without hesitation, that they have learned the fundamental skills of teaching and are no longer apprentices, but artists. The other decisions they'll still need to make every day are less about learning to use a paintbrush, and more about painting. What does that mean? Let's consider a lesson from the artist Michelangelo.

Michelangelo—or, at least, the Michelangelo imagined by Irving Stone in his best-selling *The Agony and the Ecstasy*—wasn't always the celebrated master of painting and sculpture we remember him as today. Like every other artist,

Michelangelo began as an apprentice learning the basic skills of his craft. As a young boy, even before he was a formal apprentice, Michelangelo spent time with a stone-cutter and learned the basic skills of hewing blocks of marble from the side of a mountain. When he began his first apprenticeship with a master painter, he had to learn to mix paint colors and make paintbrushes for months before being allowed to apply a single streak of paint to his mentor's fresco—let alone paint his own. Later, Michelangelo learned to sculpt wax and clay flawlessly before ever carving a piece of marble. Focusing on such menial tasks was excruciating for the young genius, who couldn't wait for the moment when he would bring his most vivid artistic visions to life.

When Michelangelo's chance came to create his own art, however, the skills he had been loath to spend so much time mastering served him well. The first piece he carved wasn't David, but it was dramatically more advanced than anything he could have created without serving his time as an apprentice. Even for the most gifted individuals in any profession, some kind of apprenticeship phase—a period of time they spend perfecting the basic skills of the trade under the guidance of an experienced master—will increase their control over their craft, the quality of their work, and the speed at which their work begins to look like an expert's.

Stretch It is all about rising to being a painter in the world of learning. By this point, teachers have learned all the foundational skills they need to begin making the spontaneity of the discussion just as rich a learning ground as the structure of the lecture. Artistry comes into play in the even more nuanced facilitation of class discussion and the content mastery that become necessary to take instruction to the next level. There's still a great deal that can go wrong during in a lesson, just as when an artist takes a chisel to a slab of marble. And yet, just like an artist who has mastered the right skills as an apprentice, a skillful teacher can use the right strategies to make learning come to life. What are these next six strategies? The pages that follow will reveal them.

> ## Core Idea
> Just like an artist who has completed an apprenticeship,
> a skillful teacher has everything it takes to paint a masterpiece.

# STRETCH IT COACHING BLUEPRINT

The two most important coaching actions during Stretch It are helping teachers maintain the skills they've already learned and getting students to do as much of the thinking as possible.

## Maintain the Skills

When you begin a fitness regimen, the hardest part usually isn't getting to your target physical condition—it's staying there. The same is true of mastering the art of teaching: the hardest part isn't learning the skills on the Scope and Sequence in the first place, but keeping them locked in as habits. Supporting the teacher in maintaining previously learned skills will be some of the most important work a leader does during Stretch It.

> ### Core Idea
>
> The hardest part of progressing as a teacher isn't mastering all the skills but keeping them locked in place.

Sometimes a skill will slip so much that you will need to return to previous phases and work on a skill from scratch. If so, just return to that section and build anew!

In most cases, however, you can use immediate real-time feedback—quick, simple reminders that get the teacher to do what he or she already knows how to do. If the teacher is able to address the issues with that feedback, then you can continue developing your teacher in new skills.

## Maintain Your Focus on Students

In Phase 4, we described the way a coach's focus this far along in the Scope and Sequence shifts to monitoring for rigor and the techniques that leaders can use to focus as fully as possible on raising the bar when it comes to student discussion. When you get to Stretch It, this remains the case—if anything, you can likely change your focus more than ever from what the teacher is doing to what the students are doing.

As you observe classrooms during the Stretch It phase, you can raise your expectations as to how much of the lesson should be student driven as opposed to teacher driven. Where your focus was once primarily on the teacher's actions, it can now be on the students' responses; where you may once have videotaped the person at the front of the classroom, you might now point the camera out at the desks and tape the students themselves. The most straightforward metric for determining the rigor of the class is this: If you turned off the teacher's voice, would the conversation still sound rigorous?

The primary focus now is on student actions; unpacking those actions and identifying how they are affected by teacher actions are secondary. When it comes to practicing with the teacher during Stretch It, you'll work predominantly on strategic interventions the teacher can use to get the students to prompt, assess, and build off of one another's responses.

In building up to the Stretch It phase, teachers and leaders have made a game-changing journey: the leader has gotten the teacher to the point where he or she can be much more independent, and now it's time for the teacher to do the same for the students. Let's dive into the specifics of what each action step in this phase calls for, and how it works to further transform the classroom to a center of intellectual rigor.

## Teaching Skills Overview

Think back to everything else we've already accomplished on the rigor side of the Scope and Sequence: we've perfected lesson planning, independent practice, and responding to student learning needs, as well as beginning work on the art of discourse. There are no new management skills to master at this point. (That's not to say management will necessarily be flawless by the time teachers reach this point on the Scope and Sequence—just that by now, the key task at hand is to polish and maintain the steps that teachers learned earlier in the year.)

Getting ready to paint means working to building masterpieces. With the skills of the first ninety days in hand, the next piece of the puzzle is to raise the rigor of the classroom: training students to have an even deeper conceptual understanding of material. We offer some general action steps here.

After mastering these action steps, the next step is for a teacher to really dive into his or her content:

- An English teacher learning the multitude of exegeses of a Shakespearean sonnet to be able to push students to a deeper analysis

- A math teacher relearning quadratic equations conceptually to make sure students do more than just memorize the procedure but understand and master the concept that will set them up for greater success in calculus and beyond

- A history teacher doing a deep dive into primary and secondary source documents around the Industrial Revolution to be able to push students deeper in their arguments and thesis statements

These are what I call content-based action steps: developing content knowledge expertise in your subject area. Unfortunately, it would take a myriad of books to highlight all the content-based action steps a teacher could learn for every subject from grades K through 12! Thankfully, there are many other resources once we've reached that point. The key is that once a teacher has mastered the skills of teaching, the content becomes the focus. And mastering content is a lifelong journey.

What follows are a few non-content-specific strategies to help the teacher on that journey.

### Stretch It Action Step Sequence

| Management Trajectory | Rigor Trajectory |
|---|---|
| None!<br><br>Once you get this far, you can focus entirely on rigor and deepening your content knowledge. | **Lead Student Discourse 201**<br><br>12. **Strategic Prompts:** Ask strategic questions to targeted students in response to student error<br><br>• Prompt students to access previously learned knowledge:<br><br>  – Point students to resources (notes, posted concepts and content, handouts).<br><br>  – "What do we know about _____ [content learned in previous classes]?"<br><br>  – Use a prompting guide (e.g., *Great Habits, Great Readers* Guided Reading Prompting Guide) to design questions. |

| Management Trajectory | Rigor Trajectory |
|---|---|
| | • Call on students based on their learning needs (data driven). |
| |   – Call on lower- and middle-achieving students to unpack the question. |
| |   – If they struggle, try a higher-achieving student. |
| |   – If they are easily unpacking, try a lower-achieving student. |
| |   – Create a sequence of students to call on based on the rigor of each prompt (e.g., first ask middle student, then low, then high, etc.). |
| | • Students prompting students: push students to use habits of discussion to critique or push one another's answers. |
| |   – Probe deeper: "[Peer], have you considered this point . . . ?" |
| | **13. Go Conceptual:** Get students to do the conceptual thinking |
| | • Ask students to verbalize a conceptual understanding of content, not just the answer to a specific question: |
| |   – "That's the procedure. Now tell me why that works." |
| |   – "Can you generalize that idea to apply to all problems like this one?" |
| |   – "Use the following terms [terms learned in previous classes] in restating your answer." |

STRETCH IT

BLUEPRINT

| Management Trajectory | Rigor Trajectory |
|---|---|
| | • Upgrade vocabulary: ask students to use technical/academic language when answering questions: |
| | – "That's the right idea generally. Now state it again using proper mathematical/historical/scientific language." |
| | – "Correct. Now state it again using your Academic Word Wall as a resource." |
| | • Stretch it: ask particular students to answer a more difficult extension to a given question: |
| | – "What would the answer be if I changed it to [change the problem to something more complex]?" |
| | – "Is there an alternative way to solve this problem/do this task?" |
| | – "What do you think is the strongest counterargument to yours, and how would you refute it?" |

# STRETCH IT RIGOR—LEAD STUDENT DISCOURSE 201

## Quick Reference Guide

| If your teacher is struggling to . . . | Jump to . . . |
|---|---|
| **Strategic Prompts** | |
| Get students to grasp concepts, despite the use of Discourse 101 techniques | Access previous understanding |
| Avoid calling on either primarily high students who already know the answer or consecutive students who all struggle to answer the question | Call on students based on their learning needs |
| Get students to prompt each other | Students prompting students |
| **Go Conceptual** | |
| Get students to probe beyond a superficial understanding of content | Verbalize a conceptual understanding of content |
| Get students to use academic or technical language | Upgrade vocabulary |
| Push students further when they comprehend content quickly | Stretch it |

## Stretch It Action Step Sequence

| Management Trajectory | Rigor Trajectory |
|---|---|
| None!<br><br>Once you get this far, you can focus entirely on rigor and deepening your content knowledge. | **Lead Student Discourse 201**<br><br>12. **Strategic Prompts:** Ask strategic questions to targeted students in response to student error<br>• Prompt students to access previously learned knowledge:<br>   – Point students to resources (notes, posted concepts and content, handouts). |

| Management Trajectory | Rigor Trajectory |
|---|---|
| |     – "What do we know about _____ [content learned in previous classes]?"<br><br>    – Use a prompting guide (e.g., *Great Habits, Great Readers* Guided Reading Prompting Guide) to design questions.<br><br>• Call on students based on their learning needs (data driven).<br><br>    – Call on lower- and middle-achieving students to unpack the question.<br><br>    – If they struggle, try a higher-achieving student.<br><br>    – If they are easily unpacking, try a lower-achieving student.<br><br>    – Create a sequence of students to call on based on the rigor of each prompt (e.g., first ask middle student, then low, then high, etc.).<br><br>• Students prompting students: push students to use habits of discussion to critique or push one another's answers.<br><br>    – Probe deeper: "[Peer], have you considered this point . . .?"<br><br>**13. Go Conceptual:** Get students to do the conceptual thinking<br><br>• Ask students to verbalize a conceptual understanding of content, not just the answer to a specific question:<br><br>    – "That's the procedure. Now tell me why that works."<br><br>    – "Can you generalize that idea to apply to all problems like this one?" |

RIGOR

STRETCH IT

| Management Trajectory | Rigor Trajectory |
|---|---|
| | – "Use the following terms [terms learned in previous classes] in restating your answer." |
| | • Upgrade vocabulary: ask students to use technical/academic language when answering questions: |
| | – "That's the right idea generally. Now state it again using proper mathematical/historical/scientific language." |
| | – "Correct. Now state it again using your Academic Word Wall as a resource." |
| | • Stretch it: ask particular students to answer a more difficult extension to a given question: |
| | – "What would the answer be if I changed it to [change the problem to something more complex]?" |
| | – "Is there an alternative way to solve this problem/do this task?" |
| | – "What do you think is the strongest counterargument to yours, and how would you refute it?" |

## Introduction to Stretch It Rigor Skills: Lead Student Discourse 201

A student error in the midst of class discussion can freeze a teacher who doesn't expect it. We first addressed this challenge in Phase 4 with universal actions that can be applied to any content: guided discourse (for example, Show Call), universal prompts (for example, "Tell me more"), and habits of discussion ("Do you agree or disagree?").

What happens, though, when the universal prompts or habits do not suffice? What happens when the students' overall lack of grasp of the task or content doesn't allow them to unpack the meaning? What can a teacher do beyond simply modeling for the students and taking over the learning?

These questions are perhaps the greatest challenge of leading a quality discussion: how to prompt students when they are still stuck, without watering down the material. Let's take a look at two different conversations—one in literacy and one in math—and see how a teacher moves from "watered down" to higher rigor.

Let's first consider the difference between two literary discussions of the science fantasy novel *A Wrinkle in Time*. In both conversations, the teacher is trying to get students to recognize that the most powerful weapon the book's villain IT uses against Meg (the protagonist) is the temptation to conform.

---

## A Literacy Case Study

*Prompting, Take 1: Watered Down*

Students are struggling to comprehend, so the teacher steps in:

*Teacher:* Think about everything IT makes the people on Camazotz do. Remember all the parents going to work and the children playing in the street, doing the same things. What does IT make them do?
*Student:* They all have to do the same things.
*Teacher:* Right. Because if they do the same things, who's in charge?
*Student:* IT.
*Teacher:* Exactly. So IT's main objective is to create uniformity. So what's powerful about Meg reciting the Declaration of Independence? We've never heard of anyone doing that in the book, correct? So what makes it different?
*Student:* She's not doing the same thing as everyone else.
*Teacher:* Right! So how do you defeat IT?
*Student:* By not doing what everyone else is doing.

---

Even though the teacher's prompting got students to verbalize the correct answer, it was so leading that the teacher did all the heavy thinking, and students really just fed back to the teacher what they heard. Look at how the conversation can change when the teacher instead uses what we call strategic prompting.

# A Literacy Case Study

*Prompting, Take 2: Strategic Prompting*

Students are struggling to comprehend, so the teacher steps in:

*Teacher:* In looking at our journals, we are struggling to understand the important message that the author is sending with the development of the character IT. When we are struggling to understand the deeper meaning of a passage, what are some actions we can take? Look at your guide for unpacking difficult text.

*Student:* We can go back into the text, find the passages on IT, and paraphrase key lines. After that, we can build a summary and synthesis from our paraphrased lines. Then we can try to answer the core question again, making sure our evidence supports our assertion.

*Teacher:* Great. Go back to work . . .

[As teacher monitors, she notes that certain students now are able to grasp the bigger ideas, but not everyone.]

*Teacher:* I am going to show-call two different summaries of the passage. Remind me: What are the keys to a good summary?

*Student:* [States the definition of a good summary that's posted on the wall.]

*Teacher:* Turn and talk to your partner: Which summary is stronger and why?

[Turn and Talk occurs and then teacher calls group back together.]

*Teacher:* OK, let's share out. Please use the definition of a good summary in defending your answer.

Before reading on, jot down your own thoughts: What are the key differences between these two conversations?

---

## Stop and Jot

What are the key actions in strategic prompting that increased the rigor of the class?

_____

_____

_____

_____

_____

_____

_____

STRETCH IT

RIGOR

Right away you'll notice that the second take embeds some of the previous actions steps learned in Phase 2 (aggressive monitoring), Phase 3 (Turn and Talks), and Phase 4 (Show Call). That already increases the rigor of the conversation.

Yet the teacher does not stop there. Every teacher prompt directs students to the learning they have already done: in this case, a resource listing the strategies they've learned for unpacking difficult passages. Too often, a student doesn't use his or her previous knowledge—and doesn't think of doing so without prompting. The prompting is for students to access *their own knowledge* rather than for the teacher to tell them what to do. That is an enormous difference in the depth of rigor required of the student.

---

### Core Idea

What is the key to overcoming student confusion?
Make sure they have the prerequisite knowledge to begin the task,
and leverage that knowledge to help them succeed.

---

These actions can look simple in a transcript, but they are quite complex to execute in real time across any content. To help us visualize them, let's take a look at another example—this time in math. I will make the errors a little more subtle, but the end result is the same.

## A Math Case Study

*Prompting, Take 1: Watered Down*

Algebra students have learned how to solve basic quadratic equations when in standard form $ax^2 + bx + c = 0$.

Now they are given a word problem that generates the following initial equation:

$$x^2 + 2x = 15$$

Students get stuck and don't realize the need to set the equation equal to zero in order to solve. Most of them end up with the following error on their paper:

$$(x)(x + 2) = 15$$
$$x = 15, \ x + 2 = 15$$
$$x = 15 \text{ or } x = 13$$

The teacher pulls the class together to address the error.

*Teacher:* I noticed most of us are struggling to set up this equation correctly. Here is the typical error. What is going wrong here?

[Given that all the students have the wrong answer, no one is able to correctly identify the error. So the students don't give a correct response.]

*Student:* They didn't show all their work as neatly as they should. And their answers don't work when they plug them back in.

*Teacher:* It's true that these answers are wrong, but you haven't told me why. Anyone have the answer? [Students shake their heads.] See, you are forgetting that for a quadratic equation you need to have zero on the right side. This is because of the zero product property: when any two numbers are multiplied together and equal zero, one or both of those numbers must be equal to zero. Juan, what is the zero product property?

*Student:* You put zero on one side so that . . . yeah . . . you can make them equal to zero when solving.

*Teacher:* You mean the factors, yes. So if I do this with this equation, I get: $x^2 + 2x - 15 = 0$. Once I do that, what's my first step for factoring?

*Student:* Find the factors of 15.

[We'll assume that students don't yet know the quadratic formula.]

*Teacher:* Great. What's the next step?

[Then they solve the rest of the problem together.]

---

Let's see the difference with strategic prompting. Note where the math teacher uses the same techniques as the literacy teacher, just with different content:

●

## A Math Case Study

*Prompting, Take 2: Strategic Prompting*

Same context: students are given a word problem that generates the following initial equation:

$$x^2 + 2x = 15$$

The same error is found in their work. The teacher pulls the class together to address the error.

*Teacher:* I see most of you are struggling with this problem. Let's come back together. Let's remember what we've learned this week: What type of equation have we generated in this problem?

[A student identifies it as a quadratic question because of the $x^2$ term.]

*Teacher:* What do we know about solving quadratic equations?

[Students mention processes for solving by factoring. When a student gets to the process of setting each factor equal to zero, teacher intervenes.]

*Teacher:* Why are we able to set each factor equal to zero?

*Student:* You put zero on one side so that . . . yeah . . . you can make them equal to zero when solving.

*Teacher:* Explain that to me in mathematical language. What property are you using that allows you to set each factor each to zero?

[Student pauses.]

*Teacher:* Use your resources. Look at the properties we have defined about equations up to this point.

*Student:* The zero product property. [Teacher gives nonverbal to elaborate in the student's own words.] It says that whenever you have a product equal to zero—two quantities multiplied by each other— then one or both of the quantities . . . in this case the factors . . . must be equal to zero. So if either factor is equal to zero, we have found a solution to the formula. That's why both answers are correct.

*Teacher:* OK. Turn and talk: How might this property help us solve this problem?

[Turn and Talk occurs and then teacher calls group back together. Students identify the error in the problem and how to set the equation equal to zero.]

*Teacher:* Excellent. So who can state the big idea we have learned when solving word problems that result in a quadratic equation? What can we generalize for solving any problem?

Rather than be the holder of the knowledge himself, the teacher gets the students to access their own knowledge learned in previous classes. A conversation like this is the culmination of all the work that has been done in Phases 1 through 4 to push for rigor. In the end, students are not just answering math questions correctly; they are articulating the "why": the conceptual understanding behind their answer that will set them up for long-term retention of the material.

Stretch It gives you the tools to guide your teacher to this level of class discussion. In this chapter, we add strategic prompting and conceptual thinking action steps to get there.

> ### 🔍 Findings from the Field: Start Universal, Then Get Specific, Then Roll Back
>
> Teachers struggle in class discussion when student confusion occurs in the moment. What was most helpful for me has been to jump in at the moment and model going from one prompt to a more complex prompt. Start with a universal prompt, then the second is usually a content-specific prompt, and the third is rolling back the error—getting the student to identify his or her own error. You might say, "So you said the denominator was three groups, but you had two in your model. What would you do differently?"
> —Adam Feiler, instructional leader, Newark, New Jersey

## Strategic Prompts

> ### Teacher Professional Development Goal
>
> **Strategic Prompts:** To unpack a difficult task, call on targeted students and give prompts that leverage their previous learning.

We saw examples of strategic prompts in the two previous case studies. What follows are the challenges teachers are most likely to face when working to respond appropriately in the moment when students provide incorrect answers:

- Despite the use of Show Call, universal prompts, and habits of discussion, students are still unable to grasp the concept/unpack the task.

- The teacher calls on primarily high-achieving students who already know the answer, and doesn't guarantee that the learning comes from all the students in his or her class.

- The teacher calls on consecutive struggling students, and the discussion stalls.

- The teacher is constantly prompting the students to use habits of discussion, but students are not building the habit of prompting one another.

# STRATEGIC PROMPTS: ACCESS PREVIOUS UNDERSTANDING

## Coaching Tips

## Teacher Context

### Challenge

Despite the use of Show Call, universal prompts, and habits of discussion, students are still unable to grasp the concept/unpack the task.

### Action Step

Prompt students to access previously learned knowledge:

- Point students to resources (notes, posted concepts and content, handouts).
- "What do we know about _____ [content students learned in previous classes]?"
- Use a prompting guide (for example, the *Great Habits, Great Readers* Guided Reading Prompting Guide) to design your questions.

### Action Step Overview

Strategic prompts, at their essence, involve getting students to leverage their knowledge to confront new material. Students regularly struggle to make the connection between previous learning and current problems when not prompted. Strategic prompts can be very difficult to develop independently: they involve a pretty deep knowledge of the content. However, certain prompts can start to get the teacher and students to that level of depth:

- "What do we know about _____ [content students learned in previous classes]?"
- "What were the key concepts/skills/strategies we learned about _____?"
- "What do we need to remember when solving these sorts of problems?"
- "Look at your resources (notes, concepts and content posted on walls, handout). What are _____ [whatever core content they should know]?"

Have the prompt starters listed earlier readily accessible for you and the teacher. Then the most important action is to make sure that the teacher knows the exemplar answer to the prompt. This connects to the Phase 2 action area of writing the exemplar, but here it is less about the exemplar response of the student work and more about the exemplar articulation of key understandings or skills from previous classes. If teachers keep that understanding in the forefront of their minds, they will know what they're listening for and will not let up until they get students to that answer.

*Quick Tip from a Coach—Use a Prompting Guide*
*When we were developing our teachers' skills in teaching guided reading, we used the Great Habits Great Readers Guided Reading Prompting Guide. We prepared teachers by making sure they knew what level students were on, and in the meeting we'd pull out the prompting guide, select the prompt according to the student error, and practice right there with the prompt. What worked best was for teachers to have four or five prompts at the ready. They had to be prompts that would help the kids as readers. For instance, if there was a picture of elephants and the text said "elephants spray," saying "think of fire trucks" wouldn't really help them read the word "spray" because they would never have thought of that otherwise. We'd talk about what would be better for making that child a better reader. That prompting guide became a sacred resource for teaching guided reading at our school, and our scholars reaped the benefits.*

*—Judy Touzin, principal, Brooklyn, New York*

STRETCH IT

RIGOR

## KEY LEADERSHIP MOVES

**Probing Questions**

- "Let's look at yesterday's lesson. What were the key understandings you wanted the students to reach by the end of the class?"
- "Where was the gap in their ability to get there?"
- "Think about your previous learning. What are the key understandings that could have helped the students unpack this task or question?"
- What are the resources you have available that have a set of prompts you can use with your kids?"

**Planning and Practice**

- Pick an upcoming lesson. After unpacking the exemplar response to the central task, name the key pieces of previous understanding that students will need to access to solve the problem.
- Prepare where students will access that knowledge:

  Chart of key terms posted in the room (key understanding itself, or previously solved problem that highlights use of the skill)

  Handout in the students' folders/binders

  Previous notes taken on the topic in the students' binders
- Plan the script to ask students to access this knowledge. Then identify critical moments in the lesson to use the script to prompt the students.

**Real-Time Feedback**

- Nonverbal: point to the resources in the room.
- Whisper prompt: "I think students are making _____ error. Ask them about _____ [previously learned knowledge or skill] to cue them to strategies that can help them solve the problem."

---

 Rewatch clip 34: Prompting: Universal (Roll Back) and Strategic (Provide a Resource) (Key Leadership Move: Plan)

---

# STRATEGIC PROMPTS:
# CALL ON STUDENTS BASED ON THEIR LEARNING NEEDS

 Coaching Tips

## Teacher Context

### Challenges

- The teacher calls on primarily high students who already know the answer, and doesn't guarantee that the learning comes from all the students in his or her class.
- The teacher calls on consecutive struggling students, and the discussion stalls.

### Action Step

Call on students based on their learning needs (data driven):

- Call on lower- and middle-achieving students to unpack the question.
- If they struggle, try higher-achieving students.
- If they are easily unpacking, try a lower-achieving student.
- Put it all together: create a sequence of students to call on based on the rigor of each prompt (for example, first ask middle student, then low, then high, and so on).

### Action Step Overview

A perfect complementary action to accessing students' previously learned knowledge is to access the varied levels of learning in the room. The starting point is to identify where the teacher normally errs: does he or she call primarily on his or her highest-achieving students and the rest are left confused and not needing to think (often the initial new teacher error)? Or does he or she stick for so long with struggling students that he or she doesn't leverage the learning of other students in the room? Once you've identified the error, you can plan the right actions to close the gap.

**Probing Questions**

- "Recall the moment when Javier, Claire, and Marta all struggled to answer the question. Based on your monitoring of their independent practice prior to the discussion, were there any other students in the room who could have provided more help? What is the advantage of calling on one of them when other students are stuck?"

- "Let's look at your recent assessment data sorted from lowest to highest performing. Think back to whom you called on in class today—where did most of the called-on students fall within your data set? What is the limitation of calling only on students in that range?"

**Planning and Practice**

- The key to effective practice is to anticipate the responses students of varying levels will give in class. After identifying the likely responses, script out the order of students the teacher will call on during the discourse:

  - Start with a medium- or lower-achieving student to see what he or she can accomplish on his or her own.

  - Call on a higher-achieving student when the previous student is struggling to answer.

  - Call on a lower-achieving student when part of the learning has been revealed but he or she can solve the rest of it or "stamp" the understanding.

- Set up the names of one high-, one medium-, and one low-achieving student for the purpose of calling those names in the simulation and your being able to monitor when the teacher is calling on each level.

- Role-play multiple times, in the following order of complexity:

  - Round 1: first student called on gets it right (forces teacher to keep calling on lower and medium students to solidify understanding).

  - Round 2: first student gets it wrong; after calling on higher students, lower students get it right.

  - Round 3: first student gets it wrong; after calling on higher student, lower student still gets it wrong.

RIGOR

STRETCH IT

| **Real-Time Feedback** | • The key to real-time feedback is monitoring student learning during independent practice. Without that, it's difficult to intervene. If you do monitor, however, you can follow Nikki Bridges's lead from clip 31, which you watched in Phase 4 (monitoring student work). |
| --- | --- |

 Rewatch Clip 31: Strategic Prompting—Call on Students Based on Their Learning Needs (Key Leadership Move: Real-Time Feedback)

STRETCH IT

RIGOR

# STRATEGIC PROMPTS: STUDENTS PROMPTING STUDENTS

 *Coaching Tips*

## Teacher Context

### Challenge

The teacher is constantly prompting the students to use habits of discussion, but students are not building the habit of prompting each other.

### Action Step

Students prompting students: push students to use habits of discussion to critique or push one another's answers.

- Probe deeper: "[Peer], have you considered this point . . . ?"

### Action Step Overview

Previous habits of discussion ensured that students were situating their response in the context of their peers' comments; here we encourage them to lead the discussion. Rather than wait for the teacher to prompt students to elaborate, students start to take on those skills themselves. The following are some of these key habits:

- Peers prompt one another with the universal prompts. ("Tell me more." "What makes you think that?" "How do you know?" "Why is that important?")
- Students summarize. ("OK. So far we have established that . . .")
- Students prompt each other to clarify. ("Can you clarify your argument for me? Are you suggesting that . . . ?")
- Peers give a hint to another student to find the answer without telling him or her. ("Remember what you mentioned earlier from page ___? Tie that in to your answer here.")

(For a full list of habits of students prompting students, look at the High School Habits of Academic Discourse Guide on the DVD.)

There are two steps to developing these habits in the students: have the teacher roll them out (just like any routine or procedure: present them and practice) and then prompt for them in the moment. In most cases, these habits will be very new, so the key will be how the teacher rolls them out at the beginning.

<table>
<tr><td colspan="2" align="center">**KEY LEADERSHIP MOVES**</td></tr>
<tr>
<td>**Probing Questions**</td>
<td>

• [Watch video of class or remember it] "Let's evaluate the class discussion from last class. Where did it lose momentum, rigor, or direction? What would have been the ideal student intervention that would have kept the discussion on point?"

• "Let's look at the guide for habits of discussion [either from *Great Habits, Great Readers* or the High School Habits of Academic Discourse found on the DVD]. Which would be the appropriate next habits to develop in the students' ability to lead the discussion?"

• "Recall how you rolled out routines and procedures at the beginning of the year. What are the key actions that we can replicate in rolling out a habit of discussion?" [Refer to action steps in Phase 1]
</td>
</tr>
<tr>
<td>**Planning and Practice**</td>
<td>

• Use a video or transcript of the previous class discussion. Diagnose the habits that students were not using and identify where the teacher could have intervened. Identify one or two common errors and the universal prompts you want students to use to address the error. Practice prompting students to use that universal prompt.

• Practice rolling out the habit. [See Phase 1 for key actions]
</td>
</tr>
<tr>
<td>**Real-Time Feedback**</td>
<td>

• Nonverbal: point to the teacher's chart for universal prompts.

• Model: "Daniela [student], look at the habits of discussion posted on the wall: What could you say to your peers to prompt a deeper response?"
</td>
</tr>
</table>

STRETCH IT

RIGOR

## Strategies for Coaching

### Strategic Prompts

| Action Step | When to Use It | Probing Questions | Scenarios to Practice | Cues for Real-Time Feedback |
|---|---|---|---|---|
| Access previous understanding | Despite the use of Discourse 101 techniques, students are still unable to grasp the concept. | • "Let's look at yesterday's lesson. What were the key understandings you wanted the students to reach by the end of the class?" <br> • "Where was the gap in their ability to get there?" <br> • "Think about your previous learning. What are the key understandings that could have helped the students unpack this task/question?" <br> • "What are the resources you have available that have a set of prompts you can use with your kids?" | • Plan: unpack the exemplar response in the upcoming lesson, & name the key pieces of previous understanding that students will need to solve the problem. <br> • Prepare where students will access that knowledge (e.g., chart posted in the room, student handout, previous notes). <br> • Plan the script to ask students to access that knowledge. | Nonverbal: point to the resources in the room. <br><br> Whisper prompt: "I think students are making _____ error. Ask them about _____ [previously learned knowledge or skill] to cue them to strategies that can help them solve the problem." |
| Call on students based on their learning needs | Teacher calls on primarily high-achieving students who already know the answer, and doesn't guarantee the learning for the rest. <br><br> Teacher calls on consecutive struggling students, and the discussion stalls. | • "Recall the moment when Javier, Claire, and Marta all struggled to answer the question. Based on your monitoring of their independent practice prior to the discussion, were there any other students in the room who could have provided more help? What is the advantage of calling on one of them when other students are stuck?" | • Plan: anticipate the responses students of varying levels will give in class. | The key to real-time feedback is monitoring student learning during independent practice. Without that, it's difficult to intervene. If you do monitor, you can follow Nikki Bridges's lead from clip 31, which you watched in Phase 4 (monitoring student work). |

| Action Step | When to Use It | Probing Questions | Scenarios to Practice | Cues for Real-Time Feedback |
|---|---|---|---|---|
| | | • "Let's look at your recent assessment data sorted from lowest to highest performing. Think back to whom you called on in class today—where did most of the called-on students fall within your data set? What is the limitation of calling only on students in that range?" | • Script out the order of students to call on during the discourse: (1) start with a medium/lower student; (2) call on a higher student when the previous student is struggling to answer; (3) call on a lower student to "stamp" the understanding.<br><br>• Rd 1: first student called on gets it right (then call on lower or medium students to solidify understanding).<br><br>• Rd 2: first student gets it wrong; after calling on higher students, lower students get it right.<br><br>• Rd 3: first student gets it wrong; after calling on higher student, lower student still gets it wrong. | |

| Action Step | When to Use It | Probing Questions | Scenarios to Practice | Cues for Real-Time Feedback |
|---|---|---|---|---|
| Students prompting students | Teacher is constantly prompting the students to use habits of discussion, but students are not building the habit of prompting each other. | • [Watch video of class or remember it] "Where did the discussion go off track? What would have been the ideal student intervention to get back on point?"<br><br>• [Use the guide for habits of discussion on the DVD] "Which would be the appropriate next habits to develop in the students' ability to lead the discussion?"<br><br>• "Recall how you rolled out routines and procedures at the beginning of the year. What are the key actions that we can replicate in rolling out a habit of discussion?" [Refer to actions in Phase 1] | • ID 1–2 common errors and the universal prompts you want students to use to address the errors. Practice prompting students to use that universal prompt.<br><br>• Practice rolling out the habit. [See Phase 1 for key actions] | Nonverbal: point to teacher's chart for universal prompts.<br><br>Model:: "Daniela [student], what could you say to your peers to prompt a deeper response?" |

## Go Conceptual

> ### Teacher Professional Development Goal
>
> **Go Conceptual:** Get students to do the conceptual thinking and understanding in each lesson.

The final action steps of this book are a culmination of all previous action steps for rigor; they simply take them deeper. At the heart of this action step is the following premise:

> ## Core Idea
>
> If you know how to do it, you understand the basics.
> If you can explain the how and why, you have mastered it.

To help explain this principle, let me share my experience with my daughters.

My two daughters are nearly polar opposites when it comes to their academic strengths in school. The first has a passionate love of literature and can easily unpack complex texts and bring ideas together in the humanities—but she struggles with math. My other daughter finds math very simple: she understands it intuitively and enjoys the challenge of resolving a difficult word problem—yet she struggles with history and generating her own thesis statement for English essays.

I cannot really explain why they ended up wired so differently coming from the same gene pool, but it has offered me a fascinating opportunity to observe up close how their two brains function.

In both of their areas of strength, they have an organic understanding of the material: they have an overall framework on which they "hang" their knowledge, allowing them to make new connections and easily build a deeper understanding. (They aren't always aware that they do this because it comes so naturally.) In their areas of growth, however, their brain stops functioning in that manner. Each piece of knowledge is a discrete object that lives in a different compartment of their brain, and because the pieces are not connected, it is extremely taxing to remember all of them and utilize them consistently.

Developing conceptual understanding is about creating a framework on which students can hang their knowledge. It allows students to understand the "why" of what they're doing, which makes it easier to internalize and retain. A humanities and a STEM example might help clarify.

For my literary-minded daughter, learning to do quadratic equations started as a procedure: just follow the steps and you're done. Of course, with that approach, all you had to do was give her a word problem with the slightest complexity and she was stumped. The procedure didn't set her up to be able to problem-solve. The most successful learning has come when she is pushed to name the conceptual understanding behind the algorithm. For example, she needed to be able to articulate the zero product property (we looked at this in the introduction to strategic prompting) in order to understand why she needed to set the factors equal to zero. This helped her catch the computational errors that she was making.

For my mathematically inclined daughter, analyzing the theme of savagery versus civilization in *Frankenstein* was overwhelming. In order to learn to analyze the text and write a quality essay, she needed to name the skills she was applying when unpacking the text and understanding themes. She needed to name the steps of annotating the text to unpack difficult passages, and the characteristics of a good thesis statement.

In both cases, my daughters needed to understand the "how" and the "why" of what they were doing in order to produce a quality answer. This is the heart of conceptual understanding. Conceptual understanding solidifies learning, takes the learning deeper, and prepares students to show mastery of the skill or content in a variety of situations.

> ### Findings from the Field: Learn the Content Together
>
> Once, I was talking to an elementary school teacher about her science lesson plans, and I realized she didn't understand the concept of density herself. So we pulled up a computer simulation, and we looked at it together. In the simulation, we manipulated the mass and volume of different blocks floating in water. We found, for instance, that if we increased the mass of one of the blocks without also increasing the volume, the density of the block increased, and the block sank. We got to a moment where the teacher said, "Ohh, now I get it!" Once that happens, then they can go in and get their students to that same point. To actually push content, in science or any subject, teachers have to dive in deeply. Sometimes that means learning the content as a student before you can teach it.
> —Christine Denison-Lipschitz, principal, Dallas, Texas

Here are the typical errors that occur when a teacher is trying to build conceptual understanding:

- The teacher moves on too quickly after asking a challenging question, possibly answering it rather than giving students a chance to do so.

- The teacher recognizes when students have made an error, but struggles to identify the deeper errors that have led them to their incorrect answers.

- The teacher does not ask students to use technical or academic language when giving answers.

- Students answer a question easily, and the teacher moves on rather than pushing them to go further.

# GO CONCEPTUAL:
# VERBALIZE CONCEPTUAL UNDERSTANDING

 *Coaching Tips*

## Teacher Context

### Challenges

- The teacher moves on too quickly after asking a challenging question, possibly answering it rather than giving students a chance to do so.

- The teacher recognizes when students have made an error, but struggles to identify the deeper errors that have led them to their incorrect answers.

### Action Step

Ask students to verbalize a conceptual understanding of content, not just the answer to a specific question:

- "That's the procedure. Now tell me why that works."
- "Can you generalize that idea to apply to all problems like this one?"
- "Use the following terms [terms learned in previous classes] in restating your answer."

### Action Step Overview

Solving a problem or completing a task is one level of student proficiency. Being able to articulate the conceptual understanding behind that task is another level altogether, one that leads toward mastery. Teachers who continually push their students to explain the "why" behind an answer will develop students to retain and deepen their understanding.

---

### KEY LEADERSHIP MOVES

**Probing Questions**

- "Let's look back at the standard aligned to this task: What are the key understandings required to master this objective?"
- "When you ask a student to explain why [the answer is correct], what is the ideal response you're looking for in this moment?"
- "What response did students give you, and how did you respond?"
- "Looking at the potential prompts for conceptual understanding, which would be most relevant to use in this context?"

**Planning and Practice**

Script the ideal response and questioning sequence to get to that response, and practice "stamping the understanding": having students articulate the key understanding after solving the problem correctly.

**Real-Time Feedback**

Model: "Mr. Smith, I'm impressed with Jordan's answer. Jordan, can you generalize the _____ [rule/strategy/skill] you used that we could use in any problem?"

---

 Rewatch clip 6: Go Conceptual
(Key Leadership Move: Real-Time Feedback)

---

# GO CONCEPTUAL: UPGRADE VOCABULARY

 *Coaching Tips*

## Teacher Context

### Challenge
Teacher does not ask students to use technical or academic language when giving answers.

### Action Step
Upgrade vocabulary—ask students to use technical or academic language when answering questions:

- "That's the right idea generally. Now state it again using proper mathematical/ historical/scientific language."
- "State it again using your Academic Word Wall as a resource."

### Action Step Overview
If you can write about it and talk about it, then you have full mastery of a concept. Too often, however, teachers leave students off the hook when it comes to talking. If the student has a general idea of the concept, they are satisfied. Demanding that students use the appropriate technical or academic language doesn't just elevate the quality of the answer: it helps make a student smarter.

## KEY LEADERSHIP MOVES

| | |
|---|---|
| **Probing Questions** | • "What is the ideal academic or technical language that you wanted students to use in their response?"<br><br>• "What was the gap between that ideal response and what students said?"<br><br>• "How can we create or leverage a resource that will push students to upgrade their vocabulary in their answers?" |
| **Planning and Practice** | • The most important part of this action step is to make sure that students have access to the right vocabulary. Focus the planning on creating a word wall or academic "cheat sheet" with key terms. That way, the practice can simply focus on pointing students to that resource when they answer the question.<br><br>• Script in moments when the teacher can punch key vocabulary terms when modeling. Script ideal student responses that include key vocabulary terms.<br><br>• Script the prompts to use when students don't use mathematical/ scientific/academic language: "That's the right idea. Now state it again using your Academic Word Wall as a resource." |
| **Real-Time Feedback** | Nonverbal: point to the academic language resource (word wall, cheat sheet, and so on). |

# GO CONCEPTUAL: STRETCH IT

*Coaching Tips*

## Teacher Context

### Challenge
Students answer a question easily, and the teacher moves on rather than pushing them to go further.

### Action Step
- Stretch it: ask particular students to answer a more difficult extension to a given question:
  - "What would the answer be if I changed it to [change the problem to something more complex]?"
  - "Is there an alternative way to solve this problem/do this task?"
  - "What do you think is the strongest counterargument to yours, and how would you refute it?"

### Action Step Overview
This action step is well placed in the Stretch It phase—it deals with students who are already learning what they most urgently need to learn, so it's secondary to getting every student to that initial level of learning. However, it's still a step that must not be underestimated or ignored. Every student needs to learn rigorously, and this is the action step that enables the teacher to raise the rigor for the students who pick up specific skills the most quickly even while keeping it at manageable level for those who might still be piecing the skill together.

**KEY LEADERSHIP MOVES**

| | |
|---|---|
| **Probing Questions** | • "What happened after you called on Jermaine and he answered your question correctly? How does that affect his learning? What could you do to raise the rigor for him without making it unmanageable for the rest of the class?" |
| | • [Watch video of a teacher using the Stretch It technique when students answer a question correctly] "What did the teacher do to stretch the learning?" |
| **Planning and Practice** | • Identify moments in the lesson plan where students might get to correct answers easily. Script "stretch it" questions to increase the rigor of those moments—for example, how/why, cite evidence, evaluate the answer. |
| **Real-Time Feedback** | • Nonverbal: pull your fingers apart—as if stretching a piece of gum—to signal that it's a good time to raise the rigor with a stretch-it question. |

## Go Conceptual

| Action Step | When to Use It | Probing Questions | Scenarios to Practice | Cues for Real-Time Feedback |
|---|---|---|---|---|
| Verbalize a conceptual under-standing of content | Teacher moves on too quickly after asking a challenging question, possibly answering it rather than giving students a chance to do so. Teacher recognizes when students have made an error, but struggles to identify the deeper errors that have led them to their incorrect answers. | • "Let's look back at the standard aligned to this task: What are the key understand-ings required to master this objective?" <br>• "When you ask a student to explain why [the answer is correct], what is the ideal response you're looking for in this moment?" <br>• "What response did students give you, and how did you respond?" <br>• "Looking at the potential prompts for conceptual under-standing, which would be most relevant to use in this context?" | • Script an ideal response and the questioning sequence to get to that response. | Model: "Mr. Smith, I'm impressed with Jordan's answer. Jordan, can you generalize the _____ [rule/ strategy/ skill] you used that we could use in any problem?" |
| Upgrade vocabulary | Teacher does not ask students to use techni-cal/ academic language when giving answers. | • "What is the ideal academic or technical language that you wanted students to use in their response?" <br>• "What was the gap between that ideal response and what students said?" <br>• "How can we create or leverage a resource that will push students to upgrade their vocabulary in their answers?" | • Create a word wall/ chart with key academic terms you will want students to use in their answers. <br>• Script in moments when the teacher can punch key vocabulary terms when modeling. Script ideal student responses that include key vocabulary terms. | Nonverbal: point to the academic language resource (word wall, cheat sheet, etc.). |

RIGOR

STRETCH IT

| Action Step | When to Use It | Probing Questions | Scenarios to Practice | Cues for Real-Time Feedback |
|---|---|---|---|---|
| | | | • Script the prompts to use when students don't use mathematical/scientific/academic language: "That's the right idea. Now state it again using your Academic Word Wall as a resource." | |
| Stretch it | Students answer a question easily, and teacher moves on rather than pushing them to go further. | • "What happened after you called on Jermaine and he answered your question correctly? How does that affect his learning? What could you do to raise the rigor for him without making it unmanageable for the rest of the class?"<br><br>• [Watch video of a teacher using the Stretch It technique when students answer a question correctly] "What did the teacher do to stretch the learning?" | • Identify moments in the lesson plan where students might get to correct answers easily. Script "stretch it" questions to increase the rigor of those moments; e.g., how/why, cite evidence, evaluate the answer. | Nonverbal: pull your fingers apart—as if stretching a piece of gum—to signal that it's a good time to raise the rigor with a stretch-it question. |

---

## Stop and Jot

What are the three top coaching ideas you plan to use to train your teachers in these Stretch It skills? Jot them down here.

_____

_____

_____

# CONCLUSION

When legendary football coach Vince Lombardi took charge of the Green Bay Packers in 1959, he delivered an opening speech that would establish his long-standing reputation as a motivational speaker. But his words did more than just motivate his players: they revealed what kind of leader he was going to be. They set an unprecedentedly high bar, and they put in place the expectation that coach and players alike would keep fighting to be their best—even though their best could never be entirely flawless.

Here's how Lombardi described his vision to his players:

> Gentlemen, we are going to relentlessly chase perfection, knowing full well we will not catch it, because nothing is perfect. But we are going to relent-lessly chase it, because in the process we will catch excellence. I am not remotely interested in just being good.[1]

> ### Core Idea
>
> To paraphrase Vince Lombardi:
> "Perfection is not attainable. But if we chase perfection, we can catch excellence."

Chasing perfection, catching excellence: I can think of no better way to describe what school leaders and their teachers are able to do when they embrace a clear pathway to improvement. We can't build perfect teachers—not in the first ninety days of teaching, not in the first year of teaching, not in ten years of teaching. But *pursuing* perfection is precisely what we do when we identify the most microcosmic ways a classroom could improve, when we tackle them one at a time to keep the stream of growth steady and sustainable, and when we role-play the moments that matter the most until they're as close to flawless as they can be before the school bell rings again. And we catch excellence when we do so.

Just ask Jackson Tobin, one of the new teachers we've gotten to know over the course of this book. Jackson always loved writing as a teacher, and at the time of the writing of this book, he channeled that energy, along with his love for teaching, into graduate student teaching in the Creative Writing department at the

University of Wisconsin-Madison. As he explained in an email to his principal, Nikki Bridges, teaching undergraduates had more in common with teaching elementary students than he had anticipated:

> I also wanted to write to let you know that last week I won the Richard Knowles Teaching Award in my program. It's a prize given to one teacher in the Creative Writing department each year.
>
> I had a meeting with my supervisor earlier in the year that left me feeling confident about my chances. The week before that meeting, he came and observed my class, taking copious notes, and when we met he went over them. He had a lot of really positive things to say, and I was flattered and very proud, but what struck me most was that so many of the things he highlighted as exceptional teaching were the things I hadn't planned for. Sure, my lecture on the line breaks of *In a Station at the Metro* was good—but what really blew him away was how I responded to one student's obviously incorrect analysis by neither agreeing nor invalidating it, and then looped in the other students to do that work for me. Yes, he liked that I used the students' own work to show strong examples of poetic images—but what was really great was that I then had the other students rank those images, and had a third group defend or oppose the rankings, so that by the end of the exercise, every student in the class had to speak.
>
> In other words: the things that made for exceptional teaching were the things I learned at Leadership Prep—things that I knew so deeply by the end of my time there, that I employed so automatically, I didn't even realize I was using them in my college classroom. Of course, I did have to train myself to stop self-interrupting them, and twice I said "track me" to a room full of undergrads, but the point is, I'm still using what you taught me. I'm using it every single day, without even thinking about it. I would never have won this award if it weren't for you.

Jackson's story shows how powerfully the tactics in the Get Better Faster Scope and Sequence can affect one teacher—and every student that teacher works with for the remainder of his career. The cycle of learning that Nikki set in place for Jackson in his very first year of teaching will matter to each of the kindergarteners Jackson worked with at Leadership Prep Ocean Hill as they make their way from elementary school, to middle school, and all the way up to and beyond their high school graduations; and what he learned will have no less profound an impact on Jackson's undergraduates' lives as they begin their careers as writers. Teach a man to fish, and he fishes for a lifetime; teach a teacher to teach, and the ripple effects are never-ending.

But what's even more powerful is how far the race to perfection can carry whole cohorts of teachers collectively. Effective coaching strategies like these are being carried out by talented instructional leaders across the country. Teachers supported by these techniques develop at a faster rate. And many of these teachers grow to take on instructional leadership roles that enable them to pass on their newfound skills to others. They're already using the coaching principles in this book as well as the teaching skills. They're sending out the ripples of excellence far beyond their own classrooms and their own students.

There's no denying it: chasing perfection is hard work, a cycle that never ends. But it is work that not only makes teachers extraordinarily good at their jobs but also honors the reasons we all became educators in the first place. If we believe in the ability of humans to learn and to grow, perpetuating this cycle of growth from new teacher to master is the *only* logical way we can approach school leadership. There's a poetic as well as a practical beauty to it: the key to granting our students access to a bright future is to give that same gift to their teachers now. We need not—must not—relent in our pursuit of perfection as long as the goal of giving this gift to every child remains unattained. The road is a long and steep one, but the excellence we'll catch along the way is its own reward.

# Get Better Faster
# Coach's Guide

Quick Reference Guide Aligned to the Get Better Faster Scope and Sequence

Printer-friendly version can be found on the DVD. Online access at my.paulbambrick.com.

# PHASE 1 (PRE-TEACHING)

## Phase 1 Management

### Develop Essential Routines & Procedures

| | Routines & Procedures 101 | | | |
|---|---|---|---|---|
| **Action Step** | **When to Use It** | **Probing Questions** | **Scenarios to Practice** | **Cues for Real-Time Feedback** |
| Plan & practice critical routines & procedures moment by moment | Teacher does not have clear routines established for the classroom. | • [Show a model video or do a live model] "What is each step the teacher takes in this routine?" "What is the teacher doing and what are the students doing?"<br>• "Describe what you want [certain routine] to look like. Ideally, what would students do during that transition/routine? What would you be doing?" | Complete a template for the key routines in the teacher's classroom (most important: student entry and exit, transitions, materials distribution, and listening). Rehearse in the classroom setting.<br>• Rd 1: basic mastery: focus on the specific words and actions the teacher will use, such as where to look and stand, and key ways to break the routine down into smaller steps for the students.<br>• Rd 2: add minor student errors in following instructions (not too much: you want to build muscle memory!). | N/A |
| Plan & practice the rollout | The routine is new for the students (beginning of the year or when changing a routine). | • [Show a model video or do a live model of an effective rollout] "What did you notice about that rollout that made it effective?" | • Focus on scripting the I Do: break it down, pregnant pause, repeat pause, repeat step-by-step.<br>• Keep the language positive and enthusiastic, including a challenge. | Model: If the teacher modeling is ineffective, prompt: "Mr. Smith, am I following your model effectively?" [then model the correct actions and narrate what you're doing]. |

| Action Step | When to Use It | Probing Questions | Scenarios to Practice | Cues for Real-Time Feedback |
|---|---|---|---|---|
| | | • "What will be the most difficult parts of the routine for you to deliver and for students to master?"<br>• "What are the key micro-actions for you to model to perfect this part of the routine?" | • Memorize the roll-out speech, then stand up and practice.<br>• Leader or peers should play roles of students to make practice more authentic. | |
| **Strong Voice** | | | | |
| **Square Up, Stand Still** | Posture: teacher undermines his/her leadership presence by slouching, shifting from foot to foot, or facing at an angle away from the students. | • [Watch video] "How does the teacher use her body language to communicate leadership in her classroom?"<br>• [Model giving directions with a relaxed posture, then while squaring up and standing still] "What is the difference in the way I communicated the first way versus the second way?"<br>• "What is the value in communicating leadership with our body language?" | • Practice maintaining a formal posture while delivering a lesson on routines and procedures. Note when the teacher is squaring up and standing still, and when the teacher's body begins to become informal/weak.<br>• Film the practice—or use a mirror—so that the new teacher can see what he or she looks like while delivering instructions. | Nonverbal: model exaggerated posture and stance—shift your body upward and arch shoulders to remind the teacher to square up and stand still. |

| Action Step | When to Use It | Probing Questions | Scenarios to Practice | Cues for Real-Time Feedback |
|---|---|---|---|---|
| **Formal register** | Tone: teacher's vocal register is too casual or informal. | • "Imagine you had to say 'it's time to leave' to three different audiences: your friend after dinner, a symphony concert audience at the end of a performance, or when a building is on fire. Speak out loud how you would deliver those words differently to each audience." [After teacher does so] "What is the value and purpose of the middle one: your formal register?"<br><br>• "When is it important to use formal register? What message does it send to the students?"<br><br>• For a teacher who knows formal register: "What are the keys to formal register?"<br><br>• [Watch video of the teacher's classroom] "What conditions lead to you drop your formal register?" | • Videotape the teacher during practice, and review the footage so the teacher can hear when he/she is maintaining a formal register, and when his/her register begins to become casual/informal.<br><br>• Practice maintaining a formal tone while delivering a lesson on routines and procedures. Note when the teacher is maintaining a formal register, and when the teacher's register becomes too informal or casual. | Nonverbal: combine Square Up, Stand Still gesture with pointing to your mouth to remind the teacher to speak in a formal register. |

## Write Lesson Plans

| | Develop Lesson Plans 101 | | | |
|---|---|---|---|---|
| Action Step | When to Use It | Probing Questions | Scenarios to Practice | Cues for Real-Time Feedback |
| Write precise learning objectives | Lesson objectives are not data driven, are not manageable and measurable, or have not been identified. | • "Let's look at the upcoming assessment and the questions related to this objective. What do students have to know and do to be able to answer one of these questions correctly?"<br><br>• "If you asked them how they know their answer is correct, what key conceptual understanding do you want them to be able to articulate?"<br><br>• [After breaking down all the skills/knowledge required to answer the assessment tasks]: "Of all the skills/knowledge, what are the most important parts for you to address in this lesson? Which do students already have some mastery of, and which are the key next skills to push them further?" | • Pull out upcoming assessments to identify the right end goal: break down too-broad objectives to make them manageable for individual lessons.<br><br>• Planning & practice are identical: plan a full week of upcoming objectives together.<br><br>• Make sure you have all materials at hand during the meeting: upcoming lesson plans, curriculum scope and sequence, interim assessment, final exam/state test released items, etc. | N/A |
| Script a basic "I Do" | Teacher stumbles or doesn't know what to say during the "I Do" part of the lesson. | • "Let's look at your objective and the key understandings that students need to have in order to master it. How will you explain those key understandings?" | • Plan: write out key understandings students must reach by the end of the lesson. | Nonverbal: hold out your palm and point to it with the other hand to indicate to the teacher to go back to his/her script and follow it. |

| Action Step | When to Use It | Probing Questions | Scenarios to Practice | Cues for Real-Time Feedback |
|---|---|---|---|---|
| | | • "What will be the key points of confusion for many of the students? Given that answer, where should you emphasize your points most clearly to address that confusion?"<br><br>• "What are the key points you want to communicate during the I Do?"<br><br>• "How can you write out your I Do to make it easy to remember and deliver in the moment?" | • Script the I Do into the lesson plan word for word. Remove extraneous words. Don't begin practice until you have fully tightened the script.<br><br>• Practice delivering: look for the teacher adding extraneous words or sentences that you could cut to reduce the model to what is essential. | |
| Design Exit Ticket aligned to the objective | Teacher's Exit Ticket doesn't align to the objective. | • "When you finish the class, what will students be able to do to show you that they have mastered the objective?"<br><br>• "What key question/task could you give them at the end of the lesson to assess that mastery?"<br><br>• "Look at the upcoming interim assessment/year-end test: How can we align your question to that level of difficulty and rigor?" | • Plan/revise a week's worth of Exit Tickets. Have the upcoming interim/year-end assessment questions in hand to help set the rigor of the Exit Ticket.<br><br>• Look at previous Exit Tickets to see where students are struggling and what skills need to continue to be assessed. | N/A |

## Internalize Existing Lesson Plans

| Action Step | When to Use It | Probing Questions | Scenarios to Practice | Cues for Real-Time Feedback |
|---|---|---|---|---|
| **Internalize and rehearse key parts of the lesson** | Teacher hasn't internalized the lesson, and may stumble when delivering it. | • "What parts of the lesson plan are most important for you to know cold? What is the value of memorizing these parts of the lesson?"<br><br>• "How do you normally prepare and internalize a lesson plan?"<br><br>• "What are the challenges to remembering these plans during delivery?" | • Give the teacher a set time to learn a specific chunk of the lesson cold, and then have him/her try delivering it to a partner without looking down at the lesson.<br><br>• Practice one chunk of the lesson at a time. Once a teacher has it cold, put those chunks together until he/she has it completely memorized.<br><br>• Build a lesson internalization routine: determine when s/he will spend time each day memorizing key parts of the lesson, how he/she will practice, and who will be his/her practice partner (even if the "partner" is as basic as a mirror). | Model: when teacher is struggling with the lesson plan, intervene and cue students to turn & talk. Give the teacher 30–60 seconds to skim the plan before jumping back into the lesson. |
| **Build time stamps into the lesson** | Teacher runs out of time, completing only part of the lesson plan and leaving large chunks untaught. | • "What is the ideal amount of time you want for independent practice at the end? What are the challenges to making sure that students have that amount of time?"<br><br>• "What are the key tasks students need to do to be able to work independently effectively? What are the parts of the lesson we could cut short if you are running out of time?" | • Write down specific time stamps in their lesson plan. Note which parts of the lesson could be trimmed or cut if teacher is running over.<br><br>• Rehearse the lesson with timer in hand. Cut unnecessary language that is slowing the teacher down. | Nonverbal: hold up fingers for how many more minutes to spend in that section of the lesson. |

# PHASE 2: DAYS 1–30

## Phase 2 Management

### Roll Out & Monitor Routines

| Action Step | When to Use It | What to Do | | |
| --- | --- | --- | --- | --- |
| | | Probing Questions | Scenarios to Practice | Cues for Real-Time Feedback |
| Economy of language | Teacher's directions are unclear or use too many words. | • "What happened yesterday when you asked your students to ___? What caused the confusion?"<br><br>• "What is the value in using fewer words to describe what students should do?"<br><br>• [Play video of teacher's instructions] "What is another way you could have restated these directions to make them clearer for students?" [or] "Write down all the directions you gave. Where did you use more words than needed?"<br><br>• [If teacher struggles, model for him/her] "Let me deliver those same instructions. [Model] What do you notice about the difference between my delivery and your own?" | • Script clear, concise instructions together. Plan them out word-by-word: don't take shortcuts! Remove all extraneous words.<br><br>• Provide feedback on clarity before practice: most errors can be fixed before your practice.<br><br>• Rehearse key directions. If necessary, model for teacher what is most effective.<br><br>• Focus on the pregnant pause between each component of the instruction: students often become confused when given too many directions at once. | Nonverbal: hold up a red card for too many words.<br><br>Nonverbal: hold up a sign that says "What to Do."<br><br>Whisper prompt: "When you bring everyone back from this assignment, just say: 'Pencils down. Eyes on me! No extra words."<br><br>Model: model giving concise directions using 3–5 words.<br><br>Model: Ask a student to repeat the teacher's instructions. |

## Routines & Procedures 201

| Action Step | When to Use It | Probing Questions | Scenarios to Practice | Cues for Real-Time Feedback |
|---|---|---|---|---|
| **Revise routines** | Students are following the routine, but it is inefficient or ineffective. | • "What has been the challenge in implementing this routine?"<br>• "Where does the breakdown begin: When is the first moment of students not following the routine?"<br>• [Watch video of a better routine] "What can you draw from this routine to make your own more effective?" | • Focus practice at the point where the routine has been going wrong. Model any student errors you anticipate.<br>• Pay attention to teacher positioning (stand in ideal location), and incorporate Strong Voice (posture, register), and What to Do.<br>• Rehearse the first words to say to nonresponsive students. | Model: "This is my favorite routine. Can I show our students the new way to do it?" |
| **Do It Again** | The routine is effective, but students aren't following it. | • "What are the keys to running a Do It Again effectively?"<br>• "Why is it important to have students repeat this routine when they haven't done it correctly?"<br>• [Watch video] "Where are the moments when students are incorrectly executing the routine? What would you like to see them do differently?"<br>• "What is challenging about noticing or stating what you want to see students change when they do it again?" | • Plan each step of the Do It Again sequence:<br>  – Use Strong Voice (Square Up, Stand Still; use formal register).<br>  – Deliver the What to Do (name the error, name the correct action).<br>  – Challenge the students to do better.<br>  – Give the signal to restart the routine.<br>• Role-play the revised routine: make the same student errors from class and have the teacher practice implementing Do It Again until the routine looks flawless. | Nonverbal: make a circle with your finger to cue teacher to have students redo that part of routine.<br>Verbal: "Ms. Smith, I know we can do that better. What would you like to see us do differently this time?"<br>Model: "Can I show our students what we'd like them to do?" Whisper to teacher what you are modeling. |

| Action Step | When to Use It | Probing Questions | Scenarios to Practice | Cues for Real-Time Feedback |
|---|---|---|---|---|
| **Cut It Short** | Teacher asks students to redo routines they have already performed sufficiently well. | • "Remember when you had students do it again for the third time? Did they perform it even better after that?"<br><br>• "What is the purpose of having your students do it again? When is it no longer valuable to do it again?" | • Practice Cut It Short the same way as you would practice Do It Again, but with extra emphasis on the conclusion of the Do It Again. As you repeat the practice, try varying how quickly you perform the routine correctly so that the teacher learns to truly evaluate when it's time to stop the Do It Again. | Nonverbal: signal to the teacher that it's time to stop repeating the Do It Again.<br><br>Model: cut short the Do It Again. |
| **Teacher Radar** | | | | |
| **Scan hot spots** | Teacher is not noticing the earliest actions of off-task behavior. | • [Watch video of class] "At what moment do the first students begin to go off track?"<br><br>• "Which students are most often off task?"<br><br>• "If you know these students are most likely to veer off track, where are your 'hot spots' that you want to scan continuously throughout the lesson?" | • Have the teacher identify hot spots and the moments in the lesson plan to scan those hot spots.<br><br>• Practice: role-play student behavior you want the teacher to be able to catch and correct by scanning. Repeat until the teacher is consistently scanning the hot spots and identifying off-task behavior. | Nonverbal: hold up sign that says "Scan."<br><br>Nonverbal: hold your hand out over a hot spot at the moment you want the teacher to notice and correct off-task behavior. |
| **Be Seen Looking** | The teacher is not scanning and watching the students; students veer off task as a result. | • [Watch video of lesson and pick key moments] "Where are you looking right now? Where should you be looking?" | • Practice scanning every row (for students' hands and eyes) of the classroom while teaching. | Nonverbal: crane your neck to indicate that teacher should do the same. |

| Action Step | When to Use It | Probing Questions | Scenarios to Practice | Cues for Real-Time Feedback |
|---|---|---|---|---|
| | | • [Model Be Seen Looking] "What did you notice about what I did when giving directions? What is the value of that body language?" | • Sit in the classroom far from the teacher. Model off-task behavior for the teacher to identify when scanning. | Model: take over the routine and crane neck/scan with your finger while scanning students. |
| Circulate with purpose (break the plane) | The teacher is stationary: lack of movement makes students go off task. | • "Where did the off-task behavior start? Where were you standing at that time? What is the challenge of not moving around during the lesson?"<br>• [Watch the video] "How much time do you spend away from the front of the room?" | • Identify the hot spots in the room (i.e., where off-task behaviors often occur).<br>• Create a pathway based on the hot spots.<br>• Practice moving along this pathway while teaching, stopping at hot spots to scan and giving students a nonverbal redirect. | Nonverbal: point to a corner of the room where the teacher should stand. |
| Move away from the student who is speaking | When one student is speaking, other students become disengaged. | • "When did the off-task behavior start? Where were you in the classroom in relation to where the problem occurred?"<br>• "What is the value of moving away from the student who is speaking?" | • Have the teacher pretend to call on an imaginary student. Then, while the imaginary student is responding, you can be playing the part of another student in another part of the room who is off task. The teacher can then practice moving around to remind the other student that he/she is still obligated to pay attention, and, if necessary, to give a silent redirect. | Nonverbal: cue the teacher to move away from the student who is speaking. |

| Action Step | When to Use It | Probing Questions | Scenarios to Practice | Cues for Real-Time Feedback |
|---|---|---|---|---|
| **Whole-Class Reset** | | | | |
| **Planned whole-class reset** | A class has slid into low engagement *over a few days* without the teacher realizing it. | • "How did you establish that routine so effectively the first time?"<br><br>• "What are the challenges in implementing the routine right now? Where does this routine break down?"<br><br>• "What are the root causes of the deterioration of this routine?"<br><br>• [Show a model: video or yourself modeling] "What did you notice: What were the key actions the teacher took to reengage the classroom?" | • Script the reset word by word: use as minimal language as possible, e.g.: pause, "Eyes on me," narrate the problem, give direction, scan, and wait for 100%. If not there, give a second direction to students not on task. Continue the lesson.<br><br>• Practice: incorporate all previous action steps, particularly: Strong Voice (posture & register), What to Do, Teacher Radar (scan).<br><br>• Rd 1: all students "comply" right away.<br><br>• Rd 2: a few students still don't comply, and teacher has to get them on target. | N/A (reset is planned in advance) |
| **In-the-moment whole-class reset** | A class has slid into low engagement *within the same class period* without the teacher realizing it. | • "When are typical moments when your students go off track?" [If teacher cannot answer, show video footage of a part of the class when students frequently go off track, and use the video to guide the teacher in identifying the moment when a reset is needed] | • From video of the teacher's classroom, practice the moment when engagement drops. | Nonverbal: create/use a cue for "reset" or hold up a sign. |

| Action Step | When to Use It | Probing Questions | Scenarios to Practice | Cues for Real-Time Feedback |
|---|---|---|---|---|
| | | • "What are the key indicators in the class that you can look for that will tell you it is time to reset the class?"<br><br>• "When have you been most successful in resetting the classroom? How could you apply those same skills to this other context?" | • Script a generic in-the-moment reset that could be used in every situation: pause, "Eyes on me," narrate the problem, give direction, scan, and wait for 100%. If not there, give a second direction to students not on task. Continue the lesson.<br><br>• Incorporate previous action steps.<br><br>• Rd 1: all students "comply" right away.<br><br>• Rd 2: a few students still don't comply and teacher has to get them on target. | Model: "Students, we need to reset ourselves right now." Model a reset for the teacher. |

**Phase 2 Rigor**

**Independent Practice**

| Action Step | When to Use It | Write the Exemplar | | Cues for Real-Time Feedback |
| --- | --- | --- | --- | --- |
| | | **Probing Questions** | **Scenarios to Practice** | |
| **Script the ideal written student response** | The teacher doesn't know what a rigorous student response looks like. | • "Let's pull out independent practice task. What do you want students to write when you give them this task? [If not yet written] Take a few minutes to write your exemplar."<br>• "What answers would be only partially correct?"<br>• "How do you want students to show or organize their work in answering this question?"<br>• "What are the advantages of writing an exemplar response? How is it different from writing objectives?" | • Write or revise exemplars for written-response questions in upcoming lessons.<br>• Spar with another exemplar: either another teacher's exemplar or the analysis of experts in the field (e.g., Shakespearean critics).<br>• Break down the exemplar: ID key things the student will need to do to produce a response of the same quality. | N/A |
| **Align independent practice to the assessment** | Independent practice activities are not as rigorous as the final assessment students are working toward. | • "Let's look at the upcoming assessment. What is the gap between the rigor of your independent practice and that of the assessment?" | • Pull up a lesson plan and upcoming assessment: write/revise independent practice to match the rigor of the upcoming assessment. | N/A |

| Action Step | When to Use It | Probing Questions | Scenarios to Practice | Cues for Real-Time Feedback |
|---|---|---|---|---|
| | | • "What can we do to make the independent practice more aligned to the rigor of the end goal?" <br> • [If teacher struggles to see the gap, use a model] "Here are two different independent practice activities. Why is activity 1 more aligned and more rigorous than activity 2?" [Teacher responds] "What are your key takeaways for designing quality independent practice tasks?" | • Write scaffolded questions that ramp up to the rigor of the final assessment question. | |
| **Independent Practice** | | | | |
| **Write first, talk second** | Class discussion begins without students having the opportunity to write first. | • "What is the value of having students write before beginning class discussion?" <br> • "What is the most important information you want to students to grapple with/write about before beginning the conversation?" | • Plan lessons that consistently place writing time before discussion time: annotate a week's worth of lesson plans with short moments to write before talking. <br> • Minimal role play: practice the launch of the writing task and bringing students back to discussion afterwards. | N/A |

| Action Step | When to Use It | Probing Questions | Scenarios to Practice | Cues for Real-Time Feedback |
|---|---|---|---|---|
| **Daily entry prompt (Do Now)** | Teacher begins class before students have had a chance to write/work independently. | • "What is the purpose of a Do Now?"<br>• Timing: "How long are students spending on the Do Now?" [If too long] "How can we reduce the Do Now so that students finish earlier?"<br>• Relevance: "What should be the purpose of your Do Now in this lesson: tell you how well students learned the content from yesterday? Or prepare them to learn the content you're teaching today?" | • Write Do Now questions for upcoming lessons: short (3–5 minutes to complete), easy to monitor (can check student work) and aligned to objective.<br>• Rehearse a start-of-class greeting that will prompt the students to begin working on the Do Now. | N/A |
| **Exit Ticket or longer independent practice** | Lessons include less than 10 minutes' worth of independent practice. | • "What is the purpose of daily independent practice/Exit Tickets?"<br>• Timing: "How long are students spending on independent practice/Exit Tickets?"<br>• Relevance: "What do you need your Exit Ticket to tell about what students learned today?" | • If challenge is quality of Exit Ticket: write Exit Tickets that confirm student mastery. Look at IP and Exit Tickets side by side to make sure they align in level of rigor/complexity.<br>• If challenge is delivery: spend time on the instructions the teacher gives to students during the times, integrating management action steps: Strong Voice, What to Do, and Teacher Radar. | N/A |

## Monitor Aggressively

| Action Step | When to Use It | Probing Questions | Scenarios to Practice | Cues for Real-Time Feedback |
|---|---|---|---|---|
| **Monitoring pathway** | Teacher monitors only a handful of students—or none at all—during independent practice. | • [Watch a model video] "What does the teacher do after launching independent practice?"<br><br>• "What do you notice about this seating chart from your peer—what about it would make it easier to monitor your students' work?" | • Pull out seating charts from other teachers to use as guides.<br><br>• Create a seating chart for this teacher's class with data in hand, & plan the monitoring pathway: start with fastest writers and then move to the ones who need more time.<br><br>• Practice: test out the seating chart walking around. Revise for anticipated management/off-task behavior. | Nonverbal or whisper prompt: cue teacher to follow his/her planned pathway. |
| **Monitor the quality of student work** | Teacher does not see patterns in student answers. | • "What were the challenges for you as you monitored during independent practice? What made it difficult for you to remember all your students' answers?"<br><br>• "If you cannot monitor everything a student writes, what are the key pieces based on today's focus?"<br><br>• "What trends did you notice as you aggressively monitored the independent work today? Who mastered it and who didn't?" | • Planning: have the teacher take out the exemplar & annotate for the keys to look for:<br>  – Humanities: the argument/thesis, evidence, or a writing technique.<br>  – STEM: a certain formula or critical step in answering a problem<br><br>• Set up a note-taking template for monitoring. | Whisper prompt: cue teacher to monitor student work. |

| Action Step | When to Use It | Probing Questions | Scenarios to Practice | Cues for Real-Time Feedback |
|---|---|---|---|---|
| | | • "What is the purpose of aggressive monitoring during independent practice? How can that help inform the rest of your lesson?" | • Practice: set out papers with student writing on desks, and give the teacher a set amount of time to fill in the note-taking template and note the patterns in student responses. | Model: walk alongside teacher and ask what trends he/she is noticing. Show teacher how to use exemplar to identify patterns and determine the trend. |
| **Pen in Hand: mark up student work** | Teacher is not giving explicit feedback to more than a handful of students, if any. | • "What is the student experiencing in the moment when you're monitoring? How many of them know if they are on the right track or not?"<br><br>• [Present a coding technique/ watch a video of a teacher marking up student work/look at a sample student work that has been marked up by a teacher] "How did the teacher give quick feedback to this student to help him/her get on track?"<br><br>• "What is the power of a coding system for allowing you to give feedback to more students?" | • Create a feedback code: simple cues to write on student work to spur self-correction.<br><br>• Practice: put out a class set of student work on all the desks. Have the teacher monitor the room and write feedback codes on as many papers as possible.<br><br>• Rd 2: ID ways to go faster<br><br>• Integrate previous actions: monitoring pathway, collecting data. | Model: walk alongside the teacher as he/she monitors and whisper, e.g., "I think you should put an E on this one" when you see him/her struggle to give the student feedback. |

# PHASE 3: DAYS 31–60

## Phase 3 Management

### Engage Every Student

| Build the Momentum | | | |
|---|---|---|---|
| **Action Step** | **When to Use It** | **Probing Questions** | **Scenarios to Practice** | **Cues for Real-Time Feedback** |
| Create a challenge | Teacher states or acknowledges the boring/hard nature of the content he/she is teaching. | • [Watch model video] "What does this teacher say to get her students so excited to complete the task?"<br><br>• "What is the value of providing a challenge to build momentum in the class?"<br><br>• "Where in your lesson did you miss an opportunity to create a challenge? What could you do differently?" | • Have teacher script challenges into lesson plan and practice delivering them. | Nonverbal: pump your hands in the air like a cheerleader. Model: model creating a challenge. |
| Speak faster, walk faster, vary your voice, and smile | Teacher's tone doesn't convey the joy and excitement that should infuse the classroom. | • [Show model video] "What do you notice about Ms. Smith's tone in this clip? What does she do to make her delivery sparkle?"<br><br>• "Now think about your own classroom. What's creating the gap between this teacher's tone and yours?" | • Have the teacher teach part of an upcoming lesson while speaking faster and smiling.<br><br>• Stop teacher and repeat what he/she has just said, while smiling and speaking more quickly.<br><br>• Have the teacher vary his/her voice, dropping lower to create tension rather than always remaining at high or low volume. | Nonverbal: point to corners of your mouth to remind teacher to smile, or gesture with your hand to remind him/her to speak more quickly. Whisper prompt: "Sparkle! Smile! Jump back into teaching!" |

| Action Step | When to Use It | Probing Questions | Scenarios to Practice | Cues for Real-Time Feedback |
|---|---|---|---|---|
| Use a timer | Teacher falls way behind the planned pacing of his/her lesson plan. | • "How much time did you want to spend on the I Do part of the lesson? What kept you from sticking to that amount if time?"<br><br>• "How much time had you planned to have left for independent work at the end of the lesson? What kept you from having enough time?" | • Plan: review time stamps for each part of the lesson. Script how to move on when the timer goes off and the teacher hasn't finished that section. Plan where teacher can cut certain parts of the lesson when falling behind.<br><br>• Practice a lesson with a timer. Rehearse what to do when timer goes off & teacher isn't finished with that section. | Nonverbal: point at watch/wrist when it's time to move on.<br><br>Nonverbal: give a hand signal of how many more minutes to stay on this activity. |
| Increase the rate of questioning | Teacher pauses too long between questions, losing the students' engagement. | • "What is the key to pacing? Given that principle, what do you think is the ideal amount of time after each student answer before you ask another question?"<br><br>• "Do you recall what happened after you called on _____ yesterday? What would you need in order to keep instruction moving more immediately after calling on a student?" | • Role-play a questioning sequence from an upcoming lesson, keeping track of the rate of questioning. Note specifically moments where the rate slows due to pauses in between questions and lack of teacher preparation.<br><br>• Key teacher actions to look for: knowing the questions cold and knowing which student to call on. | Model: model the questioning pace for the teacher. |

| Pacing | | | | |
|---|---|---|---|---|
| Use countdowns to work the clock | Students are slow to move during lesson transitions: whole class to pairs to IP, etc. | • "How much time did you want to take in this transition?" • [Watch model video] "What actions does the teacher take to go faster? How could you apply them to your lesson?" • "How could you challenge your students to work with greater purpose?" | • Script and practice Bright Lines—cues to signal switching between activities: claps, hand gestures, etc. • Play the part of students and have the teacher transition from one activity to the next using a countdown to work the clock. | Nonverbal: signal "5–4–3–2–1" with your fingers when it's time for a countdown. |
| Call & response | Students lose focus & engagement while teacher is modeling or talking. | • "What is the purpose of a choral response? How does it add value to engagement both behaviorally and academically?" • [Watch video] "Here's a video clip from your lesson yesterday. Where could you have used a choral response to increase engagement?" | • ID moments when it would be most useful to implement a choral response. • Role-play: provide occasional lackluster responses so teacher can practice having students Do It Again for choral response. | Nonverbal: create/use a cue for choral response. |
| **Engaging All Students** | | | | |
| Call on all students | Teacher tends to call on the same few students over and over. | • "Let's look at this footage from some of your questioning sequences in the past week. Which students are you calling on, and which aren't getting called?" • "What could you do to make sure you call on all students? How will you remember to do so in the moment?" | • Option 1: embed in lesson plan: write into plan which specific students to call on during plan, ensuring that students at different levels of mastery of the content are getting called on and that everyone gets to speak frequently. • Option 2: use attendance list: pull out teacher attendance list and have teacher check students off as they are called on. | Nonverbal: point to the student who would be ideal for the teacher to call on. |

| Action Step | When to Use It | Probing Questions | Scenarios to Practice | Cues for Real-Time Feedback |
|---|---|---|---|---|
| Cold Call | Some students disengage when the teacher asks a question. | • "What is the purpose of cold calling?"<br>• "Where in your lesson today could a cold call have increased engagement?"<br>• "Who are the students who would benefit the most from a cold call?" | • Have teacher choose students to cold-call in advance.<br>• Practice: run through a questioning sequence and strategically cold-calling various students. | Nonverbal: point at the ideal student for the teacher to cold-call. |
| Turn & Talk | Students become restless during a lengthy I Do or class discussion. | • "What are the benefits of having students do a Turn & Talk?"<br>• "What are the keys to an effective Turn & Talk?"<br>• "How will you know the Turn & Talk is effective?" | • Planning: ID moments in upcoming lesson to do a quick Turn & Talk.<br>• Create bright lines—make Turn & Talk entry and exit unmistakably crisp: preestablish whom students turn toward; give clear What to Do instructions and brisk signal: "Go!"<br>• Scan the room and redirect off-task students. | Nonverbal: turn forefingers toward each other.<br><br>Model: lead a Turn & Talk and then explain rationale to teacher during the Turn & Talk. |
| Use multiple methods to call on students | Teacher overrelies on just one technique for engaging all students. | • "We've discussed multiple ways to call on students: cold calling, all hands, Turn & Talks, and choral response. Which ones do you use the most? Which ones could you use more frequently in your lesson?" | • Plan a whole-group discussion: note which questions are best suited for cold call, all hands, choral response, or Turn & Talk. | Nonverbal: create/use cue for cold call, Turn & Talk, choral response, and all hands. |

| Action Step | When to Use It | Probing Questions | Scenarios to Practice | Cues for Real-Time Feedback |
|---|---|---|---|---|
| | | • "What are the times in which each technique would be best to use in your class?" | • Role-play the discussion following the script the teacher created. | Whisper prompt: "When you call the group back together, start with a choral response followed by a cold call." Model (if needed). |

### Narrate the Positive

| Action Step | When to Use It | Probing Questions | Scenarios to Practice | Cues for Real-Time Feedback |
|---|---|---|---|---|
| Narrate what students do well | Teacher's tone when addressing management problems is overly negative. | • [Watch model video] "How did the teacher get students to correct misbehaviors without being negative?"<br>• [Watch video of teacher] "What could you have done in this particular moment to increase the positivity of your tone?"<br>• "What negative phrases do you find yourself using most often?" | • Planning: re-write teacher's most frequent negative comments into positive statements.<br>• Practice: role play keeping students on track through positive narration.<br>• Focus on the positive tone: practice tone until it feels authentic: not overly positive nor too flat/negative. | Nonverbal: index card with a plus sign written on it.<br>Whisper prompt: "Narrate the positive." |
| While narrating the positive, look at off-task students | Students who are off-task don't respond to positive narration. | • [Watch model video] "Where is the teacher looking while narrating the positive? How does that affect student responsiveness?" | • Practice: you play the role of a student and model off-task behavior while the teacher looks at you and narrates the positive actions of another (imaginary) student. | Whisper prompt: "Look at off-task students while narrating positive." |
| Use language that reinforces students' getting smarter | Teacher tends to praise behavior rather than academic effort or achievement. | • [Watch model video] "What does this teacher say when her students are responding? What behavior is she reinforcing?" | • Plan: With an upcoming lesson plan, script moments when the teacher could give precise academic praise that would reinforce students' effort. | Model: praise student thinking if an opportunity is missed. |

| Action Step | When to Use It | Probing Questions | Scenarios to Practice | Cues for Real-Time Feedback |
|---|---|---|---|---|
| | | • "When do you find yourself giving positive feedback to students?"<br>• "What are the classroom culture benefits of praising academics over behavior?" | • Practice students giving a response and the teacher giving precise praise | Whisper to teacher to give precise praise after another positive academic behavior. |
| **Individual Student Corrections** | | | | |
| Least Invasive Intervention | Teacher sees the problem, but What to Do and Narrate the Positive aren't working for a few students, or teacher does not consistently or effectively provide consequences for minor misbehaviors.<br><br>Teacher uses corrections that draw unnecessary attention to the student who has been off task. | • "When a student shows ____ [insert low-level misbehavior, such as calling out, repeated head down, being off task, etc.], what is your ideal response?"<br>• "What is the challenge when you try to redirect an off-task student?"<br>• "Look at this list of interventions from least to most invasive. What is the advantage of starting with the least invasive intervention?"<br>• "When you are intervening with off-task students, which of these interventions are you using? Which ones could you add to your repertoire?" [Watch video of teaching if needed]<br>• "Which intervention is most appropriate given the behavior and the part of the lesson in which it occurs?" | You really cannot overplan and overpractice this action step. The more at-bats the better!<br>• Script the precise language of administering the consequence.<br>• Practice the tone and timing until teacher has mastered a formal tone.<br>• Role-play as a student with different types of off-task behavior. Have teacher redirect you with the least invasive interventions. Slowly progress up to persisting in off-task behavior so that teacher has a chance to escalate to every type of intervention. | Nonverbal: point to the student off task and give a redirect signal.<br><br>Whisper prompt: "This student is off task. Use ____ intervention."<br><br>Model: redirect an off-task student and wait for the teacher to repeat the action with the next off-task student. |

412     APPENDIX: GET BETTER FASTER COACH'S GUIDE

## Phase 3 Rigor

### Respond to Student Learning Needs

**Habits of Evidence**

| Action Step | When to Use It | Probing Questions | Scenarios to Practice | Cues for Real-Time Feedback |
|---|---|---|---|---|
| **Teach students to annotate with purpose** | Students don't annotate texts effectively when reading, making it difficult for them to go back and cite the best evidence. | • "What is the purpose of annotating a text? Based on your prompt/task, what would be the best focus for students' annotation?"<br><br>• "How many students are annotating the text while reading?"<br><br>• "For the students who are annotating, what are the biggest gaps in their ability to annotate for the best evidence?" | • Review text the students will be reading in the upcoming week. Have teacher create an exemplar annotation: What are the key pieces of evidence you would like them to highlight?<br><br>• Practice: monitor student work with annotated exemplar on a clipboard.<br><br>• Set up a simple written feedback/cue to give to students while monitoring their annotation (e.g., circle = look for better evidence). | Walk alongside teacher when monitoring student annotation of their reading. Look for patterns of good and weak annotations.<br><br>Whisper prompt: "Prompt [x student] to improve his/her annotations." |
| **Teach & prompt students to cite key evidence** | Students don't cite evidence from the text when answering questions. | • "What is the importance of citing evidence in answering a question?"<br><br>• "Where in your last lesson could students have been asked to cite their evidence more clearly/effectively?" | • Name key evidence from exemplar, identify additional valid evidence, and predict wrong evidence.<br><br>• Practice: prompt students when they don't cite best evidence. | Nonverbal: cue teacher to ask for evidence (e.g., hold up card with "E" printed on it).<br><br>Whisper prompt: "Ask for evidence." Model if needed. |

## Check for Whole-Group Understanding

| Action Step | When to Use It | Probing Questions | Scenarios to Practice | Cues for Real-Time Feedback |
|---|---|---|---|---|
| **Poll the room** | Teacher moves ahead without a clear vision of which (or how many) students comprehend. | • [Debrief your own intervention] "I intervened in your class and polled the room. What was the purpose of doing so? How did that help guide the rest of your lesson?"<br><br>• "What would be the best moments in your upcoming lesson to poll the room?"<br><br>• "What are the advantages of these polling techniques versus self-report thumbs up/thumbs down?" | • Script into the lesson plan key moments to conduct a poll of the room.<br><br>• Plan the rollout of the polling routine: integrate Phase 1 & 2 actions for rollouts.<br><br>• Predict the outcome for the polling of upcoming classes to help a teacher start to anticipate student error. | Nonverbal: Hold up sign that says "Poll."<br><br>Model: Poll the room yourself. |
| **Target the error** | Teacher collects data, but then moves on with his or her lesson without responding to it. Class discussion does not focus on students' common misconceptions. | • "What challenges do you anticipate during independent practice? Where is the most important area to review?"<br><br>• [Watch model video] "What actions does this teacher take to respond to students' written errors?" | • Planning: anticipate the errors students will make in upcoming lesson.<br><br>• Practice: review student work and name the error. | Whisper prompt during IP: "What patterns of error are you noticing? Plan to review only the areas of error." |

## Reteaching 101—Model

| Action Step | When to Use It | Probing Questions | Scenarios to Practice | Cues for Real-Time Feedback |
|---|---|---|---|---|
| **Give students a clear listening/note-taking task** | Teacher gives a clear model, but the students don't have a task to do while listening to the model. | • [Watch a model video] "What were the key actions the teacher took make sure the students were listening?" | • Focus on planning: include a note-taking task and a check for understanding. | Verbal prompt: "Ms. Smith, before you begin your model, I want to make sure the students have their notebooks out to take notes: this is too valuable not to write anything down!" |
| **Model the thinking, not just the procedure** | Teacher's model is confusing or unclear. Teacher tells students a procedure, but doesn't unpack the thinking behind it. | • "Let's look over your exemplar for the independent practice. Talk aloud how you would solve this problem/write this essay." [After teacher answer] "What are students struggling to do to match the quality of your exemplar? Where is their thinking or understanding breaking down?"<br><br>• "Given those gaps, what is the most important thing for you to model for them?" | • Pre-work: unpack the key errors that students are making (Phase 3 coaching tips: 1. Start with the exemplar. 2. Identify the gaps. 3. Plan the reteach.).<br><br>• Plan: design an effective think-aloud (1. Target the error. 2. Model replicable thinking. 3. Check for understanding.).<br><br>• Practice: vary tone and cadence of think-aloud/ model to emphasize key points and be as clear as possible. | Verbal prompt: "Ms. Smith, that was very interesting. Can you tell me again what you were thinking when you took that step? I want to make sure I understand."<br><br>Model: do a think-aloud yourself. |

## Reteaching 101—Model

| Action Step | When to Use It | Probing Questions | Scenarios to Practice | Cues for Real-Time Feedback |
|---|---|---|---|---|
| | | • [Watch a model video] "What were the key actions the teacher took to model the skill effectively? How do those differ from what you have been doing in class?" | | |
| **We Do/You Do: give at-bats to practice** | Teacher gives a clear model, but students don't have the opportunity to try to replicate it after the model is done. | • "What is the best way for students to practice after they have listened to your model?" | • Plan: create an at-bat where students genuinely practice what teacher just modeled. Make sure they practice the thinking involved and not just the procedure. | Nonverbal: give a cue that it's time for students to practice. |

# PHASE 4: DAYS 61–90

## Phase 4 Management

### Set Routines for Discourse

| Action Step | Engaged Small Group Work | | | |
|---|---|---|---|---|
| | When to Use It | Probing Questions | Scenarios to Practice | Cues for Real-Time Feedback |
| **Deliver explicit instructions for group work** | Groups are off task because they're confused about what to do or because not every student has something to do. | • "What do you want students doing during group work? What will they have produced if they are successful?" <br> • "How many student roles do you need in order for your students to complete their group work task? Based on that, what size should the groups be?" <br> • "What will be the hardest part to enforce? What visual evidence can you create to make it easier for you to make sure they're on track?" | • Planning: script out explicit directions for group work. <br> • Focus on visual evidence of on-task behavior: to make it easier to monitor (e.g., students chart their thoughts on the whiteboard). <br> • Practice delivery. | Model: model delivering explicit small-group work instructions. |
| **Monitor group progress & verbally enforce accountability** | Some groups are off task despite clear instructions. | • "Despite your quality instructions, you had a few groups who weren't on task today. Did you notice when they started to get off track?" | • Plan out what teacher will want to see on chart paper/ student notebooks during group work. | Nonverbal or whisper prompt: ID the off-task groups. |

## Engaged Small Group Work

| Action Step | When to Use It | Probing Questions | Scenarios to Practice | Cues for Real-Time Feedback |
|---|---|---|---|---|
| | | • "Looking back on your previously learned action steps, what sort of small-group reset or individual correction could you deliver to get the group/individual back on track?"<br><br>• "In which groups were some students shoulder-ing more of the work? What steps can you take to remedy this?" | • For resetting, script out the language for an effective reset or individual correction. Incorporate all the keys from previous action steps.<br><br>• Practice: monitor group work, and practice individual student corrections and whole-class reset. | |

# Phase 4 Rigor

## Lead Student Discourse 101

| | | Reteaching 201 | | |
|---|---|---|---|---|
| **Action Step** | **When to Use It** | **Probing Questions** | **Scenarios to Practice** | **Cues for Real-Time Feedback** |
| Show Call | Many students are struggling to identify the error in their understanding, or they struggle to generate an exemplar response.<br><br>Teacher is trying to use student work, but struggles to lead discussion around it. | • [Watch video of Show Call] "What was the value of the teacher showing a piece of student work to jump-start the conversation? How did the teacher do this effectively?"<br><br>• "What common errors are your students making when solving these problems/completing these types of tasks?"<br><br>• "When looking at student work, what do they need to see more: an exemplar response from their peer, or the error that they are making?"<br><br>• "What would an ideal answer from a student look like?" | • Planning: Look at Exit Tickets and select a strong student exemplar and a representative incorrect/incomplete student response that is indicative of an error that many students are making.<br><br>• Script out the steps: (1) post the work (either exemplar, incorrect answer, or both); (2) Turn & Talk: ask students to evaluate; (3) as a whole class: name the error and the best practice.<br><br>• Practice: rehearse the script. Focus on economy of language. | Whisper prompt: during independent practice, identify one or more student work samples that would be valuable for teacher to use during Show Call. Ask teacher which ones he/she would show-call; if teacher makes a weak choice, show him/her the ones you selected and briefly explain why. |
| **Stamp the understanding and give them at-bats** | Students can figure out their error, but they do not articulate clearly what they have to do to prevent those errors in the future and don't have time to practice. | • "Once the students identify the error or strategies in the exemplar, what is the key understanding you want them to stamp? What would the ideal answer look like?" | • Practice stamping the understanding: articulate exactly what teacher will look for in student answers. Write down that key understanding on the board. | Model: if teacher doesn't stamp the understanding, intervene to make sure students grasp the concept. |

| Action Step | When to Use It | Probing Questions | Scenarios to Practice | Cues for Real-Time Feedback |
|---|---|---|---|---|
| | | • "What would be the best form of practice for the students to get a chance to master this new strategy/understanding?" | • Plan: incorporate into lesson plan more at-bats to practice the new skill. | Nonverbal: give cue that it's time for students to practice. |
| | | **Universal Prompts** | | |
| **Provide wait time, precall, roll back** | The teacher moves on too quickly after asking a challenging question. | • "What are the possible reasons a student might not be able to answer a question you ask on the spot—beyond just not knowing the answer?"<br><br>• [Watch a video or model for the teacher] "What actions did the teacher take? Why were these beneficial?"<br><br>• "What is the purpose of repeating the student's answer back to him/her? Why not just correct the error?"<br><br>• "Which students need more time than others to formulate an answer? Which ones would benefit from a precall to give them enough thinking time?" | Integrate the practice of all three skills:<br>• Wait time: ID higher-order questions that might require more think time. Script concise directions that teacher will narrate during wait time ("This answer requires strong evidence. Everyone can be looking as we wait.").<br>• Rollback: role-play a questioning sequence from an upcoming lesson, providing student answers that would benefit from rolling back. Continue the lesson after rolling back as well. | Nonverbal: create/use a cue for wait time (e.g., hold up a hand as a stop sign).<br>Model: roll back answer to the original student, modeling for teacher. |

| Action Step | When to Use It | Probing Questions | Scenarios to Practice | Cues for Real-Time Feedback |
|---|---|---|---|---|
| | | | • Precall: ID the students who would benefit from a precall. Pick the questions in the lesson plan that would be ideal to ask those students. | |
| Ask universal prompts | The teacher doesn't know why a student got an answer wrong. | • "When the student delivered the incorrect answer, what happened next? How do you know if that student now understands at the end of the class?"<br><br>• "Let's look at this list of universal prompts. What is the value of using prompts like these?"<br><br>• "Where in your lesson could you have used one or more of these prompts?" | • Plan next lesson: predict the types of student responses that will benefit from these prompts.<br><br>• Practice: play the roles of 3 different students: 1 with a wrong answer, 2 more with limited answers. Role-play using each of the prompts. | N/A |
| Close the loop | After an incorrect answer, the teacher moves on without correcting the original error with that student. | • "When [student] delivered that incorrect answer yesterday, what did you do next? How did you know if [student] understood why he/she was wrong? What could you do next time?"<br><br>• [Watch model video] "How does this teacher guarantee that the student has learned after his original misconception?" | • Role-play a questioning sequence from an upcoming lesson, with you playing different students so that teacher has a chance to play out the process of coming back to the first student he/she has called on. | Whisper prompt: "Come back to [x student] to make sure he understands."<br><br>Model: "Jared, why is that answer right?" |

| Action Step | When to Use It | Probing Questions | Scenarios to Practice | Cues for Real-Time Feedback |
|---|---|---|---|---|
| **Habits of Discussion** | | | | |
| Keep neutral | The teacher's reactions reveal whether student responses are correct before the students can figure it out on their own. | • "Recall our recent PD on habits of discussion. What is the goal of getting students to use the habits?"<br>• [Watch video of the teacher] "Compare your responses to correct and incorrect answers. What are the differences? How do your different responses limit the rigor of the discussion?"<br>• "What actions can you take to ensure that your responses to correct and incorrect responses are the same?" | • Practice: role-play correct and incorrect responses. Focus teacher on staying neutral: eyebrows neutral, consistent nodding or not, same number of words after each response.<br>• Incorporate the use of habits of discussion and wait time. | N/A |
| Agree and build off | Student answers are disconnected from each other even when students agree. | • "What do you ideally want students to do when they agree with what a peer is saying? How could you get them to do it in the moment?"<br>• "Let's think about that moment during your lesson when [x student] shared his answer and the next student just repeated it. What training do the students need in how to build off of another student's answer?" | • Script prompts to get students to build off of another's arguments: "I agree with ___, and I would like to add that . . ."<br>• Practice: role-play a class discussion. Prompt the students to build off. | Nonverbal: Post the habits of discussion in the classroom; point to the posted habits when needed.<br><br>Model: "David [student], can you restate your answer using one of the habits posted on the wall?" |

| Action Step | When to Use It | Probing Questions | Scenarios to Practice | Cues for Real-Time Feedback |
|---|---|---|---|---|
| **Disagree respectfully** | Students either don't disagree with their peers or don't do so in a respectful manner. | • "What do you ideally want students to do when they disagree with what a peer is saying?"<br>• "What is the gap between that ideal response and what they are doing in class?"<br>• "How could you get them to do those ideal actions in the moment?" | • Script prompts to get students to respectfully disagree with one another's arguments.<br>• Practice: role-play a class discussion. Prompt the students to express respectful disagreement. | Nonverbal: point to prompts posted on the classroom walls.<br><br>Model: "Laura, can you disagree using one of the habits posted on the wall?" |

# STRETCH IT: THE NEXT STEPS

## Stretch It Rigor

### Lead Student Discourse 201

| Action Step | When to Use It | Strategic Prompts | | Cues for Real-Time Feedback |
| --- | --- | --- | --- | --- |
| | | **Probing Questions** | **Scenarios to Practice** | |
| **Access previous understanding** | Despite the use of Discourse 101 techniques, students are still unable to grasp the concept. | • "Let's look at yesterday's lesson. What were the key understandings you wanted the students to reach by the end of the class?"<br><br>• "Where was the gap in their ability to get there?"<br><br>• "Think about your previous learning. What are the key understandings that could have helped the students unpack this task/question?"<br><br>• "What are the resources you have available that have a set of prompts you can use with your kids?" | • Plan: Unpack the exemplar response in upcoming lesson, & name the key pieces of previous understanding that students will need to solve the problem.<br><br>• Prepare where students will access that knowledge (e.g.: Chart of key terms posted in the room, student handout, previous notes).<br><br>• Plan the script to ask students to access that knowledge. | Nonverbal: Point to the resources in the room.<br><br>Whisper prompt: "I think students are making ____ error. Ask them about ____ [previously learned knowledge or skill] to cue them to strategies that can help them solve the problem." |
| **Call on students based on their learning needs** | Teacher calls primarily on students who already know the answer, and doesn't guarantee the learning for the rest.<br><br>Teacher calls on consecutive struggling students, and the discussion stalls. | "Recall the moment when Javier, Claire, and Marta all struggled to answer the question. Based on your monitoring of their independent practice prior to the discussion, were there any other students in the room who could have provided more help? What is the advantage of calling on one of them when other students are stuck?" | • Plan: anticipate the responses students of varying levels will give in class. | The key to real time feedback is monitoring student learning during independent practice. Without that, it's difficult to intervene. If you do, you can follow Nikki Bridges's lead from the clip you watched in Phase 4 (Monitoring Student Work). |

| Action Step | When to Use It | Probing Questions | Scenarios to Practice | Cues for Real-Time Feedback |
|---|---|---|---|---|
| | | • "Let's look at your recent assessment data sorted from lowest to highest performing. Think back to whom you called on in class today—where did most of the called-on students fall within your data set? What is the limitation of calling only on students in that range?" | • Script out the order of students to call on during the discourse: (1) start with a medium/lower student; (2) call on a higher student when the previous student is struggling to answer; (3) call on a lower student to "stamp" the understanding.<br><br>• Rd 1: first student called on gets it right (then call on lower/medium students to solidify understanding).<br><br>• Rd 2: first student gets it wrong; after calling on higher students, lower students get it right.<br><br>• Rd 3: first student gets it wrong; after calling on higher student, lower student still gets it wrong. | |

| Action Step | When to Use It | Probing Questions | Scenarios to Practice | Cues for Real-Time Feedback |
|---|---|---|---|---|
| **Students prompting students** | Teacher is constantly prompting the students to use habits of discussion, but students are not building the habit of prompting each other. | • [Watch video of class or remember it] "Where did the discussion go off track? What would have been the ideal student intervention to get back on point?"<br><br>• [Use the guide for habits of discussion on DVD] "Which would be the appropriate next habits to develop in the students' ability to lead the discussion?"<br><br>• "Recall how you rolled out Routines and Procedures at the beginning of the year. What are the key actions that we can replicate in rolling out a habit of discussion?" [Refer to actions in Phase 1] | • ID 1–2 common errors and the universal prompts you want students to use to address the errors. Practice prompting students to use that universal prompt.<br><br>• Practice rolling out the habit [see Phase 1 for key actions] | Nonverbal: point to teacher's chart for universal prompts.<br><br>Model: "Daniela [student], what could you say to your peers to prompt a deeper response?" |
| | | **Go Conceptual** | | |
| **Verbalize a conceptual understanding of content** | Teacher moves on too quickly after asking a challenging question, possibly answering it rather than giving students a chance to do so. | • "Let's look back at the standard aligned to this task: What are the key understandings required to master this objective?"<br><br>• "When you ask a student to explain why [the answer is correct], what is the ideal response you're looking for in this moment?"<br><br>• "What response did students give you, and how did you respond?" | • Script ideal response and questioning sequence to get to that response. | Model: "Mr. Smith, I'm impressed with Jordan's answer. Jordan, can you generalize the _____ [rule/strategy/skill] you used that we could use in any problem?" |

| Action Step | When to Use It | Probing Questions | Scenarios to Practice | Cues for Real-Time Feedback |
|---|---|---|---|---|
| | Teacher recognizes when students have made an error, but struggles to identify the deeper errors that have led them to their incorrect answers. | • "Looking at the potential prompts for conceptual understanding, which would be most relevant to use in this context?" | | |
| Upgrade vocabulary | Teacher does not ask students to use technical/ academic language when giving answers. | • "What is the ideal academic or technical language that you wanted students to use in their response?"<br>• "What was the gap between that ideal response and what students said?"<br>• "How can we create or leverage a resource that will push students to upgrade their vocabulary in their answers?" | • Create a word wall/chart with key academic terms you will want students to use in their answers.<br>• Script in moments when the teacher can punch key vocabulary terms when modeling. Script ideal student responses that include key vocabulary terms.<br>• Script the prompts to use when students don't use mathematical/ scientific/academic language: "That's the right idea. Now state it again using your Academic Word Wall as a resource." | Nonverbal: point to the academic language resource (word wall, cheat sheet, etc.). |

| Action Step | When to Use It | Probing Questions | Scenarios to Practice | Cues for Real-Time Feedback |
|---|---|---|---|---|
| | | **Go Conceptual** | | |
| **Stretch It** | Students answer a question easily, and teacher moves on rather than pushing them to go further. | • "What happened after you called on Jermaine and he answered your question correctly? How does that affect his learning? What could you do to raise the rigor for him without making it unmanageable for the rest of the class?"<br><br>• [Watch video of a teacher using the Stretch It technique when students answer a question correctly] "What did the teacher do to stretch the learning?" | • Identify moments in the lesson plan where students might get to correct answers easily. Script "stretch it" questions to increase the rigor of those moments; e.g., how/ why, cite evidence, evaluate the answer. | Nonverbal: pull your fingers apart—as if stretching a piece of gum—to signal that it's a good time to raise the rigor with a stretch-it question. |

# Notes

## Introduction

1. Robert Marzano, Tony Frontier, and David Livingston, *Effective Supervision: Supporting the Art and Science of Teaching* (Alexandria, VA: ACSD, 2011), 26.

2. Daniel Coyle, *The Talent Code* (New York: Bantam Dell, 2009), 1.

3. Christina Steinbacher-Reed and Elizabeth Powers, "Coaching without a Coach," *Educational Leadership* 69, no. 4 (2011): 68–72; see also Nancy Protheroe, "Effective Resource Use—People, Time, and Money," *Principal's Research Review* 6, no. 3 (May 2011): 1–7.

4. William M. Ferriter and Nicholas Provenzano, "Today's Lesson: Self-Directed Learning . . . for Teachers," *Phi Delta Kappan* 95, no. 3 (2013): 16–21; Bryan Hassel and Emily Ayscue Hassel, "Like Peanut Butter and Chocolate, Digital Learning and Excellent Teachers Go Well Together," *EducationNext,* 18 November 2011, http://educationnext.org/like-peanut-butter-and-chocolate -digital-learning-and-excellent-teachers-go-well-together/.

5. Increasingly, the consensus in the education community is that teaching is a trainable skill. We have come a significant way since 2004, when Alexander Russo wrote in the *Harvard Education Letter* that although coaching seems on the surface as if it should succeed where other PD methods fail, we have little research to prove that it actually does. Now, a variety of educators have not only affirmed that coaching changes teacher practice but also in many cases have observed that specific best coaching practices correlate directly with increases in student achievement. Among others, Jason A. Grissom, Susanna Loeb, and Ben Master found in a 2013 survey of educational leadership practices that coaching was among the most directly linked to gains in achievement; and Elizabeth Green's 2014 book *Building a Better Teacher* documented the work of school leaders across the country whose excellent coaching practices are driving student learning in incredibly dramatic ways. Furthermore, some recent studies suggest that the "learnability" of teaching might have more power than even the most optimistic in the field once believed: although it was once said that teacher development stopped after five years, new studies suggest that it likely continues for at least ten. Sources: Jason A. Grissom, Susanna Loeb, and Ben Master, "Effective Instructional Time Use for School Leaders: Longitudinal Evidence from Observations of Principals," *Educational Researcher* 42, no. 8 (2013); Elizabeth Green,

*Building a Better Teacher: How Teaching Works (and How to Teach It to Everyone)* (New York: Norton, 2014); Joellen Killion, "High-Impact Coaching Ensures Maximum Results," *Learning System* 5, no. 3 (2010); Jim Knight, "Coaching," *Journal of Staff Development* 28, no. 1 (2007): 26–31; Alexander Russo, "School-Based Coaching: A Revolution in Professional Development, or Just the Latest Fad?" *Harvard Education Letter* 20, no. 4 (2004); Stephen Sawchuk, "New Studies Find That, for Teachers, Experience Really Does Matter," *Education Week* 34, no. 25 (2015).

6. Richard M. Ingersoll, "Beginning Teacher Induction: What the Data Tell Us," *Education Week*, 16 May 2012, http://www.edweek.org/ew/articles/2012/05/16/kappan_ingersoll.h31.html.

7. Cynthia Kopkowski, "Why They Leave, " National Education Association, 2008, http://www.nea.org/home/12630.htm, http://nces.ed.gov/pubs2007/2007307.pdf; "Teacher Attrition and Mobility: Results from the 2004–05 Teacher Follow-Up Survey," National Center for Education Statistics, 2007, http://nctaf.org/wp-content/uploads/2012/01/NCTAF-Cost-of-Teacher-Turnover-2007-policy-brief.pdf; "Policy Brief: The High Cost of Teacher Turnover," National Commission on Teaching and America's Future, 2007, http://nctaf.org/wp-content/uploads/2012/01/NCTAF-Cost-of-Teacher-Turnover-2007-policy-brief.pdf.

8. Liz Riggs, "Why Do Teachers Quit?" *Atlantic,* October 2013, http://www.theatlantic.com/education/archive/2013/10/why-do-teachers-quit/280699/2/.

9. Kopkowski, "Why They Leave."

10. Ingersoll, "Beginning Teacher Induction."

11. School Leaders Network, "Churn: The High Cost of Principal Turnover," 2014, http://connectleadsucceed.org/sites/default/files/principal_turnover_cost.pdf, 1, 12.

12. In a 2013 report, the New Teacher Project covered in great depth the different ways in which individual teachers develop. Specifically, they found that "new teachers perform at different levels and improve at different rates"; that "teachers' initial performance predicts their future performance"; that "multiple measures tend to point to the same conclusion about a teacher's effectiveness"; and, finally, that "a few specific core skills appear to be important to a first-year teacher's success." This underscores both the power of coaching and the need to use any system of coaching in a way that addresses the needs of specific teachers individually, as the Scope and Sequence allows a leader to do. Source: New Teacher Project, *Leap Year: Assessing and Supporting Effective First-Year Teachers,* 17 April 2013, http://tntp.org/assets/documents/TNTP_LeapYear_2013.pdf.

13. Valerie Strauss, "Actually, Practice Doesn't Always Make Perfect—New Study," *Washington Post*, 25 July 2014, http://www.washingtonpost.com/blogs/answer-sheet/wp/2014/07/25/actually-practice-doesnt-always-make-perfect-new teacher-study/; Nathan Collins, "Practice Doesn't Always Make Perfect," *Scientific American,* 1 November 2014, http://www.scientificamerican.com/article/practice-doesn-t-always-make-perfect/.

14. A discouraging report from the New Teacher Project underscores the necessity of providing new teachers not only with coaching but with the right coaching. *The Mirage* found that although more schools and districts are investing time, money, and energy in teacher training than we tend to assume, this training is all too often unsuccessful. "School systems shouldn't give up on teacher development," the Project concluded, "and they shouldn't cut spending on it, either. Rather, we believe it's time for a new conversation about teacher improvement—one that asks fundamentally different questions about what great teaching means and how to achieve it." Source: New Teacher Project, *The Mirage: Confronting the Hard Truth about Our Quest for Teacher Development*, 17 April 2013, http://tntp.org/assets/documents/TNTP-Mirage_2015.pdf.

15. Michael Watkins, *The First 90 Days: Critical Success Strategies for New Leaders at All Levels* (Boston: Harvard Business School Publishing, 2003), 1.

## Principles of Coaching

1.  Charlotte Danielson, *Enhancing Professional Practice: A Framework for Teaching* (Alexandria, VA: ACSD), 23.

2.  Robert J. Marzano, Tony Frontier, and David Livingston, *Effective Supervision: Supporting the Art and Science of Teaching* (Alexandria, VA: ACSD, 2011), 107.

3.  A variety of authors have been credited with this expression. The earliest trace seems to be George Loomis in the "Michigan School Moderator" in 1902, then Percy Buck in 1944, Francis Mayer in 1963, and Peter Crossley in 1971. Garson O'Toole investigates the origins of the expression in detail at Quote Investigator, http://quoteinvestigator.com/2013/08/29/get-it-right/.

4.  Grant Wiggins and Jay McTighe, *Understanding by Design* (Alexandria, VA: ACSD, 2005).

5.  Bureau of Labor Statistics, "Physicians and Surgeons," United States Department of Labor, 2015, http://www.bls.gov/ooh/healthcare/physicians-and-surgeons.htm; Anne Bennett Swingle, "Four Students and a Cadaver," *Hopkins Medical News*, Spring 2000, http://www.hopkinsmedicine.org/hmn/sp00/top.html.

6.  Eric A. Hanushek and Steven G. Rivkin, "How to Improve the Supply of High-Quality Teachers," Brookings Papers on Education Policy: 2004 (Washington, DC: Brookings Institution, 2004), 7–44.

7.  John A. Ross, "Teacher Efficacy and the Effects of Coaching on Student Achievement," *Canadian Journal of Education* 17, no. 1 (1992): 51; Barrie Brent Bennett, "The Effectiveness of Staff Development Training Practices: A Meta-Analysis" (PhD thesis, University of Oregon, Eugene, 1987).

8.  Several educators have identified giving frequent, or repeated, feedback as the key to making feedback stick. Sources: Jeannie Myung and Krissia Martinez, "Strategies for Enhancing Post-Observation Feedback," Carnegie Foundation for the Advancement of Teaching, July

2013; Min Sun, William Penuel, Kenneth Frank, Alix Gallagher, and Peter Youngs, "Shaping PD to Promote Diffusion of Instructional Expertise among Teachers," *Educational Evaluation and Policy Analysis*, September 2013, 344–369.

## Phase 1 (Pre-Teaching): Dress Rehearsal

1.  Deborah Loewenberg Ball and Francesca M. Forzani, "Building a Common Core for Learning to Teach," *American Educator,* Summer 2011, 17–39, http://www.aft.org/pdfs/americaneducator /summer2011/Mirel.pdf#page=12.

2.  If you're familiar with *Leverage Leadership,* you may notice here that the language we use to describe the learning cycle been updated. These new terms capture the cycle more straightforwardly. *Leverage Leadership 2.0* (estimated publication date 2017) will provide even more details of the new naming.

3.  Doug Lemov, *Teach Like a Champion 2.0* (San Francisco: Jossey-Bass, 2015); Lemov, *Teach Like a Champion Field Guide* (San Francisco: Jossey-Bass, 2012); Todd Whitaker and Annette Breaux, *The Ten-Minute In-Service: 40 Quick Training Sessions That Build Teacher Effectiveness* (San Francisco: Jossey-Bass, 2013).

4.  New Teacher Project, *Leap Year: Assessing and Supporting Effective First-Year Teachers,* 2013, http://tntp.org/assets/documents/TNTP_LeapYear_2013.pdf.

5.  Interview with Orhan Pamuk in *Paris Review*, no. 175 (Fall/Winter 2005). Interview transcript, http://dailyroutines.typepad.com/daily_routines/2007/08/orhan-pamuk.html.

6.  The criteria of an effective rollout are described in more detail in *Great Habits, Great Readers*.

7.  Doug Lemov, *Teach Like a Champion* (San Francisco: Jossey-Bass, 2010), 186.

8.  Brad Ermeling and Genevieve Graff-Ermeling, "Learning to Learn from Teaching: A First-Hand Account of Lesson Study in Japan," *International Journal for Lesson and Learning Studies* 3, no. 2 (2014): 170–191, http://www.academia.edu/7154219/Learning_to_learn_from_teaching _A_first-hand_account_of_lesson_study_in_Japan,http://www.marshallmemo.com/issues /da6e777fc93e2de1261d0794d1ab4333/MarshMemo541.pdf.

## Phase 2: Instant Immersion

1.  Bill Walsh, "A Method for Game Planning." (Undated lecture transcript, approximate year 1983.) In the lecture, Walsh describes the counterintuitive value of planning game plays in advance. Retrieved from http://jameslightfootball.com/2015/04/17/bill-walsh-a-method-for -planning-a-game/.

2.  For additional information about this technique and others noted here, see Doug Lemov, *Teach Like a Champion* (San Francisco: Jossey-Bass, 2010). *TLAC,* Technique 39: Do It Again, 191–194.

3.  *TLAC* Technique 37: Be Seen Looking, 177–182.

4. George Bainton, *The Art of Authorship* (New York: D. Appleton & Company, 1890), 87–88.

5. *TLAC* Technique 2: Right Is Right, 35–41.

6. *TLAC* Technique 20: Exit Ticket, 106.

7. In 2013 on the third-grade New York State Exam, Fromson's students were 80 percent proficient in math and 62 percent proficient in ELA. The following year (2014), they were 100 percent proficient in math and 80 percent proficient in ELA, ranking number one in the state of New York. Fromson then moved to Boston and to teach fifth-grade math; her student growth percentile was 92, one of the highest in the state of Massachusetts.

## Phase 3: Getting into Gear

1. Richard DuFour, along with many other educators, has written extensively over the past decade about the impact of professional learning communities (PLCs) on instruction. Specifically, advocates of PLCs cite the way they help teachers mutually increase their own expertise, and the opportunities they create to analyze data and plan reteaching strategically. Sources: Richard DuFour, "How PLCs Do Data Right," *Educational Leadership* 73, no. 3 (2015): 22–26; Richard DuFour and Mike Mattos, "How Do Principals Really Improve Schools?" *Educational Leadership* 70, no. 7 (2013): 34–40; Richard DuFour, "Work Together, But Only If You Want To," *Phi Delta Kappan* 92, no. 5 (2011): 57–61; Shirley Hord, "Evolution of the Professional Learning Community," *Journal of Staff Development* 29, no. 3 (2008): 10–13; Peter Sleegers, Perry de Brok, Eric Verbiest Fontys, Nienke Moolenaar, and Alan Daly, "Toward Conceptual Clarity: A Multidimensional, Multilevel Model of Professional Learning Communities in Dutch Elementary Schools," *Elementary School Journal* 114, no. 1 (2013): 118–137.

2. Even among the strongest advocates of PLCs, it's acknowledged that their greatest pitfall is that they sometimes fail to analyze data deeply, which prevents their fostering meaningful reteaching. Sources: Jason Brasel, Brette Garner, Britnie Kane, and Ilana Horn, "Getting to the Why and How," *Educational Leadership* 73, no. 3 (2015), http://www.ascd.org/publications /educational-leadership/nov15/vol73/num03/Getting-to-the-Why-and-How.aspx; DuFour, "How Professional Learning Communities Do Data Right"; Ronald Gallimore, Bradley Ermeling, William Saunders, and Claude Goldenberg, "Moving the Learning of Teaching Closer to Practice: Teacher Education Implications of School-Based Inquiry Teams," *Elementary School Journal* 109, no. 5 (2009), https://people.stanford.edu/claudeg/sites/default/files /ESJ2009Gallimoreetalproofs.pdf; Tamara Holmlund Nelson, David Slavit, and Angie Deuel, "Two Dimensions of an Inquiry Stance toward Student-Learning Data," *Teachers College Record* 114, no. 8 (August 2012): 42; Ronald Thomas, "Why School Teams Don't Analyze Data," *School Administrator* 68, no. 9 (2011): 24–27.

3. Doug Lemov, *Teach Like a Champion* (San Francisco: Jossey-Bass, 2010), 225–226.

4. *TLAC* Technique 22: Cold Call, 111–125.

5. *TLAC* Technique 43: Positive Framing, 204–210.

## Phase 4: The Power of Discourse

1. Steven Johnson, Steven Johnson: Where Good Ideas Come From," TED talk (July 2010), http://www.ted.com/talks/steven_johnson_where_good_ideas_come_from#t-218811.

2. Bill Graham, a communications consultant and founder of Graham Corporate Communications (www.grahamcc.com), has addressed audiences worldwide about the keys to communication. One of the biggest factors he mentions is what he calls an "open face": keeping your eyebrows neutral or slightly raised to communicate caring, neutrality, and engagement. I learned about eyebrows from him.

## Stretch It: Ready to Paint

1. First team meeting as Packers coach (1959), reported in Chuck Carlson, *Game of My Life: 25 Stories of Packers Football* (Champaign, IL: Sports Publishing, 2004), 149.

# How to Use the DVD

## SYSTEM REQUIREMENTS

PC or Mac with a DVD drive running any operating system with an HTML-compatible web browser

## USING THE DVD WITH WINDOWS

To view the content on the DVD, follow these steps:

1. Insert the DVD into your computer's DVD drive.

2. Select Home.html from the list of files.

3. Read through the license agreement by clicking the License link near the top right of the interface.

4. The interface appears. Simply select the material you want to view.

## IN CASE OF TROUBLE

If you experience difficulty using the DVD, please follow these steps:

1. Make sure your hardware and systems configurations conform to the systems requirements noted under "System Requirements" above.

2. Review the installation procedure for your type of hardware and operating system. It is possible to reinstall the software if necessary.

## CUSTOMER CARE

If you have trouble with the DVD, please call the Wiley Product Technical Support phone number at (800) 762-2974. Outside the United States, call 1 (317) 572-3994. You can also contact Wiley Product Technical Support at http://support.wiley.com. John Wiley & Sons will provide technical support only for installation and other general quality-control items. For technical support of the applications themselves, consult the program's vendor or author.

Before calling or writing, please have the following information available:

- Type of computer and operating system
- Any error messages displayed
- Complete description of the problem

It is best if you are sitting at your computer when making the call.

## ACCESS THE CONTENTS ONLINE

- Go to my.paulbambrick.com and click on New Book Activation.
- Follow the instructions on the website for registration.
- If you have any issues with Your Library account, please email us at josseybasseducation@wiley.com.

# Index

explicitly, 311–312, 315; praise, 269, 270; upgrading vocabulary, 379–380, 383–384; via body language, 85, 86, 87, 98–102, 105, *See also* Narrate the Positive; Strong Voice

Comprehension. *See* Understanding

Conceptual thinking. *See* Go Conceptual

Conroy, Ginger, 58

Corburn, Jesse, xi

Core ideas: achieving mastery, 305, 374; on action steps, 4, 304; advance planning, 56, 148; building foundation, 28; classroom function, 88; coaching, 15–16, 26, 60; creating masterpieces, 348; drawing students out, 239; expectations, 184; getting into gear, 224; importance of peer-to-peer discourse, 300; instant immersion, 130; leadership and coaching, 4–5, 7; lesson planning, 109; locking skills in place, 349; perfect practice, 12, 47; practice, 46, 80; pursuing excellence, 385–387; rehearsals, 79; responding to students, 278; use of Get Better Faster Scope and Sequence, 36

Correcting students, 235, 237, 271–274

Cosgrove, Dan, 217

Countdowns, 251, 254

Coyle, Daniel, 6

Culture: creating teacher feedback, 63, 65; positive reinforcement for students, 84

Cut It Short, 143, 159, 162

**D**

Data-driven instructional plan: ELL students and, 229; reviewing with teacher, 138; sample, 141; shifting toward, 108–109; writing objectives for, 110, 112–114, 119, *See also* Lesson plans

De La Garza, Celestina, 230

Debriefing on feedback, 63, 71–72, 73 .

Decision making, 48

Delegating coaching tasks, 133

"Delivering Real-Time Feedback" table, 72–74

Denison-Lipschitz, Christine, 174, 373

Directions, 146, 149, 150–153

Disagree Respectfully, 343, 345

Discourse: action steps, 306–307; encouraging conceptual thinking, 353–354, 355–356; leading student, 356–362; power of, 18, 301–302; reteaching strategies using, 317, 318, 319–326; setting routines for, 308, 309–310; Show Call strategies for, 317, 318, 321–323, 326; strategic prompts during, 351, 352, 354–355; student at-bats during, 324–325, 326; teaching habits for, 336–345; universal prompts during, 317, 327–336; use of evidence in, 279–283

Do It Again, 85, 143, 157–158, 159, 160–161

Do Now: coaching strategies for, 204; encouraging independent practice with, 200–201; implementing, 183; Quick Reference Guide, 181

Dowling, Kelly, 48, 81, 82

Dress rehearsals: about, 16; before school starts, 83–84; for existing lesson plans, 122–123; importance of, 77–79; topics to introduce during, 85, *See also* Phase 1

*Driven by Data* (Bambrick-Santoyo), 109

DuFour, Richard, 225

Dunbar, Kevin, 301

Dunwoody, Norvella, viii

Duru, Ijeoma, 66

Dutton, Greg, 337

DVD: clip overview for, vii–xvii; materials on, xix, 21; real-time feedback, xix, 21, 64; skills presented in, 20; using/troubleshooting, 435–436

Off-task students: individual corrections for, 235, 237, 238, 272–274; narrating positive for, 235, 236–237, 238, 268, 270; redirecting, 30–31; work groups with, 310–315

Orfuss, Kathryn, 214, 243

**P**

Pacing: about, 246; action steps, 234, 237; call and response tips, 252, 254; coaching for, 247–254; goal for, 245; Quick Reference Guide, 236; using countdowns, 251

Pamuk, Orhan, 87–88, 127

Pastore, Patrick, 40

PD goals. *See* Goals

PD. *See* Professional development

Peer-to-peer discourse. *See* Discourse

Pen in Hand, 216–218, 220

Perfect: defining, 46, 47–49; perfecting live practice, 55–56

Performance: dress rehearsals for teaching, 77–79; repeating teaching, 56–58; teaching as, 25–26, 78

Perry, Claire, xiii

Personal organization tools: calendar, 138, 142; data-driven instructional plan, 138, 141; meeting notes template, 138, 140; task management tracker, 138, 139; weekly data meeting pages, 233

Petters, Danielle, 84

Phase 1: action steps, xxxi–xxxii, 34, 85; Coaching Blueprint, 80–85; Coach's Guide for, 390–395; dress rehearsals, 16, 77–79, 83–84; DVD clips on, ix–x; overview of, 15; Quick Reference Guide, 86, 107; skills overview for, 84–85, *See also* Classroom management; Rigor; Routines and Procedures

Phase 2: action steps, xxxii–xxxiii, 34, 143–144, 146–147; Coaching Blueprint, 132–144; Coach's Guide for, 394–404; DVD clips on, x–xii; instant immersion in, 16–17, 129–131, 221; overview of, 15; Quick Reference Guide, 145; teaching skills in, 142–144; Whole-Class Reset, 173–180, *See also* Classroom management; Rigor

Phase 3: action steps, xxxiii–35, 233–235, 237–238; Build the Momentum, 234, 236, 240–245; Coaching Blueprint, 225–236; Coach's Guide, 405–414; DVD clips on, xii–xvii; Engage Students, 234, 236, 238–239, 256–263; getting into gear, 17–18, 223–224; overview of, 15; Quick Reference Guide, 236–237; responding to student learning needs, 277–279, *See also* Classroom management; Rigor

Phase 4: action steps, xxxv, 35, 306–307, 308–309, 318; coaching blueprint for, 303–307; Coach's Guide, 417–423; management routines for discourse, 308–316; overview of, 15, 305–307; power of discourse, 18, 301–302; Quick Reference Guide, 308, 317, *See also* Rigor

Phases: first ninety days in five, 15; navigating through, 22–23, *See also* *specific phase*

Plan, Practice, Follow up, Repeat principle: about, 16, 45–47; conclusions from, 58–59; core idea, 46, 56; defining "perfect", 46, 47–49; DVD clips on, vii–viii; follow up and feedback, 58, 63, *See also* Planning

Planned Whole-Class Reset, 144, 175–176, 179

Planning: backwards, 53, 186; before practicing, 46, 49–56; critical routines, 91–93, 97; data-driven instruction plans, 138; Exit Ticket, 118; follow-up meetings, 233; reteach strategies, 226, 229–230, 232; sharing and comparing, 54; Strong Voice skills, 102, *See also* Lesson plans

Playbooks. *See* Scripts

Positive framing, 94

Posture: action steps, 85, 86, 87, 100, 105; coaching leadership, 100–102; confident, 98–99

Practice: accomplishments based on, 6; characteristics of perfect, 55–56; core idea of, 46; critical routines, 91–93, 97; Exit Ticket design, 118; importance of, 80–82, 89, 241–242; internalizing existing lesson plans, 123; interrupting imperfect, 55; myths of, 11–12; planned Whole-Class Reset, 175; planning before, 46, 49–56; role-playing reteach strategies, 232; Strong Voice skills, 102, 104; student opportunities to, 297–298; taking it live, 47, 54–56; time needed for, 82; writing measurable objectives, 114, *See also* Independent Practice; Plan, Practice, Follow up, Repeat principle

Praise: affirming student's achievements, 231; reinforcing student learning, 269, 270, *See also* Narrate the Positive

Pre-teaching. *See* Phase 1

Precall strategies, 328, 329, 335

Procedures. *See* Routines & Procedures

Professional development (PD): developing effective lesson plans, 110, 119–120; dress rehearsals developing, 83–85; importance of practice, 80–82, 89, 241–242; launching real-time feedback, xix, 64; leading, 80–82, *See also* Goals

Prompts. *See* Strategic prompts; Universal prompts

## Q

Quality of student work, 212–215, 219–220

Questions: citing text when answering, 282, 283; disagreeing with answers to, 343, 345; pacing rate of, 249–250, 253

Quick Reference Guide: beginning Cheat Sheet for, 76; Independent Practice skills, 181; Phase 1, 86, 107; Phase 2, 145; Phase 3, 236–237; Phase 4, 308, 317; reteaching strategies, 275; Stretch It phase, 354, *See also* Get Better Faster Coach's Guide

## R

RACCE (Restate, Answer, Cite, Context, Explain), 217

Rainbow Guide, 22

Real-time feedback. *See* Feedback

Rector, Jesse, 233

Reflection time for students, 337

Regnier, Joshua, 89

Repetition: planning reteach strategies, 226, 229–230, 232; repeating teaching performances, 56–58, *See also* Plan, Practice, Follow up, Repeat principle

Reset. *See* Whole-Class Reset

Resources: additional DVD materials, xix, *See also* DVD

Responsive performance, 78

Reteaching strategies: action steps, 276–277; coaching, 292–298; goals for, 320; guided discourse in, 317, 318, 320–326; modeling solutions, 234–235, 237–238, 291; planning, 226, 229–230, 232; Quick Reference Guide, 275

Revise Routines, 143, 155–156, 160

Reynolds, Allyson, xiv

Ricciulli, Claudia, 82

373–376, 381, 382, 384; calling on students, 252, 254, 256, 257, 262, 366–368, 371, 372; challenging students, 95, 240–245; closing loop with students, 333–334, 336; coaching for, 7, 59–60; correcting students, 235, 237, 271–274; creating monitoring pathway, 209–211, 219; delivering clear directions, 146, 149, 150–153; disagreeing with answers, 343, 345; dress rehearsals for, 77–79; DVD resources for, xix; encouraging conceptual thinking, 352–353; encouraging discourse elaboration, 331–332, 335; ending Do It Again, 159; engaging students, 234–239, 260–261, 263; explicitly instructing groups, 311–312, 315; finding priorities for class changes, 174; focusing on, 8; helping all students excel, 228; helping students access previous learning, 362, 363–365, 371; instant immersion for, 16–17, 129–131, 221; internalizing lesson plans, 120–127; leading discussions, 341–342, 344, 356–362; locking in tasks, 58; maintaining neutrality, 339–340, 344; making decisions in advance, 147–148; marking up student work, 216–218, 220; mastering management first, 12–13; monitoring students' work, 212–215, 219–220; myths of coaching, 11–13; as performance artists, 25–26; planning for, 50–54, 55, 226, 229–230, 232; polling the room, 285–287, 290; pursuing excellence, 385–387; repeating performances, 56–58; responding to student's needs, 277–279; rigor in teaching, 207, 305–306; students as focus for, 349–350; students mirroring,

292–293; success of, 10–11; time between questions, 249–250, 253, *See also* Feedback; Teacher Radar; Voice

Teaching: identifying learning gaps, 226, 228–229, 231; importance of dress rehearsals, 77–79; instant immersion for, 16–17, 129–131, 221; laying foundation for, 27–28; mastering fundamentals of, 347–348; as performance, 25–26; practicing skills for, 2–3; students to cite evidence, 279–283, *See also* Lesson plans

Technical support, 434

*Ten-Minute In-Service, The* (Whitaker and Breaux), 82

Thinking: encouraging conceptual, 352–353, 355, 356; modeling, 294–296

Time: blocking out feedback, 132–137; saving with organization tools, 138–141; students' reflection, 335; wait time, 326–328, 333, *See also* Pacing

Time stamps, 124–126, 136

Timers, 247–248, 253

Tobin, Jackson, 1–4, 5, 6, 7, 46, 48, 67–68, 101, 130–131, 385–386

Tone: feedback meeting, 137–138, 142; narrating with positive, 266

Tools: customizing, 22; providing personal organization, 138–141; scheduling, 136

Touzin, Judy, 364

Tracking student answers, 212–213

Troubleshooting DVD, 433–434

Turn and Talk, 258–259, 263

**U**

Uncommon Schools, xxix–xxx

Understanding: articulating, 324–325, 326, 377–378, 383; checking groups', 275, 285–290; closing loop after errors in, 333–334, 336; developing conceptual, 373–379, 381–384

Universal prompts: action steps, 318; closing loop, 333–334, 336; coaching, 328–334, 335; encouraging elaboration with, 331–332, 335; goal for, 327; overview, 327; Quick Reference Guide, 317; wait time, precall, rollback strategies, 328–330, 335

Upgrading vocabulary, 379–380, 383–384

Utton, Rebecca, 271, 329

**V**

Varying voice, 243–244

Veltzé, Nicole, 112–113

Verbalizing conceptual understanding, 377–378, 383

Video clips. *See* DVD

Voice: learning skills for, 85–87, 98–106; varying, 243–244

**W**

Wait time, 328–330, 335

Walsh, Bill, 147–148

*Warriors Don't Cry* (Beals), 50–51

Waterfall approach, 43, 44

Watkins, Michael, 14

We Do/You Do, 94

Weekly data meeting pages, 233

Weishaupt, Tom, 92

*Where Good Ideas Come From* (Dunbar and Johnson), 299

Whisper prompts, 67–69, 73

Whitaker, Todd, 82

Whiteboards, 286

Whole-class discussion. *See* Discourse

Whole-Class Reset: action steps, 144, 147; case study, 37–40; implementing planned, 144, 175–176, 179; in-the-moment reset, 147, 177–178, 180; Quick Reference Guide, 145; using, 173–174

Wiggins, Grant, 53

Wilke, Kate Lynn, 110

Willey Nicole, xv

Windows computers, 435

Work groups: delivering explicit instructions to, 311–312, 315; progress and accountability for, 313–314, 315; Quick Reference Guide, 308; setting routines for, 309–310

Working clock, 251, 254

Worrell, Art, 62, 69, 294–295

Worrell, Juliana, xiv

*Wrinkle in Time, A* (L'Engle), 357

Write First, Talk Second: action steps, 182; coaching, 198–199, 204; Quick Reference Guide, 181

Writing: annotating student, 217; encouraging student's independent, 197, 198–199; exemplar, 143, 146, 181–182, 185–190; lesson plans, 16, 85, 86–87; measurable objectives, 110, 112–114, 119

Wrong answers. *See* Universal prompts

# NOTES

# NOTES

# NOTES

# NOTES

# NOTES

# NOTES

# NOTES

# NOTES

# NOTES

# NOTES

# NOTES

| If your teacher is struggling to . . . | Jump to . . . |
|---|---|
| Praise student effort rather than only student success | Script language that reinforces students' getting smarter |
| **Individual Student Corrections** | |
| Get the basic strategies of What to Do and Narrate the Positive to work for individual students | Least invasive intervention |

**Phase 3 Action Step Sequence**

| Management Trajectory | Rigor Trajectory |
|---|---|
| **Engage Every Student**<br>**7. Build the Momentum**<br>• Give the students a simple challenge to complete a task:<br>  – Example: "Now, I know you're only 4th graders, but I have a 5th-grade problem that I bet you could master!!"<br>• Speak faster, walk faster, vary your voice, & smile (sparkle)!<br>**8. Pacing:** Create the illusion of speed so that students feel constantly engaged<br>• Use a handheld timer to stick to the times stamps in the lesson & give students an audio cue that it's time to move on.<br>• Increase rate of questioning: no more than 2 seconds between when a student responds and teacher picks back up instruction.<br>• Use countdowns to work the clock ("Do that in 5, 4, 3, 2, 1").<br>• Use call and response for key words. | **Respond to Student Learning Needs**<br>**6. Habits of Evidence**<br>• Teach students to annotate with purpose: summarize, analyze, find the best evidence, etc.<br>• Teach and prompt students to cite key evidence in their responses.<br>**7. Check for Whole-Group Understanding:** Gather evidence on whole-group learning:<br>• Poll the room to determine how students are answering a certain question.<br>  – "How many chose letter A? B? C? D?"<br>  – Students answer the question on whiteboards: "Hold up your whiteboards on the count of three . . ."<br>• Target the error: focus class discussion on the questions where students most struggle to answer correctly. |

| Management Trajectory | Rigor Trajectory |
|---|---|
| **9. Engage All Students:** Make sure all students participate<br><br>• Make sure to call on all students.<br>• Cold-call students.<br>• Implement brief (15–30 second) Turn & Talks.<br>• Intentionally alternate among multiple methods in class discussion: cold calling, choral response, all hands, and Turn & Talks.<br><br>**10. Narrate the Positive**<br><br>• Narrate what students do well, not what they do wrong.<br>   – "I like how Javon has gotten straight to work on his writing assignment."<br>   – "The second row is ready to go: their pencils are in the well, and their eyes are on me."<br>• While narrating the positive and/or while scanning during a redirect, look at the student(s) who are off task.<br>• Use language that reinforces students' getting smarter:<br>   – Praise answers that are above and beyond, or strong effort.<br><br>**11. Individual Student Corrections**<br><br>• Anticipate student off-task behavior and rehearse the next two things you will do when that behavior occurs. Redirect students using the least invasive intervention necessary:<br>   – Proximity<br>   – Eye contact<br>   – Use a nonverbal<br>   – Say student's name quickly<br>   – Small consequence | **8. Reteaching 101—Model:** Model for the students how to think/solve/write<br><br>• Give students a clear listening/note-taking task that fosters active listening to the model, and then debrief the model:<br>   – "What did I do in my model?"<br>   – "What are the key things to remember when you are doing the same in your own work?"<br>• Model the thinking, not just a procedure:<br>   – Narrow the focus to the thinking students are struggling with.<br>   – Model replicable thinking steps that students can follow.<br>   – Model how to activate one's own content knowledge and skills that have been learned in previous lessons.<br>   – Vary the think-aloud in tone and cadence from the normal "teacher" voice to highlight the thinking skills.<br>• We Do and You Do: give students opportunities to practice with your guidance. |

PHASE 3

MANAGEMENT